CW01464651

TRADE AND DEVELOPMENT REPORT, 2010

Report by the secretariat of the
United Nations Conference on Trade and Development

UNITED NATIONS
New York and Geneva, 2010

Note

- Symbols of United Nations documents are composed of capital letters combined with figures. Mention of such a symbol indicates a reference to a United Nations document.

- The designations employed and the presentation of the material in this publication do not imply the expression of any opinion whatsoever on the part of the Secretariat of the United Nations concerning the legal status of any country, territory, city or area, or of its authorities, or concerning the delimitation of its frontiers or boundaries.

- Material in this publication may be freely quoted or reprinted, but acknowledgement is requested, together with a reference to the document number. A copy of the publication containing the quotation or reprint should be sent to the UNCTAD secretariat.

UNCTAD/TDR/2010

UNITED NATIONS PUBLICATION
Sales No. E.10.II.D.3
ISBN 978-92-1-112807-9 ISSN 0255-4607

Contents

List of tables

List of charts

List of boxes

xi

Explanatory notes

Classification by country or commodity group

The classification of countries in this *Report* has been adopted solely for the purposes of statistical or analytical convenience and does not necessarily imply any judgement concerning the stage of development of a particular country or area.

The major country groupings used in this *Report* follow the classification by the United Nations Statistical Office (UNSO). They are distinguished as:

» Developed or industrial(ized) countries: the countries members of the OECD (other than Mexico, the Republic of Korea and Turkey) plus the new EU member countries and Israel.

» Transition economies refers to South-East Europe and the Commonwealth of Independent States (CIS).

» Developing countries: all countries, territories or areas not specified above.

The terms "country" / "economy" refer, as appropriate, also to territories or areas.

References to "Latin America" in the text or tables include the Caribbean countries unless otherwise indicated.

References to "sub-Saharan Africa" in the text or tables include South Africa unless otherwise indicated.

For statistical purposes, regional groupings and classifications by commodity group used in this *Report* follow generally those employed in the *UNCTAD Handbook of Statistics 2009* (United Nations publication, sales no. E/F.09.II.D.10) unless otherwise stated. The data for China do not include those for Hong Kong Special Administrative Region (Hong Kong SAR), Macao Special Administrative Region (Macao SAR) and Taiwan Province of China.

Other notes

References in the text to *TDR* are to the *Trade and Development Report* (of a particular year). For example, *TDR 2009* refers to *Trade and Development Report, 2009* (United Nations publication, sales no. E.09.II.D.16).

The term "dollar" ($) refers to United States dollars, unless otherwise stated.

The term "billion" signifies 1,000 million.

The term "tons" refers to metric tons.

Annual rates of growth and change refer to compound rates.

Exports are valued FOB and imports CIF, unless otherwise specified.

Use of a dash (–) between dates representing years, e.g. 1988–1990, signifies the full period involved, including the initial and final years.

An oblique stroke (/) between two years, e.g. 2000/01, signifies a fiscal or crop year.

A dot (.) indicates that the item is not applicable.

Two dots (..) indicate that the data are not available, or are not separately reported.

A dash (-) or a zero (0) indicates that the amount is nil or negligible.

Decimals and percentages do not necessarily add up to totals because of rounding.

Abbreviations

CDS	credit default swap
CIS	Commonwealth of Independent States
CPI	Consumer Price Index
ECB	European Central Bank
ECLAC	Economic Commission for Latin America and the Caribbean
EFTA	European Free Trade Association
EIU	Economist Intelligence Unit
EMU	European Economic and Monetary Union
EU	European Union
FAO	Food and Agriculture Organization of the United Nations
FDI	foreign direct investment
GDP	gross domestic product
GFCF	gross fixed capital formation
GTAP	Global Trade Analysis Project
ILO	International Labour Organization
IMF	International Monetary Fund
ISIC	International Standard Industrial Classification
MDG	Millennium Development Goal
NAIRU	non-accelerating inflation rate of unemployment
NIE	newly industrializing economy
OECD	Organisation for Economic Co-operation and Development
R&D	research and development
RER	real exchange rate
SDR	Special Drawing Right
SITC	Standard International Trade Classification
SOE	State-owned enterprise
TDR	Trade and Development Report
TNC	transnational corporation
TVE	township and village enterprise (China)
UN COMTRADE	United Nations Commodity Trade Statistics Database
UNCTAD	United Nations Conference on Trade and Development
UN/DESA	United Nations Department of Economic and Social Affairs
UNDP	United Nations Development Programme
UNIDO	United Nations Industrial Development Organization
WTO	World Trade Organization

OVERVIEW

The global upturn from what is considered the worst economic and financial crisis since the 1930s remains fragile, and a premature exit from demand-stimulating macroeconomic policies aimed at fiscal consolidation could stall the recovery. A continuation of the expansionary fiscal stance is necessary to prevent a deflationary spiral and a further worsening of the employment situation.

It is becoming clear that not all countries can rely on exports to boost growth and employment; more than ever they need to give greater attention to strengthening domestic demand. This is especially true today, because it is unlikely that the United States' former role as the global engine of growth can be assumed by any other country or countries. The shift in focus on domestic-demand-led growth is necessary both in developed and emerging-market economies with large current-account surpluses and underutilized production potential in order to prevent the recurrence of imbalances similar to those that contributed to the outbreak of the global financial crisis. But it is also important for many developing countries that have become heavily dependent on external demand for growth and for creating employment for their growing labour force.

Unemployment is the most pressing social and economic problem of our time, not least because, especially in developing countries, it is closely related to poverty. The fallout from the global crisis has exacerbated what were already sluggish labour markets in most countries even before the crisis erupted. Since 2008, the global employment-to-population ratio has been exhibiting a sharp decline, and many countries are now facing the highest unemployment rates of the last 40 years. Therefore employment creation needs to be made a priority in economic policy.

In this context, it is important that the macroeconomic policy framework be strengthened to promote sustainable growth and employment creation in both developed and developing countries. Past experience and theoretical considerations suggest that a sustainable growth strategy requires a greater reliance on domestic demand than has been the case in many countries over the past 30 years. In such a strategy, job creation for absorbing surplus labour would result from a virtuous circle of high investment in fixed capital leading to faster productivity growth with corresponding wage increases that enable a steady expansion of domestic demand. Especially for developing countries, this may call for a rethinking of the paradigm of export-led development based on keeping labour costs low.

Global economic recovery remains fragile

After a contraction of almost 2 per cent in 2009, global real gross domestic product (GDP) is expected to grow by about 3.5 per cent in 2010, with a re-acceleration of output growth in most regions. Exceptions are the European Union (EU) and some transition economies, where recovery is proving to be much slower. But the rebound from recession will not endure if it continues to be based on temporary factors, such as inventory cycles and exceptional fiscal stimulus programmes, and if the shortcomings that caused the crisis, such as unregulated financial systems, income inequality and global imbalances, persist. Unless new sources of dynamism can be found, growth rates will probably decline again in most countries in 2011.

In developed countries, financial rescue packages by governments in 2008 and 2009 prevented the collapse of financial markets, while supportive fiscal and monetary policies partially compensated for sluggish private demand. Most of these economies returned to positive growth rates between the second and fourth quarter of 2009. However, final domestic demand has remained generally weak owing to continued high unemployment and restrained private consumption. Investment has been discouraged by idle productive capacities, uncertain demand expectations and more difficult access to credit.

Among developing and transition economies there have been wide variations in both the depth of the recession and the vigour of the recovery. The financial shock seriously affected those emerging-market economies that had been running current-account deficits and depended heavily on net capital inflows. Many of them were transition economies which were forced to apply restrictive macroeconomic policy responses, in some cases under IMF-led programmes.

The financial turmoil had little direct effect on low-income countries that are largely excluded from international financial markets and on emerging-market economies that had avoided large external deficits and accumulated significant international reserves in the years prior to the crisis. Most Asian and Latin American emerging-market economies were able to contain a rise in unemployment during the crisis and achieve a rapid recovery of domestic demand. This served to drive their output growth in 2010. Indeed, in the first quarter of this year some of the large emerging-market economies in these regions achieved two-digit growth rates.

World trade and commodity prices support growth in developing countries

World trade, which had plunged by more than 13 per cent in volume and by as much as 23 per cent in value in the first half of 2009, started to recover in mid-2009, and the recovery was much faster in developing than in developed countries. By April 2010, the volume of trade of emerging-market economies had reached its previous peak of April 2008. Higher export volumes and a rebound in primary commodity prices from their lows of the first quarter of 2009 boosted national income and fiscal revenue, especially in Africa and West Asia.

The projected growth rate for Africa in 2010 as a whole is about 5 per cent, and closer to 6 per cent for sub-Saharan Africa (excluding South Africa). In Latin America, GDP is also forecast to expand by some 5 per cent in 2010. In some countries of the region growth could exceed 6 per cent, but it is likely to be more moderate in Central America and the Caribbean. In South-East Asia, GDP should rise by about 7 per cent in 2010, and in East and South Asia most countries are on track to return to their pre-crisis growth rates. In several countries of Central and Eastern Europe and the Commonwealth of Independent States (CIS), recovery is likely to be slower owing to high unemployment, wage cuts and constraints on government spending.

Primary commodity prices began to rise once more in 2009 and the first half of 2010, particularly in metals and minerals, and energy products, especially crude petroleum. These were also the commodities that had experienced the sharpest fall in prices in the second half of 2008 as they are the most closely linked to global industrial production. The prices of agricultural commodities grew more moderately, although those of agricultural raw materials rose by more than 50 per cent from their trough. This upward trend continued partially into 2010, and in spite of their sharp decline in the second half of 2008, prices for all commodity groups during 2009 and early 2010 have been well above their average of the 2000s. Robust demand from the rapidly growing emerging-market economies, mainly China, has contributed to the recovery of commodity prices, but, as in previous years, price developments have also been strongly influenced by the behaviour of financial investors.

Food prices have remained relatively low since their fall in the second half of 2008, due mainly to bumper harvests in cereals, vegetable oilseeds and oils, and to an easing of pressure on cereal and oilseed production for biofuels. In food markets, inventories have been replenished to more comfortable levels. However, although forecasts suggest good harvests in 2010, food security is still a pressing problem in many developing countries.

Strong countercyclical macroeconomic policies in most developed and emerging-market economies helped the global economy turn the corner in mid-2009, although rates of recovery varied across regions and countries. However, during the course of 2010, there has been a reorientation towards fiscal consolidation in Europe, implying a shift towards a restrictive fiscal policy stance and thus a withdrawal from an expansionary demand stimulus from the beginning of 2011 onwards. This could compromise further recovery since, in most developed countries, especially in Western Europe, private demand, so far, has only partially recovered from its trough. It would therefore make countries overdependent on exports for their growth and could lead to the re-emergence of current-account imbalances of the kind that contributed to the build-up of the financial and economic crisis in the first place. In any case, if too many big countries rely on higher net exports, they cannot all be successful.

Developing economies lead the global recovery

The strength of the global recovery has varied in line with how aggressively stimulus measures have been applied by different countries. China, which was severely hit by the slump in its key export markets in developed economies, was the most decisive in fuelling domestic demand through stimulus measures. Its GDP growth accelerated already in the second quarter of 2009, as did growth throughout East and South-East Asia, once again contributing to an increase in employment and production capacities. China, and to a lesser extent India and Brazil, are leading the recovery, not only in their respective regions but also in the world.

As interest rates in the United States and other developed countries are near zero, and are likely to remain very low in the absence of inflationary pressures, any tightening of monetary policy in emerging-market economies as a result of their faster recovery and to avoid the risk of overheating may widen interest rate differentials in favour of these latter economies. This, coupled with a renewal of risk appetite on the part of financial investors, could well lead to an increase in net private capital flows to the emerging-market economies. Indeed, their stock market indices are already showing a substantial improvement. This, in turn, could generate upward pressure on their exchange rates and may require currency market intervention with a view to preventing exchange-rate appreciation as well as to provide "self-insurance" against speculative carry trade operations.

The recovery in developed countries resembles pre-crisis patterns

While developing countries are leading the recovery, it remains fragile and uneven in developed countries. Among the developed countries, in a repeat of global pre-crisis patterns, the United States has witnessed a stronger recovery in domestic demand than the leading current-account surplus countries – Germany and Japan. But in moving forward, the United States has to deal with the problem of 8 million crisis-related job losses, and it faces strong headwinds as the fiscal stimulus peters out in the course of 2010. In 2011, its overall fiscal stance could even become restrictive as fiscal retrenchment is expected at the state and local levels. Moreover, the housing market and house prices remain depressed.

Recovery in Germany and Japan continues to be characterized by their strong reliance on exports. The main source of export stimulus has increasingly shifted away from the United States towards China and other emerging-market economies. And weak domestic demand in Germany is no longer being offset by more buoyant domestic demand elsewhere in the EU. Europe has become the centre of the global crisis and a laggard in the global recovery, as its home-grown problems add to the vulnerability of its shaky financial markets.

Instability and uncertainty in Europe

In the first half of 2010, stress in the markets for some European countries' public debt escalated. The relevant European authorities, assisted by the IMF, responded with a support package for Greece and other European countries that may face difficulties, which helped to calm financial markets. However, doubts remain as to how the underlying real regional disequilibria in competitiveness will be addressed, and how the draconian fiscal retrenchments and wage cuts will affect recovery of domestic demand.

Following Germany's lead in committing to unconditional fiscal consolidation to regain market confidence, fiscal austerity is set to spread across Europe in 2011. The prospect of a premature exit from stimulus in Europe has heightened the risk of a double-dip recession in that region, or even worldwide. In the eagerness to embark on fiscal consolidation, it is often overlooked that a double-dip recession, through its negative impact on public revenues, could pose a greater threat to public finances than continued fiscal expansion, which, by supporting growth of taxable income, would itself augment public revenues.

A weakening of global coordination and of the G-20 process

Continued global coordination of efforts directed at crisis management and systemic reform remains an acute challenge. At this stage, coordination primarily concerns the free-rider problem. As a rule, governments should withdraw stimulus only after achieving a full recovery of private domestic demand in their country. If it is withdrawn prematurely, they have to rely on exports for recovery, thereby shifting the burden of sponsoring a demand stimulus onto others. Ideally, the timing of an exit from stimulus should contribute towards a rebalancing of global demand.

At the peak of the global crisis, the G-20 managed to agree on the need for coordinated measures, as the sheer severity of events discounted any possible alternative to stimulus. Apparently that moment has passed: views on how to tackle the current challenges vary widely, and major differences in policy visions have resurfaced. Policymakers in the euro area believe that fiscal austerity will support rather than harm growth by creating confidence. United States policymakers, on the other hand, fear that continued stagnation of domestic demand in Europe may threaten the global recovery.

In the current situation, the short-term effects of fiscal austerity, including job losses, are unlikely to be offset by sharply falling interest rates and greater confidence in long-term prospects. And the depreciation of the euro in the first half of 2010 essentially means exporting unemployment to the rest of the world. Failure to coordinate policies at the G-20 level, with a more expansionary overall stance, raises the prospect of a re-emergence of global imbalances, especially among developed countries. This would run counter to the declared objectives of the G-20 and signify a breakdown of the G-20 process of international cooperation. It would also mark a real setback: macroeconomic policy coordination among the G-20 countries is of crucial importance, as major adjustments of demand patterns are expected to occur in the United States and China that will have a considerable influence on prospects for growth and employment in the world economy.

Adjustments in opposite directions in the United States and China

In the United States, a downward adjustment of consumption will be unavoidable unless wages grow strongly, which seems unlikely. For almost 10 years before the financial crisis, personal consumption in that country had been rising considerably faster than GDP despite a decline in the share of labour compensation in GDP. Greater consumer spending by reducing savings and incurring debt was possible in a financial environment where credit was easily accessible and where a series of asset price bubbles created the illusion of increasing household wealth. But with the collapse of the United States housing market, households were forced to unwind their debt positions and cut consumer spending. This trend is set to continue. Consequently, the world economy cannot count on the sort of stimulus provided by the United States in the same way as it did prior to the crisis.

In China, a transformation from investment- and export-led growth to consumer-led growth is an official policy objective. The share of labour compensation in total income in this country also fell for some time, but has risen recently. However, overall income growth was faster than in any other economy and consumption grew rapidly, particularly over the past two years, when there was a slump in incomes and consumer spending in the other major economies. China has done more than any other emerging-market economy to stimulate domestic demand through government spending. As a result its imports have risen sharply and the current-account surplus is bound to shrink significantly in 2010.

Between 2004 and 2008, there was a sharp fall in the share of household consumption in China's GDP, reaching a low of about 35 per cent. Nevertheless, in absolute terms, the growth rates of private consumer spending have been very high since 2005. The fall in the share of household consumption was mainly the result of China's emphasis on investment and exports to fuel economic growth, and the fact that China became the hub for large-scale production by transnational corporations. Since 2009, there have been increasing signs that real wages are set to grow faster relative to productivity than in the past, and that higher government spending on social security and public investment in housing may reduce household precautionary savings. Combined with additional reforms in the financial sector, this could accelerate the increase in household consumption in China and further reduce its dependence on exports for output growth.

Risk of a deflationary rebalancing

However, there is little reason to believe that household consumption in China, which still is only about one-eighth that of the United States, could supplant United States household consumption as a driver of global growth any time soon. The net effect of United States and Chinese adjustments taken together would be deflationary for the world economy, while they would not be sufficient to unwind the large global imbalances.

Any additional contribution to a global rebalancing will therefore have to come from other countries. To the extent that it comes from other current-account deficit economies, the impact will be deflationary, as it would have to rely on import retrenchment. As for the big oil-exporting countries, the evolution of their current-account surpluses depends largely on oil revenues, which are unstable, and the size of their domestic demand is not large enough to significantly influence trade flows and employment creation at the global level. Further domestic demand growth in other large emerging-market economies in the South would certainly help to make their industrialization and employment less dependent on export markets. It might also create a larger market for other developing countries that produce consumer goods. However, the import potential of Brazil, India, Indonesia and South Africa combined is not even equivalent to that of Germany and, with the exception of Indonesia, these countries have not had current-account surpluses in recent years.

Thus the key element in demand management worldwide would have to be expansionary adjustment in the industrialized economies that have the largest surpluses, namely Germany and Japan. However, the chances of this happening are extremely remote. In Japan domestic demand growth would need to be significantly stronger, but deflation remains entrenched by wage cuts. In Germany, there is considerable scope for a rise in household consumption based on wage increases, which would also have expansionary effects in the rest of Europe. Such an expansion could make an important contribution to global rebalancing, as the size and composition of European imports of consumer goods are relatively similar to those of the United States. But the eagerness of EU governments to embark on fiscal consolidation programmes, exacerbated by wage cuts, makes it unlikely that a major contribution to global rebalancing and a substantial stimulus for global output and employment growth will come from this regional bloc. Thus the developing and emerging-market economies that had focused their export-oriented development strategies on the markets of the major developed economies may have to reconsider these strategies.

Developing countries face particular employment challenges

Employment creation is a particularly difficult challenge for developing countries. Their labour force is still growing rapidly, necessitating the constant generation of additional jobs for the new entrants within an economic structure characterized by dualism. Many of these countries have a modern sector with relatively high productivity and large economies of scale, which coexists with a sluggish traditional sector with low productivity and a predominance of constant returns to scale of production activities. The processes of economic development, in general, and of employment creation for the growing population, in particular, require an expansion of modern activities and the reallocation of labour from the traditional to the modern sectors. These need to be accompanied by enhancing productivity in all economic sectors. The modern sector, where production takes place in organized units with formal wage jobs, has often been equated with industry, particularly manufacturing, but increasingly it also includes modern services and some innovative agricultural activities.

Growth in the modern sector is associated with higher private and public investment in fixed capital as well as greater government spending for the provision of education and health services and social protection. Moreover, the more productive use of previously underemployed labour through its transfer from less remunerative traditional activities to better paid jobs in the modern sector generates higher incomes and a consequent increase in effective demand. For both these reasons, the share of non-agricultural goods and services in total demand will increase over time and support the expansion of the modern sector.

But even when activities in the modern sector expand rapidly, in poorer countries this sector is often too small to create a sufficient number of new jobs to absorb all the surplus labour. It is therefore necessary that incomes grow not only in the modern, higher productivity sectors, which frequently employ a small segment of the labour force, but also in the traditional sectors. This can be achieved by including the latter in supply chains, as far as possible, and by ensuring that incomes also rise in the agricultural sector by increasing the prices of agricultural produce in line with wage incomes in the formal sector. Without such linkages, a strategy that focuses on the development of the modern sector alone may actually widen the social and economic gap and exclude a large proportion of the population from decent employment and adequate levels of consumption and social coverage.

In the 1980s and 1990s, developing countries placed a growing emphasis on production for the world market to drive expansion of their formal modern sectors. It was hoped that this could trigger and accelerate a virtuous process of output growth, and steady gains in productivity and employment. However, that hope was seldom realized. In many countries exports did not grow as expected due to a lack of supply capacities and insufficient competitiveness of domestic producers on global markets. In others where exports grew, the domestic labour force employed in export industries did not share in the productivity gains. Instead, these gains tended to be passed on to lower prices, so that domestic demand did not increase, which would have led to higher income in the rest of the economy. As a result, employment problems persisted, or even worsened, particularly in Latin America and Africa.

Stagnation and rising unemployment in Latin America in the 1980s and 1990s

In Latin America between 1980 and 2002, per capita GDP virtually stagnated, unemployment increased and average productivity declined due to insufficient investment in fixed capital. Most of the time macroeconomic policies focused on controlling inflation through high interest rates, thereby discouraging investment. Moreover, currency overvaluation hampered export growth and favoured the use of imported components in industrial production, leading to "premature deindustrialization". Financial liberalization and an opening up of the capital account aggravated currency misalignments and economic instability, leading eventually to economic crises. As the reduction of formal employment was greater than its creation in internationally competitive sectors, the bargaining power of wage earners weakened. Moreover, wage compression aimed at restoring international competitiveness reduced wage earners' share in income distribution, which dampened the growth of domestic demand.

It was only after the experience of the Asian financial crisis in the late 1990s and the Argentinean debt crisis in 2001–2002 that a fairly radical reorientation of macroeconomic policies occurred. Governments embarked on more accommodative monetary policies and an exchange-rate policy that aimed at preserving international competitiveness. In several countries, fiscal revenues as a percentage of GDP increased, which provided them with the necessary policy space as well as the resources to spend more on infrastructure and social transfers. At the same time, specific measures for the labour market were adopted, including sizeable rises in the minimum wage, the reactivation of collective bargaining bodies and the launching of public works programmes. As a result, the employment situation improved from 2003 onwards, helped by a favourable international environment, in particular higher primary commodity prices and rapidly rising net imports by the United States. For the first time in almost 30 years, informal employment and unemployment receded and poverty fell significantly until 2008.

Persistence of a large informal sector in Africa

In Africa, employment generation, and particularly the creation of high-productivity and well-paid jobs, has been even more difficult. More than 20 years of orthodox macroeconomic policies and policy reforms have had limited success in creating the conditions necessary for rapid and sustainable growth, particularly in sub-Saharan Africa. Many countries in this subregion experienced a fall in per capita GDP and manufacturing activities during the 1980s and 1990s. By the end of the 1990s, the production structure of the subregion was reminiscent of the colonial period, consisting overwhelmingly of agriculture and mining. The extent of the impact on employment was not fully reflected in official figures on open unemployment but it was evident in the 20 per cent drop in labour productivity.

The commodity boom, debt relief and the ending of a number of civil conflicts have contributed to a recovery in income growth since 2003, which has continued in recent years despite the global crisis. However, so far there is no evidence of any significant change in the pattern of employment. Official employment rates have remained high in sub-Saharan Africa, which confirms that the unsolved problem there is not a shortage of employment in absolute terms, but the lack of productive and decent employment. Agricultural employment, which is largely informal, has diminished somewhat with progressive urbanization, but it still represents more than 60 per cent of total employment. Concomitantly there has been a rise in employment – again mainly informal – in urban services and small-scale commerce. Formal wage jobs account for only 13 per cent of employment in this subregion (excluding South Africa), and 60 per cent of the employed are "working poor", meaning that households are unable to meet their basic needs with the level of income earned. Any improvement in the employment situation resulting from a continuing trend of faster GDP growth will depend on the extent to which income growth in export industries spills over to the rest of the economy. But that in turn will depend on firms' demands for inputs, an increase in consumption of domestically produced goods, and/or a rise in government spending financed by higher taxes paid by exporters.

In North Africa, GDP growth slowed down, labour productivity stagnated and the sectoral composition of employment remained broadly unchanged between 1980 and 2000. Employment growth was not fast enough to absorb the rapidly expanding labour force. As a result, unemployment surged to two-digit figures in the 1990s. The stronger rise in official unemployment figures in North Africa is probably due to the fact that wage earners account for more than half of those employed – a much higher share than in sub-Saharan Africa. Since 2000, the acceleration of GDP growth has helped reduce unemployment in a context of rising labour productivity. But at close to 10 per cent, unemployment is high compared to other developing regions, and remains a serious problem, especially for young people and women.

Output growth and job creation in Asia

The experiences of East, South-East and South Asian countries with regard to employment creation over the past three decades differ considerably from those of Latin America and Africa. Faster capital accumulation, supported by low and stable interest rates, provided the basis for rapid increases in output, employment and productivity. Even so, open unemployment in South and South-East Asia increased, mainly in the 1990s, as urban job creation was not able to absorb all migrants from rural areas. In China and India, despite the rapid growth of GDP and exports, and employment creation in modern services and manufacturing industries, a large proportion of the labour force is still employed in low-productivity and informal activities.

Generally, the Asian economies opened up more gradually to international competition, and the process took place in a more stable macroeconomic environment, where wages grew in line with productivity. However, when financial and capital-account liberalization in East and South-East Asia opened the door to inflows of speculative capital, real exchange rates became overvalued, with attendant effects on current-account balances, which triggered the financial crisis of 1997–1998. The crisis-affected countries experienced a sharp rise in unemployment and a dramatic fall in GDP growth rates, and although the latter have picked up, particularly since 2002, they have not reached their pre-crisis levels. In most South-East Asian countries manufacturing output has been growing at less than half the rates recorded prior to the crisis.

Neglected role of domestic demand growth for employment creation

High rates of unemployment are often attributed to rigidities in the labour market that prevent wages from falling to an equilibrium level at which all excess labour would be absorbed. However, there is no empirical foundation for the proposition that the level of employment depends on the price of labour relative to that of capital. On the other hand, it can be shown that employment creation is closely associated with output growth and fixed capital formation. This means that unsatisfactory labour market outcomes are primarily due to unfavourable macroeconomic conditions that inhibit investment in fixed capital and productivity growth, as well as to inadequate growth of labour income, which constitutes the most important source of domestic demand.

There is clear evidence that in both developed and developing economies with relatively large formal manufacturing and service sectors employment generation is positively correlated with GDP growth and with investment in fixed capital. This suggests that the main consideration of entrepreneurs, in terms of its relevance for employment, is not one of choosing between varying combinations of capital and labour at a given level of output, but rather, deciding whether prevailing demand expectations are such that an increase in production capacities can be expected to be profitable or not. If the expectation is positive, they will invest in labour and capital at the same time. In many developing countries, the statistical link between an increase in employment, on the one hand, and in output and investment growth, on the other, is weaker. This is probably because a much larger proportion of the labour force is in informal employment and self-employment, which serve as buffers between productive formal employment and a status that can be defined and measured as unemployed.

Due to strong global competition and an increasing reliance on external demand, a major concern of both governments and companies in the tradables sector is the maintenance and strengthening of international competitiveness. This has induced a tendency to keep labour costs as low as possible. But if exports do not rise as expected, because other countries pursue the same strategy, or if the production dynamics in export industries do not spill over to other parts of the economy, as in many developing countries – especially in Africa and Latin America – these measures can be counterproductive for sustainable employment creation.

Given the close links between employment, output and demand growth, a strategy of keeping wages low in order to generate higher capital income to motivate fixed investment or reduce product prices in order to gain a competitive edge can be self-defeating. This is because if wages grow at a slower rate than productivity, the supply potential may end up growing faster than domestic demand, thereby discouraging innovation and productive investment.

Allowing a shrinking of the wage share is unlikely to lead to the desired outcome, unless investment and output growth are extremely dynamic. This has been the case in China in recent years. In this country, strong productivity growth was associated with two-digit increases in wage levels and a rapid growth of private consumption. The crisis since 2008, as with other – though milder – recessions in the industrialized countries before, has also revealed the limits of relying on external markets for growth and employment generation. Even if the world economy continues along its recovery path in the near future, it is unlikely that the external environment for developing countries will again be as favourable as it was in the years preceding the crisis.

Why labour income should be linked to productivity growth

In this environment, achieving more satisfactory outcomes for employment creation – and thus also for poverty reduction – requires widening the scope of policy instruments beyond what was deemed appropriate under the development paradigm of the past 30 years. Serious consideration of strategies to enhance domestic demand as an engine for employment creation is warranted for three reasons. First, the employment performances of different groups of developing countries suggest that the policy prescriptions of the past, which relied primarily – in some cases exclusively – on liberalization of product, financial and labour markets, did not lead to satisfactory levels of employment creation. Second, there is the risk of a deflationary trend in the global rebalancing process due to adjustments in the level and structure of demand that are likely to occur in the two largest economies, China and the United States. This darkens the outlook even for those developing and emerging-market economies that in the past successfully based their growth on an expansion of exports rather than domestic demand. Third, theoretical considerations suggest that a strategy of export-led growth based on wage compression, which makes countries overly dependent on foreign demand growth, may not be sustainable for a large number of countries and over a long period of time. This is because not all countries can successfully pursue this strategy simultaneously, and because there are limits to how far the share of labour in total income can be reduced.

A promising strategy for rapid employment generation could be to focus more on investment dynamics, and to ensure that the resultant productivity gains are distributed between labour and capital in a way that lifts domestic demand. This strategy was successfully pursued in most developed countries during the so-called "golden age of capitalism" between 1950 and 1973, when unemployment was at historically low levels. Labour markets were generally much more regulated than today, but central banks in nearly all developed countries were made responsible not only for maintaining price stability, but also for ensuring a high level of employment. Accordingly, real interest rates were kept low, thereby providing favourable financing conditions for investment in fixed capital. This was supplemented by financial support from public entities, along with government guarantees for bank loans, and interest subsidies for selected industries and investment projects. In addition, centralized wage negotiating mechanisms helped to ensure that productivity gains were translated into both higher profits, which stimulated innovation and investment, and higher wages, which strengthened mass purchasing power. At the same time, these mechanisms were instrumental in keeping unit labour costs from rising, and thus helped control inflation.

Although the context and circumstances differ in today's world, this strategy holds useful lessons for the design of macroeconomic and development strategies for developing countries. It can help generate an increase in demand for consumer goods and services, which would create additional demand for labour on the part of the producers of those goods and services that is sufficiently large to compensate for possible lay-offs of workers in those firms where productivity has increased. This is of particular importance for developing countries where most, if not all, capital goods have to be imported, so that the production of those capital goods does not itself create any domestic employment. However, through its effect on aggregate demand, a regime in which labour income rises in line with productivity is also supportive of investment, innovation and further gains in productivity. This is because it is the experience and expectation of rising demand, rather than a reduction in unit labour costs, which drives investment in additional or enhanced productive capacity. And such investment is a precondition for the absorption of the labour surplus in new productive activities.

The incentive for dynamic entrepreneurs to invest in fixed capital and product or process innovation is even stronger if wages follow the average productivity growth of the entire economy, rather than if the wages in each firm follow the productivity growth of that firm. The former would result in a greater differentiation of profits between capitalist firms. More dynamic entrepreneurs would be rewarded for their investments or innovations with higher pioneer rents than in a situation where they pass on the gains from their firms' enhanced productivity either to their own workers or to their customers through price reductions.

Broadening the scope of policy instruments

In the midst of the financial crisis, most governments have rediscovered the role of countercyclical fiscal policy in stabilizing aggregate demand, as reflected in the unprecedented stabilization packages that were launched to prevent another Great Depression. It would be extremely beneficial for growth and employment if the principles underlying these policy decisions continued to serve as a basis for a revised approach to fiscal policy. The public sector, as the largest purchaser of goods and services and the largest employer, has a significant influence on the expansion and functioning of goods and labour markets. Thus, if its behaviour is governed by the same principles as those of private agents, it amplifies economic fluctuations and leads to a crisis of confidence.

Moreover, governments can levy taxes on the modern sector and on highly profitable export activities to enable the provision of State financial support for productivity growth and income generation in the traditional and informal sectors. As a result, important linkages can be established between successful export industries, on the one hand, and the rest of the economy on the other. This is all the more important when such linkages are not created by market forces owing to the structural heterogeneity of a developing economy. For example, effective taxation of extractive industries' profits may often be the only way that the windfall profits resulting from an increase in international commodity prices can be channelled back into domestic demand and into greater investment in diversification of production and job creation.

Employment-friendly monetary and financial policies

While the prevention of excessive inflation is undoubtedly important, a monetary and financial policy to promote employment creation through greater fixed investment is of particular importance for developing countries where investment dynamics are weak, but where the enlargement of productive capacity and productivity growth are necessary conditions for the absorption of surplus labour. An employment-friendly monetary policy would aim at maintaining low costs of credit for investment in fixed capital and avoiding currency appreciation.

Financial policies should enable credit to be directed to sectors and activities that are of strategic importance for the structural transformation of the economy as a whole. Such financial support, which has often been used as an instrument of industrial policy, could also help solve the problem of access to adequate financing faced by many small, innovative enterprises, including those in the informal sector and agriculture. Many of these enterprises can play a key role in creating employment and linkages between modern and traditional production activities. Examples of such policies include the direct provision of credit by public financial institutions or by intervention in financial markets through such measures as interest subsidies, the refinancing of commercial loans and the provision of guarantees for certain types of credit.

Controlling inflation more effectively through an incomes policy

By shifting the emphasis of monetary policy towards growth and employment creation, the scope for central banks to pursue the objective of maintaining price stability or low inflation will be reduced. Therefore an additional instrument will be necessary to control inflation. This can be provided by an incomes policy. In the same way as it can contribute to generating greater domestic demand, such a policy can also prevent labour costs from rising faster than productivity and thus serve to control inflation.

As labour costs are the most important determinant of the overall cost level in a vertically integrated market economy, their importance in helping to stabilize the inflation rate cannot be overemphasized. If an incomes policy were to succeed in aligning wage income growth with average productivity growth plus a targeted inflation rate (not based on indexation from past inflation rates), cost-push inflation could be controlled. It would keep inflation low by preventing both increases in real production costs and demand growth in excess of the supply potential. Thus, central banks would not have to keep interest rates high to combat inflation, and consequently there would be more space for a growth-oriented monetary policy.

This is especially true for developing countries, many of which have a history of very high inflation. Backward looking indexation of nominal wages frequently contributed to bouts of inflationary acceleration. This has proved to be extremely costly, because the only way central banks can cut inflation is by applying repeated shocks to the economy through interest rate hikes and currency revaluations. Such measures imply sacrificing real investment and employment for the sake of nominal stabilization.

Institution building and public sector involvement in creating a wage-employment nexus

Alternative policy approaches for faster employment creation will have to take into account institutional frameworks that differ widely, even among countries at similar levels of per capita income. On the other hand, sustained employment creation may require reforms in these institutional conditions themselves.

Indeed, building the kind of institutions that would facilitate a productivity-led growth of labour income could be the basis for a successful development strategy that gives priority to employment creation and poverty reduction. A key element of such a strategy can be the creation and empowerment of trade unions, which should not only represent the interests of workers but also contribute to growth dynamics and macroeconomic stability. But in order to prevent an acceleration of inflation, nominal wage increases must not be adjusted to past consumer price inflation that may have resulted from increases in the prices of imported goods. Rather, the rule should be to link increases in labour compensation to past productivity increases plus a rate of inflation that is considered acceptable after taking into account price increases of imports.

This rule should ensure that the share of wage income in total income does not fall, as has frequently been the case in many countries in the past. However, situations may arise where an increase in the share of wage income is desirable. In this case, more far-reaching adjustments of labour compensation could be subject to explicit negotiations as part of a social compact. But as such a change in the functional distribution of income will often be difficult to achieve, governments may have to resort to an array of instruments to influence personal income distribution in order to correct perceived social inequalities.

Tripartite arrangements, including, for example, government recommendations for wage increases, have helped a number of countries in the past to achieve a steady increase in domestic demand. At the same time, economic policy has focused on directing investment into fixed capital, preventing undue inflationary pressure and preserving the international competitiveness of domestic producers. In the absence of, or as a complement to, a centralized negotiating mechanism for labour compensation for the entire economy, the introduction of a minimum wage and its augmentation over time, in line with productivity growth, may also help to ensure that domestic demand and the domestic supply potential rise approximately in parallel.

Since employment outside formal manufacturing and service activities constitutes a large share of total employment in most low-income developing countries, greater efforts should be made to improve earnings as well as working conditions in this segment of the economy. One way of doing this is to implement public employment schemes that establish an effective floor to the level of earnings and working conditions by making available jobs that offer such minimum employment terms.

Equally important are productivity-enhancing and income-protection measures in agriculture and the informal sector for a number of reasons besides raising income levels in such activities: they can also help strengthen the capacity of small-scale entrepreneurs or the self-employed to invest in productivity-enhancing equipment and increase demand by this segment of the population for consumer goods that are produced locally. In this context, improving and stabilizing farmers' incomes, as has been the practice in practically all developed countries for decades, is essential for enabling agricultural producers and workers to participate in economy-wide productivity and income growth. This will require a revitalization of agricultural support institutions and measures to reduce the impact on farmers' incomes of highly subsidized agricultural products imported from developed countries.

The external dimension

All these measures taken together would provide considerable scope for demand management to combat unemployment while keeping inflation in check and reducing export dependence. Especially for developing countries, broadening the menu of policy instruments and institution building would allow not only the pursuit of additional goals, but also increase the possible combinations of instruments, which in many cases will be decisive for the success or failure of a development strategy. However, a strategy of employment generation based on an expansion of domestic demand in line with productivity growth is more likely to succeed if it is embedded in a favourable coherent international policy framework.

There will be greater scope for central banks to pursue an investment-friendly monetary policy when disruptions in the financial sector and currency volatility and misalignment through speculative international capital flows are minimized. This is a systemic problem which could be solved through an appropriate multilateral framework for exchange-rate management that aims to prevent large current-account imbalances by keeping the real exchange rate relatively stable at a sustainable level. Such an exchange-rate scheme would also reduce the risk of employment losses in some countries due to undervaluation of the real exchange rate in others. In the absence of effective multilateral arrangements for exchange-rate management, the use of capital-account management techniques can contribute to regaining greater autonomy in macroeconomic policy-making, as has been done in various emerging-market economies.

A refocus on strengthening domestic demand as an engine of employment creation, and relying less on exports for growth than many countries did in the past should not be viewed as a retreat from integration into the global economy. Developing countries need to earn the necessary foreign exchange to finance their required imports, especially of capital goods with their embedded advanced technologies. Moreover, international competition can also spur innovation and investment by producers in tradable goods industries.

Supachai Panitchpakdi
Secretary-General of UNCTAD

Chapter I

AFTER THE GLOBAL CRISIS: AN UNEVEN AND FRAGILE RECOVERY

A. Recent trends in the world economy

1. Global growth and international trade

The world economy appears to be recovering from its worst crisis since the Second World War. After a marked slowdown in 2008 and a real contraction of almost 2 per cent in 2009, global GDP is expected to expand by about 3.5 per cent in 2010 (table 1.1). This would mean a return to pre-crisis growth rates in most regions, with the exception of the European Union (EU) and some transition economies where a resurgence of growth is proving to be much slower. However, these prospects are no reason for complacency: the exit from recession may seem to have been rapid but it is unlikely to be either strong or durable if it continues to be based on temporary factors, such as inventory cycles and exceptional fiscal stimulus programmes, and if the underlying causes of the crisis are still in place, such as unregulated financial systems, income inequality and global imbalances.

The global crisis in 2008–2009 was exceptional in several respects: it was the first time in the post-war period that global GDP contracted, almost all regions in the world were affected, and the time lapse between the financial shock and its impacts on the real economy was remarkably short. No region was spared by the crisis. Developed economies – where the financial

crisis originated – and transition economies were the worst affected, but developing economies also suffered GDP contractions, or at least a significant deceleration. In fact, most developed and emerging economies posted strongly negative growth rates in the last quarter of 2008 and the first quarter of 2009, including several emerging economies that had been growing at a fast pace in the first half of 2008. Even those emerging economies that avoided an outright recession (including China, India and Indonesia) could not escape a significant slowdown of economic growth at that time (see *TDR 2009*, chap. I).

As remarkable as the rapid spread of the crisis in late 2008 and early 2009, is the rapid recovery in numerous countries, particularly in developing regions. However, their relatively high growth rates in 2010 are partly due to the fact that they rebounded from low levels in 2009, a statistical effect that is set to wane in the near future. And unless new sources of dynamism can be found, growth rates will probably decline in most countries in 2011.

In developed economies, the rescue packages initiated by governments in 2008 and 2009 prevented the collapse of financial markets, while supportive fiscal and monetary policies partially compensated for sluggish private demand. With some exceptions

Table 1.1

WORLD OUTPUT GROWTH, 1991–2010

(Annual percentage change)

Region/country	1991–2003[a]	2004	2005	2006	2007	2008	2009[b]	2010[b]
World	**2.8**	**4.1**	**3.5**	**3.9**	**3.9**	**1.7**	**-1.9**	**3.5**
Developed countries	**2.5**	**3.1**	**2.5**	**2.8**	**2.5**	**0.3**	**-3.4**	**2.2**
of which:								
Japan	1.0	2.7	1.9	2.0	2.4	-1.2	-5.2	2.5
United States	3.3	3.6	3.1	2.7	2.1	0.4	-2.4	2.9
European Union (EU-27)	2.3	2.5	2.0	3.1	2.8	0.7	-4.2	1.1
of which:								
Euro area	2.1	2.2	1.7	2.9	2.7	0.6	-4.1	0.9
France	2.0	2.5	1.9	2.2	2.4	0.2	-2.6	1.2
Germany	1.7	1.2	0.8	3.0	2.5	1.3	-4.9	1.5
Italy	1.6	1.5	0.7	2.0	1.4	-1.3	-5.1	0.8
United Kingdom	2.9	3.0	2.1	2.8	2.6	0.5	-4.9	1.1
European Union (EU-12)[c]	2.7	5.6	4.7	6.5	6.1	3.9	-3.3	2.0
South-East Europe and CIS	..	**7.7**	**6.6**	**8.1**	**8.5**	**5.4**	**-6.3**	**4.1**
South-East Europe[d]	..	5.5	4.7	5.1	6.1	4.2	-3.6	1.2
Commonwealth of Independent States (CIS)	..	8.0	6.8	8.4	8.7	5.5	-6.5	4.4
of which:								
Russian Federation	..	7.2	6.4	7.7	8.1	5.6	-7.9	4.3
Developing countries	**4.6**	**7.3**	**6.7**	**7.4**	**7.8**	**5.4**	**2.4**	**6.9**
Africa	3.0	5.9	5.6	5.9	6.0	4.9	2.5	4.8
North Africa, excl. Sudan	3.4	4.8	5.2	5.7	5.2	5.2	3.3	4.7
Sub-Saharan Africa, excl. South Africa	3.0	7.6	6.5	6.3	7.2	5.3	3.8	5.9
South Africa	2.4	4.9	5.0	5.3	5.5	3.7	-1.8	3.0
Latin America and the Caribbean	2.7	6.1	5.0	5.7	5.9	4.3	-1.8	5.2
Caribbean	2.4	3.9	7.6	9.4	6.1	3.3	0.2	2.2
Central America, excl. Mexico	4.1	4.3	4.8	6.5	7.1	4.5	-0.6	3.0
Mexico	3.0	4.0	3.2	4.8	3.2	1.5	-6.6	4.1
South America	2.5	7.2	5.6	5.8	7.0	5.5	-0.2	5.9
of which:								
Brazil	2.5	5.7	3.2	4.0	6.1	5.1	-0.2	7.6
Asia	5.9	8.0	7.6	8.2	8.8	5.8	4.0	7.8
East Asia	7.5	8.3	8.1	9.2	10.2	6.8	5.3	8.9
of which:								
China	10.0	10.1	10.4	11.6	13.0	9.6	8.7	10.0
South Asia	5.1	7.5	8.1	8.4	8.7	5.0	5.5	6.6
of which:								
India	5.8	8.3	9.3	9.4	9.6	5.1	6.6	7.9
South-East Asia	4.6	6.6	5.9	6.2	6.6	4.0	0.8	7.0
West Asia	3.5	8.9	7.1	6.0	5.0	4.6	-0.8	5.2

Source: UNCTAD secretariat calculations, based on United Nations, Department of Economic and Social Affairs (UN/DESA), *National Accounts Main Aggregates* database, and *World Economic Situation and Prospects (WESP) 2010: Mid-Year Update;* ECLAC, 2010; OECD, 2010; and national sources.

Note: Calculations for country aggregates are based on GDP at constant 2000 dollars.
   a Average.
   b Preliminary estimates for 2009 and forecasts for 2010.
   c New EU member States after 2004.
   d Albania, Bosnia and Herzegovina, Croatia, Montenegro, Serbia and The former Yugoslav Republic of Macedonia.

(e.g. Finland, Greece, Iceland, Ireland, Italy, Spain and the Baltic countries), developed economies returned to positive growth rates between the second and the fourth quarter of 2009. It is estimated that in 2010, growth rates will be close to 3 per cent in Australia, Canada, Japan and the United States, but it is unlikely that developed countries as a whole will return to rapid and sustainable growth rates in the near future. The main reason is that, in general, final domestic demand remains weak owing to continued high unemployment and low private consumption. Households tend to increase savings partly for pre-cautionary reasons, but also because of declining real income and the scarcity of bank credit. Investment remains discouraged by idle productive capacities, uncertain future demand and more difficult access to credit. Indeed, it is likely that balance-sheet adjustments in financial and non-financial private sectors will continue to dampen domestic demand.

On the positive side, the inventory cycle entered an upside phase in mid-2009 as firms began to rebuild their inventories. For instance, in the United States, the main factor contributing to GDP growth since then has been the reversal from destocking to restocking, followed by private consumption; on the other hand, fixed investment, public expenditure and net exports have made little or no contribution. In Germany, the replenishing of inventories is expected to be the sole positive contribution to growth based on domestic demand in 2010. However, the contribution of restocking is by its very nature only temporary.

Several developed countries seem to be promoting net exports as a possible driver of growth. Very dynamic regional growth in Asia, and the resultant strong demand, contributed most to the significant export-led recovery of Japan – one of the developed countries severely affected by the crisis. In Western Europe, too, policies have aimed at increasing net exports, and the growth rate, albeit more modest, has also been lifted primarily by external demand. The United States, on the other hand, will find it difficult to follow an export-led growth strategy following the appreciation of the dollar. More generally, if too many big players begin to rely on net exports, they cannot all be successful, and this could lead to trade tensions among them. Moreover, there is a high risk that a withdrawal of fiscal stimulus before the return of strong domestic consumption and investment will jeopardize economic recovery.

The depth of the economic recession and the vigour of the subsequent recovery vary widely among developing and transition economies. In particular, the financial shock seriously affected those emerging-market economies that had been running current-account deficits and depended heavily on capital inflows. Such countries (many of them in Central and Eastern Europe and the Commonwealth of Independent States (CIS)) were forced to apply restrictive macroeconomic policy responses, in some cases under IMF-led programmes. By contrast, the financial turmoil had little effect on low-income countries that are largely excluded from international financial markets (such as South Asian and sub-Saharan African countries) and on emerging-market economies that had avoided large external deficits and accumulated significant international reserves in the years prior to the crisis. This not only gave their governments enough policy space to conduct countercyclical macroeconomic policies, but also their previously accumulated reserves provided a buffer against the financial shockwaves and helped them to pre-empt exchange-rate and banking crises.

As a result, most Asian and Latin American emerging-market economies were able to contain a rise in unemployment and achieve rapid recovery of domestic demand, which appear to be the main drivers of their growth in 2010. Improvements in commodity prices since mid-2009 and in the volume of exports (especially in East and South-East Asia and in some Latin American countries such as Argentina, Brazil and Mexico) have also contributed significantly to GDP growth. Latin American GDP is forecast to expand by some 5 per cent in 2010, with growth in the four MERCOSUR countries[1] and Peru at close to 7 per cent. Recovery is likely to be more moderate in Mexico, Central America and the Caribbean, with growth rates generally between 2 and 4 per cent. These countries were strongly affected in 2009 by the collapse of foreign trade, a reduction in international tourist arrivals and falling remittances. At present, their merchandise exports appear to be the main contributor to their economic upturn, as domestic demand remains weak.

Most South-East Asian economies started 2010 with very rapid growth rates, sustained by both buoyant exports and strong domestic demand. Even if some deceleration is likely in the second half of 2010 and into 2011, the subregion's GDP should expand by some 7 per cent in 2010. South and East

Asia only suffered a deceleration of their rapid pace of growth in early 2009, and most of them are on track to return to their pre-crisis growth rates in 2010. Policies aimed at boosting domestic demand in China and India, in particular, must be credited to a large extent for that outcome. Fiscal support and credit availability strengthened domestic demand, leading to both higher consumption and investment expenditure. In China, some reorientation of public expenditure is under way, which would increase the share of social expenditure and reduce that of investment in infrastructure. This, together with sustained increases in real wages, may help rebalance the composition of domestic demand and make its expansion more sustainable in the long run by increasing the share of household consumption and reducing that of investment from its very high current level. Remittances sent to South Asia continued to grow in 2009 (unlike recipient countries in Latin America, Europe, North Africa and the CIS), which added to the resilience of domestic demand. Trade flows have rebounded since mid-2009, providing a dynamic condition for these regions' economies, and contributing to the upturn in commodity prices from their lows of the first quarter of 2009.

Higher commodity prices have been playing an important role in Africa, West Asia and the CIS: they helped increase national income, generated additional fiscal revenue and relaxed foreign-exchange constraints. In oil-exporting countries in North Africa and West Asia, higher public spending in 2009 and 2010 for important investment projects was also made possible by previously accumulated funds. In several African countries, economic performance partly relies on activities such as agriculture, which are largely unaffected by short-term international trends and face generally positive prospects. In addition, investment projects related to infrastructure development, tele-communications and/or extractive industries helped maintain positive per capita income growth in 2009 and will continue to support even faster growth in 2010. In South Africa, the country in the region that was the worst affected by the international crisis, the manufacturing and mining sectors should benefit from improved foreign demand, and there is also expected to be an increase in tourism. The projected growth rate for the region as a whole is 5 per cent, and closer to 6 per cent for sub-Saharan countries (excluding South Africa). Finally, in most countries of Central and Eastern Europe and the CIS, recovery is likely to be moderate, with domestic demand weighed down by unemployment and constraints on government spending. The highest growth for these groups in 2010 will probably occur in some oil or gas exporters (e.g. Azerbaijan and Turkmenistan). The Russian Federation and Ukraine are set to grow by more than 4 per cent, and although this will not be sufficient to restore their GDP to its pre-crisis level, it will provide some relief to other CIS countries, for which the Russian Federation is a major market and the main source of workers' remittances.

International trade, which contracted sharply in both volume and value, was the main channel through which the crisis spread globally. The volume of world trade plunged by more than 13 per cent in 2009 (table 1.2). Given the overall fall in unit prices of trade (close to 11 per cent), the decline in the value of trade in current dollars was even more pronounced, reaching 23 per cent for the year.

Although the crisis-induced squeeze on trade credit played a role in reducing trade worldwide, the decline in domestic demand, amplified by the globally synchronized nature of the downturn since 2008, was the main cause of the slowdown in world trade in 2009. The sharp falls in wealth and expectations prompted households and firms to reduce or postpone spending, especially on consumer durables and investment goods, which constitute an important share of world trade. Expanded global supply chains – a dominant feature of transnational corporations in world trade today – also played an important, though unquantifiable, role in the 2009 slump in world trade. In addition, lower production of manufactures translated into lower demand for energy and industrial raw materials. As a result, all countries and regions registered significant declines in their exports of goods, with larger declines in volume in developed and transition countries than in developing countries. Since the crisis first affected the demand for durable and capital goods, it is no wonder that the impact was greatest on countries like Germany and Japan. However, in terms of the value of exports, the worst hit countries were exporters of oil and mining products, for which not only the volume, but more importantly the unit value of exports fell sharply.

In all regions, both exports and imports declined. In some cases, this was partly due to the high import component of exported manufactures, so that those countries that faced lower demand for their exports automatically reduced their demand for imports.

Table 1.2

EXPORT AND IMPORT VOLUMES OF GOODS, SELECTED REGIONS AND COUNTRIES, 2006–2009

(Annual percentage change)

Region/country	Volume of exports				Volume of imports			
	2006	2007	2008	2009	2006	2007	2008	2009
World	**9.2**	**5.8**	**3.0**	**-13.7**	**8.5**	**6.6**	**2.2**	**-13.1**
Developed countries	**8.5**	**3.9**	**2.8**	**-14.8**	**7.2**	**3.7**	**0.0**	**-14.2**
of which:								
Japan	11.8	6.8	4.9	-25.3	4.3	0.8	-0.9	-12.8
United States	10.5	6.8	5.5	-14.9	5.4	1.1	-3.7	-16.5
European Union	8.9	3.2	2.5	-13.7	8.9	4.8	1.1	-13.7
South-East Europe and CIS	**6.0**	**8.6**	**0.8**	**-15.5**	**21.4**	**26.1**	**16.0**	**-28.2**
South-East Europe	16.1	17.9	-13.3	-20.1	10.5	23.7	-9.5	-19.5
CIS	5.5	8.1	1.6	-15.2	23.6	26.5	18.9	-29.2
Developing countries	**10.8**	**8.7**	**4.2**	**-11.7**	**10.2**	**10.6**	**5.3**	**-9.5**
Africa	1.3	4.8	-2.8	-10.0	9.9	11.2	11.6	-2.4
Sub-Saharan Africa	1.1	4.7	-1.4	-10.3	12.6	8.8	3.7	-5.6
Latin America and the Caribbean	5.6	2.4	-0.6	-9.7	13.2	11.6	8.6	-17.1
East Asia	18.3	15.6	7.3	-10.2	10.6	10.2	0.6	-4.6
of which:								
China	25.4	21.8	10.5	-13.0	13.3	14.1	2.4	-0.2
South Asia	10.9	6.3	14.9	-18.9	9.9	10.9	7.2	-6.9
of which:								
India	11.3	15.2	10.7	-7.9	9.9	16.9	10.4	-7.5
South-East Asia	10.3	6.9	2.1	-9.7	7.3	6.7	8.0	-15.9
West Asia	3.8	2.0	7.4	-14.4	9.4	16.7	8.4	-12.8

Source: UNCTAD secretariat calculations, based on *UNCTAD Handbook of Statistics* database.

More generally, concurrent movements in exports and imports in all the regions show the synchronized character of economic retraction, or slowdown, and contrasts with previous episodes of localized crises. In such episodes, the economies hit by recession considerably reduced their imports but not their exports, and consequently found some economic stimulus through their foreign trade. In the present crisis, the best performers were countries that could rely on their domestic or regional markets. Thus, even though both imports and exports fell worldwide, the degree of the fall varied in different regions. In South America, the CIS and most countries exporting oil and mining products, import volumes declined more than export volumes due to terms-of-trade losses. In other countries, imports by volume declined more moderately than exports, either because a significant proportion of imports are normally funded through non-export revenues, such as public grants or private remittances (as seems to be the case in sub-Saharan Africa and South Asia), or because the countries were running large trade surpluses and/or had abundant foreign exchange reserves when the crisis erupted. In China, for example, lower exports reduced the trade surplus but only marginally affected the volume of imports.

The feared surge in protectionism has not materialized so far. New import-restricting measures imposed by G-20 countries from November 2009

Chart 1.1

WORLD TRADE BY VALUE AND VOLUME, JANUARY 2000–APRIL 2010

(Index numbers, 2000 = 100)

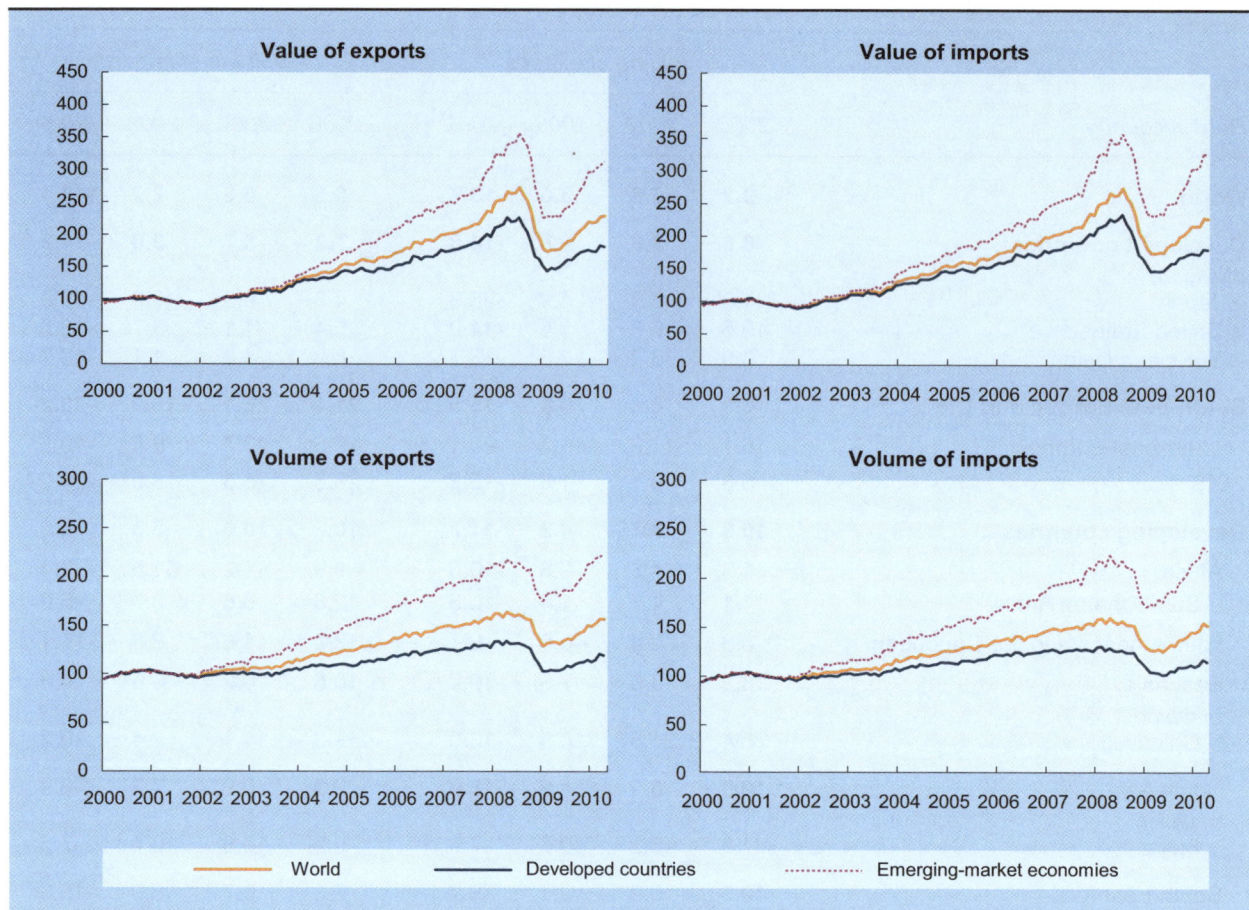

Value of exports

Value of imports

Volume of exports

Volume of imports

| World | Developed countries | Emerging-market economies |

Source: UNCTAD secretariat calculations, based on the CPB Netherlands Bureau of Economic Policy Analysis, *World Trade* database.

to May 2010 have affected at most only 0.7 per cent of these countries' imports and 0.4 per cent of world imports of goods, which represents about half the increase of the previous six months (UNCTAD, WTO, OECD, 2010; WTO, 2010). But uncertainties linked to export markets and high unemployment rates could still potentially trigger protectionist policies in the not too distant future.

Since the sharp contraction of trade in 2009 was strongly demand-driven, as demand recovers, so too should trade. In fact, trade volume started to recover from the second half of the year, led by strong demand from developing countries and relatively weaker demand from developed countries. Indeed, trade between developing countries is increasing significantly in 2010. By April 2010, the external

trade (by volume) of emerging-market economies had already bounced back to its previous peak of April 2008. External trade in developed countries has also been growing since mid-2009, although at a slower pace (chart 1.1). Overall, world trade in goods could expand in volume by more than 10 per cent in 2010, which would allow it to return to its pre-crisis levels. However, measured in current dollars, the recovery will take more time, as unit values in international trade remain, on average, clearly lower than their 2008 peaks.

Trade in services has by and large followed the same trends as that of goods. Regarding travel services, the year 2009 is viewed as "one of the most challenging periods in tourism's history" (World Tourism Organization, 2010a). The number of international tourist arrivals fell by 4.3 per cent that year, compared to 2008 which was a record year. Among world regions, international arrivals shrank above average in Europe (-5.6 per cent), partly aggravated by the then still strong euro, in West Asia (-5.4 per cent) and in the Americas, which suffered an additional blow to tourism due to the influenza A(H1N1) virus (swine flu). Worldwide tourist receipts were down by 5.8 per cent in value, which shows that tourists also cut their average expenditure at destination (World Tourism Organization, 2010b). The decline in international arrivals was the most pronounced in the first three quarters of 2009, coinciding with the period when the financial crisis reached the real economy, as reflected in rising unemployment and falling consumer confidence. The fourth quarter of 2009 saw a revival in international arrivals, although it was uneven and weak. This again corresponded to the overall economic recovery that started during that period.

International transport services also have a direct relationship with the overall performance of the global economy and total merchandise trade. Seaborne trade (which carries 80 per cent of all traded goods) declined in volume by 4.5 per cent in 2009.[2] The sharpest reduction was in containerized trade at the end of 2008 and into 2009. The bulk sector was less affected owing to large imports by China, which took advantage of low prices of commodities and freight to increase its stocks of raw materials. Prices of maritime freight plummeted by the end of 2008, when the Baltic Exchange Dry Index fell by 90 per cent from its record high in May of that year. By mid-2009 there was a partial recovery, with freight rates at around 40 per cent of their 2008 peak (UNCTAD, 2010). The world merchant fleet capacity grew by 6.7 per cent in 2008 and by another 7 per cent in 2009. Given the scheduled ship deliveries, that capacity will grow further during 2010. As a result, it is unlikely that the recovery of trade in goods will lead to a new surge in freight tariffs in the short run.

2. Recent trends in primary commodity markets

After the collapse in demand for and prices of commodities in the second half of 2008 as a result of the global financial and economic crisis, most commodity prices rebounded in 2009. This upward trend continued partially into 2010, although the behaviour of prices in the first months of the year was fairly erratic, exhibiting some downward corrections in January–February and May 2010 (chart 1.2). The prices of a large number of commodities increased significantly between the beginning and end of 2009, but they were lower than their average of 2008 (table 1.3) – an average that was very high owing to soaring prices in the first half of 2008. Overall, in spite of their sharp decline in the second half of 2008, prices for all commodity groups during 2009 and early 2010 have remained well above their average of the 2000s.

The most significant price increases in 2009 and the first half of 2010 were in metals and minerals, and energy products, particularly crude petroleum. These were also the commodities that had witnessed the sharpest slump in prices in the second half of 2008. By April 2010, the price of crude petroleum had more than doubled in comparison with the trough of early 2009, while the price index for metals and minerals had increased by 83 per cent, reaching close to its peak levels of early 2008. The prices of agricultural commodities grew more moderately, although those of agricultural raw materials rose by more than 55 per cent from their trough (chart 1.2). Thus the commodities which experienced the largest variations in prices were those that are more closely linked to the evolution of the global industrial production cycle.

Robust demand from rapidly growing developing countries, mainly China, has been the key driver of the recovery of commodity prices, particularly metals and minerals, and crude petroleum, and partly also agricultural raw materials. China's strong demand growth for minerals and metals, and energy was largely due to the success of its fiscal stimulus package and monetary policy easing in response to the crisis, as well as to its policy of building up its commodity inventories. Chinese authorities took advantage of the lower prices to increase their strategic reserves for the future, while private companies sought to replenish their inventories. As an illustration, in 2009, Chinese demand for the main base metals (aluminium, copper, lead, nickel, tin and zinc) increased by 23 per cent, whereas this demand fell by 13.5 per cent in the rest of the world (World Bank, 2010).

The monthly average of crude petroleum prices, which usually lead developments in other commodity markets, had fallen sharply to around $40 per barrel

Chart 1.2

**MONTHLY COMMODITY PRICE INDICES
BY COMMODITY GROUP, JAN. 2000–MAY 2010**

(Index numbers, 2000 = 100)

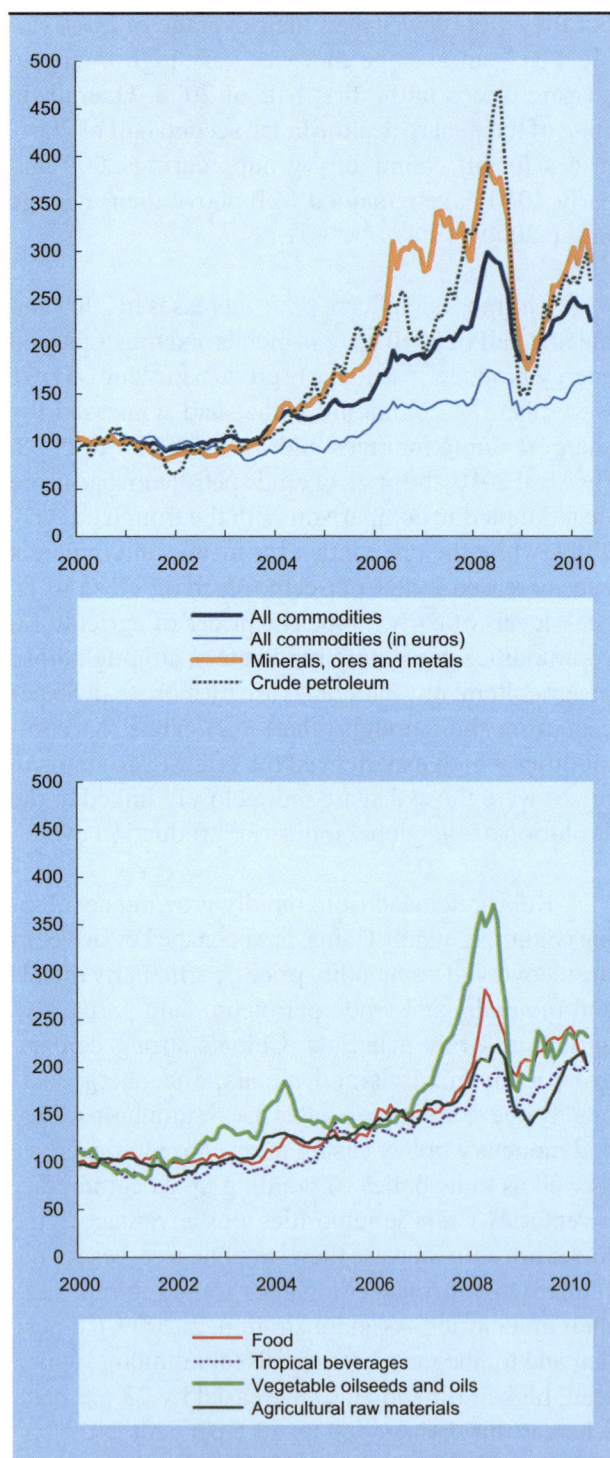

- All commodities
- All commodities (in euros)
- Minerals, ores and metals
- Crude petroleum

- Food
- Tropical beverages
- Vegetable oilseeds and oils
- Agricultural raw materials

Source: UNCTAD secretariat calculations, based on UNCTAD, *Commodity Price Statistics Online* database.
Note: Crude petroleum price is the average of Dubai/Brent/Texas, equally weighted. Prices are in current dollars, unless otherwise specified.

in December 2008–February 2009, after having reached over $130 in July 2008. By April 2010, the monthly average of Brent, Dubai and West Texas Intermediate prices was $84 per barrel. To some extent, the rebound in oil prices in 2009 was driven by the cuts in supply by members of the Organization of the Petroleum Exporting Countries (OPEC), which observed a high degree of compliance with production quotas as a reaction to the global drop in demand. Overall, in 2009 global oil demand was 1.4 per cent lower than in the previous year, mainly as a result of the 4.4 per cent decline in demand by the members of the Organisation for Economic Co-operation and Development (OECD). By contrast, oil demand in non-OECD countries rose by 2.3 per cent, with oil consumption growth in China at 7.6 per cent (IEA, 2010).

Global demand for oil has recovered since the third quarter of 2009, primarily on account of consumption growth in non-OECD countries, while oil consumption in OECD countries has remained subdued. As a result, oil prices have generally remained at around the range of $70–$80 per barrel since then. This range is widely considered among producers as high enough to provide incentives for investment in new production capacity, but at the same time low enough not to jeopardize global economic recovery, because a slow recovery would have a negative impact on demand. By the end of 2009 and early 2010 the degree of compliance with production quotas among OPEC members had declined as a result of the higher prices. In addition, production in non-OPEC countries has been increasing. Oil consumption has continued to rise in 2010, but the demand pressure on prices is being absorbed by large inventories and spare capacity. The IEA (2010) forecasts world oil demand to increase by 1.9 per cent in 2010.

While the evolution of demand fundamentals in emerging-market economies certainly will have contributed to the upturn in the prices of a large number of commodities, it does not explain the magnitude of the price increases, which seems to have been excessive given the fragility of the recovery of the world economy during 2009. An additional major factor that may have boosted commodity prices beyond market fundamentals was the strong presence of financial investors in these markets. After fleeing from commodity markets in the second half of 2008, financial investors returned in 2009, driven by their growing appetite for risk in response to indications

Table 1.3

WORLD PRIMARY COMMODITY PRICES, 2004–2010

(Percentage change over previous year, unless otherwise indicated)

Commodity group	2004	2005	2006	2007	2008	2009	2010[a]	Jan.–Dec. 2009[b]
All commodities[c]	**20.0**	**11.6**	**30.2**	**13.0**	**24.0**	**-16.8**	**13.0**	**29.4**
All commodities (in SDRs)[c]	**13.5**	**12.0**	**30.5**	**8.6**	**19.5**	**-14.6**	**14.7**	**23.6**
All food	**13.2**	**6.3**	**16.3**	**13.3**	**39.2**	**-8.5**	**2.5**	**18.3**
Food and tropical beverages	**13.2**	**8.8**	**17.8**	**8.6**	**40.4**	**-5.4**	**1.6**	**17.7**
Tropical beverages	6.4	25.5	6.7	10.4	20.2	1.9	9.1	24.9
Coffee	19.8	43.8	7.1	12.5	15.4	-6.9	9.0	15.3
Cocoa	-11.8	-0.7	3.5	22.6	32.2	11.9	12.8	33.2
Tea	2.1	9.1	11.7	-12.3	27.2	16.5	-1.5	42.7
Food	13.9	7.2	19.0	8.5	42.5	-6.0	0.9	17.0
Sugar	1.1	37.9	49.4	-31.7	26.9	41.8	12.6	86.9
Beef	17.8	4.1	-2.4	1.9	2.6	-1.2	25.5	11.4
Maize	5.0	-12.0	24.4	38.2	34.0	-24.4	-2.8	1.4
Wheat	6.8	-1.4	26.6	34.3	27.5	-31.4	-13.7	-14.2
Rice	23.1	17.1	5.5	9.5	110.7	-15.8	-8.3	-1.5
Bananas	39.9	9.9	18.5	-0.9	24.6	0.7	-3.2	-1.6
Vegetable oilseeds and oils	**13.2**	**-9.5**	**5.0**	**52.9**	**31.9**	**-28.4**	**9.6**	**23.0**
Soybeans	16.1	-10.4	-2.2	43.0	36.1	-16.6	-5.2	8.9
Agricultural raw materials	**13.4**	**3.2**	**13.3**	**12.0**	**20.5**	**-17.5**	**28.3**	**32.2**
Hides and skins	-1.7	-2.1	5.1	4.5	-11.3	-30.0	54.3	65.6
Cotton	-3.3	-11.6	5.9	10.2	12.8	-12.2	34.4	31.7
Tobacco	3.6	1.8	6.4	11.6	8.3	18.1	-2.2	16.4
Rubber	19.2	16.7	40.6	9.5	16.9	-27.0	79.0	88.3
Tropical logs	19.2	0.3	-4.7	19.5	39.3	-20.6	1.0	-5.5
Minerals, ores and metals	**40.7**	**26.2**	**60.3**	**12.8**	**6.2**	**-30.2**	**30.0**	**55.3**
Aluminium	19.8	10.6	35.4	2.7	-2.5	-35.3	30.3	54.3
Phosphate rock	7.8	2.5	5.3	60.5	387.2	-64.8	-8.5	-66.0
Iron ore	17.4	71.5	19.0	9.5	65.0	-28.2	26.1	0.0
Tin	73.8	-13.2	18.9	65.6	27.3	-26.7	29.5	36.8
Copper	61.0	28.4	82.7	5.9	-2.3	-26.3	41.5	116.8
Nickel	43.6	6.6	64.5	53.5	-43.3	-30.6	47.3	51.0
Tungsten ore	22.9	120.7	36.2	-0.6	-0.3	-8.9	0.0	0.0
Lead	72.0	10.2	32.0	100.2	-19.0	-17.7	25.8	104.9
Zinc	26.5	31.9	137.0	-1.0	-42.2	-11.7	35.3	100.0
Gold	12.6	8.7	35.9	15.3	25.1	11.6	17.4	32.2
Crude petroleum	**30.7**	**41.3**	**20.4**	**10.7**	**36.4**	**-36.3**	**26.6**	**70.6**
Memo item:								
Manufactures[d]	**8.3**	**2.5**	**3.4**	**7.5**	**4.9**	**-5.6**	..	..

Source: UNCTAD secretariat calculations, based on UNCTAD, *Commodity Price Statistics Online*; IMF, *International Financial Statistics* database; and United Nations Statistics Division (UNSD), *Monthly Bulletin of Statistics*, various issues.

Note: In current dollars, unless otherwise specified.

    a Percentage change between the average of January to May 2010 and the average for 2009.
    b Percentage change between January and December 2009.
    c Excluding crude petroleum.
    d Unit value of exports of manufactured goods of developed countries.

of better prospects for global economic activity. The increasing attractiveness of commodities as an asset class has also been reinforced by ample liquidity and low interest rates.

The volume of derivatives trading in non-precious metals increased by 132.8 per cent in 2009, while it rose by 12.9 per cent for energy products and by 3.7 per cent for agricultural products. Commodity derivatives trading is growing particularly fast in China, where the Shanghai Futures Exchange, trading mostly in futures in industrial metals, tripled its volume in 2009 (Burghardt and Acworth, 2010). Furthermore, according to Barclays Capital (2010), in 2009 commodity assets under management rose to an all-time high year-end value of $257 billion – representing the largest annual increase on record – with inflows of $68 billion. This has contributed to a 42-fold increase in commodity assets under management over the past decade. The rising trend in commodity investments is expected to continue through the next decade. Another indicator of the effect of financial investment in these markets is that in 2009, commodity inventories, particularly for metals and minerals, rose alongside prices.

Therefore, movements in commodity prices continue to be strongly influenced by financial investors' sentiment about the evolution of the markets. In January–February and in May 2010 price corrections occurred following commodity sell-offs due to concerns about falling demand associated with the European sovereign debt crisis. A tightening of monetary policy in China to prevent an overheating of the economy, particularly in the property sector, was also a factor in the retreat of investors from commodity markets, which contributed to the fall in prices.[3] At the same time, gold has been benefiting from the uncertainties about the global economic recovery: increasingly attracting investors in search of a safe haven, its price has been hitting record levels in nominal terms.

An additional factor affecting changes in commodity prices has been the evolution of the exchange rate of the dollar, in which commodity prices are usually denominated. Thus the price increases in 2009 were associated with a depreciating dollar, just as in 2010 the price declines have been occurring concurrently with a stronger dollar, particularly as the euro was weakening due to the crisis in Greece. Changes in commodity prices in euro terms are less extreme than those in dollar terms. In fact, in the first months of 2010, while the aggregate price index for all commodities in dollar terms declined, it continued to increase in euro terms (chart 1.2).

Prices of agricultural commodities, particularly food and tropical beverages, which are normally less affected by the evolution of macroeconomic variables, have been strongly influenced by supply conditions, notably the weather. Food prices, which were a major cause of the food crisis of 2008, have not recovered much since their collapse in the second half of that year. This has been mainly due to bumper harvests in cereals and in vegetable oilseeds and oils. In addition, the lower price of oil associated with the global crisis contributed to lowering the pressure on cereal and oilseed production for biofuels. Downward pressure on oilseed prices has been more modest due to strong demand, particularly for soybeans in China. Overall, the situation in food markets has been easing as inventories have been replenished to more comfortable levels. Moreover, forecasts suggest good harvests in 2010 (FAO, 2010). While this provides some relief to the global food crisis in the short term, food security is still a pressing problem in many developing countries. It is therefore critical to continue with efforts to overcome the structural causes of the food crisis (*TDR 2008*, chap. II).

Markets for tropical beverages have been tight as a result of poor harvests and rising demand. In the case of cocoa, production has been affected by recurrent underinvestment, domestic disruptions and problems of governance in Côte d'Ivoire, which accounts for about 35 per cent of global supply. Sugar prices increased sharply in 2009 and reached a 30-year high in January 2010. In 2009, bad weather seriously affected sugar production in leading sugar cane producing countries such as Brazil and India, but expectations for good crops in 2010 have led to a strong turnaround in prices (FAO, 2010). By contrast, supply conditions have not been so important in influencing agricultural raw material prices, which had fallen sharply in late 2008 and early 2009 due to the decline in global demand caused by the global recession. Natural rubber prices have increased in 2010 owing to a recovery in car production and demand in China, as well as to the increase in oil prices, which made synthetic rubber more expensive. Likewise, cotton prices have been rising as consumption has outpaced production, mainly because of the recovery of the Chinese textile sector.

In general, commodity prices have remained highly volatile, and their future evolution is extremely uncertain. As long as excessive speculation on commodity markets is not properly contained, the strong presence of financial investors will continue to add instability to these markets, as investors tend to react quickly to any financial and economic news, even if unrelated to commodity market fundamentals.[4] In the short term, developments in commodity markets will fundamentally depend on the pace of recovery of global economic activity. Given the ample inventories of most commodities at present, any increases in demand should be reasonably easy to meet, so that there is unlikely to be significant upward pressure on prices.

In the longer term, however, demand from fast growing China and other developing countries is expected to remain healthy on account of the continuing industrialization and urbanization process, and the corresponding needs for infrastructure development. On the other hand, once inventories and spare capacity begin to shrink in response to this demand, supply constraints, which contributed to the commodity price boom of 2003–2008 and have not been appropriately addressed due to the global economic crisis in 2008–2009, risk re-emerging. In fact, the crisis has most likely aggravated supply constraints in the medium term, particularly in the extractive industries. Falling demand and prices and the credit crunch led to the cancellation or postponement of a number of projects in this sector. In 2009 there was a 42 per cent drop in worldwide non-ferrous exploration budgets from their 2008 high (Metals Economics Group, 2010). As a result, although there is a revival of investment with the renewed increase in prices, due to a lag in the supply response to the increasing demand, prices are expected to remain high over the medium to long term.[5] Sustained economic and population growth in emerging-market economies as well as continued expansion of biofuel output in response to higher energy prices (and depending on government mandates) are also expected to add upward pressure on prices of food commodities during the second decade of this century. Accordingly, the risk of another food crisis cannot be ruled out (OECD-FAO, 2010).

B. Global recovery and rebalancing: current situation and prospects

When huge disruptions in global financial markets first emerged in mid-2007, policymakers were generally slow to recognize the true nature and magnitude of the unfolding calamity. Many observers had feared that the massive global imbalances posed a severe threat to global stability, but the full force of the market turmoil in August 2007 caught most policymakers off-guard. Some of them even continued to be preoccupied with perceived inflation risks, and, with few exceptions, they were only shaken out of their complacency and reluctance to act when the global economy took a nosedive in the final quarter of 2008. Coordinated policy easing by leading central banks was both a highly warranted first step and an important sign of global solidarity in what was by then finally recognized as a global crisis of potentially catastrophic proportions.

At the G-20 summit meetings in November 2008 in Washington and in April 2009 in London, Heads of State and Government committed to employing large macroeconomic stimulus packages and comprehensive support programmes for their respective financial sectors. The types and magnitudes of policy measures implemented varied significantly across countries and regions, and not always in proportion to the severity of the local downturn (*TDR 2009*). In the event, the aggregate policy impact of these measures proved sufficient to prevent the global economy from succumbing to forces that had the potential to cause another Great Depression (Aiginger, 2009).

In mid-2009, the global economy appeared to have bottomed out (see table 1.1), and has since shown some promising signs of recovery, albeit to varying degrees in different regions and countries. As a preliminary assessment, it would be fair to say that the implementation of powerful countercyclical macroeconomic policies won global policymakers an important first round in battling the crisis. However, remaining stresses and re-emerging imbalances as well as renewed fears and instabilities in global financial markets since the first quarter of 2010 indicate that the war against a global depression has not yet been won.

Despite this, calls for an "early exit" from the demand-stimulating macroeconomic policy stance have been growing louder. Such calls have been particularly prominent among European policymakers, most of whom had agreed only belatedly, and with great reluctance, to contribute to the global effort of countering the crisis in the first place. Indeed, already in 2009 some European countries embarked on retrenchment rather than stimulus programmes, and in the first half of 2010 new austerity measures aimed at balancing government budgets sooner rather than later were being announced. From a global perspective this is a risky undertaking, because it is precisely in Europe that recovery appears to be the most fragile. In fact, in mid-2010 it is becoming increasingly clear that the centre of the global crisis that originated in the United States in 2008 has shifted to Europe, creating a new hotspot of instability.

It is therefore important to stress that at this juncture any withdrawal of a stimulus policy seems rather premature, since in many countries private demand remains fragile, having only partially recovered from its trough so far, and with no sign of even approaching its pre-crisis levels. It therefore risks undermining the incipient global recovery and raises the spectre of a double-dip recession that could push the global economy into a vicious circle of debt deflation. Another risk is that countries or regions that make a premature exit from a domestic-demand-supporting policy stance could become overdependent on exports for their growth. This could result in the emergence of new divergences and renewed tensions at the regional and/or global levels, prompting retaliatory measures in the form of protectionism, which, if practiced widely, could magnify any contractionary effects and stall the recovery. Today, an increasing number of countries are under pressure from financial markets to adopt policies that would only weaken their economies further. This would simply add to the stimulus burden of the remaining countries at the regional or global level. Currently, the strongest recovery trends are apparent in developing countries.

1. Developing countries at the vanguard of a potential recovery

The global crisis spread to a large number of developing countries in the third quarter of 2008 and the ensuing free fall of growth in GDP, especially in manufacturing output, continued into 2009 in most countries and regions. World trade is estimated to have fallen by more than 13 per cent in volume in 2009 (see table 1.2). The global contagion hit some countries harder than others. Especially hard hit were several transition economies in Eastern Europe and Central Asia that had generated large current-account deficits and accumulated sizeable stocks of external debt before the crisis.[6]

Gripped by fear and panic, global finance proved quite indiscriminate in fleeing out of what were suddenly perceived as excessively risky assets and into what are conventionally considered "safe haven" assets. "Sudden stops" (or reversals) in private capital flows drove currencies down against the dollar, with only a few exceptions. China's direct exposure to "toxic assets" was limited due to prudent capital account management and tight regulation of its financial system. The latter, in conjunction with large foreign exchange reserves, provided the necessary policy space for China to maintain a stable exchange rate vis-à-vis the dollar throughout the crisis, and also to implement a massive macroeconomic stimulus programme. This helped China's recovery as early as the second quarter of 2009.

In general, the strength of the recovery varied across countries according to the aggressiveness of their respective stimulus measures (chart 1.3). China, which was severely hit by the slump in its

Chart 1.3

**CURRENT-ACCOUNT BALANCE, FISCAL BALANCE AND
REAL GDP GROWTH IN SELECTED COUNTRIES, 2005–2010**

(Per cent)

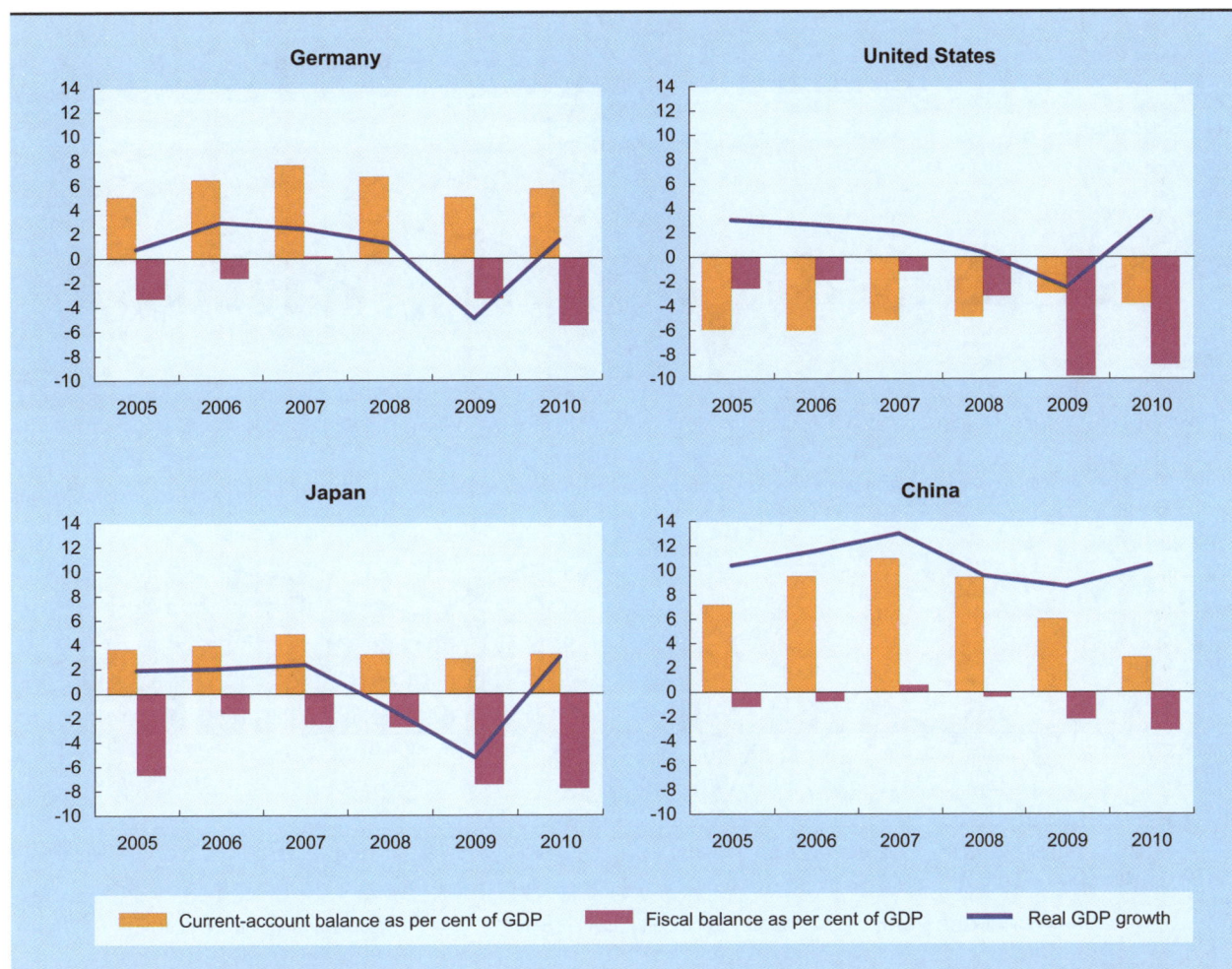

Source: UNCTAD secretariat calculations, based on table 1.1; OECD, 2010; IMF, *World Economic Outlook* database, April 2010; and Economist Intelligence Unit, *EIU CountryData* database.

key developed-country export markets, adopted the most decisive approach to boosting domestic demand through stimulus measures.[7] China's GDP growth further accelerated after mid-2009, and has since spread throughout East and South-East Asia. As some large developed economies continue to struggle with problems in their financial sector and with sluggish domestic demand due to half-hearted stimulus measures, China – and to a lesser extent India – have again achieved GDP growth rates high enough to make them global leaders in the recovery. Their GDP growth resumed quicker than elsewhere,

based on an expansion of domestic demand, and is even expected to grow faster in 2010, once again boosting employment and expansion in production capacities. In China stimulus measures fully offset the negative impact of lower net exports on GDP growth and, similar to the United States, recovery is being driven mainly or almost entirely by domestic demand, in contrast to Germany and Japan (chart 1.4).[8]

As already mentioned in section A, growth has picked up in all developing regions. In the first quarter of 2010, it approached or reached two-digit rates in

Chart 1.4

REAL GDP GROWTH AND CONTRIBUTIONS OF NET EXPORTS AND DOMESTIC DEMAND IN SELECTED COUNTRIES, 1995–2010

(Per cent)

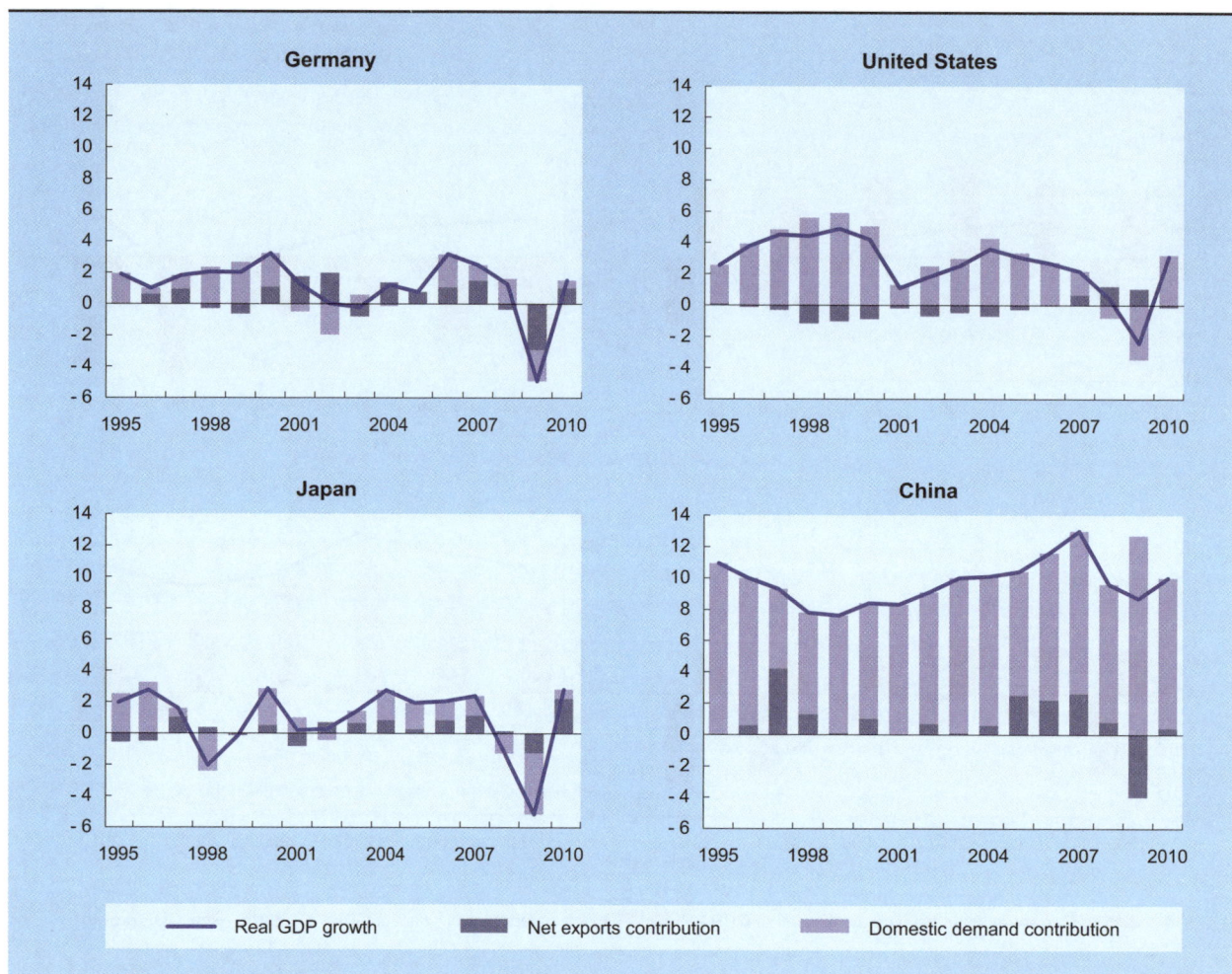

Source: UNCTAD secretariat calculations, based on table 1.1; European Commission, *Annual macro-economic* database (*AMECO*); OECD, *OECD Stat* database; National Bureau of Statistics of China, *Statistical Yearbook 2009*; and World Bank, *China Quarterly Update*, June 2010.

several economies, including Brazil, China, India, Malaysia, Singapore, Taiwan Province of China, Thailand and Turkey. Even though their performance has resulted partly from a low comparison base, this may lead to the removal, at least partially, of the domestic demand stimulus. Monetary policies may turn to a more restrictive (or less expansionary) stance, for example in Brazil, China, India, Malaysia and Peru,

and in some cases, fiscal stimulus measures may be scaled down. However, this is not mainly because of concerns about fiscal balance, but rather because of fears of possible overheating. In fact, the costs of the fiscal stimulus measures in terms of fiscal balance remain moderate, as those measures have accelerated economic activity and, accordingly, increased government revenues.

2. Coping with the vagaries of unfettered global finance

From March 2009 net private flows to emerging markets turned positive following their sudden stop – or in many cases even reversal – since mid-2008. The rebound was driven mainly by portfolio equity investment flows turning from net outflows in 2008 into net inflows again in 2009. A further increase in net private capital flows is expected for 2010 (IIF, 2010). Risk aversion gradually gave way to the return of "risk appetite" combined with the usual herding behaviour of investors. This once again led to an extremely high correlation of price movements across very different markets (chart 1.5, see also *TDR 2009*, chap. I, section C). The reduction of policy interest rates to zero or near-zero in the United States, the euro area, Japan, Switzerland and the United Kingdom, together with the gradual unfreezing of credit markets at the centre of global finance created the conditions for investors' return to risky asset markets and for the resumption of private capital flows to emerging markets.

At the peak of the crisis, pressures on their exchange rates and sharply curtailed foreign credit generally constrained the ability of emerging-market economies to promptly ease their monetary policy stance. With the improvement in international financial conditions during the course of 2009, the policy space for these economies gradually opened up, enabling them to reduce their policy interest rates to record lows. Given the generally healthier financial sector and macroeconomic conditions in these economies, and their more favourable growth outlooks compared with those for developed countries, along with positive, in some cases widening, interest rate differentials vis-à-vis developed countries, emerging-market economies again began to attract financial investors.

By the first quarter of 2010, the resurgence of net private capital inflows from their 2009 trough, although still well below their 2007 peak levels, proved sufficiently strong to pose risks and limit the policy options available to the recipient countries.[9] With sharply reduced local interest rates and plenty of domestic liquidity, many emerging-market economies do not need private capital inflows as a source of finance. Instead, "hot money" inflows act as an unruly contributory factor in pushing up asset prices, including the exchange rate.

Having been hurt by fickle capital flows in the 1990s, which provoked numerous crises, many emerging-market economies, when confronted with another surge in capital inflows after 2002, chose to intervene in currency markets. The purpose of such intervention was to prevent currency appreciation due to current-account surpluses and/or net private capital inflows and to contain the risks associated with a flood of liquidity. This strategy, often referred to as self-insurance, involved the accumulation of large amounts of foreign exchange reserves. In countries with current-account surplus positions, private capital inflows do not provide any additional finance that could be used for the purpose of increasing imports. Moreover, when their central banks intervene in the foreign exchange markets to prevent a currency appreciation, the private inflows are offset by official capital outflows as the reserves are held in foreign assets, mostly United States treasury bonds.

The effects of the global crisis are likely to reinforce the tendency among developing countries to seek such self-insurance. This may be criticized as blocking an even greater contribution of emerging-market economies with current-account surpluses to the much-needed rebalancing of global demand. But such criticism misses the point. First, resorting to self-insurance strategies is a response to systemic deficiencies in the existing global currency and financial set-up. The right way to address this issue is not to blame the countries that are the most vulnerable to these systemic flaws for their defensive responses, but to reform the global architecture in such a way as to make self-insurance strategies unnecessary. Second, these strategies reduced the vulnerability of emerging-market economies and helped them to recover from a global crisis that originated in a number of leading developed economies which are also largely responsible for the current global imbalances.

As central banks in many developed countries cut policy rates to zero or near-zero, arbitrage capital flows to emerging-market economies picked up, putting pressure on their exchange rates and reducing their room for manoeuvre in macroeconomic policy-making. At the same time, there was little pressure for adjustments in the developed economies, among which large imbalances still persist. Protracted weakness of domestic demand and a heavy reliance on exports are the most pronounced in Germany and Japan (see chart 1.4). Also, it is worth noting that Switzerland, while somewhat more successful in

Chart 1.5

EVOLUTION OF PRICES IN SELECTED MARKETS AND COUNTRIES, OCTOBER 2008–JUNE 2010

(Index numbers, 1 October 2008 = 100)

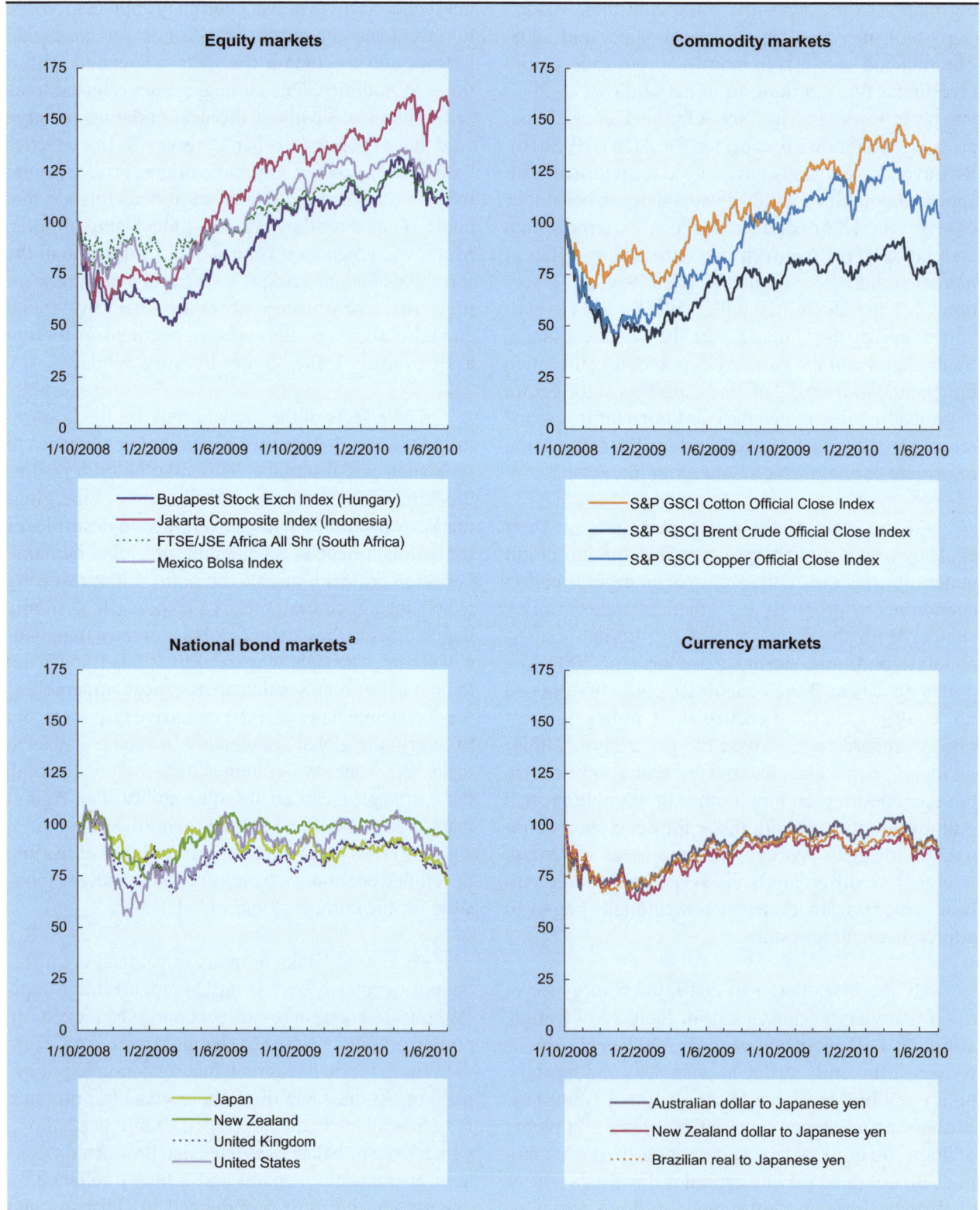

Equity markets

Budapest Stock Exch Index (Hungary)
Jakarta Composite Index (Indonesia)
FTSE/JSE Africa All Shr (South Africa)
Mexico Bolsa Index

Commodity markets

S&P GSCI Cotton Official Close Index
S&P GSCI Brent Crude Official Close Index
S&P GSCI Copper Official Close Index

National bond markets [a]

Japan
New Zealand
United Kingdom
United States

Currency markets

Australian dollar to Japanese yen
New Zealand dollar to Japanese yen
Brazilian real to Japanese yen

Source: UNCTAD secretariat calculations, based on Bloomberg.
  a Yields on 10-year bonds.

reviving domestic demand, intervened extensively in currency markets to contain an appreciation of the Swiss franc. As a result, its reserves quadrupled since the beginning of the crisis until mid-June 2010 (Garnham, 2010). Germany benefited considerably from the depreciation of the euro, which occurred as a result of the self-inflicted internal divergences in the euro area and its related debt problems. This is just the opposite of what is needed for a global rebalancing.

While developing countries have no responsibility for the global crisis, they can nevertheless play an important role in the recovery. But they cannot on their own generate the necessary stimulus for global demand and achieve global rebalancing; other countries, particularly the industrialized surplus countries, need to contribute as well (see also chapter II of this *TDR*).

In a repeat of global pre-crisis patterns, among the developed countries the United States has been experiencing a stronger recovery in domestic demand than the leading developed surplus countries (see chart 1.4). But in moving forward, the United States is likely to face strong headwinds.

3. United States: former global growth engine facing headwinds

Following a sharp contraction in domestic demand in the second half of 2008, the United States economy began to recover after mid-2009. This recovery has been driven by monetary and fiscal stimulus measures, with automatic fiscal stabilizers operating freely only at the federal level. Since the final quarter of 2009, gradual inventory restocking has been a major contributor to GDP growth. This is likely to be completed by the third quarter of 2010. By that time the fiscal stimulus too will have run its course and fiscal adjustment may once again start to drag down the economy in 2011. The crucial question, therefore, is whether private demand will be ready to take over as the driving force behind continued recovery.

The United States was among those countries that chose to counter the global crisis with a substantial fiscal stimulus programme through the American Recovery and Reinvestment Act (ARRA). Since the onset of the crisis, United States public finances have

deteriorated very sharply, largely as a direct consequence of the workings of so-called automatic fiscal stabilizers (Bilmes, 2010). As an economy goes into recession, tax revenues fall and spending on social safety nets rises without any changes in tax rates or spending parameters. In addition, discretionary measures contained in the fiscal stimulus package amounted to 5.5 per cent of GDP, spread over 2009 and 2010 (*TDR 2009*). However, public finances may have deteriorated even more if the stimulus had been smaller, or, worse still, if ill-guided austerity measures had been attempted. Failure to properly counter the crisis would have left an even larger impact on government revenues and spending commitments.

It has also been suggested that the net positive effect of the fiscal stimulus of the ARRA may have been overstated, since what appears to have been an expansionary effect at the federal level forestalled austerity measures that would have been needed at the state and local levels had the ARRA not been introduced (Aizenman and Pasricha, 2010). This is because public borrowing at the state and local levels in all states of the United States except Vermont is constitutionally constrained by balanced budget rules that require operating revenues to cover operating costs. Today, more and more states and municipalities are forced to implement fiscal austerity measures, which take the form of spending cuts and tax hikes that are bound to weaken their economies.[10] Built-in stabilizers only operate freely at the federal level through the federal income tax system, and through federal social safety nets in particular.

Also operating only at the federal level is the fiscal stimulus programme, since the balanced budget rule does not apply to the United States Federal Government. The stimulus programme includes federal grants to the states that are designed to obviate the need for state-level austerity. Unless new measures are agreed and adopted, the stimulus programme will by and large stop providing support to the recovery towards the end of 2010. Thus, state-level austerity, which is likely to increase in 2011 (McNichol and Johnson, 2010; Leachman, Williams and Johnson, 2010), could only be alleviated thereafter by federal-level automatic or built-in stabilizers.

Headwinds are also likely to arise from a number of other sources. Developments in the property market remain critical. While temporary first-buyer tax incentives, Federal Reserve purchases of mortgage-backed securities and mortgage modifications have provided some provisional support, adjustment in the housing market remains unfinished and threatens to linger on. Large stocks of unsold houses and the potential for new foreclosure waves will keep prices under pressure. And as long as house prices keep falling and foreclosures rising, lenders' and borrowers' balance sheets will continue to weaken, feeding the downward spiral that has been central to the crisis in the United States. Commercial property markets pose an additional risk.

Weakness in the labour market is likely to persist for years to come. While data indicating employment growth were a hopeful sign in March and April 2010, after more than 8 million jobs lost since the beginning of the crisis, the continued frailty of the labour market will keep growth of wages and disposable income in check. At the same time, credit growth remains feeble. It seems decidedly unlikely that the financial system, still in the process of recovery, will again augment household spending power through liberal credit creation, as it did in the pre-crisis era. In short, the former engine of global growth seems in poor shape to regain its pre-crisis strength any time soon (see also chapter II of this *Report*).

It is mainly for this reason that the United States authorities are pinning their hopes for recovery on strong growth in exports. A weaker dollar would support this strategy, which would also be in line with the needed global rebalancing. But Europe, which is the main market for United States exports and was late in joining the global boom of 2002–2007, is now also the outstanding laggard in the current global recovery.[11] This limits the scope for faster export growth in the United States. Moreover, the sharp depreciation of the euro against the dollar in the first half of 2010 will certainly not contribute to any benign global rebalancing.

4. Europe: instability and divergence

From mid-2009 a very moderate recovery began in Europe, mainly as a result of a revival of global trade, and in mid-2010 the euro area in particular remains highly dependent on exports for its meagre GDP growth. While the inventory cycle is providing a temporary boost to activity, final domestic demand growth continues to be weak. Automatic fiscal stabilizers, which are having a relatively strong impact in most Western European countries, have been the main cause of the deterioration of public finances since the start of the crisis. In Europe proactive stabilization policies are generally frowned upon, especially by the euro area authorities. Accordingly, temporary fiscal stimulus measures were applied reluctantly and unevenly across the euro area in response to the crisis. Some of the new EU member countries in Central and Eastern Europe that were particularly hard hit by the crisis responded to it by adopting contractionary policies. Among the older EU members in Western Europe, Greece, Ireland, Portugal and Spain shifted towards fiscal retrenchment in the first half of 2010. Only some core European countries opted for a mildly stimulatory fiscal policy for 2010, but this is set to be reversed, which will result in continent-wide fiscal austerity in 2011.

Instability in the euro area is largely a homegrown problem. The subprime mortgage crisis in the United States merely acted as the trigger for a series of events that led to the European debt crisis of 2010.[12] While subprime-related write-downs have certainly added to pressures for the deleveraging that is under way within European banking systems, the root cause of the European crisis can be traced to serious intraregional divergences and to the related build-up of regional imbalances that had long been negligently ignored by market participants and policymakers alike.

Upon joining the European currency union, its member countries relinquished national control over monetary policy as well as the possibility of nominal exchange rate realignments to restore trade balances. Instead, the ECB defined its primary price stability mandate as one of holding the area-wide annual harmonized consumer price inflation rate at "below but close to" 2 per cent. Maintaining a balance in intraregional competitiveness positions and trade would have required that wage trends in member countries align national nominal unit labour cost increases with the area's targeted 2 per cent inflation trend (Flassbeck, 2007).

In actual fact, national wage trends have persistently diverged from this implicit stability norm since the euro was launched in 1999. This has been the most conspicuous in Germany, where real wages have barely grown since 1999, and nominal unit labour costs have stayed virtually flat (see also chapter III, box 3.1). While trends in nominal wages and unit labour costs complied with the implicit stability norm in France, other countries such as Greece, Ireland, Italy, Portugal and Spain deviated from that norm in an upward direction, although to a much lesser extent than Germany's deviation in the opposite direction. As a result, over time, internal competitiveness positions gradually drifted out of kilter and trade imbalances in the euro area soared, with large surpluses in Germany and the Netherlands and large deficits in their Southern European intraregional counterparts.

Trade imbalances imply corresponding intraregional financial flows from the surplus to the deficit countries. These have been mainly in the form of debt flows smoothly intermediated by Europe's integrated financial system. At least this was the case until severe stress struck at the core of the leading international financial centres, which also affected Western Europe's large and globally active universal banks that engage in both traditional banking and investment activities. Triggered by the subprime mortgage crisis in the United States, regional imbalances in Europe started to unravel as credit flows in Europe dried up. Outside the euro area, in those EU countries with large current-account deficits, exchange rates were affected by a sudden stop of capital flows. Inside the euro area, financial markets concentrated on public debt markets instead. The first target of market speculators was Ireland in February 2009, which triggered ruthless fiscal retrenchment there. This was followed by speculative attacks in early 2010 on the sovereign debt of euro area member countries with large budget and current-account deficits, with Greece as their primary target.

In many ways the situation in Greece in the latest global crisis resembles the experiences of a number of emerging-market economies in earlier crises. It highlights the adjustment challenges faced by a country when its macroeconomic policy space is tightly constrained (box 1.1).

It is noteworthy that apart from Greece, other countries under attack had budget deficits below 3 per cent of GDP prior to the crisis; Ireland and Spain even had budget surpluses. In the event, the relevant European authorities responded with considerable delay to what were initially local instabilities, and then only when policymakers worldwide realized that there was a serious threat of regional contagion as well as fresh global financial stresses. First a €110 billion financial support package for Greece was agreed, conditional on its Government undertaking a ruthless fiscal retrenchment. Then a €750 billion temporary European Financial Stability Facility at the euro area level was agreed in May 2010, which includes a sizeable IMF contribution as well as small and sterilized sovereign bond purchases by the ECB in secondary markets (Reuters, 2010).

By mid-2010 the measures agreed in Europe had still failed to restore calm in global financial markets and the euro's real effective exchange rate continued to depreciate. Doubts remain as to a possible sovereign default of Greece (see also box 1.1) and whether the underlying real intraregional disequilibria will be addressed. Questions are also being raised as to the effectiveness of the draconian fiscal retrenchments in achieving fiscal sustainability when countries are pushed into deep recession, particularly as retrenchment in those countries with current-account deficits is not being offset by simultaneous expansion in surplus countries in the region. Following Germany's lead in committing to fiscal consolidation to regain market confidence, fiscal austerity is set to spread across the continent in 2011. With the prospect of a premature end to stimulus policies in Europe, there is growing fear of a possible European, or even global, double-dip recession occurring.

The crisis in Europe suggests that the euro area's current policy regime may well be unsustainable, and that member countries' uncoordinated national policies are on a collision course. It is mainly for these reasons that Europe is today's global hotspot of instability and divergence. Originating in the United States, the global crisis is now centred on Europe, and the region is slowing down global recovery, given its importance in world trade.

Box 1.1

As a member of the euro area, Greece has effectively surrendered all macroeconomic policy instruments that could potentially help it tackle its current crisis. First, due to restrictions imposed by EU treaties and the Stability and Growth Pact, as well as mounting pressures from its European partners and financial markets, the Greek Government implemented draconian fiscal retrenchment – the very opposite of what was warranted, namely a countercyclical fiscal policy. Second, while legally prohibited from rendering any monetary support to the Greek treasury, the country's central bank is also in no position to support the economy or the banking system. Third, it is no longer possible to restore the country's competitiveness by devaluing the nominal exchange rate.

This last constraint puts Greece in an even worse position than developing and emerging-market economies that have faced financial crises. In their cases, currency depreciation typically acted as a catalyst for turning their countries' fortunes around by restoring competitiveness and boosting net exports. In the case of Greece, the only avenue available for restoring competitiveness within the euro area is through nominal wage adjustments that would reduce Greek unit labour costs relative to its European partners. With nominal wage growth essentially flat in the region's largest economy, Germany, this form of adjustment would translate into outright wage-price deflation.

Not only is a drawn-out process of wage-price deflation far more painful than a one-off currency devaluation; an additional problem arises from the fact that while prices and current incomes fall in that process, the value of the debt, which is fixed in some nominal currency unit, remains unchanged, so that the real burden of the debt rises. As debtors attempt to maintain their debt service by distress selling in product and/or asset markets, the debt situation worsens further and a self-sustained process of "debt deflation" (Fisher, 1933: 337–357) is set in motion, with bankruptcies spreading among interconnected economic units and potential repercussions in other countries.

By mid-2010, the measures agreed in Europe to support the Greek economy had still failed to restore calm in global financial markets, so that a default by Greece and other EU periphery countries still seems a real possibility. Default arises when an entity can no longer meet all its obligations to make payments to other entities, including servicing its debts. Defaults by firms or households occur when current and prospective income plus assets available as collateral or for resale fail to convince potential creditors that solvency is assured for the time to maturity of the outstanding debt. But for a government the situation is quite different.

In sovereign defaults a distinction should be made between debts denominated in national currency and those denominated in foreign currencies. Sovereign default in developing countries typically arises when payment obligations in foreign currency cannot be met. Causes of difficulties that can lead to *external* default include sudden declines in export revenues, remittances or net foreign capital inflows, as well as sudden increases in foreign interest rates. As revenues denominated in foreign currency dry up or fail to keep pace with foreign currency outlays, the ability of the sovereign government to boost tax revenues in domestic currency, or issue domestic currency, is of little help in closing the foreign currency gap. With regard to sovereign debt in domestic currency, it could be argued that default is somewhat of a contradiction in terms: since national sovereignty includes the power to tax and issue a sovereign currency, it is difficult to see why a sovereign government should ever default. The position of a sovereign government is different from that of a private debtor, since, at least theoretically, it can either increase its revenues through taxes or issue more currency. However, in a democratic society, the extent to which the sovereign can make use of this prerogative is a question of political feasibility.

The Eurosystem provides a very special kind of governance with regard to the sovereignty and policy space of its member States: these States have to surrender their national sovereignty over *monetary* matters while sharing supranational monetary sovereignty over the euro. This arrangement also severely circumscribes their *fiscal* sovereignty at the national level, but at the same time it does not provide for sharing fiscal sovereignty at the supranational level. As a result, member States no longer have access to loans from their respective central banks, yet the ECB, too, is prohibited from direct lending or directly purchasing securities issued by member State governments. In addition, budget deficits and public debt outstanding of member States are subject to limits, and there is a "no bailout clause", which means that no member State shall be responsible for public debts issued by other members.

In practice, there has been a limited, indirect bailout, as the ECB has been buying a considerable amount of Greek bonds on the secondary market. Nevertheless, it is clear from the unfolding European crisis that the arrangements for macroeconomic policies and government financing need to be reviewed.

C. The need for global coordination and caution in withdrawing macroeconomic stimulus

In a globally integrated economy, international coordination of economic policies is essential. *TDR 2009* already observed that "in order to make deficit spending viable in all countries, it would be essential to ensure that no country benefits unduly from unidirectional demand spillovers emanating from deficit-spending programmes of other countries without itself making a commensurate contribution to the global demand stimulus" (*TDR 2009*, chap.I, section D). This remains a challenge in 2010 and beyond as the world community begins to reap the initial benefits of a policy-sponsored recovery.

At the current juncture, in the eagerness to embark on uncoordinated consolidation, there is a tendency to forget that a double-dip recession which could result from a premature abandoning of expansionary policies poses by far the greatest threat to public finances. Coordination does not mean that all countries should withdraw their stimulus programmes simultaneously; it primarily concerns the free-rider problem. As a rule, governments should withdraw stimulus in line with the recovery of private domestic demand in their country. Ending stimulus to domestic demand before that point means having to rely on exports for recovery, thereby shifting the burden of sponsoring demand stimulus onto others. Ideally, the timing of a stimulus withdrawal should contribute towards rebalancing global demand. From this perspective, current discussions on exit not only reveal conflicting policy visions, but also suggest that there is a lack of focus on the actual threats.

1. Fears of inflation, risks of deflation

At the peak of the crisis, policymakers mostly agreed that deflation presented the greatest threat. With the rebound of commodity prices, headline consumer price inflation has also generally returned. Yet in many economies, high levels of unemployment and depressed capacity utilization rates mean that a trend of declining wages and unit labour costs may continue to exert a downward pressure on core inflation, which is already very low. In Japan, deflation remains firmly entrenched, resulting in huge economic costs to that country for over a decade, an experience that policymakers in the United States and Europe may need to bear in mind when evaluating macroeconomic risks in the current situation. This is especially important in the euro area, where, during the period 2005–2007, rising headline inflation due to international commodity price hikes was seen as signalling inflation risks even though core inflation pressures were well contained. This led to an excessive tightening of the monetary policy stance and subdued growth of domestic demand.

A related issue concerns government bond purchases by central banks, which are sometimes viewed as posing inflation risks or as crowding out banks' bond financing needs and corporate investment plans (Barber, 2010; ECB, 2010a; Posen, 2010). In general, threats of inflation may arise when an economy is on the verge of overheating and encounters supply bottlenecks, or when important cost components or profit aspirations are out of line with productivity growth. Central banks' provision of emergency liquidity to disorderly financial markets or support for government financing on reasonable terms do not pose an inflation risk per se, if there are large spare capacities.

On the other hand, inflation risks are growing in some developing countries that have strong growth dynamics. In some of these countries, rising energy and food prices are also having a relatively strong impact on headline inflation. However, a tightening of monetary policy would be ineffective in stabilizing prices in the face of cost-push inflation pressures, while rising interest rates would provide an even greater attraction for capital inflows and threaten to destabilize their economies. In order to anchor core inflation at a low level, an incomes policy might be considered as an alternative option (see chapter V).

2. Does the G-20 process work?

The G-20 was originally created in response to the financial crises of the late 1990s. Thereafter, its role as a forum for international cooperation was strengthened in the context of the global crisis of 2008, and since then it has held regular meetings under rotating chairmanships. At their Pittsburgh Summit in September 2009 the G-20 Leaders designated the Group as the premier forum for international economic cooperation, replacing the G-8 in this role to better reflect the changed realities in the world economy. In their statement they claimed: "our forceful response helped stop the dangerous, sharp decline in global activity and stabilize financial markets" (G-20, 2009a) and they announced an agreement to launch a new Framework for Strong, Sustainable and Balanced Growth. The purpose of the framework is to commit members to "work together to assess how [our] policies fit together, to evaluate whether they are collectively consistent with more sustainable and balanced growth, and to act as necessary to meet our common objectives."[13]

In preparing the economic agenda for the Leaders Summit in Toronto in late June 2010, the G-20 Ministerial Meeting in Busan (Republic of Korea) earlier that month indicated a clear shift in emphasis in the way the G-20 is handling the crisis and on the issue of withdrawing stimulus. Media reports surrounding that meeting revealed contrasting policy views among members. The communiqué effectively denounced the previous position, that fiscal stimulus should be maintained until recovery was assured, and replaced it with fiscal consolidation as the new policy priority. According to that communiqué, "The recent events highlight the importance of sustainable public finances and the need for our countries to put in place credible, growth-friendly measures, to deliver fiscal sustainability, differentiated for and tailored to national circumstances. Those countries with serious fiscal challenges need to accelerate the pace of consolidation" (G-20, 2010).

Europe is leading the rush to the exit: immediately following the G-20 Busan Meeting, Germany passed an austerity plan, set to start in 2011, and invited its European partners to follow suit. The shift towards unconditional austerity would seem to conflict with what was agreed in the progress report prepared at the St. Andrews Summit in November 2009, namely, "to cooperate and coordinate, taking into account any spillovers caused by our strategies ..." (G-20, 2009b). Europe-wide austerity is bound to cause spillovers beyond this continent, but agreement on this issue no longer seems possible.

At the peak of the global crisis, G-20 members managed to see eye to eye on the need for coordinated measures to generate a strong demand stimulus, as the sheer severity of the events discounted any alternative. That moment seems to have passed: developments in mid-2010 have been reminiscent of the process of Multilateral Consultation on Global Imbalances that was launched in 2006, which entrusted the IMF to facilitate discussion and cooperation between China, the euro area, Japan, Saudi Arabia and the United States. Those consultations proved unsuccessful at the time: these systemically important countries failed to arrive at any "shared views on global imbalances" and hence agreed on strategies for their respective countries that did not represent any departure from the policies that had led to the global imbalances in the first place.

Today, there is a strong belief among policymakers in the euro area that fiscal austerity will not harm, but rather support, growth by boosting confidence. In contrast, policymakers in the United States fear that continued domestic demand stagnation in

Chart 1.6

REAL EFFECTIVE EXCHANGE RATE, SELECTED COUNTRIES, JANUARY 2003–MAY 2010

(CPI based; index numbers, 2005 = 100)

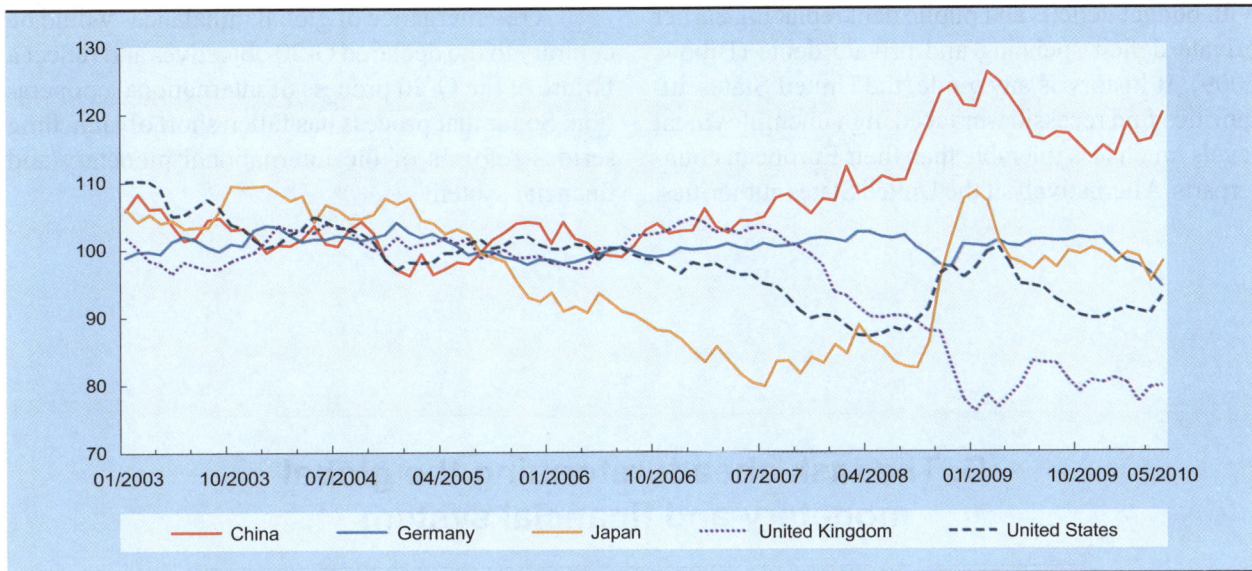

Source: Bank for International Settlements statistical database.

Europe will undermine any recovery of United States exports.[14] Failure to coordinate policies at the G-20 level raises the prospect of global imbalances re-emerging, especially among developed countries.

3. Are global imbalances set to widen again?

Global imbalances started to emerge in the early 1990s as domestic demand growth in the United States became associated with protracted weakness of domestic demand in Japan and much of Western Europe (IMF, 2001 and 2002). All along, the United States offset the deflationary forces originating in much of the rest of the world by encouraging borrowing and spending, particularly by private households. The resulting internal imbalances in the United States household and financial sectors began to implode as the property bubble burst in 2006.

Developing countries, on the other hand, staged a significant policy shift in the aftermath of the Asian financial crisis. Many of them embarked on a strategy of avoiding current-account deficits by favouring competitive exchange rates and accumulating foreign exchange reserves. After 2002, China's current-account surplus surged, and in subsequent years the oil price boom inflated oil-producing countries' surplus positions.

The immediate policy responses to the unfolding global crisis led to a sharp shrinking of global current-account imbalances (chart 1.3). However, if the global economic forces that gave rise to imbalances prior to the crisis resurface, those imbalances will again widen in due course. In principle, robust domestic demand growth in developing countries led by China, together with strengthening currencies, help global rebalancing. However, their experience with the global crisis may well convince developing countries that it would not be in their best interest to revert to tolerating sizeable current-account deficits, as they did prior to the Asian crisis. This could revive the forces that contributed to the global imbalances. At the same time imbalances among developed countries risk becoming bigger and the continued weakness of the euro also militates against global rebalancing. While China's real effective exchange rate was rising in the first half of 2010, Germany's was declining (chart 1.6).

Contrary to the pre-crisis situation, United States authorities have limited scope for recourse to expansionary monetary policy, so that sustained recovery in the United States under adverse global conditions will require greater and longer fiscal policy support, with budget deficits and public debt replacing earlier private deficit spending and private debts (Bibow, 2009). If history is any guide, the United States authorities find recession-induced high unemployment levels much less tolerable than their European counterparts. Alternatively, if the United States authorities,

too, were to succumb to the sort of fiscal orthodoxy that has quickly regained the upper hand in leading European economies, either global deflation or trade protectionism would be the likely result.

A re-emergence of global imbalances would be contrary to the declared G-20 objectives and reflect a failure of the G-20 process of international cooperation. So far that process has fallen short of launching serious reforms of the international monetary and financial system.

D. The task ahead: reforming the global monetary and financial system

1. The exchange rate problem

A major concern is that unfettered markets cannot be trusted to determine exchange rates that reflect fundamentals and allow balanced trade. Apart from generating excessive short-term volatility, currency markets systematically overshoot or undershoot, thereby causing serious trade imbalances and related instabilities. However, government policy responses to this threat may result in excessive stability of nominal exchange rates, which may have similar economic consequences. Unilateral exchange-rate management may also lead to political tensions, since it conflicts with the multilateral character of exchange rates.

Therefore, a multilaterally agreed arrangement for exchange-rate management could introduce greater stability into the world economy as well as a higher degree of coherence between the multilateral trading system and international financial governance. As discussed at greater length in previous *TDRs,* this could be achieved through a system of managed flexible exchange rates which aims for a rate that is consistent with a sustainable current-account position. Implicitly featuring the purchasing power

parity condition as the key guiding rule, nominal exchange rates would be periodically adjusted to compensate for inflation differentials. Other factors such as terms-of-trade shocks and the state of countries' development would also need to be taken into account to assure a system-wide effort to achieve balanced trade.

An internationally agreed exchange-rate system aimed at ensuring stable and sustainable real exchange rates (RERs) for all countries would go a long way towards reducing the scope for speculative capital flows. As nominal exchange rates would follow inflation differentials, containing those differentials would go even further in limiting interest rate differentials, which are the main inducement for destabilizing carry trade strategies. In addition, symmetric intervention obligations under the "stable RER" rule would greatly reduce the need for emerging-market economies to hold international reserves as a means of self-insurance against currency crises.

The current monetary non-order causes developing countries to adopt defensive strategies against fickle markets, and it allows developed countries to engage in beggar-thy-neighbour strategies, with a reliance on exports serving to offset their failure to manage domestic demand. The stable RER rule could provide a basis for the needed multilateral framework that would address both these issues.

2. Stabilizing the financial system

Closely related to exchange-rate instability and misalignment is the problem of destabilizing capital flows. Opening up to global finance implies a de facto loss of national policy autonomy for developing countries (*TDR 2006*, chap. II, section F; Akyüz, 2007; Mayer, 2008). External financial conditions, mainly influenced by monetary policies and financial players in the leading global financial market centres, largely determine the scope for domestic macroeconomic policies. Financial conditions as set in international markets are not only likely to be out of line with local requirements; they are also prone to fickleness, with floods of capital inflows and sudden reversals causing different sets of challenges.

Possible measures to deal with this problem include taxes on international financial transactions as well as various capital-account management techniques that may target both the level and the composition of inflows. In many cases, instruments directly targeting private capital flows may also be appropriately combined with, and complemented by, prudential domestic financial regulations. For instance, the Republic of Korea has recently introduced a series of measures designed to limit banks' currency exposures through forward transactions (Song Jung-a, 2010).

The global crisis has shown all too clearly that it is in the legitimate interest of countries to contain uncontrollable risks taken on by their private sectors in unfettered global financial markets. The so-called Stiglitz Commission emphasized that the host-country principle should guide countries' approach to financial regulation and supervision (UNPGA, 2009). Blindly relying on the proper conduct of foreign players that are regulated and supervised only by their home countries can prove very risky, especially since there has been limited progress in making the financial systems in the leading developed countries any safer.

One important aspect of reform of financial regulations and supervision should be to ensure the system's functional (or social) efficiency in contributing to growth and stability in the real economy. At the same time, it should eliminate products that provide no real service other than the ability to gamble and increase leverage, which is often the case with financial derivatives (see also *TDR 2009*, chap. II). For instance, credit default swaps (CDSs) are supposed to provide hedging services. But when the issuance of CDSs reaches 10 times the risk to be hedged, it becomes clear that 90 per cent of those CDSs are not providing any hedging (or insurance) service; rather, they are being used for what amounts to gambling purposes. This is why there is a need for regulations that limit the issuance of CDSs to the amount of the underlying risk, and prohibit other types of financial instruments that are conducive to gambling (see annex to this chapter).

So far, reform of financial regulations and supervision has been pursued only at the national level, without due consideration to the need for a global architecture that would guarantee a certain degree of coherence. At this juncture, financial reform in the United States is more advanced than in Europe (see box 1.2). Furthermore, United States banks have also succeeded better than those in Europe in restoring their balance sheets and capital.

Financial globalization requires proper global governance, and, officially, the G-20 members remain committed to coordinating their policies with the aim of creating a safer global financial system through the Financial Stability Board (FSB) as their coordinating platform.[15] But progress in certain areas is proving to be slow, and the mere fact that national financial reform is proceeding at different speeds and along different routes would seem to indicate that in this area too conflicting policy views and/or interests impede proper coordination by the FSB. Furthermore, it would be important to have a fundamental inquiry into why the main international institutions charged with identifying risks to global financial stability may have failed to flag early warning signs in the build-up to the global financial crisis.

Against this background, emerging-market economies and other developing countries may be obliged to erect higher protection barriers against unfettered global finance, preferably through policies other than increased self-insurance, as the latter gives rise to pressures on the key reserve currency issuer that can create systemic risks of its own.

Box 1.2

AFTER THE BAILOUT: UNITED STATES FINANCIAL REFORM

The latest financial and economic crisis forced the United States Government to commit its own credit to the survival of the financial system. The $700-billion Troubled Asset Relief Program (TARP) was only one, though very important, support measure for preventing a financial meltdown. With huge redistributive impacts, to the detriment of tax payers, the financial costs of the bailout are today shrinking with the recovery of the economy and of asset prices, as capital injections to banks are repaid at a profit to the Treasury. The true real costs of the crisis are the foregone output in its aftermath and, in particular, high levels of unemployment. These costs will continue to pile up as long as the economy fails to return to its potential growth trajectory with full employment. Apart from immediate emergency measures that successfully pre-empted a meltdown, the crisis also triggered a financial reform process that aimed at putting the system on a more solid footing to better prevent future financial crises and their impact on tax payers. The Restoring American Financial Stability Act of 2010 enacted in July stands on five pillars:

1. *Improving consumer protection* through the creation of a Consumer Financial Protection Bureau targeting the household sector, with the ability to design and enforce regulation of financial products, such as mortgages and credit cards.

2. *Addressing the "too big to fail" problem* by allowing regulators to impose capital ratios that increase with bank size, and by creating a Resolution Authority enabling the take-over, and orderly liquidation by the Government of any troubled large financial institutions which, were they to fail, could cause damages to the overall financial sector. The new legislation also imposes limits on proprietary trading by deposit-taking institutions, and limits bank ownership of hedge funds and private equity funds to 3 per cent of their tier-one capital.

3. *Regulating financial derivatives* by requiring that trading of standardized derivative products take place in organized exchanges. Banks are still allowed to trade simple derivative instruments (such as interest rate and foreign exchange swaps), but are required to move trading of more complex derivative instruments to specialized affiliates.

4. *Avoiding regulatory arbitrage and establishing an early warning system aimed at monitoring risks in the financial system as a whole* by creating a new Financial Oversight Council, and streamlining and coordinating responsibilities among existing regulators. The Council is composed of existing regulators (the Federal Reserve, the Federal Deposit Insurance Corporation and the Office of the Controller of the Currency, but not the Office of Thrift Supervision which was eliminated in the process) and chaired by the Secretary of the Treasury.

5. *Addressing incentive problems in the financial industry* by setting standards to limit excessive compensation, and by giving shareholders the right to express non-binding opinions on executive pay. Investors would be allowed to sue rating agencies for "knowing or reckless" failures in their credit assessments.

Essentially, the Act re-regulates the current system without fundamentally changing its structure (Reich, 2010). It gives regulators substantial new powers, with hardly any requirement for them to implement tougher rules. This approach has the advantage of increasing the system's flexibility, but the disadvantage of weakening regulators by not providing sufficient political backing. As a result, the ideological stance of regulators and of the administration appointing them will influence the quality of regulation. Only some of the fundamental problems of modern finance responsible for its hazardous fragility (*TDR 2009*) have been addressed; legislators were too timid to shut down the casino components of the financial system, or at least shield the banking system from its hazards.[a]

---

[a] The leniency of the Act was reflected in the market rally in bank equity prices.

E. Outlook

The global economy is at a critical juncture. Through their coordinated response to the economic and financial crisis, policymakers have won an important battle in preventing the great recession from turning into another Great Depression. However, the ongoing recovery remains highly uneven and fragile. The global industrial inventory cycle may give a misleading impression, leading to a belief in the briskness and sustainability of the turnaround. In fact, it should be a warning that businesses remain wary of the strength and durability of the rebound. It therefore behoves the world's policymakers to remain vigilant and well prepared to initiate further support measures should such a need arise.

Global growth is vital to employment creation, especially in developing countries, where the task is not only to prevent unemployment rates from rising, but also to continue the fight against poverty by absorbing a continuously growing labour force, especially in manufacturing and modern services. A faltering global recovery would mean rising unemployment and underemployment, increasing poverty, and – almost certainly – failure to meet the Millennium Development Goals.

Policy-driven recovery in the United States, fairly strong up to mid-2010, is likely to slow down in the second half of the year and faces strong headwinds ahead. In Europe, most precariously, domestic demand continues to stagnate and continent-wide fiscal austerity starting in 2011 might stall recovery in the region even before it has started. As a result, global recovery remains extremely unbalanced and fragile.

Continued policy stimulus is needed to maintain the momentum, and global macroeconomic policy coordination in this context is critical. Policies should focus on strengthening the recovery and rebalancing global aggregate demand. A process of self-sustaining growth in private spending and employment is not yet assured, while the forces that caused global imbalances in the past seem to be resurfacing. With emerging-market economies in Asia, led by China, experiencing a strong rebound from the crisis, the demand stimulus they provide to the global economy will be crucial but insufficient to restore the world economy to its pre-crisis growth path, even if the large primary-commodity-exporting countries are able to amplify the expansion in Asia. Developing countries should carefully consider all their options to prevent their development strategies from being unravelled by instabilities arising in the leading developed countries once again. In particular, developing countries with export-oriented development strategies need to prepare for the possibility of continued weakness of demand in developed-country markets. To this end, it would be advisable for them to strengthen domestic and regional demand for achieving their growth and employment objectives, an issue that is examined in greater detail in chapter III. ◼

Notes

1 Argentina, Brazil, Paraguay and Uruguay.

2 Seaborne trade volumes are measured in tons. This measure differs from the "volume of trade" presented elsewhere in this chapter, which corresponds to the value of imports or exports deflated by their corresponding unit prices.

3 Data from JP Morgan (2010) show that as growth in Chinese fixed investment, particularly in real terms, has eased significantly in 2010, growth in the volume of commodity imports has eased as well.

4 For a detailed discussion on the effects of financialization of commodity markets, see *TDR 2009*, chap. II.

5 In the medium term, offshore oil production prospects could be affected by the sinking of the Deepwater Horizon drilling rig in the Gulf of Mexico in the United States. The resultant ecologic disaster may trigger regulatory changes, with more stringent standards possibly leading to additional costs or delays in new projects (although a complete ban on offshore drilling is unlikely). This may affect oil market perspectives, since deepwater drilling accounts for roughly 13 per cent of world offshore production, which alone constitutes about one fifth of world oil reserves (See *Le Figaro*, Forage en mer : le casse-tête des pétroliers, 9 June 2010).

6 IMF stabilization programmes were arranged for: Armenia, Belarus, Bosnia and Herzegovina, Costa Rica, El Salvador, Georgia, Guatemala, Hungary, Iceland, Latvia, Mongolia, Pakistan, Romania, Serbia, and Ukraine (IMF, 2009). The current-account deficits of these countries ranged from 5 per cent of GDP to over 20 per cent.

7 China announced a 4 trillion renminbi (RMB) ($586 billion) economic stimulus package on 9 November 2008, amounting to 14 per cent of its 2008 GDP, or roughly 7 per cent of GDP over the two years covered by the plan. The headline measure included increased central government spending of RMB 1,180 billion ($172 billion), as well as local government spending and a vast lending programme by State-owned banks.

TDR 2009 estimated the magnitude of discretionary fiscal stimulus (excluding the automatic stabilizers) as amounting to 6.2 per cent of GDP. China's budget balance only deteriorated from a surplus of 0.6 per cent in 2007 to a deficit of 3.1 per cent of the GDP forecast for 2010 (chart 1.3), which shows that properly pre-emptive countercyclical fiscal stimulus partly pays for itself (Barboza, 2008; Dyer, 2008; and Yu, 2010).

8 For the impact of the global crisis on employment, see Jansen and von Uexkull, 2010.

9 In asset markets, the size of net flows may not fully reflect any potential build-up of fragility. For instance, if market participants broadly share the same views and aim at similar portfolio adjustments and market positioning, large asset price movements can also occur even with a relatively modest amount of capital flows.

10 Alluding to ill-guided attempts by the Hoover Administration to balance the federal budget during the Great Depression, Krugman (2008) stated: "But even as Washington tries to rescue the economy, the nation will be reeling from the actions of 50 Herbert Hoovers."

11 The EU is the leading destination of United States merchandise exports, with a share of 21.2 per cent in 2008, compared with Canada's share of 20.1 per cent and China's share of 5.5 per cent; for goods and services, the EU's share in 2008 was over 25 per cent compared with China's share which was less than 5 per cent (UNCTAD, *Handbook of Statistics* database; and United States Bureau of Economic Analysis database).

12 What started as a subprime crisis in the United States quickly turned into a global crisis mainly because of the high degree of vulnerability of European banks. The European Central Bank (ECB) is often credited with having responded promptly to the emerging stress in the euro area money market in August 2007, which was caused by banking problems that had remained undetected. Germany's Industrie Kredit

Bank (IKB) and France's BNP Paribas were leading examples of banks with considerable exposure to the United States mortgage market. McGuire and von Peter (2009) point out that, in addition, the vast international expansion of European banks since 2000 had also left them with a huge dollar funding gap. It was the need for frequent rollovers in wholesale markets and a reliance on foreign exchange swap markets for that purpose that caused those euro money market dislocations, which then prompted the ECB to provide emergency liquidity in euros, and later also in dollars through central bank swap arrangements. Fender and McGuire (2010) report that at the end of 2009 the dollar funding gap persisted, and that German banks maintained the largest gap among European banking systems.

13   At the G-20 Ministerial meetings in St. Andrews in November 2009 and in Washington, DC, in April 2010, further details were worked out concerning the consultative mutual assessment process of national and regional policy frameworks, programmes and projections. The IMF was charged with preparing a report on alternative policy scenarios based on members' inputs, for consideration at the G-20 Leaders Summit in Toronto in late June 2010.

14   Giles (2010) and Giles and Oliver (2010) reported on conflicting views on policy at the Busan Ministerial in June. In an op-ed in the *Financial Times* on 23 June 2010, German Finance Minister Schäuble asserted that the German "course could be described as one of 'expansionary fiscal consolidation'". This idea of expansionary fiscal consolidation is also central to the ECB's analysis of past experiences with fiscal consolidations in Belgium, Finland, Ireland, the Netherlands and Spain (ECB, 2010b; on this issue see also Alesina and Ardagna, 2009). An important "fallacy of composition" (Keynes, 1936) is involved here, as the experiences of individual small countries are irrelevant when the EU as a whole is embarking on unconditional fiscal austerity. The contrast in policy visions became even clearer in the run-up to the Toronto Summit of the G-20 in June 2010, with the United States and Germany representing the two opposing poles in the stimulus versus austerity debate (Walker and Karnitschnig, 2010). The G-20 Toronto Summit Declaration states that "the G-20's highest priority is to safeguard and strengthen the recovery and lay the foundation for strong, sustainable and balanced growth, and strengthen our financial systems against risks" but also announces that "advanced economies have committed to fiscal plans that will at least halve deficits by 2013 and stabilize or reduce government debt-to-GDP ratios by 2016."

15   The Financial Stability Board was created by the G-20 Summit in London in April 2009 as the successor to the Financial Stability Forum founded in 1999. Its task is the international coordination of the work of national financial authorities and international standard setting bodies, along with the development of effective regulatory, supervisory and other financial sector policies, and promoting their implementation.

References

Aiginger K (2009). The Great Recession vs. the Great Depression: Stylized facts on siblings that were given different foster parents. WIFO Working Paper 354, Austrian Institute of Economic Research, Vienna.

Aizenman J and Pasricha GK (2010). On the ease of overstating the fiscal stimulus in the US, 2008-9. NBER Working Paper 15784, National Bureau of Economic Research, Cambridge, MA.

Akyüz Y (2007). Global rules and markets: Constraints over policy autonomy in developing countries. *Global Economy Series* 10. Penang, Third World Network.

Alesina AF and Ardagna S (2009). Large changes in fiscal policy: Taxes versus spending. NBER Working Paper 15438, Cambridge, MA, October.

Barber T (2010). Markets rally runs out of steam. FT.com, 10 May.

Barboza D (2008). China unveils $586 billion stimulus plan. *New York Times*, 10 November.

Barclays Capital (2010). The commodity refiner: Ghost in the machine. London. January.

Bibow J (2009). Toward Bretton Woods 3? Prospects for global rebalancing. New America Contract Policy

Paper, New America Foundation, Washington, DC, 7 October.

Bilmes LJ (2010). The fiscal crisis in state government – and what should be done about it. Next Social Contract Policy Paper, New America Foundation, Washington, DC, 17 June.

Burghardt G and Acworth W (2010). Volume trends: Decline in the West, surge in the East. *Futures Industry Magazine*, March.

Dyer G (2008). Beijing offers just quarter of stimulus funds. FT.com, 14 November.

ECB (2010a). *Financial Stability Review*. Frankfurt, European Central Bank, June.

ECB (2010b). Fiscal consolidations: past experiences, costs and benefits. *Monthly Bulletin*, June: 83–86.

ECLAC (2010). *Economic Survey of Latin America and the Caribbean 2009–2010*. Santiago de Chile, Economic Commission for Latin America and the Caribbean, July.

FAO (2010). *Food Outlook*. Rome, Food and Agriculture Organization of the United Nations, June.

Fender I and McGuire P (2010). European banks' US dollar funding pressures. *BIS Quarterly Review*, June: 57–64.

Fisher I (1933). The debt-deflation theory of great depressions. *Econometrica,* 1, October: 337–357.

Flassbeck H (2007). Wage divergences in Euroland: Explosive in the making. In: Bibow J and Terzi A, eds. *Euroland and the Global Economy: Global Player or Global Drag?* Basingstoke, Palgrave Macmillan.

G-20 (2009a). Leaders' Statement, the Pittsburgh Summit, 24–25 September.

G-20 (2009b). Progress report on the economic and financial actions of the London, Washington and Pittsburgh G20 Summits. Prepared by the United Kingdom Chair of the G-20, St Andrews, United Kingdom, 7 November.

G-20 (2010). Communiqué of the Meeting of Finance Ministers and Central Bank Governors, Busan, Republic of Korea, 5 June.

Garnham P (2010). Swiss central bank emerges as key supporter of euro. FT.com, 9 June.

Giles C (2010). G20 countries aim to reach consensus on global recovery. FT.com, 4 June.

Giles C and Oliver C (2010). G20 drops support for fiscal stimulus. FT.com, 5 June.

IEA (2010). Oil market report. Paris, International Energy Agency, June.

IIF (2010). Capital flows to emerging market economies. IIF Research Note, Institute of International Finance, Washington, DC, 15 April.

IMF (2001). *World Economic Outlook*. Washington, DC, May.

IMF (2002). *World Economic Outlook*. Washington, DC, September.

IMF (2009). Review of recent crisis programs, 14 September. Available at: http://www.imf.org/external/np/pp/eng/2009/091409.pdf.

Jansen M and von Uexkull E (2010). Trade and employment in the global crisis. Geneva, International Labour Office and New Delhi, Academic Foundation.

JP Morgan (2010). *Global Data Watch*, 18 June.

Keynes JM (1936). The General Theory of Employment, Interest and Money. London, Macmillan.

Krugman P (2008). Fifty Herbert Hoovers. *The New York Times*, 29 December.

Leachman M, Williams E and Johnson N (2010). Failing to extend fiscal relief to states will create new budget gaps, forcing cuts and job loss in at least 34 states. Washington, DC, Center on Budget and Policy Priorities, 10 June.

Mayer J (2008). Policy space: What, for what, and where? *UNCTAD Discussion Paper* no. 191. Geneva, UNCTAD, October.

McGuire P and von Peter G (2009). The US dollar shortage in global banking and the international policy response. BIS Working Papers, no 291. Basel, October.

McNichol E and Johnson N (2010). Recession continues to batter state budgets; state responses could slow recovery. Washington, DC, Center on Budget and Policy Priorities, 27 May.

Metals Economics Group (2010). World exploration trends. A special report from Metals Economics Group for the Prospectors and Developers Association of Canada (PDAC) International Convention 2010, Toronto.

OECD (2010). *Economic Outlook* No. *87*, May.

OECD-FAO (2010). *Agricultural Outlook 2010–2019*. Paris and Rome.

Posen A (2010). When central banks buy bonds: Independence and the power to say no. Speech delivered to Barclays Capital 14th Annual Global Inflation-Linked Conference, New York, NY, 14 June.

Rcich R (2010). The Senate finance bill merits two cheers. *Financial Times*, 24 May.

Reuters (2010). EU announces 750 billion euro crisis shield with IMF, 10 May.

Song Jung-a (2010). South Korea restricts currency forwards. FT.com, 13 June.

UNCTAD (2010). *Review of Maritime Transport 2010*, Geneva (forthcoming).

UNCTAD (various issues). *Trade and Development Report*. United Nations Publication, New York and Geneva.

UNCTAD, WTO, OECD (2010). UNCTAD-OECD-WTO Report on G-20 Trade and Investment Measures. Paris and Geneva, 9 March.

UN/DESA (2010). *World Economic Situation and Prospects 2010* (update as of mid-2010). New York, NY, United Nations.

UNPGA (2009). Report of the Commission of Experts of the President of the United Nations General Assembly on Reforms of the International Monetary and Financial System. Final Report, 21 September. Available at: http://www.un.org/ga/econcrisissummit/docs/FinalReport_CoE.pdf.

Walker M and Karnitschnig M (2010). Merkel rejects Obama's call to spend. *Wall Street Journal*, 23 June.

World Bank (2010). *Global Economic Prospects*, Summer 2010: Appendix. Washington, DC.

World Tourism Organization (2010a). *World Tourism Barometer*, 8(1). Madrid, January.

World Tourism Organization (2010b). *World Tourism Barometer*, Interim update. Madrid, April.

WTO (2010). Report to the TPRB from the Director-General on Trade-related developments. WT/TPR/OV/W/3, World Trade Organization, Geneva, 14 June.

Yu Y (2010). Asia: China's policy responses to the global financial crisis. *Journal of Globalization and Development*, 1(1).

Annex to chapter I

CREDIT DEFAULT SWAPS

A credit default swap (CDS) is a derivative financial instrument in which one party buys protection against the default on a given debt instrument. This annex describes the main characteristics of CDSs and discusses their potential costs and benefits.

The origin of the CDS market dates back to the early 1990s when, in the aftermath of the Exxon Valdez oil spill of March 1989, the United States bank, JP Morgan, bought protection against a possible Exxon default from the European Bank for Reconstruction and Development (EBRD). This contract reduced JP Morgan's exposure to Exxon and increased the return on EBRD reserves that could only be used to lend to high rated borrowers (Tett, 2009).

In the second half of the 1990s, regulators and internal risk managers agreed that CDSs were an effective means of dispersing risk, and allowed banks to use these instruments to reduce their capital. As a result, the CDS market started to grow very rapidly: in 2005, the notional value of all CDSs tracked by the Bank for International Settlements (BIS) was about $10 trillion, and by the end of 2007 it had surpassed $58 trillion (about $3 trillion higher than the world GDP in that year).

Before the latest financial crisis, many regulators, especially in the United States, were enthusiastic about the risk diversification properties of CDSs. For instance, in 2006 Alan Greenspan argued that what CDSs did was "lay-off all the risk of highly leveraged institutions … on stable American and international institutions" (quoted in Das, 2008). However, many of these institutions did not turn out to be as stable as expected and are now either bankrupt or in life support. As a consequence, many observers now share UNCTAD's original scepticism on the social value of innovative financial instruments (*TDR 2009*) and the regulation of CDS and other derivative instruments plays a prominent role in the global debate on financial reform.[1]

Description and terminology

In a CDS, the *buyer* makes periodic payments (*the spread*) to the *seller* in order to be protected against default (*credit event*) on a debt instrument (the *reference obligation*) by a given borrower (the *reference entity*). The difference between a bond spread and the CDS spread is usually referred to as the *basis*.[2]

The reference entity can be a corporate borrower or a sovereign State. CDS contracts written on sovereign States are usually referred to as sovereign CDS. A CDS contract on a corporate borrower can be triggered by the bankruptcy of the reference entity. As the concept of bankruptcy does not apply to sovereign States, a sovereign CDS can only be triggered by one of the following three events: (i) failure to pay the interest or principal on a bond or loan; (ii) an announcement of the intention to suspend payments (moratorium); or (iii) a change in the contractual terms in a way that puts creditors at a disadvantage (for instance, a change in the currency of denomination of the debt instrument or an extension of the maturity of the debt instrument).

If a credit event does take place, the CDS can be settled either by physical delivery or in cash. When settling by physical delivery, the buyer delivers the defaulted debt instrument to the seller and receives a payment equal to the face value of the instrument (this is the *notional principal* of the CDS). When settling in cash, the seller makes a payment to the buyer equal to the difference between the par value and the market price of the reference obligation. CDS contracts specify how the market price of the reference obligation is to be measured. Originally, CDS contracts were tailored to the specific needs of their buyers and sellers; now most CDS contracts follow standard forms designed by the International Swaps and Derivatives Association.

When a CDS is used to hedge or transfer an existing credit risk, the party that buys protection eliminates (or reduces) its credit risk and the party that sells the CDS increases its total credit risk. By contrast, a naked CDS is a contract which is not matched by the underlying credit risk. After the transaction, the buyer is short on credit risk and the seller is long on credit risk. Naked CDSs are normally used to short the underlying instrument with the aim of making a profit if the value of the instrument decreases or a default does indeed happen.

CDS and insurance contracts

Insurance and CDS contracts are similar in the sense that in both cases the buyer makes a periodic payment and receives a much larger sum of money if a given event takes place.

Even though CDSs operate like insurance contracts, they are not classified as insurance and thus escape regulation.[3] CDS contracts are thus exempt from regulation that requires the presence of an insurable interest (which would make naked CDSs illegal) and that the insurer holds adequate reserves based on actuarial risk. Since unregulated sellers of CDSs do not need to hold reserves and do not use actuarial models to price their instruments, they try to hedge their risk with other market operations, and price

and value CDS contracts on a mark-to-market basis by using arbitrage relationships with other market instruments. However, CDS contracts can transfer but cannot eliminate credit risk. Therefore, the credit risk remains in the system but it becomes more difficult to track and identify. Consequently, CDSs may reduce transparency and amplify counterparty risk and price volatility especially because fluctuations in CDS spreads feed back into market prices leading to a vicious circle of high volatility.

CDS price and default risks

There are several problems with the assumption that market signals like CDS spreads (or bond spreads) are good measures of default risk. The most basic problem is that spreads are too volatile to reflect changes in slow moving fundamentals.[4] Price volatility is driven jointly by changes in the expected loss from default and changes in the overall risk premiums, with the latter factor accounting for approximately four fifths of the volatility of all spreads (Remolona, Scatigna and Wu, 2007). In the case of sovereign debt, risk premiums are driven mainly by global factors and have little to do with domestic fundamentals (González-Rozada and Levy Yeyati, 2008). Therefore, it is hard to conclude that sovereign spreads are a good measure of default risk.

Moreover, price discovery in the CDS market is limited by the fact that trading in this market tends to be thin. Even though arbitrage imposes a tight long-run relationship between CDS spreads and bond spreads, the short-run relationship between these two spreads (as measured by the basis) is far from being stable; it is affected by liquidity in the two markets and by contractual details (such as the definition of the trigger event and the deliverable obligation). Based on the observations that CDS spreads are more volatile than spreads in the cash markets, and that the volume of activity on the CDS markets is correlated with the level of the spreads, a recent study by Barclays Capital (2010) concludes that CDS spreads are dubious indicators of default risk.

That CDS spreads are not a good measure of default risk is evident on examining sovereign CDSs for the United Kingdom or the United States. These CDSs had a positive value in February 2009 (when the spread on United Kingdom sovereign CDSs peaked at 175 basis points and that for United States CDSs peaked at 100 basis points) indicating that there were economic agents willing to pay up to $17,500 each year for a contract that would deliver $1,000,000 if the Government of the United Kingdom defaulted. However, since almost all debt of the United Kingdom is denominated in pound sterling, which that country's Government can print, the probability that the United Kingdom will default is basically zero. (In the worst-case scenario, the country can inflate away its own debt; however, a devaluation of the currency is not considered a credit event.) In the United States, the fact that spreads on its sovereign CDSs have a positive value is even more puzzling. In this case, not only is the probability of a credit event negligible, but also the counterparty risk is close to being infinite. If the United States were to default on its debt, the ensuing financial calamity would probably lead to a general state of default throughout the world. CDS contracts would become completely worthless because no seller of CDSs would be able to deliver on its obligation.[5] To sum up, markets are giving a positive value to an instrument that is supposed to deliver a payment if a near-zero probability event occurs in the full knowledge that if the event were to occur the counterparty would not honour its obligation to make the payment. Even the shadiest Las Vegas casino seems to offer better odds!

As the fundamental value of an asset is the expected net present value of the income stream of the asset, sovereign CDSs for the United States should have zero value. And yet in February 2009 they were trading at a spread of 100 basis points. How is this possible? While there are theoretical models that justify rational bubbles in which assets are priced well above their fundamental value (Blanchard, 1979), these models require a certain degree of uncertainty at the precise moment when the asset will reveal its true value. In the case of a CDS contract with no fundamental value, such uncertainty does not exist because all players know that the true value will be revealed on the day the CDS expires. It is then legitimate to ask why investors are willing to pay a positive price for an asset with zero value.

The answer to this puzzle lies in the fact that most banks have internal regulations aimed at limiting their exposure to corporate and country risk. A European bank with a large exposure to the United States corporate sector can reduce its exposure by buying corporate CDSs, but it also needs to buy sovereign CDSs in order to reduce its exposure to the overall United States risk. Even though these sovereign CDSs are completely useless (for the reasons explained above), the bank will buy them anyway in order to satisfy its own internal rules and reduce the need to hold internal reserves.[6] This suggests that the demand for high-rated CDSs is purely due to the presence of (internal) regulatory arbitrage.[7] Once the demand for these types of instruments becomes established, market participants have an incentive to start trading them and making bets on their short-run movements. In fact, the popularity of naked CDSs indicates that the huge success of the CDS market is not due to the need to cover a certain exposure, but to the desire to bet on the short-term volatility of country spreads.

Valuation problems are even more acute for certain classes of corporate CDSs. In these cases, both the CDS and the reference obligation (which may also be a derivative instrument like a collateralized debt obligation) are thinly traded or not traded at all. Consequently, prices are fully model driven, without price discovery but with large, self-reinforcing and destabilizing feedback amplified by the fact that, in many cases, the notional value of CDS contracts on a given instrument is a multiple of the face value of the reference obligation.

Summing up, CDS spreads overreact to information and market sentiments, and are more likely to amplify fluctuations than to provide accurate information on default risk.

Are CDSs socially useful?

The credit crisis triggered a debate on the social benefits of financial innovation (*TDR 2009*), and CDSs have been at the very centre of that debate. While most economists agree that there are several problems with the current structure of the CDS market (especially with its lack of transparency and centralized clearing), they are divided on the issue of the social benefits of CDSs, especially naked CDSs. Both sides started from the observation that a naked CDS is the best instrument for market participants interested in shorting an asset.[8] Those who emphasize the benefits of CDSs argue that the possibility to go short facilitates price discovery and may either prevent bubbles or make bubbles burst earlier (Zingales, 2010). They liken CDSs to medical tests, which may reveal painful news, but the sooner one knows, the better. Those who emphasize the costs of naked CDSs argue that these instruments increase volatility and make coordinated runs, speculative attacks and "bear raids" easier (Portes, 2010; and Soros, 2010). As CDS spreads are mostly driven by short-term market sentiments and appear to do a poor job at discovering and measuring default risk, the latter view seems to be more appropriate than the former.

Moreover, while CDSs are often praised for increasing market liquidity, there is evidence that at times of widespread financial distress, speculators become users rather than providers of liquidity (Das, 2010). For all these reasons, in an analysis which applies network theory to financial markets, Haldane (2009) points out that CDSs are akin to horizontal networks that are known to increase interconnectedness and reduce the stability of the system.[9]

While most of the current discussion has focused on the alleged costs and benefits of naked CDSs, there are also potential problems with CDSs used for hedging purposes.

Litan (2009) argues that these derivative instruments provide several advantages in terms of risk sharing, as they allow banks to reduce credit concentration without severing their relationships with well-established customers. While there is some merit to this argument, one should also consider that banks tend to have a large amount of information on their customers, and, when a bank makes a loan and then buys a CDS, the bank is effectively transferring the risk to a party that has less information than the bank (Baker, 2010). This looks more like insider trading than like a transaction with the potential to increase economic efficiency and risk sharing.

CDSs may also be a source of moral hazard. One of the pitfalls of the "originate and distribute" model is that banks that do not plan to keep a credit on their books have limited incentive to invest in credit screening procedures and their lending standards may be more lax (*TDR 2009*). The same applies to lenders that decide to use CDSs to transfer their credit risk to non-regulated third parties. Consequently, CDSs issued for hedging purposes may lead to systemic problems through three channels: (i) an increase in total risk taking; (ii) the transfer of risk to less informed, less regulated and, possibly, less capitalized players; and (iii) an increase in opacity.

Finally, CDSs may increase instability because, in case of default, insured creditors do not have the incentive to avoid socially costly, value destroying liquidation of the collateral. ■

Notes

1   For instance, the G-20 Declaration on Strengthening the Financial System of 2 April 2009 includes a commitment to "promote the standardization and resilience of credit derivatives markets, in particular through the establishment of central clearing counterparties subject to effective regulation and supervision." However, the G-20 effort has yet to produce any concrete results, especially as global coordination has since given way to uncoordinated national initiatives.

2   If the risk-free rate on 5-year loans is 5 per cent and 5-year bonds issued by reference entity x pay 7 per cent, the bond spread for entity x is 2 per cent. If the 5-year CDS spread for reference entity x is 2.3 per cent, the basis for reference entity x is 0.3 per cent. The basis is not fully arbitraged because of counterparty risk, liquidity and investor preferences. There are in fact instances in which the basis widens because bond spreads and CDS spreads move in opposite directions.

3   The financial services industry lobbied against any attempt to extend insurance regulations to the CDS market or have CDSs regulated by any other body. The market for these instruments expanded very rapidly after the United States Commodity Futures Modernization Act of 2000 exempted them from regulation and supervision by the United States Securities and Exchange Commission.

4   Shiller (1981) was the first to demonstrate that stock prices exhibit greater volatility than the present value of realized dividends.

5   Nassim Taleb put it well in an interview with the *Wall Street Journal* (Heard on the Street, 17 May 2004) when he said that buying sovereign CDSs for the United States is like buying insurance on the Titanic from someone on the Titanic.

6   Alternatively, consider the case of a bank that is exposed to a distressed United States company which is considered too big to fail. It is likely that CDSs on this distressed company will have high spreads. But if the company is indeed too big to fail, internal risk managers may consider a much cheaper sovereign CDS to be equivalent to the more expensive corporate CDS.

7   Basel II regulations do not affect the demand of CDSs for highly rated sovereign debt because there is no capital charge for the debt of highly rated sovereigns.

8   Without CDSs, shorting assets becomes complicated and requires capital. A CDS allows shorting an asset by simply paying the CDS spread.

9   The bankruptcy of the car parts maker Delphi offers a good example of these network effects. At the time of default, Delphi's debt was approximately $4 billion and CDS contracts on Delphi's debt were estimated to range between $20 and $30 billion. A centralized clearing house would have solved some of the problems associated with the large gross CDS positions.

References

Baker D (2010). Financial innovation: What is it good for (II)? Credit default swaps. TPM blog, 11 March.

Barclays Capital (2010). Sovereign CDS. The canary or the cat? Barclays Capital Global Rates Strategy, 15 February.

Blanchard OJ (1979). Speculative bubbles, crashes and rational expectations. *Economics Letters*, 3: 387–389.

Das S (2008). CDS market may create added risk. *Financial Times*, 5 February.

Das S (2010). Swap tango, a derivative regulation dance. *Eurointelligence*, 3 March.

Haldane A (2009). Rethinking the financial network. Speech delivered at the Financial Student Association, Amsterdam, April.

González-Rozada M and Levy Yeyati E (2008). Global factors and emerging market spreads. *Economic Journal*, 118(533): 1917–1936.

Litan R (2009). In defense of much, but not all, financial innovation. Washington, DC, Brookings Institution.

Portes R (2010). Ban naked CDS. *Eurointelligence*, 18 March.

Remolona E, Scatigna M and Wu E (2007). Interpreting sovereign spreads. *BIS Quarterly Review*, March: 27–39.

Shiller R (1981). Do stock prices move too much to be justified by subsequent changes in dividends? *American Economic Review*, 71(3): 421–36.

Soros G (2010). America must face up to the dangers of derivatives. *Financial Times*, 22 April.

Tett G (2009). Fool's Gold. New York, NY, Free Press.

UNCTAD (2009). *Trade and Development Report*. United Nations Publication. New York and Geneva.

Zingales L (2010). Credit default swaps on trial. Project Syndicate, 19 April. http://www.project-syndicate.org/commentary/zingales2/English.

POTENTIAL EMPLOYMENT EFFECTS OF A GLOBAL REBALANCING

A. Introduction

There is widespread agreement that the persistently large imbalances in the world economy – with sizeable current-account deficits in some countries, particularly the United States, and sizeable current-account surpluses in others, notably China, Germany, Japan and a number of oil-exporting countries – contributed to the outbreak of the current economic and financial crisis and facilitated its global spread (see also *TDR 2009,* chap. I). There is also agreement that a smooth and non-deflationary reduction of these imbalances is indispensable for ensuring that the recent global economic upturn continues. This chapter focuses on the effects of global rebalancing on the patterns of global demand and trade flows.

Although the United States accounted for about 50 per cent of the aggregate current-account deficits in the world economy, and China for about 22 per cent of all surpluses in pre-crisis 2007, the global imbalances are far from being just a bilateral problem between the United States and China. China began to show a strong current-account surplus only from 2003 (Yu, 2007); prior to that the main counterparts to the United States' long-standing current-account deficit were surpluses in Germany and Japan. However, while so far there is little evidence that adjustments in the two countries would be able to help bring about a global rebalancing, in the United States there appears

no alternative to adjusting household consumption unless another asset bubble is allowed to occur, and in China, the need to embark on major structural transformation from investment- and export-led growth to consumer-led growth has been officially recognized.[1] It is against this background that this chapter concentrates on adjustments in the United States and China to illustrate the effects of rebalancing on international trade flows and employment.[2]

The recent growth trajectories of the United States and China appear to have moved in opposite directions. Consumption as a share of gross domestic product (GDP) increased in the United States but fell in China; investment rose dramatically in China while its importance shrunk in the United States. Thus the United States current-account deficit has been associated with a low national savings rate and a continuously rising share of private consumption in GDP, while along with China's current-account surplus there has been a very high national savings rate and a very low share of household consumption in GDP. However, the external position of neither of these two countries is sustainable.

A correction of the current-account imbalances and – their mirror image – the savings-investment disequilibria in both countries will affect the entire world economy. One reason for this is, of course, the large size of these two economies. But equally important for the overall outcome is the big difference in their levels of per capita income, since the level and structure of world trade is influenced by the relative importance of rich and poor countries in global economic growth. As long as per capita income growth in rich countries drives global growth, their demand patterns will largely determine global trade patterns: given their already high levels of industrialization and per capita incomes, growing demand in these countries will be directed more at non-tradable services and manufactured consumer goods, whereas industrial raw materials, energy and food products will feature more prominently in the demand patterns of rapidly industrializing developing countries. Thus, if the latter assume greater weight in the world economy, the resulting changes in the pattern of global demand growth are likely to influence the trends in commodity prices and terms of trade. This, in turn, will guide investment decisions and lead to changes in the sectoral focus of investment, productivity, output and employment growth.

> A non-deflationary reduction of global imbalances is indispensable for the global recovery to continue.

Major developments in the global economy since the beginning of this millennium may well have strongly influenced sectoral output growth and employment in developing countries. The three main developments were: the decline in national savings and the rapid increase in household consumption in the United States; the growing importance of investment and exports for growth in large Asian developing countries, particularly China; and the unprecedented surge in the prices of primary commodities after 2002. In particular, the rapid growth of consumer demand in the United States provided a growing market for manufactured exports from the industrializing developing countries. The consequent rapid industrialization in these countries, in turn, provided export opportunities for primary commodities from other developing countries. The overall expansionary nature of these three developments contributed to sustained output growth in the world economy for several years, making it easier to combine productivity-enhancing investment with a general expansion of employment.

This overall favourable external economic environment, combined with judicious policies, also allowed some developing countries to emerge as drivers of global growth, thereby, at least temporarily, reversing the previously observed divergence of economic performance between the industrialized and developing countries. It is now widely accepted that in order to recreate a favourable external environment for development, the challenge for policymakers is to achieve a non-deflationary and durable rebalancing of demand in the world economy. Such rebalancing will probably have to include a decline in the share of consumption in aggregate income in the United States and an increase in that share in China. Such a process of global rebalancing will undoubtedly cause a change in both the level and composition of international trade, with implications for structural change and employment in all countries. This chapter analyses these implications, for the demand side and for employment.

The chapter first discusses issues related to developments in the United States, where they are crisis-related (section B), before addressing developments in China (section C), where they are more closely associated with a gradual shift in the sectoral composition of output and employment. This discussion is followed by a simulation of the likely effects of rebalancing in the United States and China on global trade flows and sectoral employment shifts (section D). The results of this simulation suggest that such rebalancing in these two countries alone will not be sufficient to bring about an unwinding of global imbalances in a non-deflationary manner. Section E draws policy conclusions, stressing that for global rebalancing to occur in conjunction with sustained economic growth, adjustments in the level of composition of demand will also be necessary in other major economies and that developing countries may be well advised to take these global changes into account when defining or revising their post-crisis strategies to raise output growth and employment.

B. Rebalancing growth in the United States

1. Relationship between the current-account balance and consumer demand in the United States

While there are different views on the causes and effects of global imbalances, there can be little doubt that the saving and consumption patterns of United States households have been a key determinant of those imbalances.

A decomposition of the national income and product accounts in the savings-investment balance, with the components of net national savings disaggregated, highlights the secular decline in the United States household savings rate since the beginning of the 1980s, with a particularly sharp drop around the year 2000 (chart 2.1). It also indicates that the pattern of the United States current account from 1992 onwards correlates with that of household savings rather than government savings.[3] In the second half of the 1990s, a sizeable improvement of the government's fiscal position prevented the fall in the household savings rate from reducing overall national savings. The increase in public savings was matched by an equal increase in private investment, linked to the information and communications technology boom and to related expectations of more rapid productivity growth. This situation changed radically in 2001. From 2001 to 2003, investment fell sharply. Meanwhile, the deterioration in the United States

> The increase in household consumption in the United States was unsustainable because it was not supported by a similar expansion of labour compensation.

budget deficit over the same period reduced national savings. Given that the increase in fiscal deficits and continued fall in household savings exceeded the fall in investment, the United States current-account deficit remained high.

The decline in the United States household savings rate went hand in hand with a rapid expansion of private consumption. Since the late 1990s, the share of personal consumption in GDP has considerably exceeded its average long-term trend of about 66 per cent, reaching a peak in early 2009, when it accounted for 71 per cent of GDP (chart 2.2).

More importantly, the increase in United States household consumption was largely debt financed. Facilitated by easy consumer credit, lax lending standards, a proliferation of exotic mortgage products, the growth of a global market for securitized loans and soaring house values, burgeoning household spending created strongly growing household debt and led to a sharp decline in the United States household savings rate to almost zero.[4] The ratio of debt to personal disposable income reached an all-time high in 2007, exceeding 130 per cent. As a result, household leverage was 27 percentage points above where it would have been had it maintained its 1975–2000 trend (chart 2.3). This difference, which corresponds to about $2.8 trillion, indicates the potential magnitude of United States household deleveraging that could be achieved through debt reduction and increased savings.

Chart 2.1

NET SAVINGS AND INVESTMENT BALANCES IN THE UNITED STATES, 1980–2009

(Per cent of GDP)

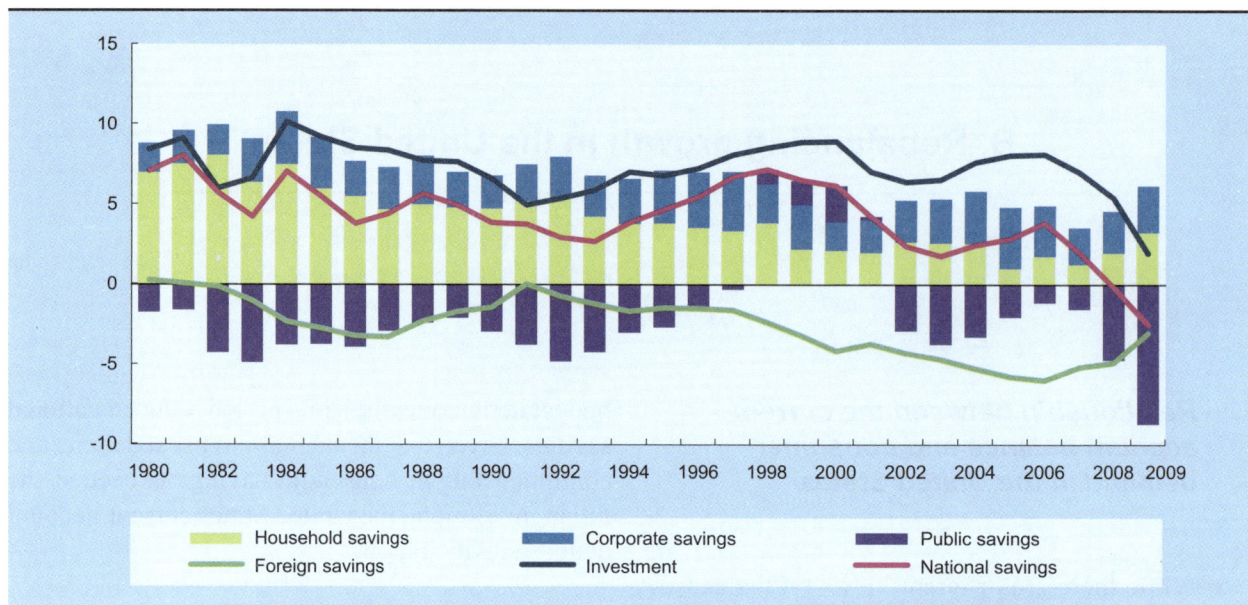

Source: UNCTAD secretariat calculations, based on the United States Bureau of Economic Analysis database.

Chart 2.2

PERSONAL CONSUMPTION IN THE UNITED STATES, 1950–2010

(Per cent of GDP)

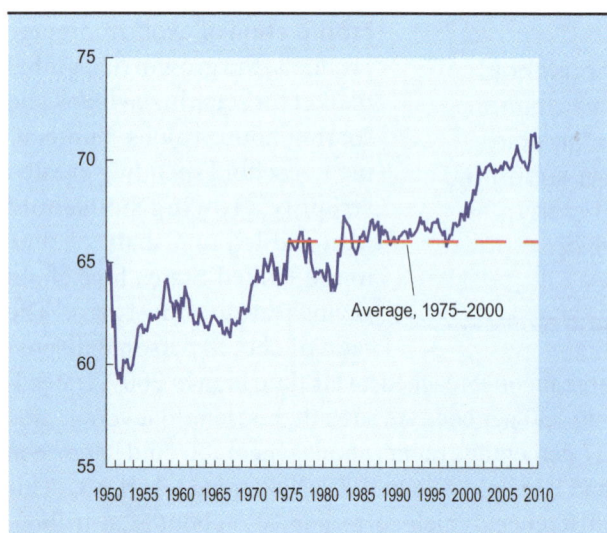

Source: UNCTAD secretariat calculations, based on the United States Bureau of Economic Analysis database.
Note: Data for 2010 refer to the first quarter.

The increase in private consumption was unsustainable because it was not supported by a similar expansion of labour compensation in the private sector. Compared to previous upswings, the economic expansion that ended with the onset of the current crisis had been characterized by a low increase in employment – a phenomenon sometimes referred to as "jobless growth" – and by the relative stagnation of real wages. As a result, private sector labour compensation grew at an unusually sluggish pace and fell short by more than $800 billion (in real terms) relative to the trajectory of the previous four business cycles (Roach, 2009: 14). Low- and middle-income households that intended to maintain their relative standards of consumption thus turned from income- to debt-financed expenditure. While the share of consumer credit in disposable personal income oscillated around an average of about 18 per cent between the mid-1960s and the mid-1990s, it reached a peak of over 25 per cent in the 2000s due to an average annual rate of growth of consumer credit of 8 per cent between 1992 and 2006 (Barba and Pivetti, 2009: 115). Low interest rates, asset price inflation (first for equities and then for housing) and financial deregulation were responsible for this shift

Chart 2.3

HOUSEHOLD LIABILITIES, DISPOSABLE PERSONAL INCOME AND LABOUR COMPENSATION IN THE UNITED STATES, 1965–2009

(Per cent)

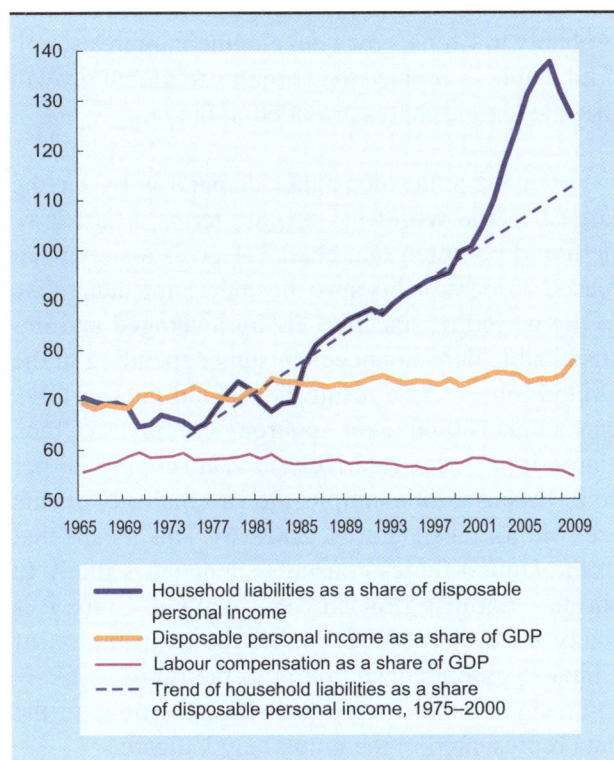

- Household liabilities as a share of disposable personal income
- Disposable personal income as a share of GDP
- Labour compensation as a share of GDP
- Trend of household liabilities as a share of disposable personal income, 1975–2000

Source: UNCTAD secretariat calculations, based on the United States Federal Reserve, *Flow of Funds* database (tables B100, F6 and F7).

Note: Data for 2009 are preliminary.

from wage to non-wage income (i.e. income from property and government transfers) and loans as the sources of purchasing power, used increasingly by low- and middle-income households. Resort to non-wage income allowed households to maintain the share of disposable personal income in GDP at around 74 per cent, despite the long-term decline in the share of labour compensation in GDP since the early 1980s (interrupted by only a brief upswing in the late 1990s) (chart 2.3). Efforts to maintain relative standards of consumption, despite sluggish growth in labour compensation, led many households to lower their savings or increase their debts, causing a marked fall in the household savings rate.[5]

In the final two quarters of 2008, real personal consumption expenditure fell sharply, marking a departure from the trend of a steady increase in the consumption rate since the 1980s. Thereafter, it picked up again, but this is most likely due to the one-off effects of transfers related to various government programmes such as the "cash-for-clunkers" programme, food stamps and extended unemployment benefits, as well as tax cuts. This suggests the recovery is only temporary. Indeed, there is good reason to believe that the decline in household consumption as a share of GDP has only just begun. It has fallen by only about one percentage point from its peak of 71.5 per cent – still more than five percentage points above its pre-bubble average of 66 per cent during the period 1975–2000. This fall corresponds to only about 20 per cent of the shift that would take household consumption as a share of GDP back to the historic average. The decline in asset prices and the associated wealth effects for households, a sharp tightening of credit availability and a large increase in unemployment risk are widely expected to have a lasting downward impact on household spending. According to recent estimates (Lee, Rabanal and Sandri, 2010: 3), the current changes in the respective shares of household consumption and savings in total income are likely to settle at the levels of the early 1990s, which "implies a significantly lower share of private sector demand in GDP by about 3 percentage points compared to the pre-crisis (2003–2007) average".[6]

2. United States consumption spending and imports

Buoyant consumer demand in the United States was the main driver of global economic growth for many years in the run-up to the current global economic crisis. A return of United States household savings to about 4 per cent of disposable income – the average of the mid-1990s (i.e. before those households went on a spending spree) – would translate into a fall in household consumption of about 3 per cent of that country's GDP. Given that before the crisis household consumption in the United States accounted for about 16 per cent of global output and that imports constituted a sizeable proportion of that consumption, this would imply both a reduction in world output and a decline in other countries' export opportunities. From 2000 to 2007, United States imports as a share of its GDP grew from 15 per cent to

Chart 2.4

HOUSEHOLD CONSUMPTION IN SELECTED COUNTRIES AND COUNTRY GROUPS, AVERAGE FOR 2007–2008

(Billions of dollars)

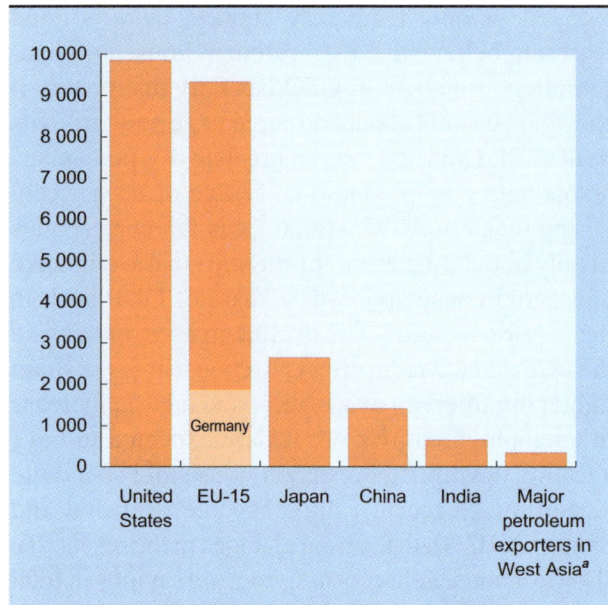

Source: UNCTAD secretariat calculations, based on *UNCTAD Handbook of Statistics* database.
a Bahrain, Iraq, Kuwait, Oman, Qatar, Saudi Arabia, Syrian Arab Republic and United Arab Emirates.

17 per cent, boosting aggregate demand in the rest of the world by $937 billion, in nominal terms. Moreover, as a result of global production sharing, United States consumer spending increases global economic activities in many indirect ways as well (e.g. business investments in countries such as Germany and Japan to produce machinery for export to China and its use there for the manufacture of exports to the United States). In short, the future path of United States consumption spending has macroeconomic implications, not only for economic recovery in the United States but also for global growth.[7]

The question arises as to which countries' consumer demand could make up for the decline in United States consumer demand. This raises at least two issues: the importance of the absolute level of United States household consumption at the global level, and the composition of United States imports, especially its imports of consumer goods. For instance, discussions about decoupling of economic

performance in developing countries from that in developed countries have often focused on whether and when China could supplement the United States as an engine of global growth. The remainder of this section focuses on these issues. The key finding of this discussion, supported by empirical evidence, is that fostering consumption growth in China, while probably in China's own development interests, will not be able to replace the stimulus to global growth that the United States provided in the past.

United States consumer demand is by far the largest in the world in absolute terms (chart 2.4). It should be noted that chart 2.4 gives a somewhat biased impression because the underlying data relate to the period of sizeable, highly leveraged and unsustainable debt-financed consumer spending in the United States. As a result, household debt to GDP was about 100 per cent, in strong contrast to China where it has been relatively low, at roughly 20 per cent (because, for example, the vast majority of cars are sold for cash) (Lardy, 2009: 6). This means that in the United States consumer demand is likely to shrink – not just grow slower – while in China it is likely to grow rapidly. Hence, the contribution of China to global consumption in the future is likely to be significantly larger than extrapolations of the data represented in the graph may indicate.

What would be the impact of a reduction in United States consumer demand on the country's current-account balance? The deterioration in the United States current-account balance up to 2006 and its recent improvement have been largely driven by changes in the trade account.[8] Indeed, merchandise trade is by far the most important component of the United States current account. With a deficit of about $800 billion, which corresponds to 6 per cent of GDP, the trade deficit has been responsible for an average of about 110 per cent of the current-account deficit in the past five years.[9]

However, these aggregate data mask important features that are of particular importance for the link between household consumption and current-account imbalances. While capital goods and industrial supplies and materials (excluding energy) are the largest categories on both sides of the United States trade account, a disaggregation of the United States trade deficit by main end-use categories shows that consumer goods, including automotive products, accounted for over 85 per cent of the increase in the non-energy

Chart 2.5

**CURRENT-ACCOUNT BALANCE AND TRADE BALANCE BY
END-USE CATEGORY IN THE UNITED STATES, 1980–2009**

(Billions of dollars)

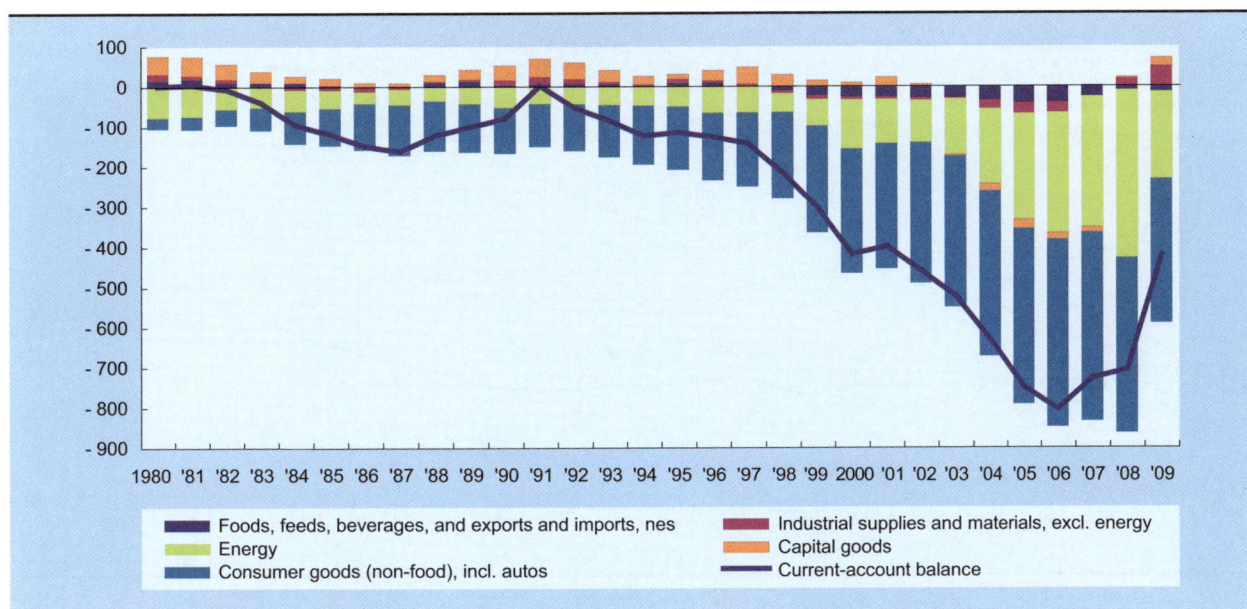

Legend:
- Foods, feeds, beverages, and exports and imports, nes
- Energy
- Consumer goods (non-food), incl. autos
- Industrial supplies and materials, excl. energy
- Capital goods
- Current-account balance

Source: UNCTAD secretariat calculations, based on the United States Bureau of Economic Analysis database.
Note: nes = not elsewhere specified.

trade deficit between 1997 and 2008 (chart 2.5). A loss in competitiveness may partly explain the worsening balance of trade in consumer goods. But the rapidly expanding household consumption has most likely been the major cause of the large and widening deficit in the consumption categories of United States trade, and thus in its current account.

It is unlikely that the sharp decline in United States imports of consumer goods could be compensated by an increase in consumer spending and associated imports of consumer goods by China or any other developing country. Given that China's consumption was only about one eighth of United States consumption and that its GDP at current exchange rates is only one third that of the United States, there is little reason to believe that household consumption in China could supplant United States household consumption as a driver of global growth any time soon. In order for

> Higher consumption in China or other developing countries cannot compensate for the lower imports of consumer goods by the United States.

Chinese consumption to compensate for the reduction in United States consumption, the share of consumer spending in GDP in China would need to increase by at least 10 percentage points – an unlikely occurrence in the foreseeable future.[10] Domestic demand could also expand in other relatively large and rapidly growing developing countries, notably Brazil and India. However, compared to the United States economy, the economies of these countries are still small, making it unlikely that they could compensate fully for the decline in United States consumption. Rather, household consumption in developed countries in the European Union (EU), particularly Germany, as well as Japan, would be better placed to achieve this.

What is more, the import content of domestic consumption in China is less than 8 per cent – three times smaller than in the United States (Akyüz,

Chart 2.6

**PERCENTAGE OF SIMILARITY IN THE COMPOSITION OF IMPORTS OF SELECTED
COUNTRIES WITH THE IMPORTS OF THE UNITED STATES, 1992–2008**

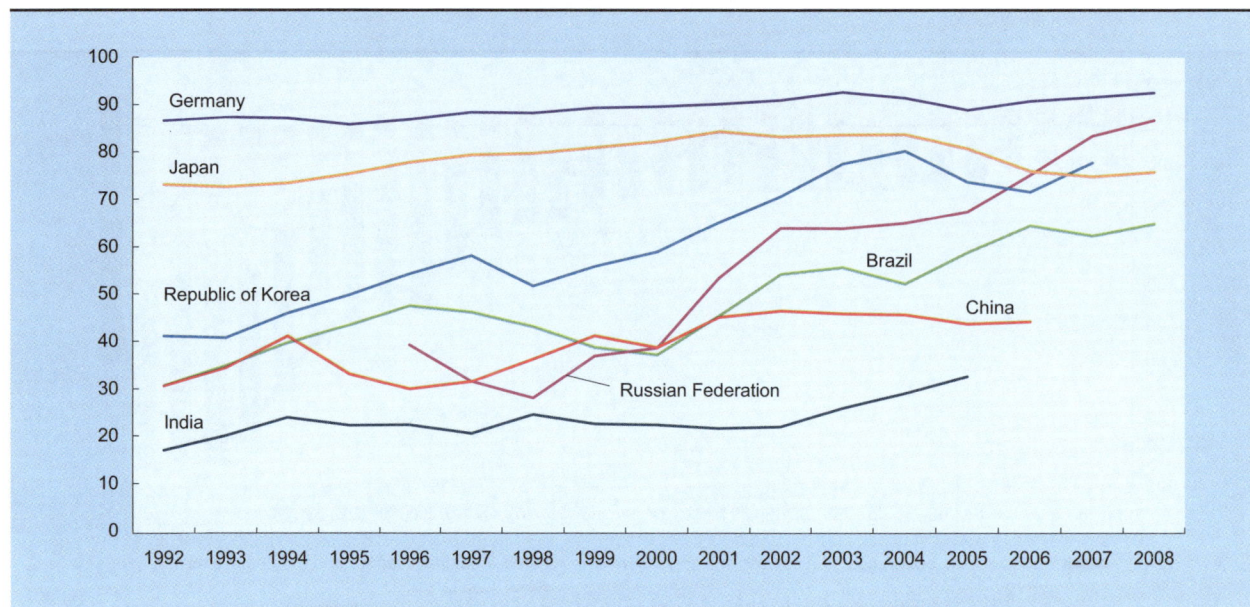

Source: UNCTAD secretariat calculations, based on United Nations, *UN COMTRADE* database.

2010: 11). Perhaps even more importantly, the composition of United States imports of consumer goods differs greatly from that in other countries. An import similarity index based on 428 different consumer goods indicates that China's basket of imported consumer goods overlaps that of the United States by only about 45 per cent (chart 2.6).[11] This index also indicates that the composition of imports of consumer goods by major developed countries with current-account surpluses, namely Germany and Japan, is very similar to that of the United States. Combined with the evidence on the size of household consumption shown in chart 2.4, this shows that these two developed countries would be in a better position than China to compensate for the decline in United States consumer goods imports.

C. Rebalancing growth in China: potential employment effects

1. Introduction

The skilful management of growth processes in a globalizing economy and a pragmatic use of sometimes unconventional economic policies have enabled China to achieve a more than fivefold increase in real per capita income since 1990, and to lift some 390 million citizens out of poverty (Chen and Ravallion, 2008; *TDR 2005*). However, important domestic challenges persist, such as the continued need to generate employment and raise living standards of all segments of the population and in all regions of the country. It has therefore been suggested that, in order to continue its rapid economic growth and progress in reducing income gaps and poverty, China may need to address these domestic imbalances, quite independently of the shocks from the current global economic and financial crisis and of efforts at global rebalancing (Yu, 2007).

The domestic imbalances have arisen in parallel with, and perhaps occasionally exacerbated by, China's emphasis on an investment- and export-led growth path, which has also been linked to sizeable trade surpluses and the accumulation of massive foreign exchange reserves. This section attempts to identify the major challenges that China is facing in redressing its internal and external imbalances, the potential trade-offs and sequencing of different policy options, as well as the potential impact of rebalancing in China on other developing countries. The intention here is not to provide policy prescriptions; rather, it aims to contribute to a better understanding of a number of adjustment-related issues, including the potential impact on both China and other developing countries of policies proposed in the recent international debates on global imbalances.

The analysis in this chapter is based on the recognition that the greatest challenge to China's continuation along its development path is to foster internal integration through the expansion of internal markets based on a much more rapid growth of consumption than that witnessed since the early 2000s. An increase in consumer spending that compensates for slower export growth would also reduce the country's vulnerability to adverse changes in external demand.[12]

With these considerations in mind, this section discusses, first, to what extent Chinese employment depends on exports and, second, the reasons for the relatively small and recently further declining share of household consumption in aggregate demand. It goes on to discuss two policy areas which are frequently mentioned in the rebalancing debate: a currency revaluation, and the range of measures more directly designed to increase total household disposable income, including government transfers and reform of the financial system.

2. How dependent is Chinese employment on exports?

The most internationally visible characteristic of China's development path has been its strong export growth. The nominal value of China's exports has increased more than 100-fold since the country's economic opening in 1979, and its exports accounted for over one third of its GDP during the period 2005–2008. Such emphasis on foreign demand for economic growth inevitably increased China's vulnerability to a downturn in its major export markets. Thus it is not surprising that China's exports fell sharply with the onset of the global economic crisis. This has led to renewed calls for a rebalancing of the composition of its aggregate demand, which would give less importance to investment and exports and more to a greater reliance on domestic consumption.

An important reason for Chinese policymakers to place greater emphasis on foreign demand was the relatively low level of per capita income and, thus, domestic demand, when the country started its economic catch-up growth. While the importance of exports to China's output growth is well recognized, the contribution of exports to employment creation has been less clear. The close link between exports and foreign direct investment (FDI) enabled relatively easy access to state-of-the-art technology and rapid growth of labour productivity. This high labour productivity translated into lower prices. The ensuing competitive advantage boosted external demand, and hence domestic output and employment. On the other hand, China's exports contain a sizeable share of imported intermediate goods. Domestic value added, which is the part that is comparable to GDP, is generally estimated to account for only about half of total gross revenues (see, for example, Koopman, Wang and Wei, 2008; and Chen et al., 2009).[13]

This comparatively low share of domestic value added in export earnings points to a correspondingly smaller contribution of exports to employment generation in China, although it has had an employment generation effect in other countries in East and South-East Asia. Data from a recent study by Feenstra and Hong (2007) indicate that in China only about 70 million jobs are in export activities, including jobs indirectly related to exports through the production of domestically supplied intermediate inputs.[14] This corresponds to less than 10 per cent of total employment, but may be equivalent to about 20 per cent of wage and salary employment.[15] It has also been estimated that the decline in export-oriented production in 2008 and 2009 caused a loss of about 40 million jobs in China, of which 14.6 million were in agriculture and 15.1 million in manufacturing.

The latter corresponds to about 4 per cent of non-agricultural employment in 2007 (Cai, Wang and Zhang, 2010).

The direct contribution of exports to employment generation in China is likely to have remained small relative to total employment in that country. The long-term development of China's export ratio is difficult to predict from cross-country comparisons because China is much larger than the next largest countries, except India, but India has remained a relatively closed economy. However, worldwide, the domestic value-added content of exports accounts for about one fifth of GDP, on average, and is much lower in large countries than in small ones.[16] In developed countries, value added per worker is much the same in traded as in non-traded sectors. Taken together, this suggests that in the long run export-oriented industries will employ about 10 per cent of all workers in China. In other words, employment in China is much less dependent on exports than is commonly supposed.

> Employment in China is much less dependent on exports than is commonly supposed.

3. Household consumption and the share of labour compensation in total income

Private consumer spending in China is low by international standards, regardless of whether it is measured in per capita terms or as a share of GDP (chart 2.7). In 2008, per capita consumption was only $758 (in real 2000 terms), much lower than that of many other developing countries, including in Asia.

However, a low and declining share of private consumption in aggregate demand is a characteristic frequently observed in rapidly industrializing economies during their early phase of economic take-off. The industrialization experiences of Japan and the Republic of Korea indicate that the share of private consumption in GDP tends to fall during about the first 20 years after economic take-off, before turning to a slow upward trend thereafter. And this may happen in spite of stable positive

> Private consumer spending in China is low by international standards.

Potential Employment Effects of a Global Rebalancing

PER CAPITA HOUSEHOLD CONSUMPTION EXPENDITURE AND SHARE OF HOUSEHOLD CONSUMPTION EXPENDITURE IN GDP IN SELECTED COUNTRIES, 2008

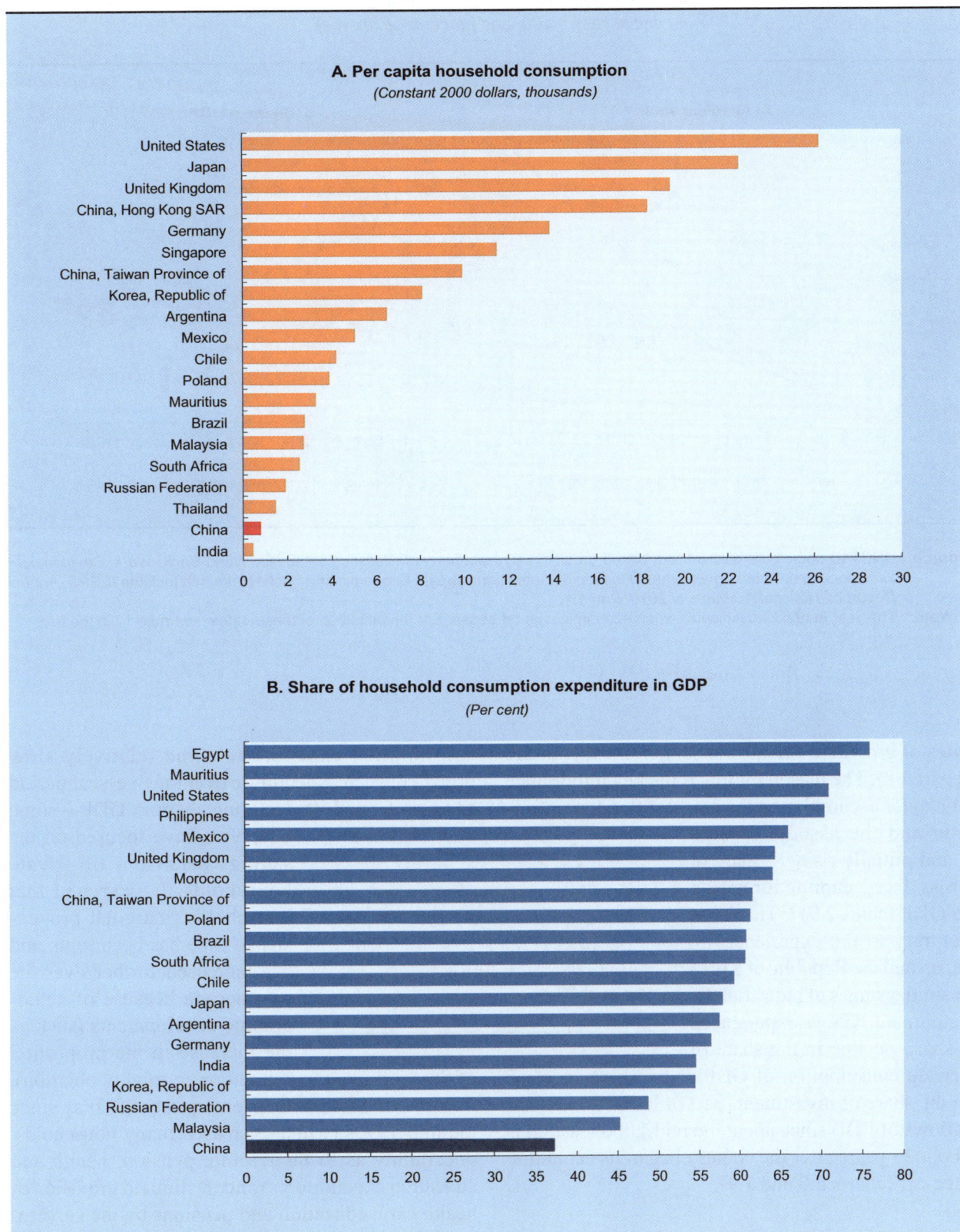

A. Per capita household consumption
(Constant 2000 dollars, thousands)

United States	
Japan	
United Kingdom	
China, Hong Kong SAR	
Germany	
Singapore	
China, Taiwan Province of	
Korea, Republic of	
Argentina	
Mexico	
Chile	
Poland	
Mauritius	
Brazil	
Malaysia	
South Africa	
Russian Federation	
Thailand	
China	
India	

(x-axis: 0 2 4 6 8 10 12 14 16 18 20 22 24 26 28 30)

B. Share of household consumption expenditure in GDP
(Per cent)

Egypt	
Mauritius	
United States	
Philippines	
Mexico	
United Kingdom	
Morocco	
China, Taiwan Province of	
Poland	
Brazil	
South Africa	
Chile	
Japan	
Argentina	
Germany	
India	
Korea, Republic of	
Russian Federation	
Malaysia	
China	

(x-axis: 0 5 10 15 20 25 30 35 40 45 50 55 60 65 70 75 80)

Source: UNCTAD secretariat calculations, based on *UNCTAD Handbook of Statistics* database.

Chart 2.8

HOUSEHOLD CONSUMPTION IN CHINA, JAPAN AND THE REPUBLIC OF KOREA FROM START OF ECONOMIC TAKE-OFF

*(Index numbers on a logarithmic scale,
initial year = 100, and percentage shares)*

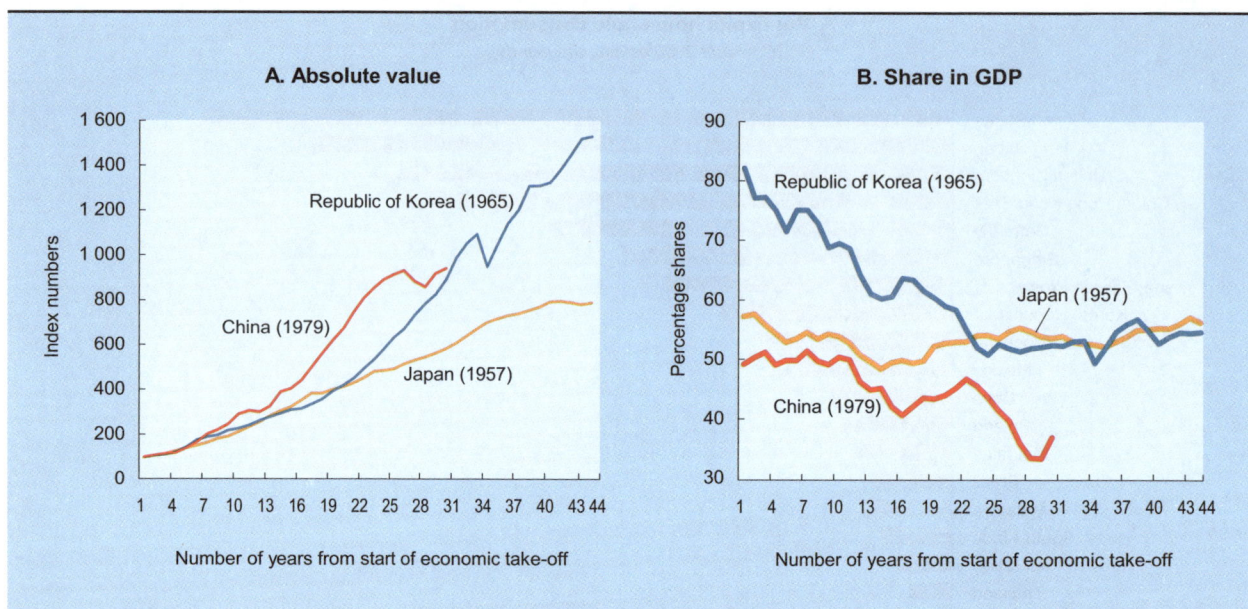

A. Absolute value

B. Share in GDP

Number of years from start of economic take-off

Number of years from start of economic take-off

Source: UNCTAD secretariat calculations, based on *UNCTAD Handbook of Statistics* database; World Bank, *World Development Indicators*, and *Global Development Finance* database; and Japan, Economic and Social Research Institute (ESRI), *Annual Report on National Accounts of 2010*, Part 1.1.

Note: The year in brackets indicates when economic take-off began. For the definition of these dates, see note 17 in the text.

rates of growth in private consumption expenditure (chart 2.8). The reason for this is the key importance of capital accumulation for successful industrialization and the associated high – and initially rising – share of gross fixed capital formation in GDP (chart 2.9).[17] However, contrary to the experiences in Japan and the Republic of Korea at similar stages of industrial development, China experienced a sharp decline in the share of private consumption of GDP and a sharp increase in the share of investment (part of it due to buoyant inflows of FDI) since about the mid-2000s, which is about 25 years after the country began its economic take-off (charts 2.8 and 2.9).

In order to explain the two features observed since the mid-2000s with regard to China's private

> The share of labour in national income in China has declined since the mid-1990s ...

consumption expenditure – the relatively slow growth of such expenditure over the five-year period as a whole, and its declining share in GDP – some observers have focused on the savings behaviour of private households. It is argued that households' marginal propensity to save has been high, and has increased further over the past decade because of demographic developments (such as the increase in the proportion of the working age population in total population), reforms of State-owned enterprises (SOEs) since the mid-1990s (which increased many households' uncertainty as to their future pension, health and education expenditures) and the limited provision of health care, education and pensions by the Government (see, for example, Modigliani and Cao, 2004; and Blanchard and Giavazzi, 2006).[18]

Chart 2.9

SHARE OF GROSS FIXED CAPITAL FORMATION IN GDP IN CHINA, JAPAN AND THE REPUBLIC OF KOREA FROM START OF ECONOMIC TAKE-OFF

(Per cent)

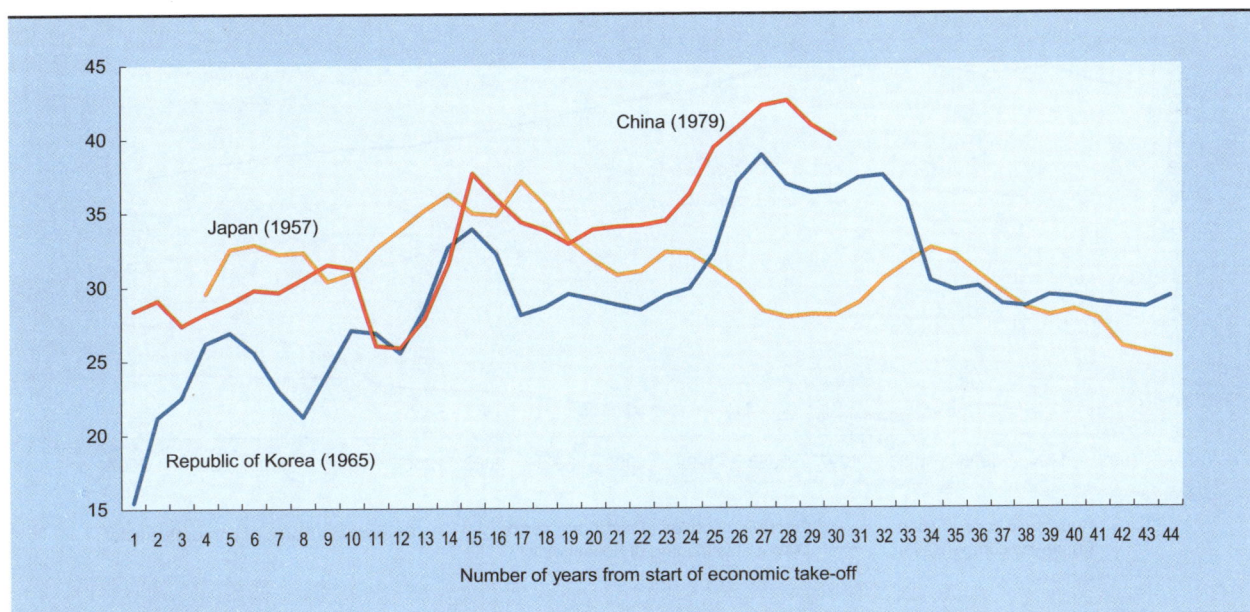

Source: See chart 2.8.
Note: See chart 2.8.

These factors are undoubtedly important explanations for the increase in the savings rate of Chinese households (see, for example, McKinsey Global Institute, 2009). But it is far less likely that they played a major role in the decline of the share of consumption in aggregate demand. Calculations based on regression analysis suggest that the 5 percentage point increase in China's household savings since the early 1990s has been responsible for only one ninth of the 9 percentage point decline in the share of consumption in GDP that has occurred since then. The same calculations suggest that it is the decline in the share of households' disposable income in GDP that is largely responsible for the relative decline in consumer demand (Aziz and Cui, 2007).

The share of labour income in national income reached a peak in the mid-1990s and has been consistently declining since then.[19] This decline has been closely mirrored by the decline in the share of household consumption in GDP. At the same time,

.... as has the share of household consumption in GDP.

the share of corporate profits in national income has been increasing (chart 2.10). To be sure, this evidence does not suggest that labour compensation in China has been falling, but only that household income and employee compensation have been growing slower than GDP.[20]

At first glance, this evidence would suggest that the low and declining share of household consumption in GDP reflects an imbalance between employee compensation and corporate profits (Hung, 2009). However, this evidence is likely to be the result of a greater number of potentially overlapping factors whose relative quantitative importance is difficult to disentangle.

While statistical factors[21] explain the one-off drop in the share of labour compensation in GDP between 2003 and 2004, structural change has probably been a key determinant of the tendency of this share to decline since the mid-1990s. A recent study

Chart 2.10

HOUSEHOLD CONSUMPTION, EMPLOYEE COMPENSATION, CORPORATE PROFITS AND DISPOSABLE INCOMES OF HOUSEHOLDS AND FIRMS IN CHINA, 1993–2007

(Per cent of GDP)

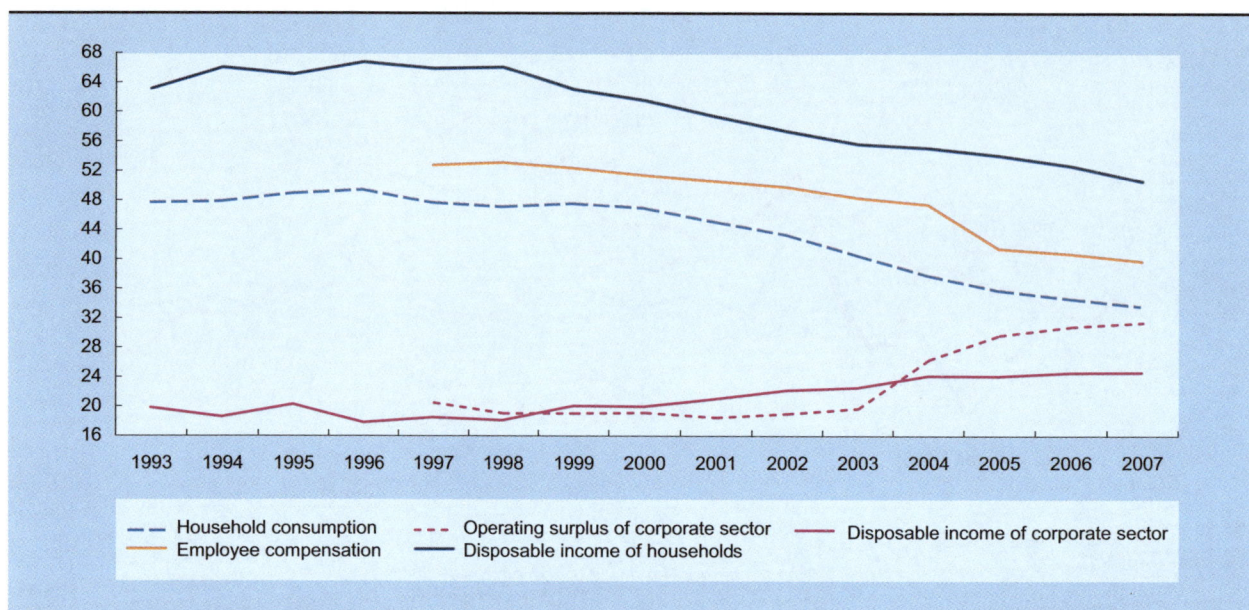

Source: UNCTAD secretariat calculations, based on National Bureau of Statistics of China database; and Bai and Qian, 2009a: table 4.

decomposes the change in the aggregate share of labour compensation in GDP into changes stemming from shifts in aggregate output structure and those caused by differences in sectoral employment shares (Bai and Qian, 2009b). On the basis of this analysis, the authors argue that the main cause of the falling share of household disposable income and labour compensation in GDP since the mid-1990s has been the declining importance in total value added of agriculture and the growing importance of industry and services, with the employment share being much larger in the former than in the latter sectors. They also show that the lower share of employment in the industrial sector has been an amplifying factor since the mid-1990s. A large part of the decline in the wage share in this sector during the late 1990s and early 2000s was most likely due to the reform of SOEs. Moreover, for the entire 15-year period, the exceptionally high investment rate, the sizeable FDI inflows and the resulting capital-intensive structure of industrial production, combined with rapid technological progress and very high rates of labour productivity in Chinese manufacturing, must have contributed significantly to the relatively slow pace

of employment growth in manufacturing, and hence in total labour compensation.[22]

Another factor that might have slowed down the growth rate of total employee compensation was the continued abundant supply of very low-cost workers – a factor that is often assumed to be a defining characteristic of the Chinese economy. There can be little doubt that the existence of surplus labour makes it difficult for workers (and in particular migrants) to bargain for wage increases. While this may explain the relatively slow wage growth (see below), it is more difficult to see why it should have prevented rapid employment growth, and thus contributed to the decline in the share of employee compensation in GDP. The decline in the share of labour compensation in aggregate income had such a sizeable effect on Chinese households' disposable income because the non-wage components of household income were of only marginal importance. Disaggregating household disposable income into wage income, investment income and government transfers shows that government transfers and investment income were very small (chart 2.11).[23] As a corollary, a very

Chart 2.11

**HOUSEHOLD DISPOSABLE INCOME, HOUSEHOLD INCOME FROM DIFFERENT
SOURCES AND HOUSEHOLD SAVINGS IN CHINA, 1992–2006**

(Per cent of GDP, unless otherwise indicated)

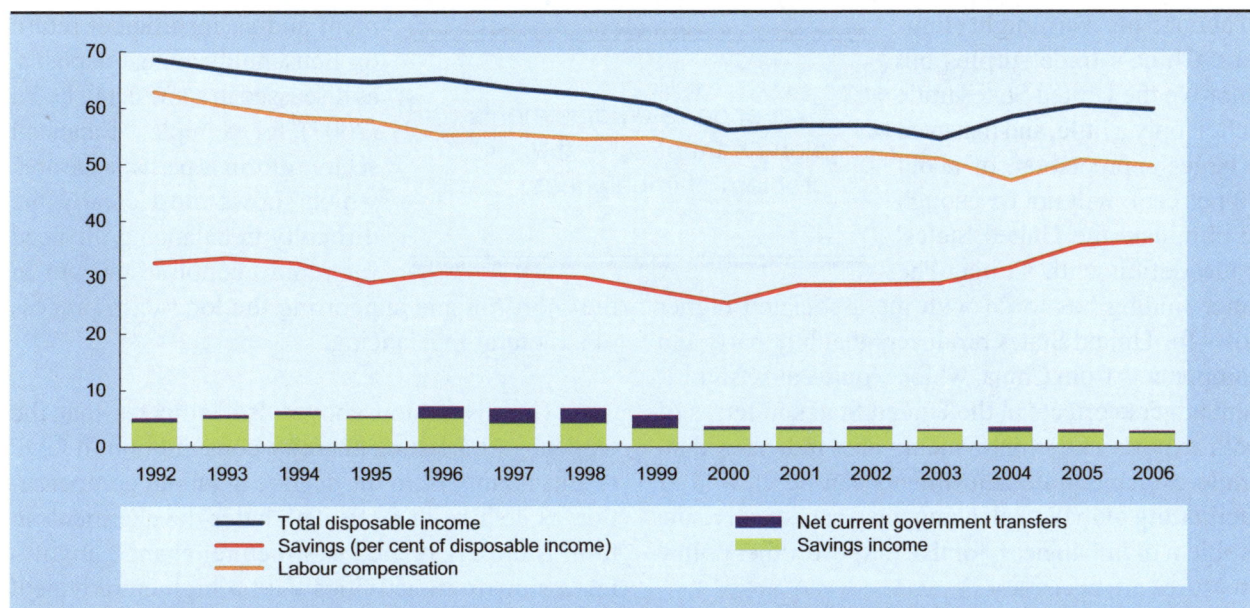

- Total disposable income
- Savings (per cent of disposable income)
- Labour compensation
- Net current government transfers
- Savings income

Source: UNCTAD secretariat calculations, based on National Bureau of Statistics of China database.
Note: Labour compensation and total disposable income refer to flow of funds accounts.

large proportion of household disposable income in China consists of wages. Households' savings income has been adversely affected by the low level – and further decline between the mid-1990s and mid-2000s – of interest rates on bank deposits, which have been the main vehicle of savings for Chinese households. Moreover, there is no strong link between household income and developments on the stock market because dividend payments are low, and because only a small percentage of Chinese households actually hold shares in Chinese firms, either directly through the stock market or indirectly through institutional investors and pension funds (Aziz and Cui, 2007). The recent decline in labour compensation was accompanied by some, but by no means a strong, increase in households' propensity to save (chart 2.11), especially since the early 2000s following reforms of SOEs, due to increased uncertainty over old-age pensions, health and education that these enterprises had previously provided. Taken together, this evidence suggests that in order to increase households' disposable income, and hence consumer demand, there might be a case for larger

budgetary transfers. Increased public spending on health, education and housing may be useful for combating any tendency towards increased precautionary savings.

4. Prospects for increasing household consumption in China

It is often argued that a strong appreciation of the renminbi is the most important, if not the only, policy measure for achieving rebalancing in China. It would sharply reduce the country's external surplus, and, as a side effect, also the United States current-account deficit (e.g. Krugman, 2010). This is clearly overly simplistic for at least two reasons. First, while most observers would agree that China's strong external position has been supported by a competitive exchange rate, it is not clear whether the renminbi is highly undervalued as is frequently suggested: one recent study suggests that China's currency may be undervalued by somewhere between 2.5 per cent and 27.5 per cent (Evenett, 2010). This can hardly provide the basis for clear policy guidance on such a controversial matter. Second, the same study supports findings of earlier simulations (e.g. *TDR 2005*) showing that a small appreciation of the renminbi, of about 5 per cent, might eliminate China's trade surplus but improve the United States trade deficit only a little, and that even a larger appreciation, of about 10 per cent, will not be enough to eliminate the United States' trade deficit with China. The latter finding has to do with the associated higher costs for United States producers that buy parts and components from China, which would cause significant adverse effects in the United States in terms of both exports and employment. This indicates that, while exchange-rate adjustments can be viewed as facilitating global rebalancing, they cannot solve the problem of imbalances; for that purpose, other policy measures are necessary.

> Exchange-rate adjustments alone cannot solve the problem of imbalances.

There is widespread agreement that measures such as an increase in government spending on social security (including pensions, health and education) and public investment in housing could help reduce household precautionary savings and may help increase consumer spending in China. The additional government expenditures could be financed at least partly by dividend payments from SOEs (World Bank Beijing Office, 2006: 15–17; Yu, 2007; McKinsey Global Institute, 2009). This would help reverse the adverse effects resulting from the extensive reforms of SOEs in the 1990s, which substantially reduced the public provision of health care, education, pensions and housing, and shifted this responsibility to households. For example, the proportion of health spending by households increased from less than 20 per cent in the 1980s to over 60 per cent in the 2000s (Blanchard and Giavazzi, 2006), despite the fact that in the mid-2000s government spending on health had increased by 125–140 per cent (Hong, Vos and Yao, 2008: 46).

> It will be difficult to sustain rapid industrialization without a faster growth of real wages.

Further reform of the financial sector may also help boost household consumption. The most important measure so far has probably been the large-scale recapitalization of the State-owned commercial banks, which removed the sizeable overhang of non-performing loans from banks' balance sheets. Nevertheless, the institutional set-up of the financial sector and the lending policy of China's largest banks may have provided overly strong incentives for investment and an insufficient return on household savings deposits, as discussed in some detail by Yu (2007), for example.[24] Financial sector reform is perhaps the area which shows most clearly the difficulty in balancing the need for rapid economic growth in the short run and supporting the long-term process of structural rebalancing.

The discussion above also indicates that the tendency of a falling share of consumption in GDP results mainly from the decline in labour compensation as a share in GDP. The latter development, in turn, is closely related to structural change, involving a shift from activities with a high employment share (particularly agriculture) towards industrial activities with a generally lower employment share, and to an emphasis on capital-intensive production in the manufacturing sector. However, achieving such structural change – which is a natural process in a country's economic development – without real wages growing more rapidly relative to productivity than in the past may become increasingly difficult. Ongoing rapid economic growth, combined with slower growth of the working-age population, due to the one-child policy adopted in the early 1980s, may well signal a situation in China where demand for labour starts increasing more rapidly than the workforce, and the rural labour surplus grows less rapidly than in the past (Cai, 2007, see also box 2.1).

One way of estimating developments regarding surplus labour is by looking at the age structure of a country's labour force.[25] While the size of China's total labour force (i.e. the population aged 15 years and older), is likely to peak only in the mid-2030s, its pre-retirement labour force (the population aged between 15 and 64 years), can be expected to peak at around 2015 (chart 2.12). Perhaps more importantly, the size of the population entering the labour force defined broadly

Box 2.1

CHINA: SKILL COMPOSITION OF NEW JOB SEEKERS

The number of additional workers entering the labour market is only one element of the supply-demand balance on the labour market; another is the skill level of workers. China has a sharply growing number of college graduates, and it might not always be easy for these higher skilled job seekers to fulfil their career expectations. Earlier catch-up experiences in East Asia suggest that changes in the sectoral structure of an economy, for example linked to the technological upgrading of its export sector, can absorb part of the increased supply of educated workers (*TDR 2003*). This is likely to happen also in China: the slower growth of the labour surplus could make unskilled labour relatively more expensive, and the growing supply of skilled labour could make skilled workers relatively less expensive. As a result, the country's comparative advantage could shift towards more skill-intensive manufactures and services, thereby absorbing part of the increased skill supply. This mechanism clearly has implications not only for China itself but also for other developing countries, particularly those that participate in vertical supply chains across East and South-East Asia. On the other hand, there are indications that in rural areas (i.e. the sources of another significant segment of job seekers), the quality of education is relatively low (Knight, Li and Deng, 2009). However, a gradual lifting of the household registration system (discussed intensely in the Chinese media prior to the Party conference in spring 2010, reflected in dozens of articles and op-ed contributions in *China Daily*), and in particular, a growing demand for simple service activities associated with the increasing importance of household consumption for economic growth as well as with urbanization, is likely to absorb much of these relatively low-skilled workers.

Chart 2.12

CHINA'S LABOUR FORCE BY AGE STRUCTURE, 1990–2050

(Million)

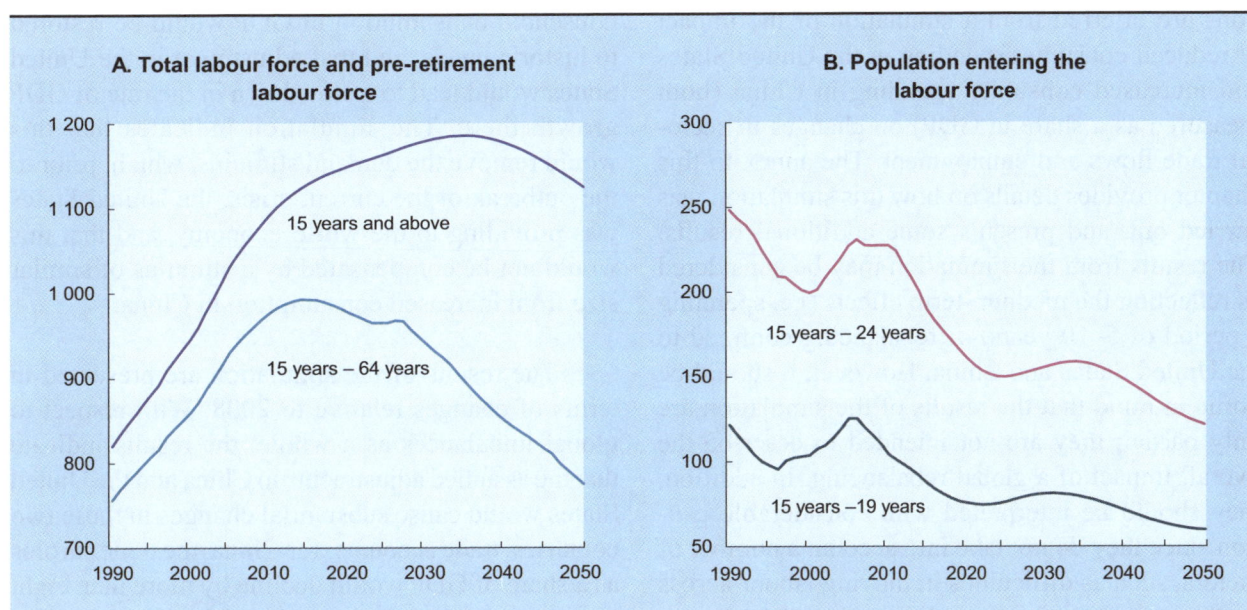

A. Total labour force and pre-retirement labour force

B. Population entering the labour force

Source: UNCTAD secretariat calculations, based on the United States Census Bureau database.
Note: Data from 2010 are estimates.

(i.e. the 15–24 year age group) reached its peak of 224 million people in 2009, and that of the population entering the labour force defined narrowly (i.e. the 15–19 year age group) reached its peak of 125 million people in 2005. Taken together, this evidence is indicative of an ageing labour force in China, which tends to be less mobile. Consequently, employers will need to pay a higher wage premium to get and retain workers,[26] so that real wages are likely to grow more rapidly relative to productivity than in the past. Indeed, according to media reports, minimum wages have been rising strongly in several provinces (Mitchell and Dyer, 2010). While this evidence suggests a broad tendency towards rising wages, it must be interpreted with caution. Part of it could be a reaction to more supportive agricultural policies, such as the abolition of the agricultural tax (Knight, 2007). But in any case, although not for demographic reasons, this would have increased the premium for employers to induce workers to migrate from rural to urban areas. All of these factors taken together could be a powerful stimulus to domestic consumption.

D. The potential impact of a global rebalancing on trade flows and employment

The discussion in the two preceding sections examined issues relating to rebalancing in the context of the national economies in the United States and China. This section focuses on the implications of these processes for other countries. These implications are inferred from a simulation of the impact of reduced consumer spending in the United States and increased consumer spending in China (both measured as a share in GDP) on changes in sectoral trade flows and employment. The annex to this chapter provides details on how this simulation was carried out, and presents some additional results. The results from the simulation may be considered as reflecting the medium-term effects (i.e. spanning a period of 5–10 years) of rebalancing confined to the United States and China. However, it should be borne in mind that the results of the simulation are only partial; they are not intended to describe the overall impact of a global rebalancing. In addition, they should be interpreted with considerable caution since they do not take into account a number of factors, such as difficulties in moving labour across sectors, subsidies and problems of market access. Nevertheless, simulations are useful for identifying the countries and sectors that are vulnerable to global rebalancing and for forming an idea of the order of magnitudes involved.

The simulation is based on the assumptions that in both China and the United States the share of household consumption in GDP would be restored to historic levels, and that adjustment in the United States would lead to a slowdown in the rate of GDP growth there. The simulation indicates that this would remove the demand stimulus, which, prior to the outbreak of the current crisis, the United States was providing to the world economy, and that this would not be compensated by a stimulus of similar size from increased consumption in China.

The results of the simulation are presented in terms of changes relative to 2008. With respect to global imbalances as a whole, the results indicate that the assumed adjustments in China and the United States would cause substantial changes in these two countries' trade accounts: for China, the trade surplus as a share of GDP would decline by more than eight percentage points, so that only a fairly small surplus position would remain, while for the United States, the trade balance as a share of GDP would improve

Tuesday 18th October 2011

Royal Geographical Society
with IBG

Advancing geography
and geographical learning

● A2 Study Day
● Programme

10.00 – 10.30	**Delegate registrations open** Complimentary squash and biscuits for all delegates in the main hall
10.30- – 10.55	**A short introduction to the objectives and structure of the day followed by opening presentation 'What every good geographer should understand'** Please sit in the front section of the Ondaatje only
11.00 – 12.00	**Presentation one: Go to your pre chosen group** • Understanding the development process : SUNLEY ROOM with Philippa • Biodiversity and ecosystems : LOWTHER ROOM with Andy • Tectonic hazards: ONDAATJE LECTURE THEATRE with Tom • Superpowers and Conflict: EDUCATION ROOM with Iain
12.00-12.15	**Refreshments break:** Complimentary tea, coffee, squash and biscuits for all delegates in the main hall and the map room
12.15- 1.15	**Presentation two: Go to your pre chosen group** • Understanding the development process: ONDAATJE LECTURE THEATRE with Philippa • Biodiversity and ecosystems : EDUCATION ROOM with Andy • UCAS and geography at university advice: SUNLEY ROOM with Kate
1.15 - 1.45	**Lunch** For those who have ordered one a packed lunch will be served in the MAIN HALL and the MAP ROOM. Complimentary tea, coffee, squash and biscuits for all delegates in the MAIN HALL and additional cold drinks in the MAP ROOM **'Geography in the News'** drop in sessions and **geography ambassadors** available to chat informally about studying geography at university all in the SUNLEY ROOM
1.45 – 2.30	**Presentation three:** ONDAATJE LECTURE THEATRE **Exam success - Making the grade:** Iain Palot Robust advice and top tips for succeeding in your examinations next summer
2.30 - 2.45	Q and A and summing up. All delegates leave at 2.45pm

A2 Study Day 2011
Map of the RGS-IBG

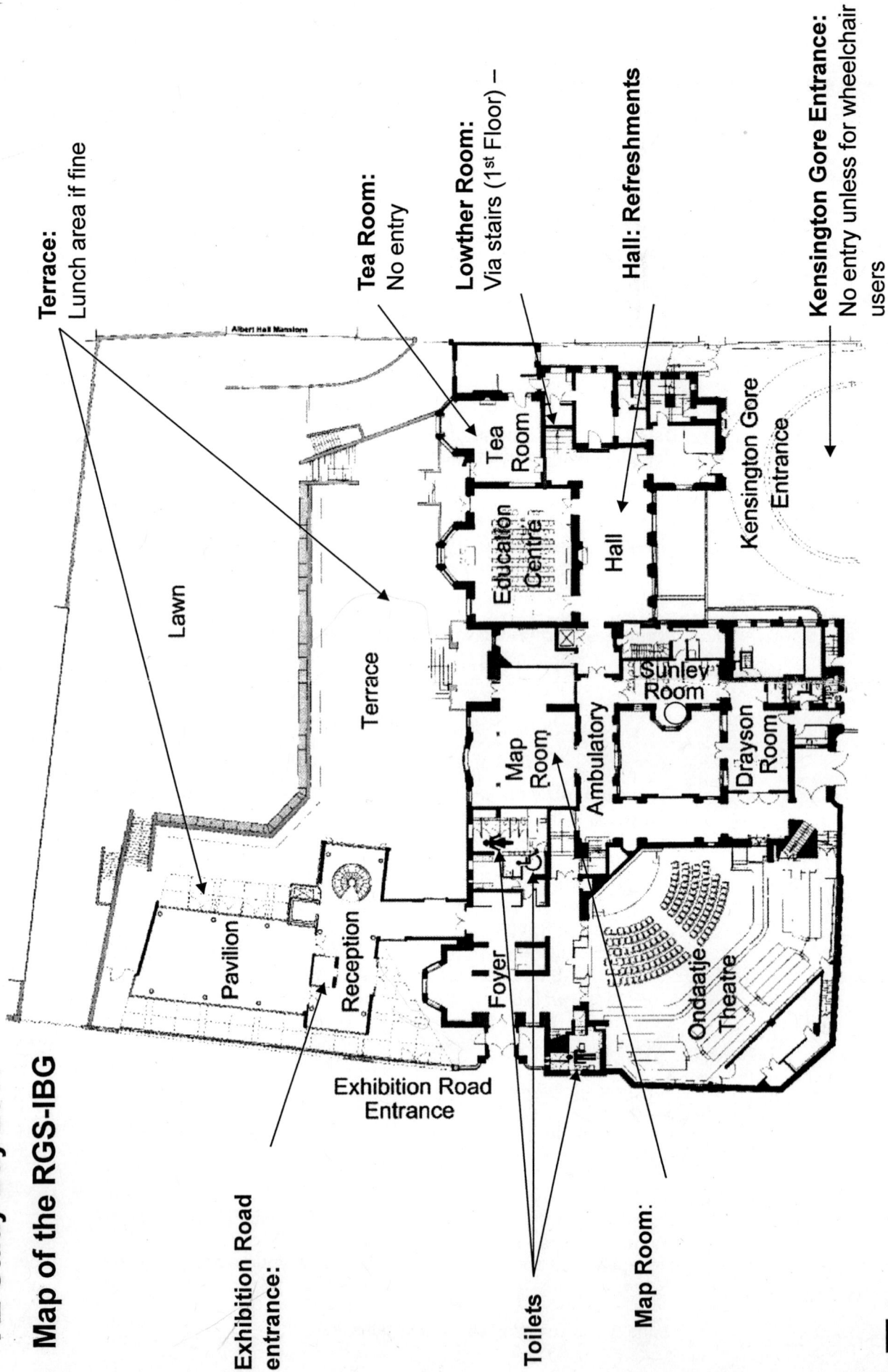

Terrace:
Lunch area if fine

Tea Room:
No entry

Lowther Room:
Via stairs (1st Floor) –

Hall: Refreshments

Kensington Gore Entrance:
No entry unless for wheelchair users

Exhibition Road entrance:

Toilets

Map Room:

Albert Hall Mansions

Lawn

Terrace

Tea Room

Education Centre

Hall

Kensington Gore Entrance

Sunley Room

Map Room

Ambulatory

Drayson Room

Reception

Pavilion

Foyer

Ondaatje Theatre

Exhibition Road Entrance

○ Ambassadors and geography in the news at lunchtime

by more than five percentage points and transform the trade balance into a slight surplus (columns 2 and 3 in table 2.1). However, important trade imbalances would persist in other countries: for example, trade surpluses would decline only a little in Germany, in a number of developing countries in East and South-East Asia, and in the countries in the group comprising West Asia and North Africa. As mentioned in the two preceding sections, this is because the absolute value of China's household consumer spending is much smaller than that of United States households, its import content is smaller, and the composition of China's imports of consumer goods differs greatly from that of the United States.[27] The net effect of the two adjustments taken together would be deflationary for the world economy, while they would not be sufficient to unwind the large global imbalances.

Looking at developments in exports and imports separately (columns 4 and 5 in table 2.1), the results indicate that for the United States a sharp decline in imports would be accompanied by an even sharper increase in exports. Apart from China, whose trade balance would deteriorate mainly because of its own adjustment efforts, the greatest decline would occur in Thailand, followed by Mexico, Japan (which would experience the strongest percentage decline in exports), Germany and Singapore. In most countries, particularly developing countries in Asia – notably China, India and Thailand – the deterioration in the trade balance would be caused mainly by a decline in exports rather than by an increase in imports, as indicated by the difference in the growth rates reported in columns four and five of the table. The strong increase in United States exports (a large proportion of which consists of machinery and electronic equipment, as well as services) and the strong decline in its imports would be facilitated by the sharp depreciation of the dollar (column 7 in table 2.1).[28] Additional results (not shown here) indicate that the bulk of the increase in United States exports would be directed to developed countries, namely EU members and Japan, while the bulk of the decline in United States imports would particularly affect EU members, China and Japan.

> The net effect of adjustments in China and the United States on the world economy will be deflationary ...

> ... and yet insufficient for the unwinding of global imbalances.

Turning to changes in the sectoral structure of trade, the percentage changes in the trade balance of the United States would be largest for machinery and equipment and electronic equipment (table 2.2). This improvement would be mirrored by a sizeable deterioration in the trade balance for these sectors in all Asian economies included in the table, as well as Mexico and Germany. The strong improvement in the United States trade balance for chemicals (which includes pharmaceuticals – the single most important item in United States consumer goods imports) would be mirrored by a substantial deterioration in the trade balance for these products in China, Germany and Singapore. The strong improvement in the United States trade balance for motor vehicles and other transport equipment would be mirrored by a sizeable deterioration in the trade balance for these products in Argentina, Brazil, Mexico, Germany, Japan, the Republic of Korea, and Singapore (though most of these effects for Singapore are likely to be due to trans-shipment, as witnessed by the strong deterioration in Singapore's trade balance for commercial services and trade and transport).

To determine how the changes in sectoral trade balances would affect employment, it may be useful to relate these changes to sectoral differences in labour intensity. Concentrating on the changes in world exports of industrial products (shown in the last column of table 2.2) suggests that the simulated adjustments in the economies of China and the United States would lead to sizeable adverse employment impacts in the world economy as a whole. This is indicated by the fact that world exports would decline in the majority of industrial sectors.[29] Perhaps more importantly, the largest declines would occur in the most labour-intensive industrial sectors (chart 2.13).[30]

The decline in world exports of labour-intensive industrial goods will have different implications for different countries, depending on their sectoral production and trade structure. The simulation results for changes in sectoral employment suggest that in China employment would decline in most industrial sectors (but substantially increase in agriculture,

Table 2.1

GTAP SIMULATION RESULTS OF THE IMPACT OF REBALANCING IN THE UNITED STATES AND CHINA ON TRADE FLOWS AND FACTOR PRICES, SELECTED COUNTRIES/GROUPS

	Change in trade balance	Share of trade balance in GDP	Change in export volume	Change in import volume	Change in terms of trade[a]	Appre-ciation[b]	Change in wages[c] Unskilled labour	Skilled labour
	(Percentage points)				(Per cent)			
(1)	(2)	(3)	(4)	(5)	(6)	(7)	(8)	(9)
China	-8.2	1.8	-17.6	3.7	2.9	7.1	6.6	8.8
United States	5.2	0.6	41.9	-15.4	-7.2	-8.2	-8.1	-8.5
China, Hong Kong SAR	-1.4	14.9	-1.2	0.6	-0.1	2.3	2.3	2.2
China, Taiwan Province of	-1.0	14.3	-0.6	1.4	0.3	2.1	2.1	2.0
Indonesia	-1.1	0.8	-2.8	1.0	0.3	2.7	2.7	2.7
Malaysia	-1.6	42.4	-0.5	1.3	0.3	2.3	2.1	1.9
Philippines	-1.3	3.6	-1.4	0.8	-0.1	2.1	2.1	2.0
Republic of Korea	-1.6	1.5	-3.4	1.5	0.8	2.9	3.1	2.9
Singapore	-1.7	-2.6	-0.3	1.3	0.5	2.7	2.7	2.7
Thailand	-3.7	5.8	-3.7	1.9	0.4	2.9	2.9	2.9
Rest of East and South East Asia	-1.6	2.0	-2.2	0.1	-0.1	2.1	2.0	1.7
India	-1.2	-7.7	-6.6	2.7	1.1	3.6	3.8	3.8
South Asia, excl. India	-1.2	-17.1	-6.7	1.7	0.8	3.3	3.2	3.3
West Asia and North Africa	-1.5	13.8	-1.7	2.6	0.7	2.8	2.9	2.6
Sub-Saharan Africa	-1.7	1.2	-2.5	3.1	0.7	3.1	3.2	3.3
Argentina and Brazil	-1.8	0.8	-7.7	5.2	2.1	4.1	4.0	4.1
Mexico	-2.1	-2.1	-6.0	4.9	3.3	3.2	3.3	3.4
Rest of developing America	-1.6	-1.8	-3.8	3.4	1.5	2.7	2.8	2.9
Canada	-1.7	-2.7	-2.9	5.7	3.1	2.3	2.4	2.4
Germany	-1.9	3.8	-3.8	2.3	0.6	3.2	3.1	3.1
Rest of EU-25 and EFTA[d]	-1.6	-3.5	-3.6	2.0	0.7	3.2	3.2	3.2
Australia and New Zealand	-1.5	-1.8	-5.5	3.8	1.5	3.6	3.7	3.6
Japan	-2.0	-1.0	-12.7	5.7	2.3	4.3	4.3	4.4
CIS, excl. the Republic of Moldova	-0.8	6.6	-1.2	1.4	0.4	2.9	3.0	2.8
Rest of the world	-1.8	-9.6	-2.3	1.7	0.3	2.9	2.9	2.6

Source: UNCTAD secretariat calculations.
Note: All changes are relative to 2008.
  a An improvement in the terms of trade indicates that the price of exports increased more (or fell less) than the price for imports.
  b An appreciation indicates an increase in the price for primary factors, which may be likened to an appreciation of the real exchange rate.
  c The definition of skilled and unskilled labour and the wage ratio between skilled and unskilled labour is explained in note 2 of the annex to this chapter.
  d EFTA - European Free Trade Association.

utilities and services) (table 2.3). By contrast, in the United States, employment would increase in most industrial sectors, as well as in agriculture, but decline in utilities and services. The United States is also the only country shown in the table (except Singapore) which would experience an increase in employment in the two labour-intensive sectors for

which the estimations indicate an increase in world exports (see chart 2.13): "machinery and equipment not elsewhere classified", and "transport equipment not elsewhere classified". This contrasts with the results for most countries, especially those in Asia, for which the simulations indicate that adverse employment effects are likely to be concentrated in the

Table 2.2

GTAP SIMULATION RESULTS FOR CHANGES IN SECTORAL TRADE BALANCE, SELECTED COUNTRIES/GROUPS

(Per cent of GDP in 2008)

	China	United States	Argentina and Brazil	CIS[a]	Germany	Japan	Malaysia	Mexico	Rep. of Korea	Singapore	Thailand	Sub-Saharan Africa	Memo item: Change in world exports relative to base year
Grains and crops	-0.22	0.07	-0.06	-0.01	-0.01	-0.01	0.00	-0.10	-0.02	-0.00	0.06	-0.09	1.46
Forestry and fishing	-0.02	0.00	-0.00	0.01	-0.00	-0.00	0.03	-0.00	-0.00	-0.00	0.00	-0.00	1.03
Mining	-0.08	0.05	-0.01	-0.01	-0.01	-0.02	0.02	0.04	-0.00	-0.09	-0.14	-0.08	-0.18
Livestock and meat products	-0.13	0.05	-0.07	-0.02	-0.00	-0.00	0.01	-0.08	-0.01	-0.00	-0.01	-0.01	0.34
Processed food	-0.24	0.14	-0.11	-0.01	-0.02	-0.02	0.16	-0.19	-0.01	0.00	-0.16	-0.05	-0.93
Textiles	-0.51	0.10	-0.03	-0.00	-0.01	-0.01	0.05	-0.14	-0.02	0.05	-0.01	-0.02	-1.85
Wearing apparel	-0.40	0.11	-0.01	0.00	0.00	0.00	-0.07	-0.11	-0.02	-0.02	-0.17	-0.06	-4.95
Leather products	-0.42	0.05	-0.03	0.01	0.00	-0.00	-0.01	0.02	0.01	0.01	0.01	0.00	-4.30
Wood products	-0.31	0.11	-0.08	-0.00	-0.02	-0.02	0.02	-0.13	-0.01	-0.01	-0.09	-0.01	-3.41
Paper products and publishing	-0.11	0.11	-0.06	-0.01	-0.03	-0.02	-0.01	-0.08	-0.04	-0.04	-0.03	-0.02	0.09
Petroleum and coal products	-0.02	0.01	-0.01	-0.01	0.00	0.01	-0.00	-0.00	0.01	0.07	-0.00	-0.01	-0.29
Chemicals, rubber, plastic products	-0.62	0.68	-0.21	-0.13	-0.34	-0.23	-0.33	-0.28	-0.22	-0.42	-0.37	-0.14	-0.72
Mineral products, nes	-0.09	0.05	-0.04	-0.00	-0.01	-0.01	0.03	-0.04	-0.01	-0.01	-0.03	-0.01	0.35
Ferrous metals	-0.11	0.04	-0.06	0.02	-0.00	-0.02	0.03	-0.02	0.01	0.01	-0.07	-0.04	0.46
Metals, nes	-0.08	0.07	-0.05	-0.09	-0.02	-0.01	0.02	-0.06	-0.00	-0.01	0.02	-0.12	0.27
Metal products	-0.33	0.12	-0.04	-0.00	-0.03	-0.03	-0.00	-0.11	-0.02	-0.02	-0.08	-0.03	-0.52
Motor vehicles and parts	-0.20	0.40	-0.15	-0.02	-0.18	-0.32	-0.00	-0.41	-0.26	-0.04	-0.11	-0.11	-1.23
Transport equipment, nes	-0.25	0.37	-0.20	-0.10	-0.17	-0.10	-0.24	-0.03	-0.20	-0.67	-0.15	-0.15	4.18
Electronic equipment	-1.38	0.68	-0.13	-0.02	-0.18	-0.49	-0.77	-0.36	-0.33	-0.23	-0.72	-0.10	0.04
Machinery and equipment, nes	-2.05	1.40	-0.45	-0.17	-0.66	-0.64	-0.54	-0.71	-0.38	-0.45	-1.10	-0.37	1.85
Manufactures, nes	-0.58	0.20	-0.02	-0.01	-0.02	-0.03	0.01	-0.02	-0.02	0.01	-0.22	-0.04	-3.87
Utilities and construction	-0.02	0.03	-0.02	-0.03	-0.01	-0.02	-0.01	0.00	-0.00	-0.01	-0.01	-0.02	4.27
Trade and transport	-0.47	0.34	-0.07	-0.11	-0.08	-0.09	-0.10	-0.11	-0.09	-0.15	-0.32	-0.15	-0.21
Commercial services	-0.15	0.51	-0.12	-0.10	-0.13	-0.11	-0.11	-0.10	-0.22	-0.47	-0.19	-0.17	1.10
Other services	-0.17	0.29	-0.08	-0.10	-0.10	-0.07	-0.16	-0.13	-0.13	-0.14	-0.14	-0.16	3.85

Source: UNCTAD secretariat calculations.

Note: Trade balance refers to volumes. Percentage shares of trade volumes and values in GDP in the base year are identical, as prices are assumed to equal one.

nes = not elsewhere specified.

a Excluding the Republic of Moldova.

Chart 2.13

GTAP SIMULATION RESULTS FOR CHANGES IN WORLD EXPORTS
AND LABOUR INTENSITY BY INDUSTRIAL SECTOR

(Per cent)

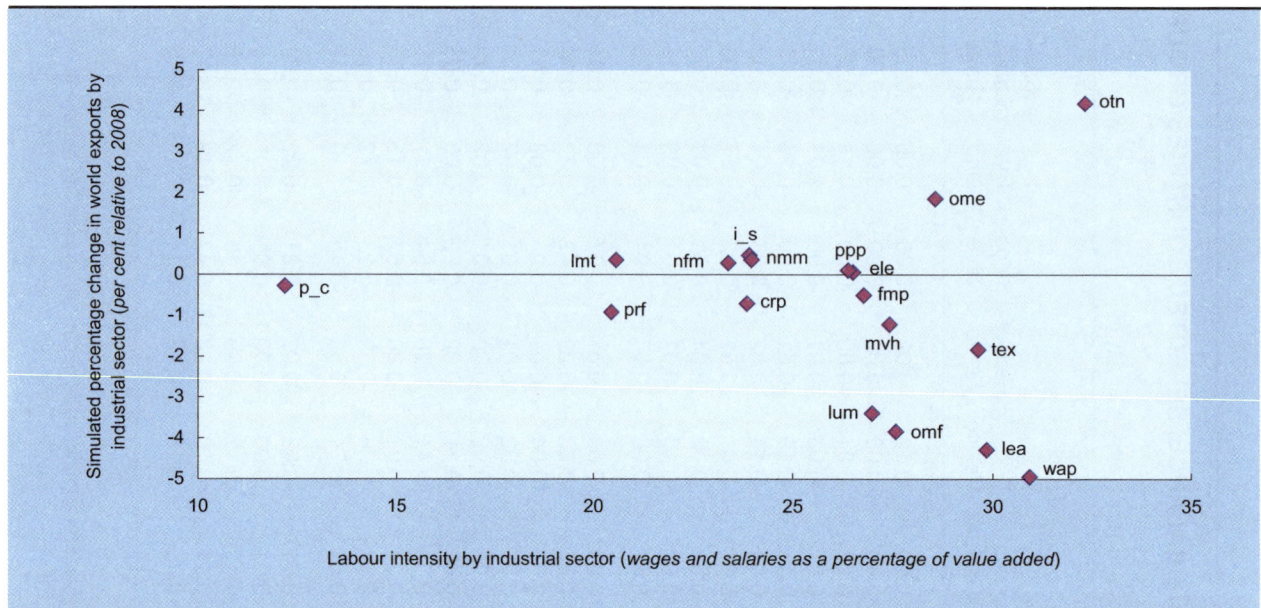

Source: UNCTAD secretariat calculations, based on GTAP simulations; and UNIDO, *Industrial Statistics* database, CD-ROM 2009.
Note: Labour intensity is measured as the unweighted world average of the share of wages and salaries in sectoral value added during the period 1995–2005.

crp	=	Chemicals, rubber and plastic products	nmm	=	Non-metallic mineral products
ele	=	Electronic equipment	ome	=	Machinery and equipment not elsewhere classified
fmp	=	Metal products	omf	=	Manufactures not elsewhere classified
i_s	=	Ferrous metals	otn	=	Transport equipment not elsewhere classified
lea	=	Leather products	p_c	=	Petroleum and coal products
lmt	=	Livestock and meat products	ppp	=	Paper products, publishing
lum	=	Wood products	prf	=	Processed food
mvh	=	Motor vehicles and parts	tex	=	Textiles
nfm	=	Metals not elsewhere classified	wap	=	Wearing apparel

most labour-intensive sectors. For example, among the countries shown in table 2.3, Japan, Malaysia, the Republic of Korea and Thailand may experience a reduction (or only a very slight increase) in employment in labour-intensive sectors such as apparel, transport equipment, textiles, and machinery and equipment (which includes domestic appliances). As

already noted, these results should not be taken as quantitatively precise predictions. Nonetheless, they provide useful qualitative information that indicates broad directions of the possible employment effects of a global rebalancing resulting from adjustments only in China and the United States.

Table 2.3

GTAP SIMULATION RESULTS FOR CHANGES IN SECTORAL EMPLOYMENT, SELECTED COUNTRIES/GROUPS

(Per cent)

	China	United States	Argentina and Brazil	CIS[a]	Germany	Japan	Malaysia	Mexico	Republic of Korea	Singapore	Thailand	Sub-Saharan Africa
Industrial goods												
Petroleum and coal products	1.1	-2.7	-0.4	-0.1	-0.3	0.2	0.1	0.6	-0.8	0.7	0.5	0.5
Processed food	4.8	-3.7	-0.9	-0.0	0.2	-0.1	1.8	3.5	-0.2	0.6	-0.9	-0.2
Livestock and meat products	7.2	-1.3	-2.1	-0.3	0.3	-1.6	0.9	0.9	-1.2	0.2	-0.4	0.3
Metals, nes	-11.7	30.4	-6.7	-2.4	-2.7	-4.1	1.1	-1.8	-1.7	1.0	-3.0	-4.4
Chemicals, rubber, plastic products	-7.4	14.7	-4.3	-2.8	-3.3	-4.9	-2.0	1.7	-3.0	-1.9	-3.7	-1.6
Ferrous metals	-5.7	21.2	-4.1	0.3	-0.7	-2.8	2.6	3.6	0.1	4.7	1.0	0.3
Non-metallic mineral products, nes	-0.6	7.8	1.2	1.0	1.8	1.6	3.0	3.0	2.3	3.8	4.1	2.2
Paper products and publishing	-3.1	3.3	-2.8	-0.6	-0.8	-0.9	-0.7	1.8	-1.9	-1.2	-1.8	-0.4
Electronic equipment	-11.4	27.2	-1.8	0.1	-0.8	-4.7	0.1	-4.1	-1.6	0.5	-2.1	1.1
Metal products	-7.4	12.2	-2.5	0.2	0.4	0.6	1.5	-2.4	0.2	1.3	-0.0	1.8
Wood products	-11.7	4.9	-4.5	0.4	1.2	2.0	0.6	-6.6	0.7	1.6	-3.5	0.5
Motor vehicles and parts	-2.3	4.1	-0.6	0.9	-0.3	-5.4	1.1	0.4	-2.1	4.0	4.0	1.5
Manufactures, nes	-9.5	17.3	0.8	-0.5	0.6	0.3	-0.0	-1.0	-0.7	3.0	-3.2	-0.5
Machinery and equipment, nes	-10.3	21.3	-5.2	-0.2	-2.3	-5.7	-2.2	-3.0	-1.7	1.3	-4.0	-0.8
Textiles	-8.6	13.7	-2.2	0.2	0.3	-1.7	1.5	-4.1	-1.2	3.5	-1.3	-0.2
Leather products	-12.9	29.6	-3.8	2.9	1.4	-0.4	-3.1	5.4	1.4	2.6	1.0	2.2
Wearing apparel	-4.4	4.2	0.1	0.5	1.0	0.7	-6.3	-3.5	-1.4	-4.7	-2.6	-1.9
Transport equipment, nes	-7.1	22.4	-10.3	-7.7	-8.3	-10.4	-12.5	-0.8	-8.8	-6.7	-9.9	-8.7
Memo items:												
Agriculture and mining												
Grains and crops	3.6	7.7	-1.6	-0.1	-0.5	-1.3	-0.1	-0.3	-0.5	-0.2	-0.9	-0.6
Forestry and fishing	3.9	3.7	-1.4	0.7	0.3	-0.1	1.1	0.3	0.4	0.3	-0.6	0.5
Mining	-2.3	6.8	-1.3	0.0	0.3	-0.6	0.5	3.0	1.0	1.8	1.4	-0.3
Utilities and services												
Utilities and construction	3.3	-2.4	5.8	1.3	5.4	5.7	4.2	1.5	3.8	4.4	8.8	5.2
Trade and transport	1.6	-1.5	0.3	-0.2	-0.6	0.4	-0.2	-0.8	-0.5	-0.1	0.3	0.1
Commercial services	1.6	-0.6	-0.2	-0.5	0.4	0.2	-0.5	-0.6	-0.3	-0.9	-0.8	-0.3
Other services	8.6	-5.7	0.4	-0.3	0.3	-0.2	-0.7	0.2	-0.4	0.0	-0.1	-0.1

Source: UNCTAD secretariat calculations, based on GTAP simulations; and UNIDO, *Industrial Statistics* database, CD-ROM 2009.

Note: The data in the table refer to percentage changes in the demand for unskilled labour relative to 2008. The percentage changes in the demand for skilled labour are very similar, and thus are not shown. Industrial goods are listed by increasing labour intensity, measured as the unweighted world average of the share of wages and salaries in sectoral value added during the period 1995–2005.

    nes = not elsewhere specified.

    a   Excluding the Republic of Moldova.

E. Conclusions: the need for a global macroeconomic reorientation for growth and employment creation

Before the outbreak of the financial and economic crisis, strong consumer spending by United States households and the associated sharp increase in that country's imports of consumer goods led to a rapid growth of its current-account deficit, but also served as a significant demand stimulus to the world economy. However, much of this consumer spending was debt-financed and proved to be unsustainable. Households could initially sustain rising debt burdens and maintain, or even increase, consumer spending, despite a declining share of labour compensation in income. This was because a series of asset price bubbles contributed to increasing their wealth. With the collapse of the United States housing market, households were forced to unwind their debt positions and cut consumer spending. This trend is set to continue unless another asset bubble occurs. Consequently, the world economy cannot count on the sort of stimulus provided by the United States prior to the crisis.

China has been the other major engine of growth in the world economy since the turn of the millennium. Here, the share of labour compensation in income declined as well, but in a context of much faster overall income growth. Household disposable income and real consumption each rose at average annual rates of about 8 per cent over the past two decades. Thus, consumption and income growth in China were faster than in any other economy, either developed or developing, particularly over the past two years when many of the other economies recorded negative growth rates in these areas. Despite this, the share of household consumption in GDP in China fell due to that country's growth and development strategy. This strategy placed strong emphasis on investment and exports as the main drivers of economic growth, largely motivated by

China's relatively low level of per capita income when economic take-off began. Like consumption and income growth, employment growth in China has lagged behind the average annual growth rate of GDP of around 10 per cent over the past two decades.

In the United States, the slowdown in consumer spending between 2007 and late 2009 sharply reduced that country's imports of consumer goods, thereby contributing to a sizeable decline in its current-account deficit. This led to a fall – or at least considerably slower growth – of exports in a number of developing and emerging-market economies, particularly China. However, in China there are signs that faster growth of domestic demand could replace much, if not all, of the stimulus to economic growth and employment creation that had been provided by exporting to the United States in the past. The expansionary macroeconomic policy stimulus has succeeded in rapidly pushing the level of GDP beyond its pre-crisis peak, and GDP growth has returned to its high pre-crisis trajectory. Owing to this policy stimulus, China's imports have grown well in excess of its exports, resulting in a sharp decline in its external surplus. The structural shift in demand from exports to domestic consumption, while helping the Chinese economy recover from the crisis, also indicates a shift in China's future growth strategy. This will have a longer term effect on China's role in the world economy.

Taking the adjustments in the two large economies of China and the United States together, the analysis in this chapter suggests that the net effect for the world economy will be deflationary, but at the same time insufficient to bring about an unwinding of the large global imbalances. This is due to the fact that not only the absolute value of the consumer goods bought by Chinese households but also their import content is much smaller than that of goods bought by United States households. Moreover, the composition of consumer goods imported by China differs considerably from that of the goods imported by the United States. As a result, there will be a tendency towards a deterioration in the trade balance of many other countries in the world economy, unless the necessary adjustments in the United States and the structural changes in China are accompanied by rebalancing efforts in other economies. On the other hand, primary commodity prices and the export prospects of many of China's trading partners may not be negatively affected by China's structural shift towards a stronger emphasis on domestic demand growth. This is because such a shift is unlikely to change the growth trajectory of China's imports of primary commodities as long as the pace of its overall output growth can be maintained.

Since world exports are set to decline, especially for industrial goods, with the largest declines likely to occur in the most labour-intensive industrial sectors, the net effect of adjustments by China and the United States could well have a sizeable adverse impact on employment worldwide. The impact will differ across countries, depending on their sectoral production and trade structure. In China itself employment would probably decline in most industrial sectors, but substantially increase in agriculture, utilities and services. In most developing countries, especially in Asia, negative employment effects are likely in labour-intensive sectors. Thus, apart from Japan, employment in countries such as Malaysia, the Republic of Korea, Singapore and Thailand may fall (or increase only very slightly). A positive employment impact in other sectors, particularly the extractive industries, will be comparatively weak, since those industries provide little employment. With regard to services, the Indian experience suggests that rapid expansion of modern, information technology-based business services is unlikely to create a large number of jobs,

Some European economies could replace the United States' role in providing growth stimulus to the global economy ...

... through expansionary monetary and fiscal policies and higher domestic consumption.

and that these jobs require comparatively high skill levels (Nayyar, 2009).

The expansionary policy responses to the economic and financial crisis by both China and the United States have provided vital support to the global recovery. In particular, the vigorous rebound in industrial production led by China has contributed significantly to buoyant commodity prices, and hence to recovery in commodity-producing countries, both developed and developing, such as Australia, Brazil, Canada, the Russian Federation and South Africa. However, even if China were to further reduce the contribution of exports and increase that of household consumption to output growth and employment, this adjustment still would not replace the stimulus to global growth that the United States provided in the past.

It needs to be re-emphasized that unbalanced growth among developed countries was the root cause of global imbalances prior to the crisis. Indeed, these imbalances were not a bilateral phenomenon between China and the United States. The peculiar form of uneven development brought about by the process of globalization cannot be ignored. The fact that in today's globalized world capital and technology are freely mobile across borders, while labour is not, has resulted in the targeted location of production for global markets in a selected (and changing) set of countries, motivated by lower labour costs and other locational advantages. In recent years, China has been the most popular among such destinations. In addition, its domestic firms have been importing technologies and developing the capabilities to produce for global markets. Not surprisingly, its exports have grown rapidly, along with a rising trade and current-account surplus. However, China's very large current-account surplus occurred only relatively recently: it rose sharply only after 2003, at which time it was still comparable to that of Switzerland.

However, it should be pointed out that low-wage developing countries like China are not the only beneficiaries of globalization. Germany, for example, where innovation and technical progress were accompanied by stagnant or even falling real wages, has been able to increase exports both inside and outside the euro area. Several members of that currency area, that no longer have the possibility of currency devaluation to make their exports cheaper and imports more expensive, have found it increasingly difficult to compete with Germany and sustain their growth.

The two large industrialized economies of Germany and Japan have also recorded sizeable and more long-lasting current-account surpluses as a counterpart to the United States deficit. In 2007, the share of Germany in the aggregate current-account surplus worldwide was around 16 per cent, and that of Japan was 14 per cent. Both these countries have been notorious for slow growth of their domestic demand and they are again at the heart of imbalances among developed countries in the context of the current recovery.

The evolution of the current-account surpluses of the Russian Federation, Saudi Arabia and other oil-exporting countries has been determined largely by oil price developments; besides, the size of these countries' domestic demand is not large enough to influence global trade flows and employment creation. Moreover, the price of oil, like those of other primary commodities, is highly volatile, and, in the context of slower growth in the G-7 economies than in the past, the surpluses of these countries are likely to shrink anyway. Other countries that are often suggested as possible future markets for countries that pursue export-oriented growth strategies are some large emerging-market economies in the South, particularly India which has the second largest population in the world and has recorded fast and stable growth over many years (box 2.2). If domestic demand in these countries were to expand, it would certainly help to make their industrialization less dependent on export markets, and might also create a larger market for other countries that produce consumer goods. However, the import potential of

> Shifts in the demand structure in China are unlikely to adversely affect its primary commodity imports.

> Developing countries should not rely on export growth alone – they should also give more support to domestic demand growth.

Brazil, India, Indonesia and South Africa combined is not even equivalent to that of Germany, and with the exception of Indonesia, these countries have not had current-account surpluses in recent years.

China has done more than any other emerging-market economy to stimulate domestic demand, and as a result its imports have expanded significantly. Private consumption rose by more than 15 per cent in real terms in 2009 and is forecast to rise by more than 20 per cent in 2010 (CLSA, 2009: 37), dwarfing attempts by all other major economies to revive their domestic markets. The Chinese economy is again growing vigorously and unit labour costs have been rising more than elsewhere, which has undermined its competitive advantage, even with a fixed nominal exchange rate. Thus any additional contribution to global rebalancing will have to come from other major deficit and surplus countries. To the extent that it comes from other deficit economies, the impact will be deflationary, as it would have to rely on import retrenchment. Hence, to achieve a recovery of global output growth and employment creation without reproducing the large imbalances that had built up in the run-up to the crisis, the key element in demand management worldwide would have to be expansionary adjustment in the major industrialized surplus economies, namely Germany and Japan.

Japan suffered the sharpest GDP contraction among the large economies in 2009, owing to its export dependence. Its recovery since then has also been driven mainly by exports, together with some revival of private consumption. Due to only moderate growth in its former prime export market, the United States, Japan reoriented its exports towards East Asian markets, where demand has been growing rapidly following their brisk recovery. But Japan could make a much greater contribution to the recovery of global output and employment by overcoming its deflation. Domestic demand in Japan is forecast to grow at a moderate pace of 1.5–2 per cent in 2010 and 2011 (OECD, 2010). In order to compensate for the sharp fall in the global demand

Box 2.2

GLOBAL REBALANCING AND THE INDIAN ECONOMY

India has benefited from the opportunities offered by globalization, mainly as an exporter of tradable services, while growth in its manufacturing sector has been driven primarily by domestic demand at much lower though creditable rates. India's manufacturing industry has grown much more slowly than China's, but growth was significant and relatively stable even after the Asian crisis of 1997. Over the three periods 1980–1989, 1990–1996 and 1997–2003 (the years after the Asian financial crisis), China's manufacturing value added grew at average annual rates of 2.1, 11.8 and 14.1 per cent respectively, whereas the corresponding figures for India were 5.6, 8.7 and 4.7 per cent.[a]

In India, during the period 1997–2003, fewer industries were as export dependent as those in China. All of these were traditional industries, such as apparel, leather goods and textiles. In most manufacturing categories (at the three-digit SITC level) exports accounted for less than one fifth of production. But apparent consumption (which takes into account imports) was significantly higher than domestic production, indicating a sizeable share of imports in domestic consumption. This can be attributed to the demand for imported luxury goods, resulting from trade liberalization, a growing middle and upper middle class of consumers and the inability of Indian producers to meet this demand. Therefore, India provides a market for a number of manufactured and semi-manufactured imports, and will continue to do so.

From this structural perspective, if growth remains high or accelerates further in India, it may have a positive effect on global demand. This means that India may play an equally (if not more) important role as China as a future engine of growth and employment creation in other countries. However, so far it is nowhere near being a powerful engine because of the relatively small size of its home market for manufactures and the rate of growth of that market, which falls well short of that of China. Moreover, India, unlike China, runs trade and current-account deficits in its balance of payments, and therefore growth of domestic demand in that country would not contribute to global rebalancing in the short term.

[a] UNCTAD secretariat calculations, based on Centre d'Etudes Prospectives et d'Informations Internationales (CEPII), *TradeProd* database.

stimulus of the United States, Japan's domestic demand growth would need to be significantly stronger to offset the temporarily negative growth contributions of its net exports, unless the adjustment is facilitated through a further yen appreciation.

Germany could compensate for a substantial share of the decline in the demand stimulus to the world economy through strong growth of household consumption and attendant expansionary effects in the rest of Europe. Europe's imports of consumer goods are relatively similar to those of the United States in terms of both size and product composition. But in Germany, even more so than in Japan, recovery until mid-2010 has been entirely export-driven, while domestic demand, especially private consumption, has been shrinking. Moreover, there are no indications that Germany will shift its emphasis from export-led growth to domestic-demand-led growth any time soon, despite its dependence on exports, its low rate of investment and stagnant consumption in recent years. What was mentioned above about the requirements for a Japanese contribution to global rebalancing applies even more to Germany, where domestic demand is forecast to fall by 0.3 per cent in 2010 and to grow by only 1 per cent in 2011 (OECD, 2010).

With Germany's key European export markets hammered by spreading fiscal austerity, the country's heavy export orientation is shifting towards markets in China and other developing countries. The sharp depreciation of the euro, driven by the region's home-grown crises and inadequate policy responses, may lend support to this strategy. However, this will not contribute to the needed global rebalancing, especially since Europe provides the major market for United States exports.

As mentioned, China cannot replace the United States' pre-crisis role of providing the growth stimulus to the global economy because of the size and composition of its imports. Major EU economies could fill this role, but it would require them to continue with their expansionary monetary and fiscal policy stance as well as increase domestic consumer demand, especially through wage increases in Germany. However, Germany's status as the main surplus economy in the euro zone has been built largely on wage restraint (see also chapter III) and its serious problem of unemployment also persists. Moreover, the stagnation of private consumption in Europe, exacerbated by the tendency for EU governments, especially the German Government, to hasten towards fiscal consolidation programmes makes it unlikely that a major contribution to global rebalancing and

a substantial stimulus for global output and employment growth will come from the European surplus economies.

This means that the developing-country exporters that had focused their export-oriented development strategies on the markets of the major developed economies should perhaps adapt to the new situation. China provides a leading example, not only of successful fiscal policy support to domestic demand for bridging the adjustment from export towards domestic demand orientation while sustaining a high rate of GDP growth, but also for the sustained rapid expansion of real private consumption based on strong productivity growth and two-digit level wage increases.

A reorientation towards private consumption, accompanied by a corresponding refocus on investment expenditure, would reduce developing countries' dependence on GDP growth in developed countries. How a reorientation of development strategies by which income growth and employment creation could be made to rely more on domestic demand than has been the case in the past is discussed in greater detail in the subsequent chapters of this *Report*. ■

Notes

1   See China's 11th Five Year Plan enacted in 2006.
2   For a general discussion of the issues involved in moving from a current-account surplus to a more balanced external position, see IMF, 2010.
3   It should be pointed out that the sustainability of a deficit position depends very much on whether it is held by the government or the private sector. The dynamics of public debt affect the growth rate of aggregate income, but changes in households' indebtedness do not influence the course of their level of income. Moreover, the public sector can resort to the central bank and raise taxes in order to repay its debt, but households may

be forced to default when their debt-to-income ratio increases (see also Palley, 2006).
4   Glick and Lansing (2010) show that large increases in household leverage (as measured by the ratio of debt to disposable personal income) and the housing bubble were not unique to the United States; they also occurred in other developed countries.
5   For further discussion on the development of income inequality and the relationship between income distribution and the maintenance of relative, rather than absolute, standards of consumption in the United States, see Barba and Pivetti, 2009.

6 Carroll and Slacalek (2009) use a different simulation model but arrive at similar conclusions. They also note that retail sales have declined particularly sharply, and considerably more than in any previous recession since the Second World War.

7 The adverse demand effect on the rest of the world would also occur if household consumption was replaced by government consumption. This is because much of government consumption relates to public sector service activities which have a low import content.

8 The current account is the sum of the trade balance, the balance on labour income, the balance on international investment income and unilateral transfers (foreign aid and remittances).

9 While the balance on unilateral current transfers has been slightly negative, the balance on income and on trade in services has been positive, so that the trade deficit exceeds the size of the current-account deficit as a whole (statistics presented in the text have been calculated from the Aggregate Income and International Transactions databases of the Bureau of Economic Analysis).

10 According to the Bank for International Settlements (BIS, 2007: 56) "final consumption goods constitute only 4% of China's total imports and calculations suggest that the elasticity of demand for its ordinary imports (i.e. those not used for processing in the export sector) with respect to domestic spending is insignificant."

11 For this analysis, consumer goods are identified on the basis of the United Nations Classification by Broad Economic Categories (BEC), codes 61, 62 and 63, which cover durable, semi-durable and non-durable consumer goods, respectively (United Nations, 1971). Using concordance tables, these codes were translated into 428 products at the 5-digit level of the Standard International Trade Classification (SITC), Revision 3. The import similarity index between two economies $j_{1,2}$ is:

$$100 \sum_i s(i,j_1) s(i,j_2) \left(\sqrt{\sum_i s(i,j_1)^2} \sqrt{\sum_i s(i,j_2)^2} \right),$$

where $s(i,j)$ is the share of good i in the imports of country j.

12 A similar view has been expressed by leading policymakers in China, such as Premier Wen Jiabao, and prominent Chinese academics such as Yu (2007) and Cai and Wang (2010), in addition to a wide range of international observers, including Blanchard and Giavazzi (2006), World Bank Beijing Office (2006), Aziz and Cui (2007) and Akyüz (2010).

13 According to Koopman, Wang and Wei (2008), those Chinese exports that are often labelled as "relatively sophisticated", such as electronic devices, have a particularly high foreign content, corresponding to about 80 per cent of their nominal export value.

14 This figure results from combining the export data and employment coefficients in tables 2 and 3 of Feenstra and Hong (2007), which used employment coefficients from an earlier version of Chen et al. (2009). The estimated number of jobs may be rather low because official statistics exclude some migrant workers employed in export sectors. However, it is unlikely that an inclusion of such migrants would significantly alter this estimate.

15 This percentage corresponds to about 28 per cent of urban employment in 2002. However, it is most probably an overestimate, since it is unlikely that all the 70 million jobs were in urban areas to which the data on wage and salary employment refer. While this estimate is based on data for 2002, it is unlikely to have increased substantially in more recent years. This is because the increase in the share of exports in GDP since 2002 has in all likelihood been accompanied by an increase in the relative productivity of workers in the sector, so that the net effect on the share of employment in export industries will have changed only marginally.

16 This figure of one fifth is derived by adjusting downwards the world average ratio of exports to GDP (which is about one quarter) by the world average share of domestic value added in the gross value of exports, using data from Nicita and Olarreaga (2007). See *TDR 1998*, table 48, for an example of the many cross-country regressions that confirm that trade/GDP ratios decline with country size.

17 *TDR 2005* provides a more detailed discussion of these comparisons for the first 20 years from the start of economic take-off (i.e. for China between 1979 and 1999). The dates used here to determine the beginning of economic take-off are those of *TDR 2005*. They were determined through a breakpoint analysis of productivity growth series, measured by growth rates of GDP per worker, as is frequently used in the literature on catching up and integration (Maury and Pluyaud, 2004; IMF, 2004). These dates closely correspond to (but do not coincide with) the dates used by the IMF (2005) for growth take-off. However, the IMF study determines the beginning of economic take-off by the start of an economy's rapid integration into international trade; it is defined by the IMF (2004) as "starting when the three-year moving average of constant-price export growth first exceeded 10 percent".

18 A more innovative approach finds a close link between the increase in household savings and China's one-child policy and the surplus of men, because it produced a highly competitive marriage market (Wei and Zhang, 2009).

19 For a detailed discussion of the data issues involved in these calculations, see also Aziz and Cui, 2007.

20 It should be noted that analyses of wage trends in China face "the lack of systematic, consistent

aggregate data that cover wages and labor compensation over a wide basis and an extended period of time" (Yang, Chen and Monarch, 2009: 5). This is probably why headlines about double-digit growth rates of wages in China (e.g. JP Morgan, 2010; EIU, 2010: 27) frequently cause confusion: they refer to the 13 per cent growth between 1998 and 2007 or to the 12 per cent rate of growth in real wages between 2003 and 2009 calculated on the basis of data for *urban* wages and salaries. The problem with these data is not only that they exclude non-urban manufacturing activities (such as in township and village enterprise (TVEs)), where wages are much lower, but also that they mainly cover the urban workforce in SOEs, where wages tend to be higher than in the private sector (Yang, Chen and Monarch, 2009: 9). Perhaps the most detailed study on labour cost developments in China (Lett and Banister, 2009: 36), which takes into account both manufacturing urban units and manufacturing TVEs, found that between 2002 and 2006, employee compensation (including wages, social welfare contributions, housing and other benefits) in urban manufacturing units grew by an average annual rate of 12 per cent and in TVEs by 7 per cent; with two thirds of manufacturing employees categorized as TVE workers, "total manufacturing compensation in China more closely reflects the compensation costs of TVE workers than it does urban unit compensation costs." Another study provides supportive evidence: it also indicates an average annual rate of real wage growth in urban manufacturing of about 11.4 per cent between 2002 and 2006, which significantly exceeds the increase of about 4.7 per cent for rural migrants during the period 2003–2006 (Park, Cai and Du, 2010).

21 According to international practice (such as followed in the United Nations System of National Accounts) the proceeds from self-employed work are treated as operating surplus (i.e. capital income), unless the self-employed receive wages from their own enterprises or unless individuals create their own enterprises. Given the difficulty in distinguishing between capital income and labour income in the proceeds from self-employed work, China's national statistics used to categorize both as labour income (Aziz and Cui, 2007). One rationale for this might have been that in poor countries the self-employed tend almost entirely to provide labour services. This changed in 2003–2004: since 2004, the income of self-employed individuals engaged in non-agricultural activities has been counted as capital income (Bai and Qian, 2009a). As a result, more than half of the steep decline in the share of employee compensation (the orange line shown in chart 2.10) for 2004 was most probably due to this change in statistical reporting (Bai and Qian, 2009b).

22 According to standard economic theory, a high and increasing rate of investment and a growing capital intensity of production reduce the return on capital. As a result, the total income accruing to capital would decline and that accruing to labour would increase. This is the opposite of what happened in China. A possible explanation is that rapid technological progress accompanied the intensive use of capital and prevented additional investment from becoming less efficient.

23 The data series for total disposable income and labour compensation shown in this figure differ from those shown in the previous figures. This is because the evidence shown here reflects data based on national data, while that in the previous figures is based on aggregated provincial data. For a discussion of these data issues, see Bai and Qian (2009a); and Aziz and Cui (2007).

24 Recent reports in the media suggest that the lending policy of China's largest banks may also have played a role in the resurgence of non-performing loans over the past few months (Anderlini, 2010).

25 A complementary measure relates to the unemployment trend. However, data available for China provide conflicting evidence of this trend: while data from the 2000 census and from the 2005 mini census point to a decline in unemployment, from 8.1 per cent to 5.2 per cent over this period of time, labour force survey data for the same period suggest that in 2002 there was a reversal of the initial decline in unemployment, but that, nonetheless, unemployment declined from 7.6 per cent in 2000 to 7 per cent in 2005 (Park, Cai and Du, 2010).

26 This evidence does not mean that China's total labour supply is shrinking and that the country will be facing a labour shortage any time soon. On the other hand, the radically altered age structure of the labour force means that wages are almost certain to rise faster relative to productivity growth than they have over the past 20 years.

27 The first two of these three elements also underlie the simulation exercise in Zhang, Zhang and Han (2010), who otherwise focus on financial linkages, rather than the trade linkages emphasized in this chapter.

28 The set-up of the Global Trade Analysis Project (GTAP) model implies that external imbalances caused by an exogenous shock are removed and the external balance is restored by changes in the prices of primary factors, downwards to spur exports and reduce imports, or upwards to reduce exports and increase imports. The relationship between the prices of primary factors across different countries may be likened to an exchange rate. Real and nominal exchange-rate changes coincide because GTAP, as most other computable general equilibrium models, deals with real variables, with no money involved.

29 This analysis is based on the methodology proposed by Rajan and Subramanian (2006), who measure the labour intensity of a sector by the unweighted average across countries of the share of wages and salaries in value added for specific industrial sectors. The averages used here refer to the period 1995–2005 and cover all countries for which data are available in the *Industrial Statistics database* CD-ROM, 2009 of the United Nations Industrial Development Organization (UNIDO). The mapping of industrial sectors at the three-digit level of the International Standard Industrial Classification (ISIC) Revision 3 into the sectors used for the GTAP-simulations is based on the concordance table made available on the GTAP-website (https://www.gtap.agecon. purdue.edu/databases/contribute/concordinfo.asp). The data-points shown in chart 2.13 are unweighted averages based on a total of 10,210 country-sector observations of which 5,227 refer to developed countries, 4,573 to developing countries and 410 to transition economies. The distribution of the data-points in chart 2.13 changes only marginally if the period is limited to 2000–2005 or if averages are calculated only for developed or developing countries. The sample period ends in 2005 because no comprehensive data were available for more recent years.

30 There are two exceptions to this: (i) the category "machinery and equipment not elsewhere classified" includes, for example, machinery, domestic appliances, optical instruments, watches and clocks; (ii) the category "transport equipment not elsewhere classified" includes railway vehicles, aircraft and associated equipment, and ships and boats.

References

Aizenman J (2007). Large hoarding of international reserves and the emerging global economic architecture. Working Paper No. 13277, National Bureau of Economic Research. Cambridge, MA, July.

Akyüz Y (2010). Global economic prospects: the recession may be over but where next? Research paper No. 26, South Centre, Geneva.

Anderlini J (2010). Chinese banks forced to increase reserves. *Financial Times*, 3 May.

Aziz J and Cui L (2007). Explaining China's low consumption: the neglected role of household income. Working Paper No. 07/181, International Monetary Fund, Washington DC, July.

Bagnai A (2009). The role of China in global external imbalances: some further evidence. *China Economic Review*, 20(3): 508–526.

Bai C and Qian Z (2009a). Who is the predator, who the prey? An analysis of changes in the state of China's national income distribution. *Social Sciences in China*, 30(4): 179–205.

Bai C and Qian Z (2009b). Changes in factor income distribution in China: Facts, reasons, and policy responses. Presentation made at the Stanford Center for International Development's China Mirror Conference 2009, Tsinghua University, 13 April. Available at: //scid.stanford.edu/system/files/shared/ Factor_Income_Share_English.pdf.

Bank for International Settlements (BIS) (2007). *Annual Report 2007*. Basel.

Barba A and Pivetti M (2009). Rising household debt: its causes and macroeconomic implications – a long-period analysis. *Cambridge Journal of Economics*, 33(1): 113–137.

Bernanke B (2005). The global saving glut and the US current account deficit. Speech delivered for the San-dridge Lecture, Virginia Association of Economists, Richmond, VA, 10 March.

Blanchard O and Giavazzi F (2006). Rebalancing growth in China: A three-handed approach. *China & World Economy*, 14(4): 1–20.

Cai F (ed.) (2007). The China Population and Labor Year-book, Vol. 1: *The Approaching Lewis Turning Point and its Policy Implications*. Beijing, Social Sciences Academic Press.

Cai F, Wang D and Zhang H (2010). Employment effectiveness of China's economic stimulus package. *China & World Economy*, 18(1): 33–46.

Cai F and Wang M (2010). Growth and structural changes in employment in transition China. *Journal of Comparative Economics*, 38(1): 71–81, March.

Carroll CD and Slacalek J (2009). The American consumer: reforming, or just resting? Working Paper No. 2009/12. Frankfurt, Center for Financial Studies, Frankfurt University, June.

Chen S and Ravallion M (2008). China is poorer than we thought, but no less successful in the fight against poverty. Working Paper No. 4621, World Bank, Washington DC, May.

Chen X et al. (2009). Domestic value added and employment generated by Chinese exports: A quantitative estimation. Working Paper 09/07, University of California at Santa Cruz, Santa Cruz Institute for International Economics. Available at: http://sciie.ucsc.edu/workingpaper/2009/KC_PaperforReStat.pdf.

Chinn MD and Ito H (2007). Current account balances, financial development and institutions: Assaying the world "savings glut". *Journal of International Money and Finance*, 26(4): 546–569.

CLSA (Credit Lyonnais Securities Asia) (2009). Eye on Asian Economies, 1st quarter 2010, Hong Kong (China).

Cooper R (2008). Understanding global imbalances. In: Little JS, ed. *Global Imbalances and the Evolving World Economy*. Boston, MA, Federal Reserve Bank of Boston.

Dimaranan BV and Narayanan BG (2008). Skilled and Unskilled Labor Data. In: Center For Global Trade Analysis, ed. GTAP 7 Data Base Documentation. West Lafayett, IN, Purdue University. Available at: https://www.gtap.agecon.purdue.edu/resources/download/4183.pdf.

Dooley MP, Folkerts-Landau D and Garber P (2004). The revived Bretton Woods System: the effects of periphery intervention and reserve management on interest rates and exchange rates in center countries. Working Paper No. 10332, National Bureau of Economic Research. Cambridge, MA.

EIU (Economist Intelligence Unit) (2010). *Country Forecast: China*. London, April.

Evenett S (ed.) (2010). *The US-Sino Currency Dispute: New Insights from Economics, Politics and Law*. London, Centre for Economic Policy Research (a VoxEU.org publication).

Feenstra RC and Hong C (2007). China's exports and employment. Working Paper No. 13552, National Bureau of Economic Research, Cambridge, MA, October.

Glick R and Lansing KJ (2010). Global household leverage, house prices, and consumption. *Economic Letter 2010-01*, Federal Reserve Bank of San Francisco, 11 January.

Hertel TW (ed.) (1997). *Global Trade Analysis: Modeling and Applications*. Cambridge, Cambridge University Press.

Hong P, Vos R and Yao K (2008). How China could contribute to a benign global rebalancing? *China & World Economy*, 16(5): 35–50.

Hung HF (2009). America's head servant? *New Left Review*, 60: 5–25, November-December.

IMF (2004). The global implications of the U.S. fiscal deficit and of China's growth. *World Economic Outlook*, chapter 2, April.

IMF (2005). Globalization and external imbalances. *World Economic Outlook*, chapter 3, April.

IMF (2010). Getting the balance right: Transitioning out of sustained current account surpluses. *World Economic Outlook*, chapter 4, April.

JP Morgan (2010). China: Rising wages not expected to trigger spike in CPI. Economic Research Note, Global Data Watch, 5 March.

Knight J (2007). China, South Africa and the Lewis model. Research Paper No. 2007/82, United Nations University, World Institute for Development Economics Research, Helsinki.

Knight J, Li S and Deng Q (2009). Education and the poverty trap in rural China: Setting the trap. *Oxford Development Studies*, 37(4): 311–332.

Koopman R, Wang Z and Wei SJ (2008). How much of Chinese exports is really made in China? Assessing domestic value-added when processing trade is pervasive. Working Paper No. 14109, National Bureau of Economic Research, June.

Krugman PR (2010). Taking on China. *New York Times*, 15 March.

Lardy N (2009). Statement at the Hearing before the U.S.-China Economic and Security Review Commission on China's Role in the Origins of and Response to the Global Recession, Washington, DC, 17 February.

Lee J, Rabanal P and Sandri D (2010). U.S. consumption after the 2008 crisis. IMF Staff Position Note SPN/10/01, International Monetary Fund, Washington, DC.

Lett E and Banister J (2009). China's manufacturing employment and compensation costs: 2002–06. *Monthly Labor Review*: 30–38, April.

Mann C (2002). Perspectives on the U.S. current account deficit and sustainability. *Journal of Economic Perspectives*, 16(3): 131–152.

Maury T and Pluyaud B (2004). Breaks in per capita productivity trends in a number of industrial countries. Working Paper No 111, Banque de France, Paris.

McKinsey Global Institute (2009). If you've got it, spend it: Unleashing the Chinese consumer. Seoul, McKinsey & Company, August.

Mitchell T (2010). 'Invisible fetters' cling to migrants. *Financial Times,* 16 April.

Mitchell T and Dyer G (2010). Inflation surge spurs fears of Chinese wage increases *Financial Times*, 8 February.

Modigliani F and Cao S (2004). Chinese saving puzzle and the life-cycle hypothesis. *Journal of Economic Literature*, 42(2): 145–170.

Narayanan B and Walmsley TL (eds.) (2008). *Global Trade, Assistance and Production: The GTAP 7 Data Base*. West Lafayett, IN, Center for Global Trade Analysis, Purdue University. Available at: https://www.gtap.agecon.purdue.edu/databases/v7/v7_doco.asp.

Nayyar G (2009). The nature of employment in India's services sector: Exploring the heterogeneity. Discussion Paper 452, Department of Economics, University of Oxford, Oxford, September.

Nicita A and Olarreaga M (2007). Trade, production, and protection database, 1976–2004. *The World Bank Economic Review*, 21(1): 165–171.

OECD (2010). OECD Economic Outlook No. 87, Paris, June.

Park A, Cai F and Du Y (2010). Can China meet her employment challenges? In: Oi JC, Rozelle S and Zhou X, eds. *Growing Pains: Tensions and Opportunity in China's Transformation*. Stanford, Walter H Shorenstein Asia-Pacific Research Center Books.

Palley T (2006). The fallacy of the revised Bretton Woods hypothesis: Why today's international financial system is unstable. Public Policy Brief No 85, Levy Economics Institute of Bard College, Annandale-on-Hudson, NY.

Rajan R and Subramanian A (2006). What undermines aid's impact on growth? Working Paper No. 11657, National Bureau of Economic Research, Cambridge, MA, September.

Roach S (2009). Statement at the Hearing on China's Role in the Origins of and Response to the Global Recession before the U.S.-China Economic and Security Review Commission, Washington, DC, 17 February.

Roubini N and Setser B (2005). The sustainability of the US external imbalances. *CESifo Forum,* 1/2005: 8–15.

The Economist (2010). China's misunderstood economy, 14 January.

UNCTAD (various issues). *Trade and Development Report*. United Nations publications, New York and Geneva.

United Nations (1971). Classification by Broad Economic Categories. Statistical Papers, Series M, No. 53. Sales No. E.71.XVII.12. New York, NY.

United Nations (2010). *World Economic Situation and Prospects 2010*. Update as of mid-2010. New York, NY. Available at: http://www.un.org/esa/policy/wess/wesp2010files/wesp10update.pdf.

Wei SJ and Zhang X (2009). The competitive saving motive: Evidence from rising sex ratios and savings rates in China. Working Paper No. 15093, National Bureau of Economic Research, Cambridge, MA, June.

World Bank, Beijing Office (2006). *China Quarterly Update*, November.

Yang DT, Chen V and Monarch R (2009). Rising wages: Has China lost its global labor advantage? Economics Program Working Paper No 09-03, The Conference Board, New York, NY.

Yu Y (2007). Global imbalances and China. *Australian Economic Review*, 40(1): 3–23.

Zhang W, Zhang Z and Han G (2010). How does the US credit crisis affect the Asia-Pacific economies? Analysis based on a general equilibrium model. *Journal of Asian Economics*, 21(3): 280–292.

SIMULATION OF THE TRADE AND EMPLOYMENT EFFECTS OF GLOBAL REBALANCING: A TECHNICAL NOTE

The simulation employs the standard model of the Global Trade Analysis Project (GTAP) – a computable general equilibrium model of the global economy which emphasizes the role of intersectoral factor mobility in determining sectoral output supply, and which assumes output to be produced with constant returns to scale.[1] The model also assumes product differentiation between imported and domestic goods, and among imports from different regions. This assumption allows for two-way trade in each product category, depending on the ease of substitution between products from different regions. The model's demand system allows for differential price and income responsiveness across countries. An assumed "global" bank mediates world savings and investment. In addition to five production factors (land, capital, unskilled and skilled labour,[2] and natural resources), the GTAP database covers 113 countries (or regions) and 57 product sectors, which for this simulation have been aggregated to 25 regions and 25 sectors (see tables 2.1 and 2.2).

The simulation assumes: (i) a 5 percentage point decline in United States consumption as a share of GDP (i.e. equivalent to the difference in 2008 between the actual share and the long-term average share as shown in chart 2.2 in this chapter), and (ii) a 7 percentage point increase in China's household

consumption as a share of GDP (i.e. equivalent to the decline between 2005 and 2008 as shown in chart 2.8 in this chapter). In technical terms, conducting simulations based on these assumptions requires, for both the United States and China, (i) the variable "private consumption expenditure (yp)" to become exogenous and the "private consumption distribution parameter ($dppriv$)" to become endogenous, and (ii) the "savings distribution parameter ($dpsave$)" to become exogenous and the "average distribution parameter shift ($dpav$)" to become endogenous. These two modifications ensure that any change in the share of income used for private consumption will be reflected entirely in changes in the share of savings in income.

The simulation further assumes (iii) a reduction in the United States' potential output by 1 percentage point relative to 2008 (i.e. the starting point of the simulation). This reduction is implemented by assuming a respective decline in output-augmenting technological change. The motivation for this assumption is that the decline in household consumption leads to a slowdown in aggregate domestic demand in the United States which, over the medium term, cannot be compensated in a sustainable manner by an increase in another element of aggregate demand.[3] This slowdown in United States domestic demand, in turn, has spillover effects on other econo-mies, since a greater emphasis on consumption-led growth relative to export-led growth in China and a shift in the opposite direction in the United States would reduce aggregate imports of these countries from the rest of the world. In other words, global rebalancing confined to adjustment in the United States and China would remove the demand stimulus that, prior to the outbreak of the current crisis, the United States was providing to the world economy without replacing it with a stimulus of similar size from increased consumption in China, as already mentioned in the main text.

The GTAP model's most updated database re-fers to 2004. Given that both global current-account imbalances and the share in GDP of consumption in the United States and China have changed sig-nificantly since 2004, the ratios of trade balances to income were updated to 2008 (i.e. roughly the onset of the current global economic and financial crisis). More precisely, each region's current-account bal-ance as a share of income was updated on the basis of the respective growth rates between 2004 and 2008, calculated from the IMF's *World Economic Outlook* database. This was done by treating the change in the ratio of the trade balance on goods and services to re-gional income (*dtbalr*) as an exogenous variable, and the slack variable that represents the risk premium on investment (*cgdslack*) as an endogenous variable. These modifications cause investment to adjust such that it compensates for the assumed changes in the trade balance, thus ensuring that the savings-invest-ment balance equals the trade balance. Given that the sum of all regions' trade balances must be zero, so that *dtbalr* cannot be treated as exogenous for all regions, the trade balances of two groups (West Asia and North Africa and Rest of the World) were left to be determined endogenously. This methodology may be considered broadly equivalent to simulating a shock to real exchange rates. The simulation uses this updated database as the baseline scenario (i.e. the benchmark against which the impact of the assumed changes is measured). To test the robustness of the results obtained in this way, the simulation was run also on the original 2004 database with adjustment in United States consumption assumed to be equivalent to 4 percentage points and that in China's consump-tion equivalent to 5 percentage points. While the

changes resulting from this alternative simulation are quantitatively smaller, partly because the underlying current-account imbalances in 2004 were smaller than in 2008, they are qualitatively identical.

Simulations were undertaken for a scenario that assumes adjustments in the United States and China occur at the same time (the results of which are re-ported in the main text), as well as with a scenario that assumes adjustments occur separately in China and the United States. Doing so gives some indications as to the importance of adjustment in either of these two countries for global rebalancing. The results for the scenario in which adjustment is confined to China (table 2.A1) indicate that the assumed increase in the share of China's consumption in GDP would have a minor impact on trade flows for individual countries, except for China itself. They also indicate that the countries in East and South-East Asia taken together would benefit the most. This latter finding is probably due to the fact that these countries and China are part of the same international production networks, so that the simulated adjustments, helped by an appreciation of the renminbi by about 5 per cent, would imply a relocation of the exit point of these networks from China to other developing countries in the region. This finding also mirrors the results generally ob-tained from GTAP models that simulate an increase in China's exports, where adverse effects are usually concentrated in the other Asian developing countries (*TDR 2002*, chapter V).

Given the relatively small overall impact of adjustment when confined to China, it is no surprise that the results for the scenario in which adjustment is confined to the United States (not shown) are similar to those for the scenario that assumes simultaneous adjustments in China and the United States, shown in table 2.1. The only major difference is that the impact on China's trade balance in the scenario where adjustment is confined to the United States is much smaller than in the scenario in which adjustment oc-curs in both countries at the same time. The fact that the impact on China also is significantly smaller than for the vast majority of the other regions shown in table 2.1 suggests that the United States trade deficit is indeed multilateral in nature, rather than the result of bilateral trade flows between the United States and China. In terms of employment, these results

Table 2.A1

GTAP SIMULATION RESULTS OF THE IMPACT OF REBALANCING IN CHINA ON TRADE FLOWS AND FACTOR PRICES, SELECTED COUNTRIES/GROUPS

	Change in trade balance	Share of trade balance in GDP	Change in export volume	Change in import volume	Change in terms of trade[a]	Appre-ciation[b]	Change in wages[c]	
							Unskilled labour	Skilled labour
	(Percent-age points)				(Per cent)			
(1)	(2)	(3)	(4)	(5)	(6)	(7)	(8)	(9)
China	-6.7	3.4	-14.6	2.9	2.8	4.8	4.3	6.4
United States	0.2	-4.4	1.4	-1.2	-0.4	-0.3	-0.3	-0.3
China, Hong Kong SAR	0.2	16.5	0.1	-0.3	-0.1	0.4	0.5	0.4
China, Taiwan Province of	0.2	15.5	0.1	-0.2	0.0	0.2	0.2	0.1
Indonesia	0.2	2.2	0.5	-0.2	-0.1	0.2	0.2	0.1
Malaysia	0.3	44.3	0.0	-0.3	-0.1	0.1	0.0	-0.1
Philippines	0.3	5.3	0.3	-0.3	-0.1	0.0	-0.0	-0.1
Republic of Korea	0.3	3.5	0.6	-0.3	-0.2	-0.1	-0.2	-0.2
Singapore	0.3	-0.6	0.1	-0.2	-0.1	-0.2	-0.2	-0.2
Thailand	0.7	10.3	0.6	-0.5	-0.0	0.0	0.0	-0.1
Rest of East and South East Asia	0.4	4.0	0.4	-0.4	-0.2	0.1	0.0	-0.2
India	0.2	-6.3	1.1	-0.3	-0.1	0.0	0.0	-0.1
South Asia, excl. India	0.2	-15.6	0.9	-0.4	-0.0	0.0	0.0	-0.1
West Asia and North Africa	0.2	15.6	0.3	-0.3	-0.1	-0.1	-0.0	-0.1
Sub-Saharan Africa	0.3	3.3	0.4	-0.6	-0.2	-0.1	-0.1	-0.2
Argentina and Brazil	0.3	2.8	1.3	-0.5	-0.1	-0.2	-0.2	-0.3
Mexico	0.2	0.2	0.7	-0.1	0.0	-0.1	-0.1	-0.2
Rest of developing America	0.3	0.1	0.6	-0.4	-0.1	-0.1	-0.1	-0.2
Canada	0.2	-0.8	0.6	-0.2	-0.1	-0.1	-0.2	-0.2
Germany	0.3	6.0	0.6	-0.5	-0.2	-0.2	-0.2	-0.2
Rest of EU-25 and EFTA	0.3	-1.6	0.6	-0.4	-0.1	-0.2	-0.2	-0.2
Australia and New Zealand	0.3	-0.1	0.9	-0.6	-0.2	-0.1	-0.1	-0.1
Japan	0.4	1.4	2.0	-1.7	-0.7	-0.4	-0.4	-0.4
CIS, excl. the Republic of Moldova	0.1	7.5	0.3	-0.2	-0.1	-0.1	-0.1	-0.1
Rest of the world	0.3	-7.5	0.5	-0.2	-0.0	-0.1	-0.1	-0.2

Source: UNCTAD secretariat calculations.

Note: All changes are relative to 2008.

a An improvement in the terms of trade indicates that the price of exports increased more (or fell less) than the price for imports.

b An appreciation indicates an increase in the price for primary factors, which may be likened to an appreciation of the real exchange rate.

c For the definition of skilled and unskilled labour and the wage ratio between skilled and unskilled labour, see note 2 of this annex.

suggest that rebalancing China's growth trajectory will do little for other developing countries in terms of compensating for adverse effects stemming from adjustment in the United States. This is because China imports mainly intermediate goods (including parts and components), and primary commodities (primarily energy products and metals), which are not very employment intensive.

Notes

1   For documentation of the model, see Hertel (1997), and for the GTAP-7 database, see Narayanan and Walmsley, 2008.

2   In the GTAP-model, the split between skilled and unskilled labour is based on occupational data. Skilled labour refers to professional workers (managers and administrators, professionals and para-professionals), while unskilled labour refers to production workers (tradespersons, clerks, salespersons and personal service workers, plant and machine operators and drivers, labourers and related workers, and farm workers). The relationship between the wages of skilled and unskilled workers in the GTAP model is determined on the basis of an econometric estimation, as explained in Dimaranan and Narayanan, 2008.

3   This assumption is consistent with the simulations by the United Nations (2010) which indicate that the ratio of the United States current-account deficit to GDP would increase, rather than shrink, over the coming five years if the United States economy were to grow at a rate similar to that prior to the current crisis. It is also in line with earlier experiences of rebalancing in countries with an external deficit that is typically associated with a slowdown in output growth, as noted by the IMF (2010). Another main finding of the IMF study is that policy-induced reversals of external surpluses are not typically associated with lower growth, which accords with the assumptions made here with regard to China. However, to the extent that exporting brings dynamic external benefits (e.g., through learning-by-doing effects) that are not present in output production for the domestic market, rebalancing from exports to domestic consumer demand may imply a slowdown in output growth.

References

Dimaranan BV and Narayanan BG (2008). Skilled and Unskilled Labor Data. In: Center For Global Trade Analysis, ed. GTAP 7 Data Base Documentation. West Lafayett, IN, Purdue University. Available at: https://www.gtap.agecon.purdue.edu/resources/download/4183.pdf.

Hertel TW (ed.) (1997). *Global Trade Analysis: Modeling and Applications*. Cambridge, Cambridge University Press.

Narayanan B and Walmsley TL (eds.) (2008). *Global Trade, Assistance and Production: The GTAP 7 Data Base*. West Lafayett, IN, Center for Global Trade Analysis, Purdue University. Available at: https://www.gtap.agecon.purdue.edu/databases/v7/v7_doco.asp.

United Nations (2010). *World Economic Situation and Prospects 2010*. Update as of mid-2010. New York, NY. Available at: http://www.un.org/esa/policy/wess/wesp2010files/wesp10update.pdf.

Chapter III

MACROECONOMIC ASPECTS OF JOB CREATION AND UNEMPLOYMENT

A. Introduction: globalization and employment

Most observers acknowledge that the period from the early 1990s until around 2007 delivered some economic successes, such as satisfactory or even rapid output growth in a number of developing countries (although average growth rates were still lower than in the 1960s and 1970s) and relatively low inflation. However, all of them agree that labour market outcomes were generally unsatisfactory in this period of accelerated globalization: employment typically grew at much lower rates than output – or in some cases did not grow at all – and the share of wages in national income generally declined in both developed and developing countries.

In this chapter, it is argued that employment creation and a declining wage share are interdependent, in the sense that if wage growth does not keep pace with productivity growth, the expansion of domestic demand and employment creation will be constrained, and that this constraint can only be lifted temporarily, if at all, by reliance on external demand.

Some analysts have attributed the relative slowdown in wage growth to the integration of global markets for products, capital and labour. According to one view, globalization implies that 1.5 billion workers in developing and emerging-market economies which have a small endowment of capital have been added to the existing workforce for producing goods on world markets, thereby disturbing previous labour market equilibriums and exerting downward pressure on wage levels, particularly for low-skilled labour (Freeman, 2008). A more nuanced position holds that the impact comes essentially from workers involved in producing traded goods and services (see, for example, Blinder, 2006), and that the greater participation of the more populous developing countries in global trade in goods and services has served to increase the supply of labour-intensive manufactures, thus reducing world market prices. This is assumed to have lowered the compensation of labour involved in such activities.

However, apart from an increase in merchandise trade, the impact of low-wage labour in developing and emerging-market economies on the labour markets of the industrialized countries is much weaker

> Wage formation may have been influenced by the "threat" of companies being able to relocate parts of their production abroad.

than is often alleged in these latter countries. Although recent evidence suggests that short-term migration for work has been increasing (UNDP, 2009), in general the international mobility of labour is still low, with migrant workers accounting for only about 1 per cent of the global labour force (ILO, 2009). Compared to total fixed capital formation, the international mobility of fixed capital in the form of greenfield investment, not to be confused with short-term financial flows, is also rather limited. Wage equalization remains a distant mirage for the populations of many developing countries, where economic catch-up and improvements in living standards have continued to advance at a frustratingly slow pace, if at all.

Nevertheless, wage formation and bargaining in the more advanced economies may indeed have been influenced by the "threat effect" of companies being able to relocate or outsource parts of their production in one form or another to lower wage economies (Blinder, 2006; Pollin, 2007). Indeed, the adoption of export-led growth strategies based on the advantage of labour costs appears to have changed the nature of competition between countries. This has led to calls for protectionist measures against goods produced under low-wage conditions, and to attempts in industrialized countries to prevent an increase in wages or even reduce them in order to withstand such competition. These responses are misguided. They are based on textbook neoclassical theory, which posits that relative factor price equalization through trade is possible under perfect competition. More importantly, models used in this context fail to recognize the critical role of effective demand in shaping both current economic activity and future growth possibilities, because they do not grasp the complex dynamics of investment, productivity growth, wage formation and employment.

In this chapter it is argued that export-led growth strategies tend to lead to relative wage compression, which may seem indispensable for strengthening or maintaining the international competitiveness of producers in any economy. But if many or all countries adopted this strategy it would lead to a "race to the bottom" with regard to wages. This would translate into insufficient growth of workers' purchasing power, which itself is an important determinant for

> Export-led growth strategies tend to lead to relative wage compression.

aggregate demand growth and job creation. A more sustainable growth strategy would be one that relies on domestic demand from wage increases linked to aggregate labour productivity increases. Such a strategy would build on a virtuous circle whereby a favourable environment for fixed capital formation enables productivity growth, the gains from which are distributed equally between labour and capital, so that the share of wages does not decline over time and domestic demand rises at least at the same pace as productivity. This way additional employment, new wage income and incentives for further investment in real productive capacity can be created.

By arguing for introducing a strong element of wage-led growth into macroeconomic and development strategies, this chapter questions the logic underlying the orthodox reasoning about employment and labour markets. It argues that a general macroeconomic analysis of employment and unemployment should take into account the conditions in which labour markets actually function in the real world. To that end, it relies upon the following stylized facts:

- Labour markets are organized and regulated at the national level, and are linked in various ways to other markets.

- Labour market outcomes depend on the level of investment in real productive capacity, which in turn depends mainly on demand expectations, the availability and costs of finance, and the complementarity of public and private investment. And all these interact in various ways, depending on the historical and structural features of each country.

- Wages, through their impact on the level of consumption, have a strong influence on the level and structure of aggregate demand and product markets. Therefore, they have an impact on corporate profits from both the cost and the demand side, with attendant effects on investment in real productive capacity. This in turn feeds back into the demand for labour.

- The exchange rate has a strong influence on the level of exports and the share of imports in domestic absorption, and hence on labour market outcomes. In a global monetary system that allows large fluctuations and persistent misalignments of exchange rates, trade performance is often distorted and does not always correctly reflect the "competitiveness" of producers from different countries.

- The level and growth rate of wages depend on country-specific institutional frameworks for wage determination and national labour-market regulations. In most developing countries, where institutional control over wages is weak, the level and growth of wages and incomes from self-employment are affected by patterns of aggregate demand.

- Productivity in an economy and its growth over time are determined by the stock of productive capital, the technology embodied in that capital stock as a result of domestic research and development (R&D), access to the foreign technology embodied in imported capital goods (and its expansion over time), as well as the quality of labour resulting from education, vocational training and learning by doing (and its improvement over time).

- Markets for long-term capital are interlinked internationally, but national long-term interest rates are strongly influenced by national monetary policies which determine the short-term interest rate.

- Foreign direct investment (FDI) can play a role in the catching up process, but in most developing countries this role is only complementary to that of domestic investment. Both domestic and foreign investment tend to apply the most up-to-date technology available, irrespective of the labour endowment and wage level in each country.

- Short-term capital flows have an increasingly strong influence on prices in many important markets, like those for commodities and currencies, and cause major price distortions in the international markets for goods and services.

Based on these stylized facts, this chapter sets out to look at the basic relationships between growth, investment, productivity and wages. It argues that unsatisfactory labour market outcomes are more likely to be due to insufficient investment in real productive capacity and inadequate wage growth than to insufficient "flexibility" in labour markets and the replacement of labour by capital. The laissez-faire capitalism of the last 30 years, with its emphasis on liberalization of labour markets to achieve "greater flexibility" in contractual wages and employment conditions, has not delivered the promised results in terms of labour market performance. Obviously, the institutional conditions for employment and labour market policies differ between developed countries, emerging-market economies and low-income developing countries (and within each of these groups), as discussed further in chapter V of this *Report*. However, it is suggested that macroeconomic conditions favourable to fixed capital formation and the full participation of labour in the productivity gains emerging from innovative investment are necessary for achieving and maintaining a high level of decent employment, irrespective of the stage of development of an economy.

> **Growth of workers' purchasing power is an important determinant of aggregate demand growth and job creation.**

B. The neglected role of aggregate demand growth for employment creation

1. The problem with microeconomic reasoning about the labour market

Rising and persistent unemployment in many countries has prompted a variety of explanations based on new and old ideas concerning the rigidities and malfunctioning of labour markets and the role of the welfare state in generating such "inflexibilities". According to neoclassical employment theory, the only explanation for high or rising unemployment is that real wages are too high or are rising too fast because strong labour unions or excessively high legal minimum wages prevent wages from falling sufficiently to absorb an excess supply of labour. This reasoning is based on a microeconomic concept that is transposed to the macroeconomic level. However, for prices to balance supply and demand, the supply and demand functions have to be independent of each other. This holds for the microeconomic level, but is not valid at the macroeconomic level.

For example, if the decision of a sufficiently large number of households to buy less bread does not affect the income situation of any of these individual households, the fall in the demand for bread should lower its price and result in new and stable relative prices between bread and other products. From a microeconomic perspective this is valid reasoning if prices are determined by market demand. By contrast, if the income situation of all households

> Neoclassical theory blames rising unemployment on real wages being too high.

depends, directly or indirectly, on the value added that is generated by all producers in an economy, and the latter have to adjust their production downwards in reaction to a fall in household demand, this adjustment itself will feed back into aggregate household income through lower total wage income.

This is not a new insight: Marshall (1890: 437) observed this 120 years ago, as did Schumpeter when he stated: "an analysis that uses the simple demand-supply apparatus is essentially partial analysis, that is to say, it takes as independently given the factors that determine the demand and supply schedules. This is inadmissible in the case of so important an element of the economic system as is labour as a whole" (Schumpeter, 1976: 942).

The argument frequently made, that a strong welfare state and powerful labour unions are the main reasons for rising unemployment (e.g. Siebert, 1997; IMF, 2003; St. Paul, 2004), is based on a comparison of unemployment in the United States and a number of European economies (chart 3.1). Following peaks in 1975 and 1982-1983, the unemployment rate in the United States returned to its former, or even lower, levels, whereas in Europe it continued to remain high, and rose even further for more than a quarter century. A frequent explanation for this experience is that in European welfare states, with a relatively high degree of wage rigidity, the pressure of increasing globalization caused greater unemployment, as labour was increasingly

Chart 3.1

UNEMPLOYMENT RATES IN THE EU-6, THE UNITED STATES AND THE EURO AREA, 1960–2009

(Per cent of labour force)

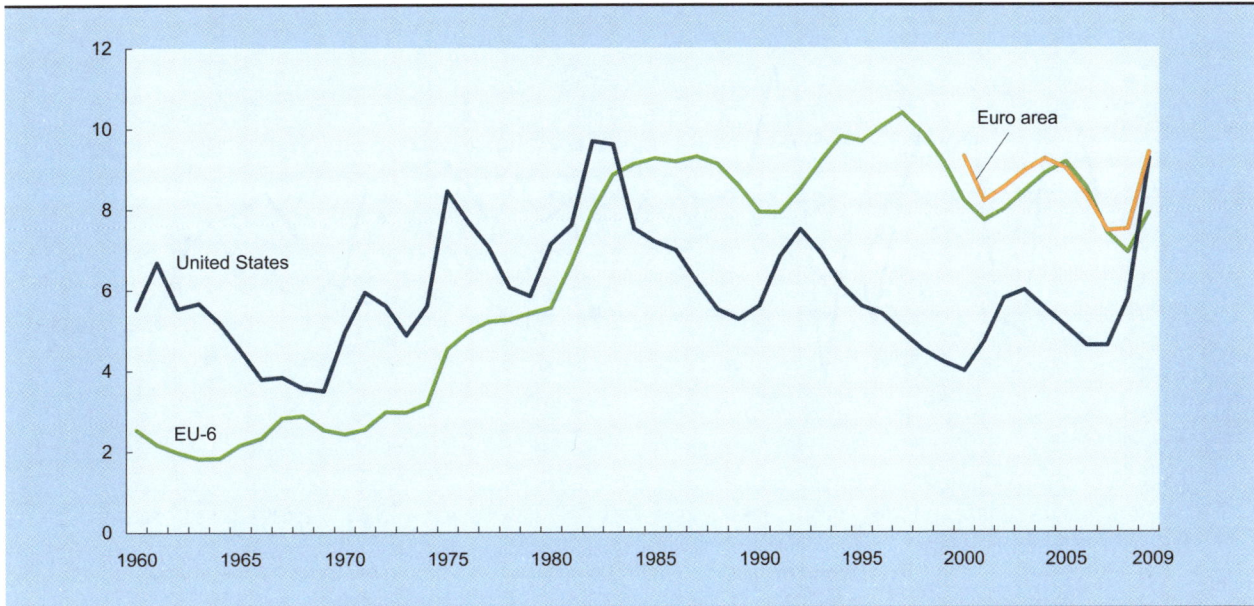

Source: UNCTAD secretariat calculations, based on OECD.*Stat Extracts*, *Annual Labour Force Statistics* and *Main Economic Indicators* databases; and ILO, *LABORSTAT* database.

Note: EU-6 comprises: Belgium, France, Germany, Italy, Luxembourg and the Netherlands.

substituted by capital. By contrast, in the United States, globalization pressures led to lower wages, but, allegedly because of a more flexible labour market, unemployment remained lower than in Europe (even though this was associated with the emergence of a class of "working poor"). Although the view that legal employment protection, trade union power and generous unemployment benefit schemes are responsible for higher unemployment has become very widely accepted, it has been shown to be empirically unfounded (Howell et al., 2007).

It is certainly true that the rate of unionization of the workforce and the level of social protection traditionally have been much higher in Europe than in the United States. Consequently, in a slack labour market situation, to the extent that European workers could defend their wage position with the assistance of trade unions, they were much less obliged to accept

> The view that employment protection and social-security institutions are responsible for higher unemployment is empirically unfounded.

lower wages in the same or new jobs. However, this explanation for the higher unemployment in Europe is dubious because it builds on a partial analysis of the labour market, which treats the latter as if it was disconnected from the rest of the economy. In reality, there is a strong interdependence between the labour market, on the one hand, and product and financial markets on the other. Only if these other markets had performed identically in the two regions in terms of output growth, could the hypothesis of labour market "flexibility" provide a plausible explanation. Although nominal wages may be more flexible in the United States, wages do not stabilize employment there either. In a recession, employment falls in the United States as well. The key difference is that the United States authorities respond by providing macro stimulus to boost demand and employment, whereas European authorities tend to ascribe high unemployment to structural

Chart 3.2

REAL GDP GROWTH IN THE EU-6 AND THE UNITED STATES, 1970–2009
(Per cent)

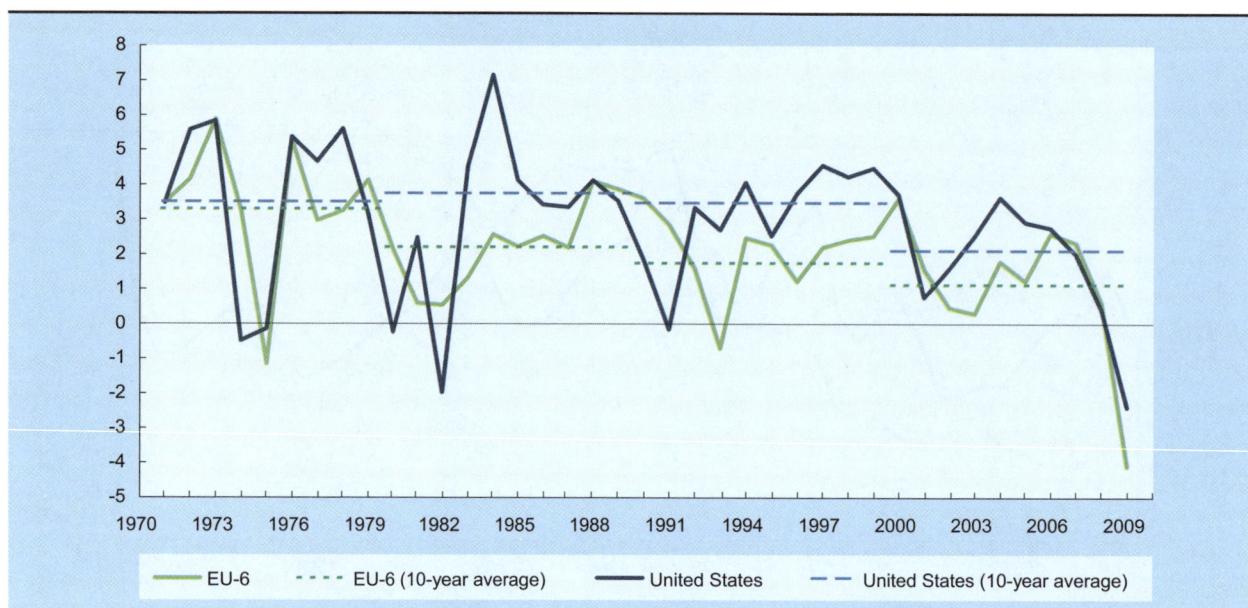

Source: UNCTAD secretariat calculations, based on United Nations Department of Economic and Social Affairs (UN/DESA), *National Accounts Main Aggregates* database; and the United States Department of Commerce, Bureau of Economic Analysis database.

problems. The authorities in the United States may feel more obliged to take countercyclical action to combat unemployment because the welfare system in that country provides much less support than in Europe. But that does not make European welfare systems the cause of high unemployment.

2. Macroeconomic trends are key to employment

Starting in the early 1980s, the average growth performance of the EU-6 fell significantly behind that of the United States (chart 3.2). Whereas the average annual growth rates of these two economies were about the same in the 1970s, at around 3.4 per cent, they began to diverge over time, reaching a differential of 1.6 percentage points during the 1990s. Since the turn of the century this has narrowed to 0.9 points. These growth differentials imply that, while labour markets may indeed function differently in diverse institutional settings, the macroeconomic environment

also evolves quite differently. Consequently, employment performance in these two economies cannot be explained using a neoclassical labour market model in which labour and capital are substituted at a given level of output according to their relative prices. Such a model is based on microeconomic reasoning and ignores the macroeconomic factors that determine the demand for goods and services, and labour.

The proposition that employment has to be analysed in connection with output growth, instead of treating the labour market in isolation, draws additional justification from the remarkable cyclicality of unemployment and growth in both economies. The greater frequency and longer duration of the cyclical upswings as well as the shorter downswings in the European unemployment curve are as apparent as the longer duration of the periods of unemployment decline in the United States (charts 3.1 and 3.2).

Generally, in developed countries employment cycles are very closely associated with output growth cycles: employment growth is typically associated with growth of aggregate demand and output

Chart 3.3

GROWTH OF EMPLOYMENT AND REAL GDP IN DEVELOPED COUNTRIES, 1970–2009

(Per cent)

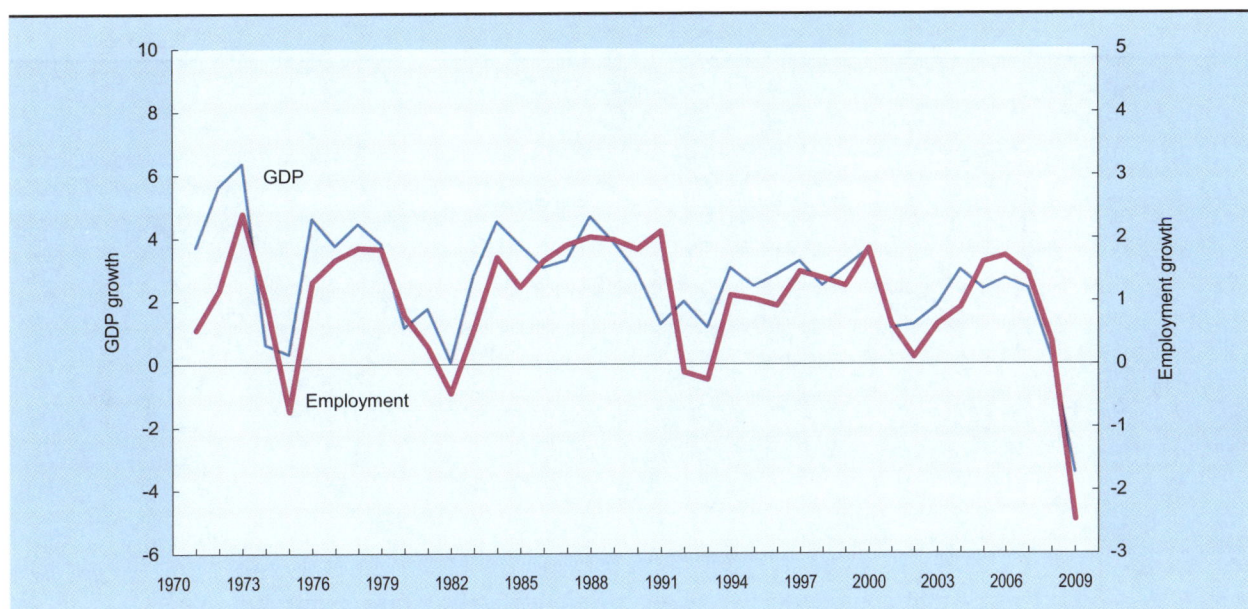

Source: UNCTAD secretariat calculations, based on table 1.1; UN/DESA, *National Accounts Main Aggregates* database; ILO, *LABORSTAT* and *Key Indicators of the Labour Market* (*KILM*) databases; OECD.*Stat Extracts*, *Annual Labour Force Statistics* and *Main Economic Indicators* databases; and ECLAC, *CEPALSTAT* database.

Note: Developed countries comprise: Australia, Austria, Belgium, Canada, Denmark, Finland, France, Germany, Greece, Iceland, Ireland, Israel, Italy, Japan, Luxembourg, the Netherlands, New Zealand, Norway, Portugal, Spain, Sweden, Switzerland, the United Kingdom and the United States.

(chart 3.3). Such a strong correlation of growth and employment would be highly improbable if the better employment record in the United States compared to Europe were due to the greater flexibility of wages in the United States. A more plausible explanation is that both the United States and Europe have needed a number of strong and long recoveries to bring the unemployment rate down, but Europe has been unable to generate such output recoveries. This means that wage flexibility and the absence of the kind of "distortions" associated with the welfare state can no longer be used to explain that country's superior employment record.

There is also a strong positive correlation between investment in fixed capital and employment creation in developed countries (chart 3.4).

> Employment needs to be analysed in connection with output growth.

The evident explanation is that companies invest and disinvest in labour and capital at the same time, depending on the overall state of the economy, since capital and labour are not substitutes, the use of which is left to the employers' discretion, but complementary factors of production that are combined quite independently of their relative prices.

Clearly, the elasticity of employment in relation to growth differs from country to country, and from period to period, but the close link between growth, employment and investment must challenge the belief that a significant number of new jobs can be created without a critical level of output growth. Once it is recognized that it is not primarily the relative cost of labour but the pace of output growth that is the key determinant of the level of employment, it follows that investment in real productive capacity and the

Chart 3.4

**GROWTH OF EMPLOYMENT AND GROSS FIXED CAPITAL FORMATION (GFCF)
IN DEVELOPED COUNTRIES, 1970–2008**

(*Per cent*)

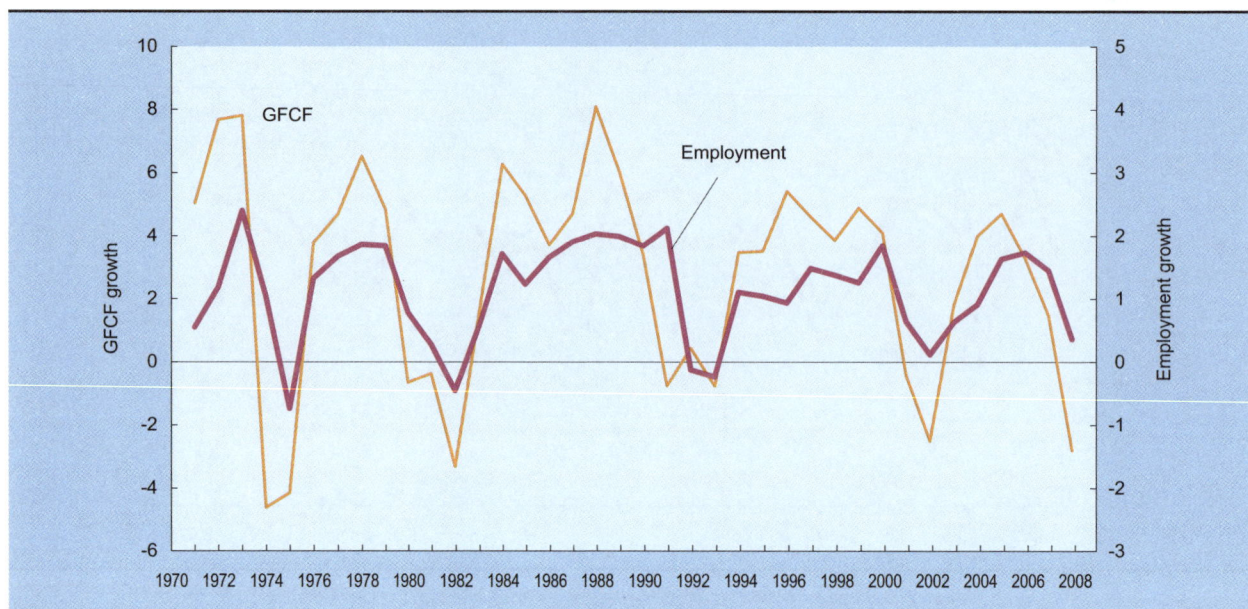

Source: See chart 3.3.
Note: See chart 3.3.

demand expansion that motivates such investment are the drivers of both income growth and employment creation.[1]

This is not to deny that the dynamics of new technology creation are likely to be influenced by the wage level in those economies where the technology is developed. At the firm level, new investments embodying advanced technologies – aimed at reducing the "disutility" of labour[2] – may be driven partly by an interest in saving on labour when unit labour costs rise. But in general, productivity growth results from the introduction of process or product innovations, which are the main driving force of a capitalist economy. Macroeconomic reasoning also has to take into account additional factors. First, new technologies do not fall from the sky: prior to the "productivity shock" from the introduction of new technologies in a dynamic economy, employment is created in the firms and institutions where research and development (R&D) is carried out. Second, in the process of introducing new products or production processes, employment is created for the production of the new capital goods. The net employment effect will still be negative if the destruction of jobs resulting from the introduction of new processing technologies is greater than the creation of jobs in the technology producing and capital goods sectors.[3] This is likely to be the case, particularly in developing countries, many of which import most, if not all, their capital goods requirements. However, a further, and the most important, employment creating effect will result when overall productivity increases translate into higher factor incomes which create additional demand for goods and services. In that case, the net effect in a growing economy can be positive, because the production of the additional goods and services requires the employment of additional factors of production, including labour.

> Companies invest and disinvest in labour and capital at the same time.

Whether or not aggregate demand rises sufficiently to create net employment depends crucially on the distribution of the gains from productivity growth, which in turn is greatly influenced by policy choices. The policies generally adopted over the past 25 years have sought to keep wages low, and have served to translate productivity gains either into higher capital income or into lower prices. They are based on the assumption that the demand for labour will behave in the same way as the demand for most goods (i.e. the lower the price, the greater the demand). But keeping wages low in order to generate higher profits is self-defeating, because without a stronger purchasing power of wage earners, domestic demand will not rise sufficiently to enable owners of capital to fully employ their capacity and thereby translate the productivity gains into profits. A potentially more successful strategy would be one oriented towards ensuring that the gains from productivity growth also accrue to labour: wages rising in line with productivity growth will cause domestic effective demand to increase and nourish a virtuous cycle of growth, investment, productivity increases and employment over time (Stockhammer et al., 2009).

> **Keeping wages low in order to generate higher profits is self-defeating.**

3. Do macroeconomic trends matter equally in developing countries?

An important question is whether the same mechanisms at work in developed and highly industrialized economies also operate in developing and emerging-market economies where capital endowment is much weaker and there is a large amount of surplus labour.

Structural unemployment or underemployment is undoubtedly a prominent feature in most developing countries, and labour-market and social-security institutions are much less developed than in industrialized countries. These conditions lead to different behaviours of actors on both sides of the labour market. But in today's developed countries, the creation of such

> **The creation of labour-market and social-security institutions was part of the process of structural change that accompanied industrialization.**

institutions was itself part of the process of structural transformation that accompanied industrialization, and the participation of labour in productivity growth was a necessary condition for the advancement of this process and for achieving higher standards of living. Between today's developing countries and the countries that industrialized and created labour-market and social-security institutions before the globalization of production and investment, the main differences are not in the macroeconomic processes but in the context of corporate decision-making on production and investment. Earlier, such decisions were taken primarily with reference to demand and competition in domestic markets, even when the rest of the world provided markets for some of the increasing production as well as outlets for some labour through migration. By contrast, in most developing countries today such decisions are taken primarily with reference to external demand and global competition. Moreover, these countries can import advanced technologies from the North. The problem of combining technological progress, investment and productivity growth with employment creation is more pronounced when labour-saving technology is introduced in an economy that produces neither the capital goods nor the embodied technology. Since this is a typical situation for developing countries, it is even more important for employment creation that productivity gains translate into higher demand for domestically produced goods and services.

In developing economies that are still highly dependent on the production and export of primary commodities, the link between growth and employment creation can be quite loose. This is because short-term growth is often influenced more strongly by movements in internationally determined prices for primary commodities than by an expansion in the volume of domestic output. Strong increases in commodity prices, as witnessed during the period 2002–2008, can lead to income growth without an increase in real output, and thus do not result in higher employment in the commodities sector. To the extent that higher

Chart 3.5

GROWTH OF EMPLOYMENT AND REAL GDP IN DEVELOPING ECONOMIES, 1970–2009

(Per cent)

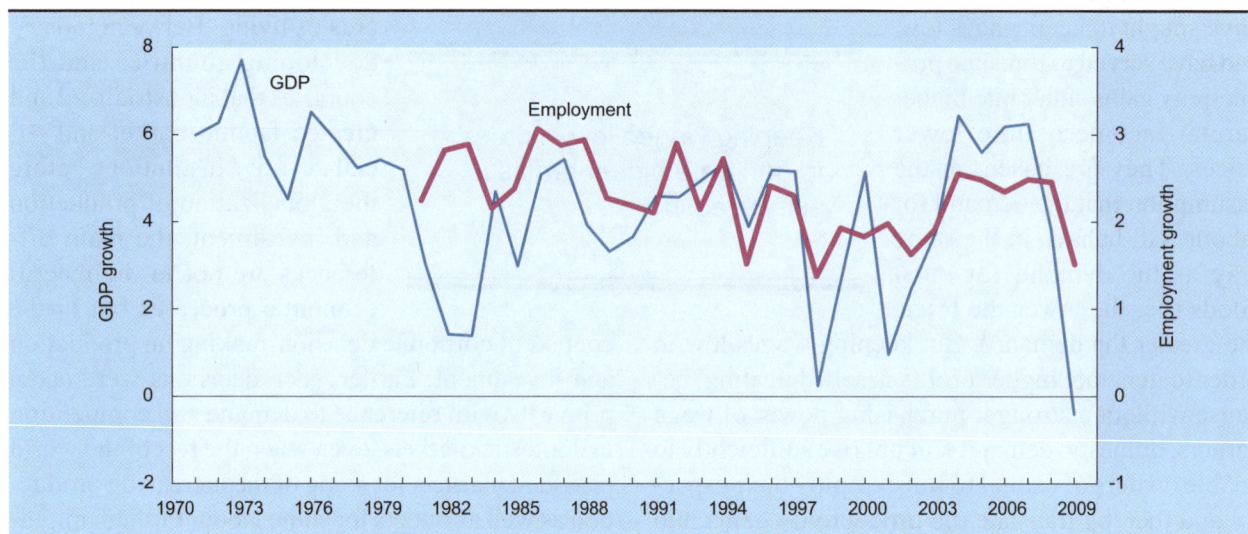

Source: See chart 3.3.

Note: Developing economies comprise: Argentina, the Bolivarian Republic of Venezuela, Bolivia, Brazil, Chile, Colombia, Costa Rica, Cuba, Ecuador, Egypt, El Salvador, Guatemala, Honduras, Hong Kong (China), India, Indonesia, Jamaica, Malaysia, Mauritius, Mexico, Nicaragua, Pakistan, Panama, Paraguay, Peru, the Philippines, the Republic of Korea, Singapore, Taiwan Province of China, Thailand, Trinidad and Tobago, Tunisia, Turkey, Uganda and Uruguay.

commodity prices increase profits in that sector, they tend to have a very small impact, if any, on domestic demand, and thus on employment. However, to the extent that rising commodity prices translate into higher wages (or larger fiscal revenue and expenditure), they could have the same effect as productivity growth resulting from technological innovation: they could boost demand and employment in other parts of the economy. The latter situation is rare because of the frequent monopoly position of capital owners in the primary sector, especially in mining, and the particularly weak position of labour. Transforming productivity gains resulting from commodity price increases into a sustained process of growth and employment throughout the economy would require changing this situation to ensure that higher prices or productivity growth in the primary sector translate into greater domestic demand and/or more investment (see also chapter V for a discussion on distribution of rents).

> In commodity-dependent developing economies the link between growth and employment creation can be quite loose.

The situation is different in those developing and emerging-market economies that have achieved a more diversified production structure and sometimes also generated significant productivity increases. In some of these economies technological catching up has led to rapid growth in their tradable goods industries through an expansion of net exports. Productivity changes are often passed on in the form of lower prices, while keeping wages depressed in the context of falling world market prices or in the hope of increasing world market shares. However, if an economy depends entirely on external markets for growth, the scope for employment creation is circumscribed by the ability to benefit from demand expansion in other countries or to increase market shares, both of which are limited. Since wages do not increase, domestic demand does not grow, and so domestic employment creation is also more limited. As a result, this type of growth does not necessarily generate more desirable

Chart 3.6

**GROWTH OF EMPLOYMENT AND GROSS FIXED CAPITAL FORMATION
IN DEVELOPING ECONOMIES, 1970–2008**

(Per cent)

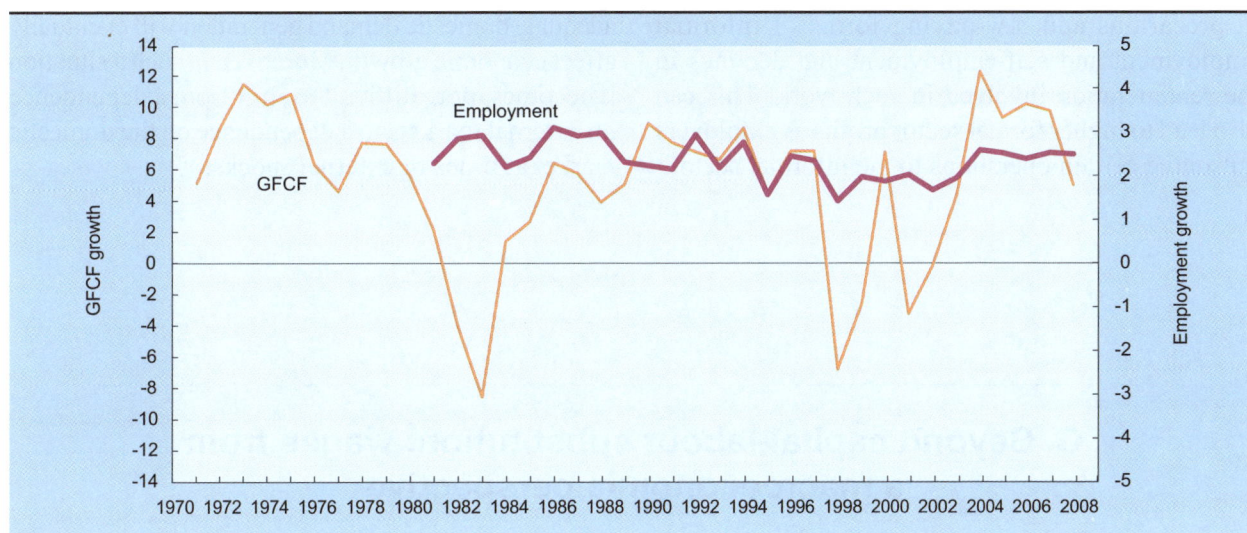

Source: See chart 3.3.
Note: See chart 3.5.

employment, which means that informal and less remunerative activities may persist, and even expand, during what may be a dynamic output growth process (Ghosh, 2010).

Therefore, in developing countries, as in developed countries, the ability to achieve sustained growth of income and employment on the basis of productivity growth depends critically on how the resulting gains are distributed within the economy, how much additional wage income is spent for the consumption of domestically produced goods and services, and whether higher profits are used for investment in activities that simultaneously create more employment, including in some service sectors, such as the delivery of health and education (see chapter IV of this *Report* for some examples).

Conclusive statistical evidence for developing countries is difficult to find due to the scarcity of

> Changes in informal employment and self-employment dampen the effects of growth cycles on formal employment.

statistical data on employment and labour market conditions. Where such data are available, the statistical evidence suggests that the link between growth and formal employment is weaker in developing countries than in developed countries. This can probably be explained partly by the fact that changes in informal employment and self-employment dampen the cyclical effects.[4] In developing countries more than in developed countries, workers who are laid off in the formal sector of the economy in bad times often tend to move into the informal economy because of the lack of social safety nets.

Nevertheless, for those developing countries for which reliable data are available, employment growth is also positively correlated with growth of both GDP and investment in fixed capital (charts 3.5 and 3.6; see also chapter IV), although the cyclicality of employment generation is less pronounced in developing than in developed countries.[5]

Since in most developing countries the distinction between the formal and informal sectors is often blurred, with the former shading into (and often dependent on) the latter, wage stagnation or reduction does not always involve actual declines in wage rates in the formal sector. Rather, it can reflect increases in precarious and low-paying forms of informal employment and self-employment and declines in the remuneration involved in such work. This can also lead to higher formal sector profits as employers outsource certain operations to the informal sector.

Competition in external markets then results in these two sides of the process – informal employment with low wages, and export success – reinforcing each other. However, since there are several limits to such a process, as mentioned above, this can only be sustained for a short period of time; the lack of adequate domestic demand generation will eventually affect economic growth. Moreover, in such a situation it becomes more difficult to shift from a dependence on external markets to a dependence on the domestic market at times of external shocks.

C. Beyond capital-labour substitution: wages from a macroeconomic perspective

1. The "price of labour" and employment

Labour compensation has a dual character. On the one hand, it constitutes the largest proportion of production costs. The wage rate is a key variable in the macroeconomic process, because in vertically integrated economies final, intermediate and capital goods are all produced by the domestic labour force, except for those goods that are imported. Thus, at the macroeconomic level the only cost factor affecting overall production costs, apart from wages, is the price of the imported products (Flassbeck and Spiecker, 2007: 53). On the other hand, labour compensation determines, to a very large extent, the level of demand of private households (Bhaduri and Marglin, 1990).

Distributing productivity gains between labour and capital at constant factor income shares will create new jobs ...

use of labour because of the fall in the price of labour in relation to capital. In this way, the lower wage per worker would be immediately balanced by a rising number of workers that are employed to replace capital and to produce the same amount of goods and services; hence no demand gap would occur.

There are two problems with this approach. Firstly, owing to strong competition on goods markets, prices may fall by the full amount of the nominal wage reduction, so that real wages may not fall. Secondly, if the latter do fall because prices on the goods markets are more rigid than nominal wages,[6] the drop in real wages will induce a reduction in overall final demand long before any substitution of capital with labour can take effect. As such substitution implies a change in the technology used for the production of similar goods as before, with a more labour-intensive combination of the factors of production, the effect, even if intended by the owners of capital, would take a significant time to materialize. By contrast, a reduction in total real wages will

Downwardly flexible wages induce a fall in demand from wage earners. According to neoclassical theory, a fall in nominal wages would reduce real wages and increase the incentive for entrepreneurs to change their production processes towards a greater have the immediate effect of inducing workers to cut down on their consumption because they will have no expectation of a quick return to their former standard of living (Weeks, 1989: 123–124).

It could be argued that a fall in wages would redirect existing resources towards the remuneration of capital (i.e. profits), and thus cause investment to rise. But the same logic as above applies in this case as well: a reduction in real wages will trigger a fall in demand, so that profits will not rise. In a context of unchanged profits and falling demand it cannot be assumed that companies will invest more than before and in this way compensate for the fall in workers' consumption. Hence, overall income will decline.[7]

… and compensate for possible job losses in the firms where productivity has increased the most.

In a relatively closed economy this outcome can be prevented temporarily if the fall in wages is accompanied by an increase in non-wage sources of income, for example through asset price inflation, or when wage-earning households save less or incur additional debt in their efforts to maintain or even increase their consumption. A prominent example is that of households in the United States over the past decade, but it has also been observed in several other countries. It is evident that such a situation cannot be sustained for long, as household debts will eventually reach unsustainable levels or asset price bubbles will burst.

For a more open economy, this reasoning needs to be slightly modified. If nominal wages fall in one country but remain constant in others, the former gains a competitive (absolute) advantage if the implied fall in unit labour costs is not balanced by an appreciation of its currency. With permanently lower prices, the country will gain international market shares and raise its income and employment as the external contribution to its overall income increases, normally moving the current-account balance into surplus (see box 3.1, comparing France and Germany). This may be an attractive option for countries that follow an outward-oriented growth strategy that seeks to attract foreign demand, as opposed to mobilizing domestic demand. However, increasing income and employment this way will be possible only if the same strategy is not simultaneously pursued by many other countries. When the strategy succeeds in one country,

in the sense that higher external demand compensates for lower domestic demand so that domestic employment is stabilized or increased, this success will be at the expense of the other economies, where incomes and employment will fall as a result of their loss of international market shares. Thus, from the global perspective there is a fallacy of composition.

Moreover, such a strategy is only feasible if the international monetary system allows a significant misalignment of real exchange rates, which occurs when differences in the rate of inflation or in the rate of increase of unit labour costs are not fully compensated by adjustments in the nominal exchange rate. In fact, as recent events in Europe show, even in a unified currency regime like the euro zone, real exchange rates between members of the currency area may get misaligned when relative wages and prices between them change.

2. Productivity growth and employment

As argued above, a key economic variable for the determination of aggregate demand growth and employment is the distribution of the gains from productivity growth among profits and wages. This distributional question has critical significance for a sustainable trajectory of growth with employment creation.

Like wage growth, productivity growth has a dual character. On the one hand, it is the most important source of income growth for all economies which lack a rich endowment of natural resources. On the other hand, it has a labour-saving effect and is a potential source of unemployment. However, the destructive part of it can be overcome if the higher proceeds from the deployment of new technologies that are more productive than older ones can be deployed to enhance mass incomes in the economy, which will induce an increase in demand for goods and services.

The distribution of productivity gains between earners of capital and labour incomes can take two

Box 3.1

THE LINK BETWEEN WAGES AND EMPLOYMENT:
THE EXPERIENCES OF FRANCE AND GERMANY COMPARED

Germany's experiment with a restrictive wage policy has been the subject of economic debate in Europe for over a decade. However, so far policymakers do not appear to have drawn lessons from this experience.

A comparison of the wage policies of Germany and France offers important insights into the interdependence of productivity, wage and employment growth. The two countries are comparable in size and both have been members of the European Economic and Monetary Union (EMU) since 1999. Their common target for price stability is an annual inflation rate of about 2 per cent, as set by the European Central Bank. In the years before the EMU was established, both France and Germany had rather high unemployment rates. After 1999, Germany suffered significant employment losses, with the unemployment rate reaching an all-time high of more than 11 per cent in 2005. In France, the unemployment rate fell below that of Germany as France achieved higher GDP growth rates than Germany.

The better employment performance of France was accompanied by a constant share of wages in total income, whereas the German wage share dropped. In Germany, particularly between 2002 and 2007, wage policy was very restrictive. From 1999 onwards unit labour costs in Germany fell consistently compared to those of France, so that by 2007 the difference amounted to 20 percentage points (chart 3.B1.1). In France, although real wages rose much more than in Germany, new jobs were created and the unemployment rate fell.

Chart 3.B1.1

**LABOUR PRODUCTIVITY, REAL WAGES AND UNIT LABOUR COSTS
IN FRANCE AND GERMANY, 1999–2009**

(Index numbers, 1999 = 100)

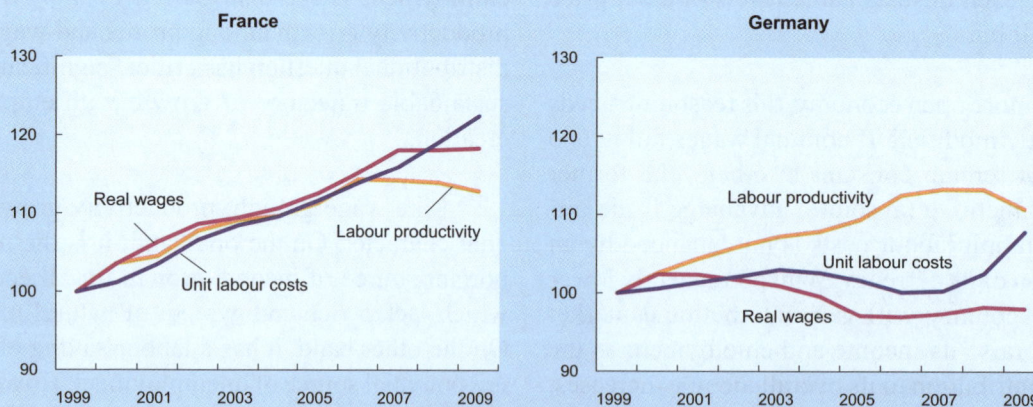

Source: UNCTAD secretariat calculations, based on *AMECO* database.

As Germany is part of the EMU, its competitiveness increased without a currency devaluation, resulting in a much larger growth of its exports than those of France, but sluggish domestic consumption growth (chart 3.B1.2). France, on the other hand, achieved a better performance in terms of a higher rate of investment and faster GDP growth than its neighbour.

Box 3.1 (concluded)

Chart 3.B1.2

PRIVATE CONSUMPTION AND EXPORTS IN FRANCE AND GERMANY, 1999–2009
(Index numbers, 1999 = 100)

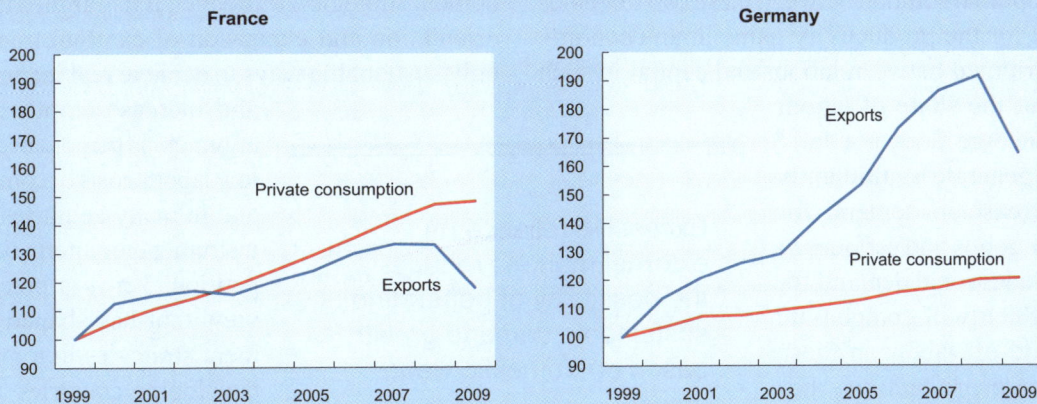

Source: See chart 3.B1.1.

Lower nominal wage increases in Germany did not produce a positive effect on investment or employment. Indeed, there is evidence that wage restraint – inspired by the neoclassical model that emphasizes substitution of capital and labour – turned out to be detrimental not only from a social but also a macroeconomic perspective.

Wage restraint was beneficial for the German economy only in terms of boosting its international competitiveness and exports, an effect that was supported by Germany's membership of the European currency union. However, inside the euro area the effects of German wage restraint on the country's real exchange rate and external trade are being felt in many countries in the form of current-account deficits. This is causing a deflationary threat for the currency area as a whole, because sooner or later wage restraint will become unavoidable in the deficit countries, especially Greece, Portugal and Spain.

extreme forms, or turn out to lie somewhere between these two. At one extreme, the owners of capital may try to appropriate the entire productivity gains by resisting both wage increases and price reductions. This attempt will fail because demand for their products will decline if they cut the redundant jobs. As a result, the expanded productive capacity will not be fully used, investment will tend to fall, and a deflationary effect will result. If workers' bargaining position is weak but there is strong competitive pressure in the goods market, the technological pioneers may choose, or be forced, to pass on the productivity gains to consumers through lower prices while keeping nominal wages unchanged. Consequently, real wages will increase, but the price reduction could induce consumers to delay their purchases, and this could also feed a deflationary spiral with negative implications for employment.

At the other extreme, if workers have strong bargaining power, they may obtain an increase in nominal wages that absorbs the entire productivity gain, so that unit labour costs will rise. As capital owners normally are not willing to accept a reduction in the share of profits, firms will increase prices in order to maintain that share. If they do not succeed, demand will rise more than the productivity-induced increase in supply potential. This means that there will be inflationary pressure from both the cost and the demand side with no real wage growth. This may stimulate further investment, but will also trigger an inflationary acceleration, even in the presence of unemployment.

An optimal solution between these two extremes would be for the productivity gains in an economy to be distributed between labour and capital in such a way that the share of labour in total income does not fall.[8] This will generate a sufficiently large increase in demand for consumer goods and services to create an additional demand for labour, which will compensate for the laid-off labour in those firms where productivity has increased. And there will be no risk of inflation from either the cost or the demand side.[9]

As supply and demand on the labour market cannot be separated from what is happening in the other markets of an economy, the problems of cyclical and structural unemployment in developing countries appear in a different light. It could even be argued that one reason why structural unemployment and underemployment have remained very high over many decades is that the link between domestic demand growth and employment creation did not receive the attention it deserved. If low wages dictated by powerful employers are regarded as a "natural" labour market outcome in an economy that has an excess supply of labour, this tends to lock in high unemployment.

This is more likely to happen when employment generation is not a central focus of growth and development strategies. Moreover, if it is argued that export orientation and expansion of external trade are the only sustainable ways to achieve real income growth and increase employment, the argument is perpetuated, because low labour costs become a major, and in many countries the only, instrument for international competition. Yet it is precisely this view that has shaped development strategies in a majority of developing countries as well as some developed countries over the past three decades. It is true that many developing countries, especially those with lower levels of per capita income, do not have sufficient domestic purchasing power to benefit from the scale economies necessary for a vibrant manufacturing sector, and therefore must rely on external demand even to diversify their production base. However, their excessive reliance on external markets may prevent them from generating more sustainable output growth and employment on the basis of rising domestic wages.

> Excessive reliance on external markets reduces the possibility of generating sustainable demand growth based on domestic wage growth.

D. Productivity-oriented wage growth supports investment and innovation

In addition to playing a key role in employment creation, wage incomes are also closely related to the dynamics of real productive investment and innovation. This is because profits drive investment, and the level of profits is fundamentally driven by demand rather than by a reduction in production costs.

A large part of investment is motivated by the possibility of gaining competitive advantages by introducing technological advances in the production process. As Schumpeter (1911) noted nearly a century ago, technological progress arises from entrepreneurs' interest in earning higher profits, which they seek to achieve by gaining competitive advantages resulting from a process of innovation and imitation, in the course of which new cost-saving production techniques are introduced or new products are launched that are more attractive to consumers than those already on the market.

> Profits are driven by demand rather than by a reduction in production costs.

At the firm level, successful innovative investment will be reflected in growing market shares if the investor chooses to pass on the rents from innovation in the form of lower prices; or it will lead to (temporary) monopoly profits if the investor chooses to leave sales prices unchanged and enjoy the rents from innovation until competitors succeed in imitating the innovator. The choice of the strategy will largely depend on the intensity of competition.

If wages paid to workers with the same qualifications are uniform throughout the economy, changes in competitiveness will result from changes in relative labour productivity across different firms. For this process to unfold, it is essential for pioneer investors to be able to increase their productivity without being forced to increase wages at the level of the individual firm. This implies that technological progress and the ensuing growth in labour productivity are associated with what might be called "workable" rather than "perfect" competition in the markets for goods and services (Clark, 1962), allowing temporary monopoly rents to accrue to pioneer firms. In the labour market, this process requires more or less uniform wages for workers with similar qualifications across the entire economy (i.e. the "law of one price"), rather than each production plant (or sector) determining wages in accordance with its marginal productivity. However, this is conditional on having a highly mobile labour force or, alternatively, a highly centralized process of wage formation, for example through nationwide collective bargaining or through the government setting or recommending wage targets.

The dynamic development of an economy is then driven by profit differentials, rather than wage differentials. Indeed, as noted by Keynes (1930: 141), "the departure of profits from zero is the mainspring of change in the ... modern world ... It is by altering the rate of profits in particular directions that entrepreneurs can be induced to produce this rather than that, and it is by altering the rate of profits in general that they can be induced to modify the average of their offers of remuneration to the factors of production." Hence, the closer the actual conditions on the labour markets get to the law of one price, the stronger will be the effects of profit differentials on the evolution of economic systems.[10] Or, the more rigid the wages, the more flexible will be the profits and the stronger will be the dynamic forces in the economy.

This potential for generating extra profits through product or process innovation is the major incentive for starting and sustaining a process of "creative destruction" along Schumpeterian lines. To the extent that wages in each firm grow in line with firm-specific productivity gains, innovative investors will receive lower extra profits, and will thus have less incentive for innovative investment.

> The more rigid the wages, the more flexible will be the profits and the stronger will be the dynamic forces in the economy.

In developed countries, innovative investment extends the technological frontier, whereas in developing countries it mostly entails the adoption, imitation and adaptation of technology invented elsewhere. However, this does not undermine the importance of productivity-enhancing investment to boost competitiveness at the firm level, or significantly alter the determinants of investment decisions. Technological catch-up can take place in different ways and through diverse mechanisms, such as the transfer of a physical plant as part of a process of industrial relocation through FDI, local investment in R&D that allows the adoption and adaptation of off-the-shelf technologies, or other forms of innovation. This can play a critical quasi-Schumpeterian role in the growth process also in developing countries, if these productivity gains enlarge the domestic market and trigger a process of wage-led growth. It is important to bear in mind that productivity improvements can take place at all levels of production and in different kinds of enterprises, and often increases in productivity among small-scale producers in agriculture and informal sector activities may be the most crucial for overall economic advancement. Thus, while technological upgrading in developing countries is usually associated with a painstaking and cumulative process of learning, there is scope for it to occur in various ways and at different levels. However, since the development of skills per se cannot create additional jobs (except in the education sector), investment in real productive capacity remains crucial to enable the absorption of surplus labour.

E. Conclusions

This chapter has argued that employment growth critically depends on an expansion of aggregate demand, and much less – if at all – on the price of labour relative to that of capital. The conventional wisdom about "export-led growth" advocates a reliance on export markets rather than on domestic markets for aggregate demand growth. Consequently, export-led growth strategies have tended to suppress wage growth with the aim of lowering unit labour costs to improve a country's competitive position in global markets. This strategy may work for some economies for some time, but the more economies that follow such a strategy, the less it can be successfully sustained by all of them. The relative longevity of this strategy over the past decade and more has been possible mainly because of the fast growth of import demand from the United States, which, however, generated large external deficits in that economy. As attempts are made to trim these deficits, other countries in the world will also have to rebalance (as discussed in chapter II of this *TDR*). It is therefore important that the macroeconomic and growth strategies adopted in most countries in recent decades be reconsidered.

In any case, a more sustainable growth strategy would be one that relies, more than it did in the past, on domestic demand based on wage increases in line with aggregate labour productivity increases. At the same time, an increase in domestic demand for wage goods needs to be accompanied by a dynamic process of investment and new capacity creation for absorbing surplus labour.

Despite apparent differences in structure, institutions and types of constraints on growth, there are important similarities between developed and developing countries in terms of the relationship between investment, output and employment. In all countries, sustainable growth trajectories are those that are based on the synergies between employment and output growth.

For a virtuous circle of investment, productivity growth, income growth and employment creation to occur, policies need to be oriented towards ensuring that the income gains from productivity growth are distributed equally between labour and capital, so that the share of wages in national income does not decline over time. This basic insight is just as relevant for developing countries as it is for developed countries, though for the former countries wage shares need to be broadly interpreted to include incomes from self-employment in agriculture and non-agricultural informal activities, and it may also include the public provision of wage goods.

> Faster employment growth cannot be achieved by greater wage flexibility, but by changes in the general wage level along the path of average productivity growth in the economy.

From this perspective it is not greater wage flexibility that leads to faster employment growth, but rather the opposite: an orientation of changes in the general wage level along the path of average productivity growth in the economy. This will not only create additional jobs that produce additional value added, but also allow for the emergence of profit differentials strengthening the dynamic forces in the economy, and thus investment in productive capacity.

The policy implications of an alternative and more employment-friendly growth and development strategy that relies more on domestic demand growth are discussed in chapter V of this *Report*. It is more important than ever that such policies be considered seriously; otherwise both developed and developing countries face the real risk of a downward spiral into recession and economic instability. ∎

Notes

---

1   See also Weeks (1989: 160), who shows that what may be true at the level of the firm (higher real wages lead to less employment) is not true in the aggregate, even if capital is assumed to be perfectly malleable.

2   This notion goes back to Marshall (1890), Edgeworth (1894), Pigou (1933) and Keynes (1936).

3   Job losses are likely to occur at the level of the individual firm when new technologies are introduced for the production of traditional goods. But when new technologies are associated with the introduction of new products that cater to new customers, there are likely to be few, if any, job losses even at the microeconomic level.

4   While underemployment and low-wage informal employment have been seen as typical features of developing countries, in recent years, the meaning of unemployment has also changed somewhat in statistics for developed countries as new forms of underemployment have proliferated. The recent

economic and financial crisis has led to employment adjustments at the firm level: short-time working and work time reduction has been combined with wage reduction, thereby avoiding open unemployment; however, "unemployment on the job" has increased.

5   The correlation weakens considerably or even disappears, depending on the periodization, when China is included in the sample. Some of the main reasons for this could be that: (i) growth cycles in that country have been less pronounced than in most other countries, (ii) the large share of FDI – often including leading-edge technology – in total investment in China creates extremely large productivity gains, and (iii) rural-urban migration (and reverse migration), and the way in which it is recorded in statistics, dampen the impact of changes in investment on employment.

6   Indeed, if nominal wages (i.e. the price on the labour market) were as flexible as the prices on all the other markets, the neoclassical edifice would collapse. If an exogenous shock, say a fall in export demand, were to occur, the prices on all of these markets would react in the same way, and the real wage would not fall. Unemployment would rise but the labour market would have no means to cope. This only supports the contention (explained earlier in this chapter) that the labour market should not be treated as a separate market.

7   Another perspective on the relationship between wages and investment, which leads to the same conclusion, is provided by Leijonhufvud (1968: 335): "Observing unemployment, the 'classical' economist draws the conclusion that wages are too high and 'ought' to be reduced. In Keynes' theory, the maintenance of full employment depends upon the maintenance of a 'right' relation between...asset prices and the wage ... Keynes' point is that when

the appropriate price relation does not obtain, it is in general not wages but asset demand prices that are out of line...".

8   The application of this rule would ensure that the functional income distribution will not change at the expense of labour incomes as a result of productivity increases. Of course, there may be specific situations in particular countries where the current distribution of income between capital and labour as a result of past policies is considered unfair. In this case, shifts in that distribution towards labour would need to be subject to negotiation and consensus-building at the national level. Moreover, the creation of a more equitable society is mainly the outcome of public policy choices, including with regard to taxation and the provision of public services.

9   To the extent that this implies an increase in imports, the greater demand will boost output and employment not only in the country where the productivity increases, but also abroad. If the distribution of productivity gains is similar in all countries, unit labour cost relations will remain unchanged, ensuring that trade remains in balance. If, however, inflation differentials lead to a divergence in unit labour costs, an adjustment of the nominal exchange rate will be necessary to prevent the emergence of trade imbalances.

10 Looking at developed countries, Scarpetta and Tressel (2004) point out that in addition to wage bargaining regimes, two main aspects of labour-market policy and institutional settings are closely related to the incentives for firms to undertake investment with a view to expanding and innovating production facilities: (i) the stringency of employment protection legislation, which influences the costs of hiring and firing; and (ii) the possible interactions between this legislation and industry-specific technology characteristics.

References

Bhaduri A and Marglin S (1990). Unemployment and the Real Wage: The Economic Basis for Contesting Political Ideologies. *Cambridge Journal of Economics* 14 (4): 375–393.

Blinder AS (2006). Offshoring: The next industrial revolution? *Foreign Affairs,* 85(2): 113–128.

Clark JM (1962). *Competition as a dynamic process.* Washington, DC, The Brookings Institution.

Edgeworth FY (1894). Theory of international values. *The Economic Journal,* 4(16): 606–638.

Flassbeck H (2004). Saving, investment and government deficits: A modern Kaleckian approach. In: Sadowski ZL and Szeworski A, eds. *Kalecki's Economics Today.* London and New York, Routledge.

Flassbeck H and Spiecker F (2007). Das Ende der Massenarbeitslosigkeit, Mit richtiger Wirtschaftspolitik die Zukunft gewinnen. Frankfurt, Westend.

Freeman R (2008). The new global labour market. *Focus* 26(1). University of Wisconsin, Madison, WI, Institute for Research on Poverty.

Ghosh J (2010). *Growth, macropolicies and structural change.* Background paper for UNRISD Report on Strategies for Poverty Reduction (forthcoming).

Howell DR et al. (2007). Are protective labor market institutions at the root of unemployment? A critical review of the evidence. *Capitalism and Society,* 2(1): 1–71.

ILO (2009). Facing the global jobs crisis: Migrant workers, a population at risk. Available at: http://www.ilo.org/global/About_the_ILO/Media_and_public_information/Feature_stories/lang--en/WCMS_112537/index.htm.

IMF (2003). *World Economic Outlook.* Washington, DC, April.

Keynes JM (1930). *A Treatise on Money.* London, Macmillan.

Keynes JM (1936). The General Theory of Employment, Interest and Money. London, Macmillan.

Leijonhufvud A (1968). *Keynesian Economics and the Economics of Keynes.* Oxford, Oxford University Press.

Marshall A (1890). *Principles of Economics.* London, Macmillan.

Pigou AC (1933). *The Theory of Unemployment.* London, Macmillan.

Pollin R (2007). Global outsourcing and the U.S. working class. *New Labour Forum,* 16(11): 122–125.

Scarpetta S and Tressel T (2004). Boosting Productivity via Innovation and Adoption of New Technologies: Any Role for Labour Market Institutions? World Bank Policy Research Paper 3273. Washington, DC, World Bank.

Schumpeter JA (1976). *History of Economic Analysis.* New York, Oxford University Press.

Schumpeter JA (1911). Theorie der wirtschaftlichen Entwicklung: Eine Untersuchung über Unternehmergewinn, Kapital, Kredit, Zins und den Konjunkturzyklus. Berlin, Duncker and Humbold.

Siebert H (1997). Labor Market Rigidities: At the Root of Unemployment in Europe. *Journal of Economic Perspectives,* 11(3): 37–54.

St. Paul G (2004). Why are European countries diverging in their unemployment experience? *Journal of Economic Perspectives,* 18(4): 49–68.

Stockhammer E, Onaran Ö and Ederer S (2009). Functional income distribution and aggregate demand in the Euro area. *Cambridge Journal of Economics,* 33(1): 139–159.

UNCTAD (2009). The global economic crisis: Systemic failures and multilateral remedies. Task Force Report. United Nations publications, New York and Geneva.

UNCTAD (various issues). *Trade and Development Report.* United Nations publications, New York and Geneva.

UNDP (2009). *Human Development Report 2009.* Basingstoke and New York, Palgrave Macmillan.

Weeks J (1989). *A Critique of Neoclassical Macroeconomics.* London and New York, Macmillan and St. Martins Press.

Chapter IV

STRUCTURAL CHANGE AND EMPLOYMENT CREATION IN DEVELOPING COUNTRIES

A. Introduction

Employment creation is a particularly difficult challenge for developing countries. Their labour force is still growing rapidly, necessitating the constant generation of additional jobs for the new entrants within an economic structure characterized by dualism. Typically, these countries have a modern sector with relatively high productivity and large economies of scale, which coexists with a sluggish traditional sector with low productivity and mostly constant returns to scale. Economic development, in general, and employment creation for a growing population, in particular, require an expansion of modern activities and the reallocation of labour from the traditional to the modern sector. The more productive use of previously underemployed labour through its transfer from less remunerative traditional activities to better paid jobs in the modern sector generates higher incomes and a consequent increase in effective demand.

The modern sector, where production takes place in organized units with formal wage jobs, has often been equated with industry, particularly manufacturing, but increasingly it also includes modern services and some innovative agricultural activities. Since the early 1980s developing countries have sought to expand this sector through a growing emphasis on production for the world market. It was hoped that this could trigger and accelerate a virtuous process of

output growth, and steady gains in productivity and employment. However, in many countries exports did not grow as expected due to a lack of supply capacities and insufficient competitiveness of domestic producers on global markets. In others where exports grew, the domestic labour force employed in export industries did not share in the productivity gains. Instead, firms tried to use such gains to raise the profit share or passed them on to lower prices, so that domestic demand did not increase, which would have led to higher income in the rest of the economy. As a result, employment problems persisted, or even worsened, particularly in Latin America and Africa.

The employment situation generally improved between 2003 and 2008, partly as a result of a reorientation of macroeconomic policies, and partly due to a more favourable international environment with higher prices for primary commodities and rapidly rising import demand from the United States, China and some other fast-growing emerging-market economies. But the global financial and economic crisis has caused unemployment and underemployment to rise again and they are likely to persist in the changing global economic environment, as discussed in chapter II. Since 2008, the global employment-to-population ratio has been exhibiting a declining trend and unemployment rates have been rising. Global unemployment reached its highest level on record in 2009, and the share of workers in vulnerable employment[1] worldwide is estimated to represent over half of the world's labour force (ILO, 2010a).

This chapter examines the issue of employment in the structural context of developing and emerging-market economies and how the employment situation has evolved in developing countries over the past 30 years. An analysis of employment and unemployment in developing countries is made difficult by the scarcity of statistical data on employment and labour market conditions in many countries, and by the problem of distinguishing unemployment from underemployment. In developing countries more than in developed countries, workers who are laid off in the formal sector of the economy in bad times often tend to move into the informal economy, where productivity and earnings are lower. This informal sector is often quite large in the absence of social safety nets. Therefore changes in the quality of employment are as much a reflection of changing labour market conditions as changes in the quantity of employment and unemployment.

Section B of this chapter takes a general look at employment trends in developing and transition economies, and how they are related to specific characteristics of different groups of countries as well as the process of their structural transformation. Section C then discusses in greater detail the growth and employment performance in three developing regions, Latin America, Africa and East, South-East and South Asia in the context of the macroeconomic and development strategies pursued by countries in these regions.

B. Employment, productivity growth and structural change in developing countries

1. The employment challenge in developing countries

The nature of the employment challenge in developing countries differs greatly from that in developed countries. In most developing countries a deficiency of effective demand may cause the underutilization of capital equipment and labour, but there is more to it than that. According to Kalecki (1976), "the principal problem is deficient productive capacity and not the abnormality of it being underutilised", so that even if all existing equipment were fully employed, it would still be insufficient to provide decent jobs to all the available labour force. The solution therefore lies in increasing investment and accelerating economic growth. However, even this may not be enough because of the probable "dynamic insufficiency" of the development process (Prebisch, 1963: 27–29) which is unable to provide productive employment to an abundant labour force that, in addition, may be growing at a rapid pace.

Several developing regions are at an early stage of demographic transition, with rapid growth rates of their population. In sub-Saharan Africa and West Asia, the average annual growth rate of the population was well over 2 per cent during the period 2003–2009, compared with less than 1 per cent in developed regions since the mid-1960s, and it has been close to zero in the transition economies. In China, there has been an active policy to keep population growth under control; consequently, the population growth rate in East Asia as a whole has

Table 4.1

TOTAL POPULATION AND LABOUR FORCE, SELECTED REGIONS, 1981–2009

(Average annual growth rates)

	Population	Labour force	Population	Labour force	Population	Labour force
	1981–1990		*1991–2002*		*2003–2009*	
Developed economies	**0.6**	**1.3**	**0.6**	**0.9**	**0.6**	**1.0**
North America	1.1	1.7	1.2	1.3	1.0	1.0
Asia	0.6	1.2	0.4	0.5	0.1	-0.4
Europe	0.3	0.9	0.3	0.7	0.5	0.6
Developing economies	**2.1**	**2.7**	**1.7**	**2.0**	**1.4**	**1.9**
East Asia	1.5	2.6	1.0	1.2	0.6	0.9
South Asia	2.4	2.5	2.0	2.3	1.6	2.4
South-East Asia	2.1	3.1	1.6	2.3	1.3	1.9
West Asia	2.9	4.2	2.5	2.7	2.2	2.3
North Africa	2.7	3.0	1.9	2.9	1.7	2.9
Sub-Saharan Africa	2.9	3.0	2.7	3.0	2.5	2.8
Latin America and the Caribbean	2.0	2.9	1.6	3.0	1.2	2.2
Transition economies[a]	..	..	**-0.1**	**-0.1**	**-0.1**	**0.8**

Source: UNCTAD secretariat calculations, based on ILO, *LABORSTAT* and *KILM* databases; OECD, *Annual Labour Force Statistics* in *OECD.Stat Extracts* database; ECLAC, *CEPALSTAT* database; EIU, *EIU CountryData* database; UN/DESA, *World Population Prospects: The 2008 Revision Population Database*; and national sources.

a   1991–2002 refers to 1993–2002.

declined significantly, from 1.5 per cent in the 1980s to 0.6 per cent in the 2000s – a rate similar to that of developed countries. In the other developing regions, namely North Africa, South and South-East Asia and Latin America and the Caribbean, there has been a deceleration of demographic growth, from an average annual rate of 2–2.7 per cent in the 1980s to a nevertheless significant 1.2–1.7 per cent in the period 2003–2009 (table 4.1).

In general, the labour force increases at a considerably faster rate than the total population (table 4.1). Even if total population growth were to further decelerate in most developing regions, growth of the working age population would only begin to slow down after a time lag of several years. Moreover, in many countries the labour force is growing more rapidly than the working age population owing to social factors, the most important being the increasing participation of women in labour markets (table 4.2). Women's participation in paid or recognised work increased globally by more than 18 per

cent between 1997 and 2007 (ILO, 2008a; Horton, 1999; Çağatay and Özler, 1995). In some countries, this evolution has been partially counterbalanced by a longer period of time spent by youth in education, which delays their entry into the active population, and by some reduction in the rates of men's participation in the labour force. But in general, the effect of the increasing participation of women on the overall participation rate is greater than that of the declining participation of youth and men (box 4.1).

In all the regions, in the long run total employment seems to have increased at a fairly similar rate as the labour force, even though GDP growth rates have varied widely (tables 4.1 and 4.3). This may have prevented the emergence of large-scale open unemployment in regions where the labour force has been expanding and GDP growth has been slow, but at the cost of overall productivity which has barely increased, or even declined. Moreover, there has been little improvement in the quality of jobs in terms of remuneration and working conditions.

Table 4.2

LABOUR PARTICIPATION RATES AND SHARE OF WOMEN IN TOTAL
LABOUR FORCE, SELECTED REGIONS, 1980–2009

(Per cent)

	Labour force in total population	Women in total labour force	Labour force in total population	Women in total labour force	Labour force in total population	Women in total labour force	Labour force in total population	Women in total labour force
	1980		1990		2002		2009	
Developed economies	**43.9**	**39.6**	**47.0**	**42.4**	**48.7**	**44.2**	**49.5**	**45.1**
North America	46.8	41.1	49.6	44.3	49.6	45.9	49.6	46.2
Asia	48.0	38.7	51.3	40.6	52.0	40.9	51.4	42.1
Europe	40.5	39.1	43.5	41.8	46.8	44.0	48.5	45.2
Developing economies	**41.2**	**36.4**	**43.6**	**37.7**	**44.9**	**38.5**	**45.3**	**38.6**
East Asia	51.3	43.0	56.7	44.6	58.1	45.5	59.1	45.7
South Asia	36.4	26.6	36.9	27.8	38.3	28.4	40.4	29.4
South-East Asia	41.9	40.9	45.3	42.1	48.8	41.5	50.8	41.5
West Asia	28.4	20.4	31.8	22.3	32.6	21.9	32.6	21.7
North Africa	27.2	20.3	28.0	23.5	31.1	25.9	33.5	28.2
Sub-Saharan Africa	38.2	42.6	38.5	43.0	40.0	43.5	40.8	44.2
Latin America and the Caribbean	34.9	30.4	38.0	32.2	44.7	39.4	47.7	41.7
Transition economies[a]	..	..	**50.4**	**48.1**	**50.4**	**48.4**	**53.2**	**48.8**

Source: See table 4.1.
   a   1990 refers to 1992.

In some regions, the agricultural sector absorbed a significant proportion of new entrants to the labour market, but in low quality jobs. The labour force in agriculture is still growing significantly in sub-Saharan Africa and South Asia, although at a slower rate than overall employment. On the other hand, it has declined rapidly in developed countries and in the transition economies, and has also begun to fall in absolute terms in Latin America and East Asia (table 4.4). But rather than going into manufacturing, workers have been moving disproportionately into traditional service activities, where they often take up informal jobs for wages that may be higher than in agriculture. However, there is limited scope for sustained growth of productivity in these activities, and consequently little potential for the creation of a virtuous cycle of industrialization, whereby fast productivity growth enables real income growth and an expansion of domestic demand, which in turn motivates additional fixed investment for further industrialization. While a select group of countries were able to industrialize using interventionist policies and relying on dynamic export demand, many others could not adopt a similar approach. This was partly because of their inability to compete in global markets, but also because they adopted strategies that relied primarily on market forces for growth. And even when such growth occurred it did not necessarily translate into an accelerated generation of formal and well remunerated employment.

2. Unemployment in developing countries: an overview

Open unemployment is a persistent problem in several regions, both developed and developing. In most regions, unemployment rates displayed an upward – although irregular – trend, and were significantly higher in 2009 than in 1980, with the

Box 4.1

INCREASING FEMALE PARTICIPATION IN THE LABOUR FORCE

The participation rate of the total labour force (the share of the labour force in total population) has been increasing in parallel with the share of women in the labour force. The concomitant rise of total and female participation rates has been particularly strong in Latin America and the Caribbean, and, although from a low initial level, in North Africa as well as in Europe. In these regions, the greater participation of women in labour markets contributed to maintaining the growth rate of the labour force well above that of the total population. Female participation rates remain relatively low in West Asia, South Asia and North Africa (despite a recent increase in the latter), which implies that the labour force in these regions could continue to grow rapidly in the coming years, depending on the evolution of social and cultural norms.

In contrast, developed economies, transition economies and developing East and South-East Asia already have high participation rates, together with a large proportion of women in the labour force. A special case is that of the sub-Saharan region, where female participation has been traditionally high, at a level comparable to that of developed economies. This apparent paradox can be explained by the high incidence of self-employed or unpaid family workers, particularly in agriculture, where women's participation rate is close to that of men. Conversely, there is a lower proportion of women among wage earners and the urban labour force. Thus it seems that women's participation in this region is more in informal employment.

It is worth noting that the increased share of women in the labour force coincides with changes in the structure of employment – associated specifically with economic growth and development – limited growth in formal industrial employment and the more rapid increase in the share of services and informal forms of employment. More and more women around the world are employed in service activities (ILO, 2008a) that are often poorly paid and more precarious. While export growth in many developing countries since the mid-1980s has resulted in an expansion of low-skill, labour-intensive and female-intensive manufacturing industries, continued feminization of employment in manufacturing in Latin America has been due to the low levels of initial female participation and slower industrial upgrading. By contrast, defeminization in manufacturing in South-East Asia was found to be related to the dramatic industrial upgrading in the region in the last couple of decades following high levels of female participation in the 1980s. This suggests that the "high-road" of industrialization may be associated with defeminization, while the "low road" could be associated with a continued heavy reliance on women for low-paid jobs (Ghosh, 2004; Jomo, 2009).

exception of East Asia (table 4.5). There appears to have been a negative correlation between the trend in unemployment rates and GDP growth rates (with a lag of one or two years) in developed and transition economies, though less so, or not at all, in developing regions, except East Asia (table 4.6). In many developing economies there exist "cushions" of informal, low-quality employment as an alternative source of employment for workers who lose their jobs or are unable to find formal jobs due to economic recession.

With economic recovery, many of these workers may shift from informal to formal employment, instead of moving from open unemployment to employment. The existence of such "cushions" reduces the growth elasticity of employment in the short run. This does not imply that there is no relationship between growth and unemployment, but rather that changes in growth rates affect unemployment more gradually, and that output growth is not the only factor explaining the level and evolution of unemployment rates.

Table 4.3

REAL GDP AND EMPLOYMENT, SELECTED REGIONS, 1981–2009

(Average annual growth rates)

	GDP	Employ-ment	GDP	Employ-ment	GDP	Employ-ment
	1981–1990		1991–2002		2003–2009	
Developed economies	**3.3**	**1.3**	**2.5**	**1.0**	**1.7**	**0.9**
North America	3.6	2.0	3.3	1.5	2.0	0.8
Asia	3.9	1.2	1.1	0.2	1.1	0.1
Europe	2.6	0.8	2.3	0.9	1.5	1.1
Developing economies	**3.6**	**2.7**	**4.7**	**1.9**	**6.3**	**2.0**
East Asia	9.1	2.8	7.6	1.1	8.0	0.8
South Asia	4.8	2.1	5.1	2.3	7.5	2.6
South-East Asia	5.1	2.9	4.7	1.9	5.7	2.2
West Asia	1.2	4.2	3.5	2.6	5.6	2.4
North Africa	3.0	2.7	3.5	2.7	5.6	3.6
Sub-Saharan Africa	1.7	2.9	2.8	2.9	5.1	2.9
Latin America and the Caribbean	1.6	3.1	2.8	2.6	4.4	2.8
Transition economies[a]	..	..	**-0.4**	**-0.4**	**5.6**	**1.1**

Source: See tables 1.1 and 4.1.
   a 1991–2002 refers to 1993–2002.

Table 4.4

LABOUR FORCE IN AGRICULTURE, SELECTED REGIONS, 1981–2009

(Average annual growth rates)

	1981–1990	1991–2002	2003–2009
Developed economies	**-2.4**	**-3.0**	**-3.3**
North America	-1.2	-1.9	-2.0
Asia	-2.8	-5.0	-5.8
Europe	-2.6	-3.0	-3.3
Developing economies	**1.6**	**0.9**	**0.7**
East Asia	1.8	0.3	-0.1
South Asia	1.1	1.5	1.3
South-East Asia	2.1	1.1	0.7
West Asia	1.0	1.2	0.5
North Africa	0.3	1.2	0.9
Sub-Saharan Africa	2.1	1.9	1.8
Latin America and the Caribbean	0.0	-0.2	-0.7
Transition economies	**-1.2**	**-2.2**	**-1.9**

Source: UNCTAD secretariat calculations, based on FAO, *FAOSTAT Resources PopSTAT* database.

Very slow or even negative growth of per capita GDP in the 1980s and 1990s in Latin America and the Caribbean, West Asia and North Africa contributed to pushing unemployment rates up to two-digit levels by the early 2000s. But while unemployment did not surge in the 1980s, when per capita GDP growth rates were negative, it did in the 1990s, despite a recovery in economic growth. In these cases, changes in policy orientation, including privatizations, trade liberalization and the deregulation of capital flows affected the capacity for job creation. Similarly, although sub-Saharan Africa did not perform better in terms of per capita GDP growth, the economic depression was not clearly reflected in open unemployment statistics. This has to do with the high incidence of informal and rural employment in most countries of that subregion, so that changes in GDP growth have a greater effect on productivity than on employment. It should be pointed out that reliable and comparable statistics on unemployment and underemployment are scarce in sub-Saharan Africa. In some cases, statistics merely assume that informal sector workers are employed, although many workers in the rural sector are only seasonally employed (Nkurunziza, 2007: 166).[2] But even with these caveats, available national surveys

Table 4.5

UNEMPLOYMENT RATES, SELECTED REGIONS, 1980–2009

(Unemployed as a percentage of total labour force)

	1980	*1990*	*2002*	*2007*	*2009*
Developed economies	**5.7**	**6.4**	**6.7**	**5.8**	**8.4**
North America	7.2	5.9	6.0	4.8	9.1
Asia	2.1	2.3	5.5	4.0	5.2
Europe	5.8	7.9	7.5	6.9	8.8
Developing economies	**5.5**	**5.9**	**7.1**	**6.4**	**6.9**
East Asia	4.9	2.5	2.6	2.9	3.4
South Asia	6.1	10.4	10.3	9.1	9.8
South-East Asia	2.9	3.8	7.7	6.6	5.7
West Asia	9.0	9.0	11.1	9.6	12.0
North Africa	8.7	11.1	13.5	9.8	9.7
Sub-Saharan Africa	7.3	7.9	8.4	7.9	8.0
Latin America and the Caribbean	6.2	5.8	11.1	7.9	8.3
Transition economies[a]	..	**5.7**	**7.9**	**6.3**	**7.2**

Source: See table 4.1.
    a 1990 refers to 1992.

show clear differences between African countries and also within each country. In particular, unemployment rates are much higher in urban than in rural areas.[3]

East, South and South-East Asia present a very different picture, with much higher GDP growth in the past few decades. However, only in East Asia has the unemployment rate been very low. In South Asia, open unemployment rose from 6 per cent in 1980 to 11 per cent in 1991, and has since remained close to 10 per cent. In South-East Asia, the unemployment rate increased progressively from very low levels in 1980, especially in Indonesia and the Philippines, where it remained relatively high until 2005.

This global overview shows that generating jobs at a pace rapid enough to absorb the unemployed and employ the new entrants into the labour market remains an enormous challenge for developing economies. Even in countries where the total labour force has been growing slowly, such as China, internal migration from rural areas makes it necessary to provide greater employment opportunities in the cities, or alternatively, to create new job opportunities in the countryside.[4]

Table 4.6

CORRELATION BETWEEN ANNUAL GDP GROWTH AND UNEMPLOYMENT RATES, SELECTED REGIONS, 1980–2009

	Correlation coefficient	*Time lag (years)*
Developed economies		
North America	-0.57	1
Asia	-0.66	1
Europe	-0.39	2
Developing economies		
East Asia	-0.51	0
South Asia	-0.28	2
South-East Asia	-0.21	2
West Asia	-0.13	2
North Africa	-0.14	2
Sub-Saharan Africa	0.11	0
Latin America and the Caribbean	0.01	1
Transition economies	**-0.49**	**2**

Source: See tables 1.1 and 4.1.

3.   *Quality of employment*

Developing countries not only need to create enough employment in quantitative terms; they also need to improve the quality of jobs. Indeed, a major characteristic of the labour structure in developing countries is the large number of informal low-productivity jobs and the relatively few modern, high-productivity jobs. This kind of segmentation is important enough to affect the entire functioning of their labour markets, although the relative weight of the different segments varies widely from country to country. The structural heterogeneity of employment is evidenced by a number of dual characteristics: high/low productivity, qualified/non-qualified, formal/informal, with/without social security, stable/transitory, wage earners/self-employed or unpaid family worker, urban/rural, unionized/non-unionized, and employment in big/small firms. These varying forms of employment are naturally related to the structural heterogeneity of an economy. For example, there tend to be more jobs with high productivity and social security coverage in manufacturing, modern services and the public sector than in traditional agriculture and the retail trade. In the latter two sectors, the borders between employment, underemployment and open unemployment are frequently blurred.

Employment status varies widely from one region to the other (table 4.7). In developed countries, wage earners ("employees") constitute 85 per cent or more of the total employed population, followed by self-employed workers that constitute almost 9 per cent. This preponderance of wage earners is the result of a long process involving the gradual decline of farmers (their share in total employment now ranging from 1.5 per cent in the United States to 4 per cent in Japan) and the replacement of individual storekeepers by commercial chains. Self-employed workers also include a number of qualified workers, professionals, and, in some countries, even employers. Wage earners are also the largest category in the employment structure of transition economies, particularly in Europe, where the structure by status is very similar to that of developed countries. By contrast, the share of self-employed and unpaid family workers remains significant in the transition economies of Central Asia, where informal employment is higher and employment in agriculture in many of these countries exceeds 25 per cent of total employment.

The employment status in developing countries varies widely, reflecting different levels of development and also the different sectoral composition of employment. In sub-Saharan Africa, the share of wage earners in employment is particularly low, at only 13 per cent (excluding South Africa), and there is an overwhelming predominance of self-employed and unpaid family workers. By contrast, countries in North Africa (especially Algeria, Egypt and Tunisia) and parts of Southern Africa (South Africa, Botswana and Namibia) have a high proportion of wage earners. Much of this difference is due to the share of employment in agriculture, which is still predominant in most sub-Saharan countries, while it has fallen dramatically in North and South Africa. Wage earners constitute the largest proportion of the workforce in small island States, such as Mauritius and Seychelles, where employment related to tourism and assembly manufacturing has expanded.

Asian countries also present a mixed picture. West Asia, has a very high proportion of wage earners, exceeding 95 per cent of the total workforce in Kuwait, Qatar and the United Arab Emirates. Such a high proportion of salaried workers is partly explained by the large participation of foreign nationals in total employment, since these workers normally arrive with formal contracts and require monetary payments to be remitted to their home countries. Lebanon, the Syrian Arab Republic and Turkey also have a high share of wage earners, although self-employed, family workers and employers account for a significant share in sectors such as retail trade, personal services and agriculture. In East, South and South-East Asia, much of the labour force is still linked to agriculture: more than 40 per cent in Indonesia and Thailand, close to 50 per cent or even more in Bangladesh, Cambodia, China, India, the Lao People's Democratic Republic, Nepal, Pakistan and Viet Nam. In all these countries, self-employed and family workers constitute the majority of the employed, although the proportion of wage earners is increasing and already exceeds one third of all workers in most of them. Salaried and wage workers are the largest category in the most industrialized economies of the region, such as Taiwan Province of China, the Republic of Korea, Malaysia, Hong Kong (Special Administrative Region of China) and Singapore, and to a lesser extent, the Islamic Republic of Iran and the Philippines. There is a much smaller share of employment in agriculture in these countries.

Table 4.7

EMPLOYMENT STATUS BY REGION, 2008[a]

(Per cent)

	Employees	Employers	Self-employed	Members of producers' cooperatives	Contributing family workers	Workers not classifiable by status
Developed economies	**87.0**	**2.8**	**8.7**	**0.0**	**1.3**	**0.2**
North America	92.1	0.0	7.8	0.0	0.1	0.0
Europe	83.6	4.7	9.8	0.1	1.7	0.2
Asia and Oceania	86.7	2.7	7.3	0.0	2.9	0.4
Transition economies	**83.8**	**2.2**	**12.1**	**0.2**	**1.7**	**0.0**
Europe	89.0	2.3	8.1	0.1	0.6	0.0
Asia	53.2	1.8	35.6	0.7	8.6	0.0
Developing economies	**43.1**	**3.1**	**36.8**	**0.2**	**16.1**	**0.7**
Africa	27.3	2.5	47.0	0.0	22.9	0.3
North Africa	55.8	8.7	20.3	0.0	14.6	0.6
South Africa	81.7	5.2	9.3	0.0	3.7	0.0
Other Sub-Saharan Africa	13.0	0.4	58.9	0.0	27.4	0.3
Latin America and the Caribbean	62.1	4.2	25.1	0.6	5.9	2.1
South America and Mexico	62.7	4.3	24.8	0.5	5.6	2.1
Central America	48.3	4.6	30.4	0.0	12.6	4.2
Caribbean	70.3	2.0	24.1	2.2	1.3	0.1
Asia	40.5	2.7	46.6	1.8	8.4	0.1
East Asia	38.6	2.8	52.6	2.8	3.1	0.0
South Asia	31.1	1.6	46.1	0.0	20.9	0.3
South-East Asia	37.7	2.6	39.7	0.0	20.1	0.0
West Asia	61.7	5.6	20.9	2.6	9.2	0.0
Memo item:						
Asia, excl. China	40.5	2.8	38.2	0.0	18.4	0.1

Source: UNCTAD secretariat calculations, based on ILO, *LABORSTAT* database; Ghose, 2005; and national official publications.

a Or latest year for which data were available.

Latin America and the Caribbean has the highest proportion of wage earners among developing regions owing to a relatively early process of urbanization, industrialization and development of government institutions and public services. This is particularly true for Argentina, Barbados, Brazil, Chile, Costa Rica, Cuba, Mexico, Panama, Trinidad and Tobago and Uruguay, where between 65 and 75 per cent of the employed population are wage earners. On the other hand, in Bolivia, Colombia, Paraguay, Peru and several Central American countries, self-employed and unpaid family workers remain a significant proportion of the employed population. Most are unqualified workers in agriculture – which still employs a significant percentage of the population in these countries – or in low-productivity services in urban areas.

4. Structural change and employment: recent evidence

Economic development is closely related to structural change, particularly the growing importance of non-agricultural sectors in production and employment (Kuznets, 1966). As the share of labour in agriculture falls continuously over time, that of services increases, while the share of labour in manufacturing follows an inverted U-shaped pattern: increasing in the early stages of development and decreasing in the later stages (Chenery, Robinson and Syrquin, 1986).

For many years, the development process was equated with industrialization. The importance of manufacturing for economic development relates, on the supply side, to its potential for strong productivity growth, and on the demand side, to the high income elasticity of demand for manufactures. The productivity growth potential in manufacturing activities derives from their growing tendency towards specialization, learning and agglomeration economies, as well as from static and dynamic economies of scale. As labour and capital move into these activities, average productivity in the economy climbs. This further enhances the demand for services and industrial products, which generates profitable new investment opportunities in these areas and growing demand for labour (Lluch, Powell and Williams, 1977).

While these mechanisms remain valid even today, their functioning is likely to have been affected by recent external developments, which may require a re-examining of the role of services and primary production in development. One external factor is the pattern of international demand. A sharp increase in demand for manufactured imports in the United States provided a strong stimulus to exporters of manufactures and further supported the role of industrializing Asian economies, particularly China, in global growth and trade flows. This in turn reinforced growing demand and soaring prices for primary commodities between 2002 and 2008, which temporarily reversed the usually bleak demand prospects for primary commodity production.

Another factor has to do with the substantial changes that have occurred in the services sector over the past few years. For example, the information and communications technology (ICT) revolution has increased the tradability of services, as well as the potential for productivity growth of ICT-based services. In addition, several services based on new technologies and standardization of delivery enable substantial productivity gains in some activities (Baumol, Blackman and Wolff, 1989). Thus, productivity growth in transport services, financial operations, wholesale trade and renting services has become similar to that in the most dynamic manufacturing sectors (Maroto-Sánchez and Cuadrado-Roura, 2009).[5] This has led some observers to argue that the services sector may have turned into a growth engine (Dasgupta and Singh, 2007). However it must be borne in mind that this is a particularly heterogeneous sector. Recent studies point to two waves of growth in services: the first one occurs at modest levels of per capita income and is associated with traditional

services, and a second wave starts at middle-income levels and is associated with more modern services (e.g. financial, communications, computing, legal, technical and business) (Eichengreen and Gupta, 2009).

In this context, it is worth examining which sectors have driven labour productivity growth and employment generation in developing and transition economies, and how productivity growth has interacted with employment generation. Four economic sectors are identified: agriculture (which also includes hunting, forestry and fishing), mining (which also includes utilities), manufacturing and services.[6] Two periods are distinguished: (i) from 1995 to 2002, when several emerging-market economies experienced slow growth and financial crises; and (ii) between 2002 and 2008, when economic growth accelerated in a number of emerging-market economies, in particular the large and populated "BRIC" countries (i.e. Brazil, the Russian Federation, India and China) that joined the United States as major drivers of global demand, which boosted the demand for primary commodities.

In the vast majority of developing and transition economies that have experienced rapid per capita income growth, this has been associated with above-average growth of output in manufactures and/or services (chart 4.1), particularly in China and India. In countries where aggregate growth rates have been negative or low, so also have been the growth rates of manufactured output. During the first period, in most regions per capita growth was slow, without a clear sectoral pattern: primary production performed somewhat better than manufactures in South America, sub-Saharan Africa and South-East Asia, since it was less exposed to cyclical movements, while manufactures grew faster in Central America, North Africa and South Asia (excluding India), partly due to the introduction of assembly industries. When overall growth accelerated after 2002, growth rates in the manufacturing and services sectors exceeded those in the agricultural and mining sectors – a somewhat surprising development in a context of rapidly rising primary commodity prices in global markets. Several factors could explain this result. First, primary production tends to be relatively price inelastic, at least in the short run: agriculture depends heavily on climate, and investment in extractive industries typically involves long gestation periods. Second, it could be that a significant share of windfall revenues

Chart 4.1

PER CAPITA OUTPUT BY SECTOR, SELECTED COUNTRIES AND COUNTRY GROUPS, 1995–2008

(Average annual growth rates)

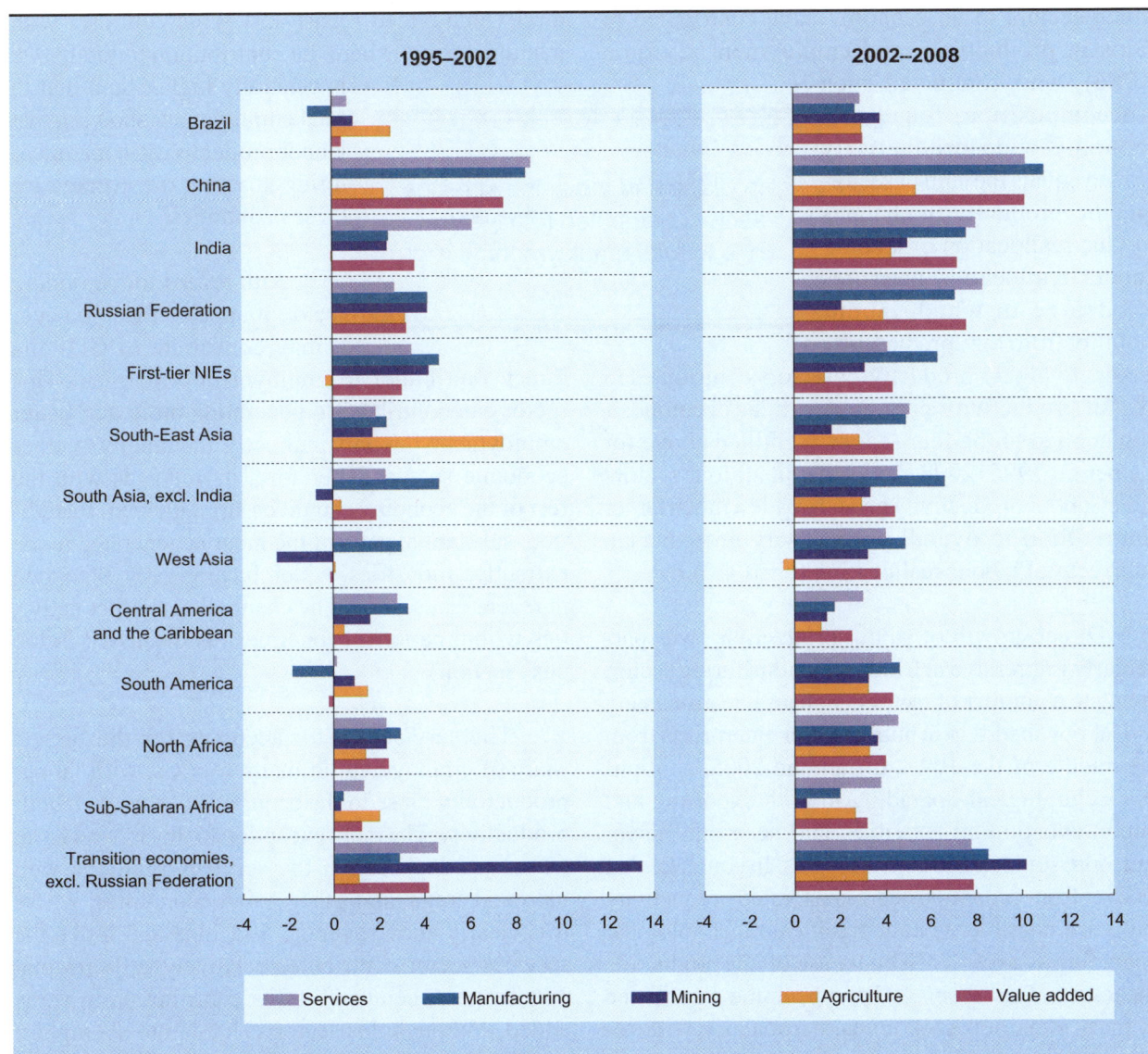

Source: UNCTAD secretariat calculations, based on *UNCTAD Handbook of Statistics* database; and UNECE, *Economic Statistics* database for the Russian Federation in 2002.

Note: South-East Asia excludes Singapore. West Asia comprises: Jordan, Kuwait, Qatar, Saudi Arabia and the United Arab Emirates. North Africa excludes Sudan. First-tier newly industrializing economies (NIEs) are: Hong Kong (China), the Republic of Korea, Singapore and Taiwan Province of China. For China, mining is included in manufacturing due to the lack of disaggregated output data for mining.

was not reinvested in the primary activities that generated them, either because foreign enterprises chose to repatriate most of their gains or because governments managed to appropriate a larger share of those revenues and used them for diversifying their economies. Supplementary income obtained from

primary activities can thus generate demand for the entire domestic economy.

It has already been noted that in the process of structural change job losses can be prevented when output growth in the higher productivity sectors is sufficiently strong to compensate for productivity growth, or if those sectors have significant linkages with other sectors for employment to be generated in the rest of the economy. With this in mind, decomposition techniques can be used to examine which sectors of an economy have contributed to gains in productivity and employment. Syrquin (1986), who conducted such a decomposition, found that economy-wide productivity growth equals the sum of sector-specific productivity changes and the reallocation of labour.[7] Labour reallocation measures the degree to which labour mobility from low-productivity sectors to higher productivity sectors contributes to overall productivity growth. A similar decomposition applied to the four sectors identified above for the period 1995–2008 shows that in all four sectors direct labour productivity growth made a much larger contribution to overall productivity growth than intersectoral labour reallocation (chart 4.2).[8]

Direct growth of labour productivity was particularly impressive in China's manufacturing sector, owing to a number of factors: industrial restructuring and labour shedding in public sector enterprises from the middle of the 1990s till around 2005, continuous technological upgrading in both exporting and import-substituting activities, and access to newer and more sophisticated technologies. In countries that recover from economic depression, rapid productivity gains are possible without significant technological upgrading as a result of a better use of idle productive capacities. This seems to have been the experience in most transition economies, particularly with respect to manufacturing and services. By contrast, productivity gains through labour reallocation among sectors have been very limited. In particular, labour reallocation in agriculture had an overall negative effect on productivity growth in India, other South Asian countries, South-East Asia, North Africa and South America (chart 4.2).[9] In these countries, agriculture appears to have become a "refuge" sector for unemployed or underemployed labour to a greater extent than services.

While the figures in charts 4.1 and 4.2 indicate percentage changes over the past 15 years, the absolute number of jobs that these four sectors have provided depends on their relative weight in

each economy. Agriculture accounts for a significant share of total employment in several regions, particularly in Asia, North Africa and the Central Asian Commonwealth of Independent States, a share that is much larger than its relative contribution to total value added (chart 4.3). This contrasts with manufacturing, where the contribution to total GDP is generally higher than that to total employment, showing that labour productivity in manufacturing is above the average for these economies.

> In China and India, the services sector contributed relatively little to total employment.

With regard to the mining sector, it appears that whatever it may contribute to GDP, its direct contribution to employment is marginal. This sector can contribute to generating more and better employment, but only indirectly and mainly in other economic sectors. Therefore, its linkages with the rest of the economy should be strengthened. In addition, substantial parts of the income generated in the extractive industries, which have greatly expanded in recent years, should be channelled to other activities within national economies (as discussed in the next section).

The services sector accounts for the largest share of employment in many regions, with labour productivity close to the economies' average labour productivity. The main exception to this is West Asia, where productivity in the services sector is well below average, and other Asian economies, where it is clearly above average. In China and India, the services sector contributed relatively little to total employment, compared to its contribution to value added. Although that sector's share in total employment has increased since the late 1970s (Bosworth and Collins, 2008: table 4), in international comparisons it has remained unusually small.[10] In India, services are clearly the most dynamic sector in output terms, but their potential to offer adequately productive and remunerative employment is not clear: the number of jobs in modern services, such as communication and business services, doubled between the mid-1990s and the mid-2000s, but they still only account for around 5 per cent of total services employment and less than 1 per cent of total employment (Chandrasekhar and Ghosh, 2010; Nayyar, 2009). This pattern is probably mainly due to the fact that both China and India (and many other Asian and African countries) remain largely rural societies, and modern

Chart 4.2

AVERAGE SECTORAL CONTRIBUTIONS TO ECONOMY-WIDE LABOUR PRODUCTIVITY GAINS, SELECTED COUNTRIES AND COUNTRY GROUPS, 1995–2008

(Per cent)

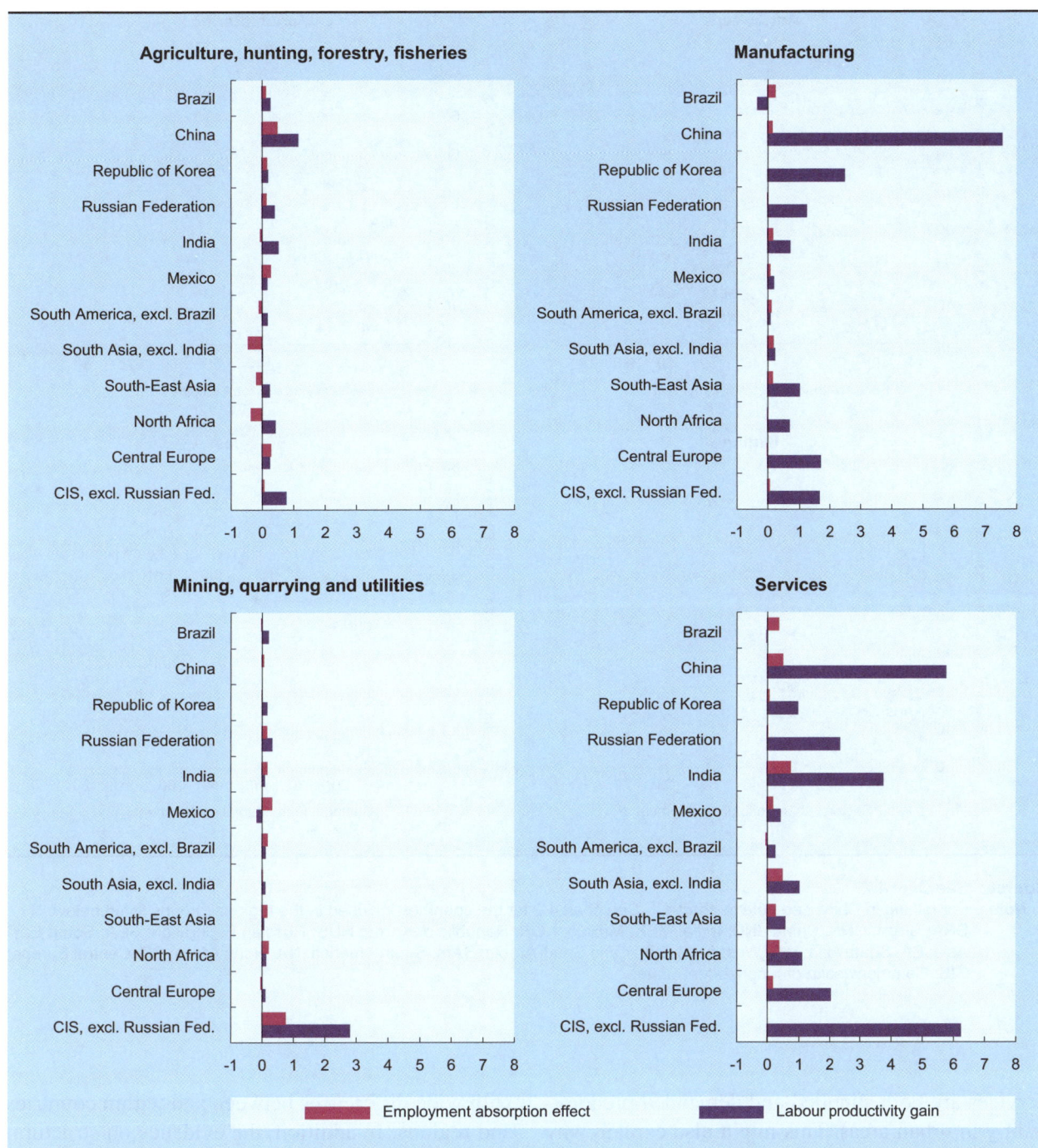

Source: UNCTAD secretariat calculations and estimates, based on United Nations, *National Accounts* database; and ILO, *Employment* database.

Note: South America refers to: Argentina, the Bolivarian Republic of Venezuela, Chile, Colombia, Ecuador and Peru. South Asia refers to: Pakistan and Sri Lanka. South-East Asia refers to: Indonesia, Malaysia, the Philippines and Thailand. North Africa refers to: Egypt and Morocco. Central Europe refers to: Czech Republic, Hungary and Poland. CIS refers to: Azerbaijan, Georgia, Kazakhstan and Kyrgyzstan.
Time periods vary: 1995–2007: China, Republic of Korea, South Asia and North Africa. 1995–2006: India. 1998–2007: CIS. For China, labour productivity gain in mining is included in manufacturing due to the lack of disaggregated output data for mining.

Chart 4.3

AVERAGE SECTORAL SHARES IN TOTAL VALUE ADDED AND EMPLOYMENT, SELECTED COUNTRIES AND COUNTRY GROUPS, 1995–2008

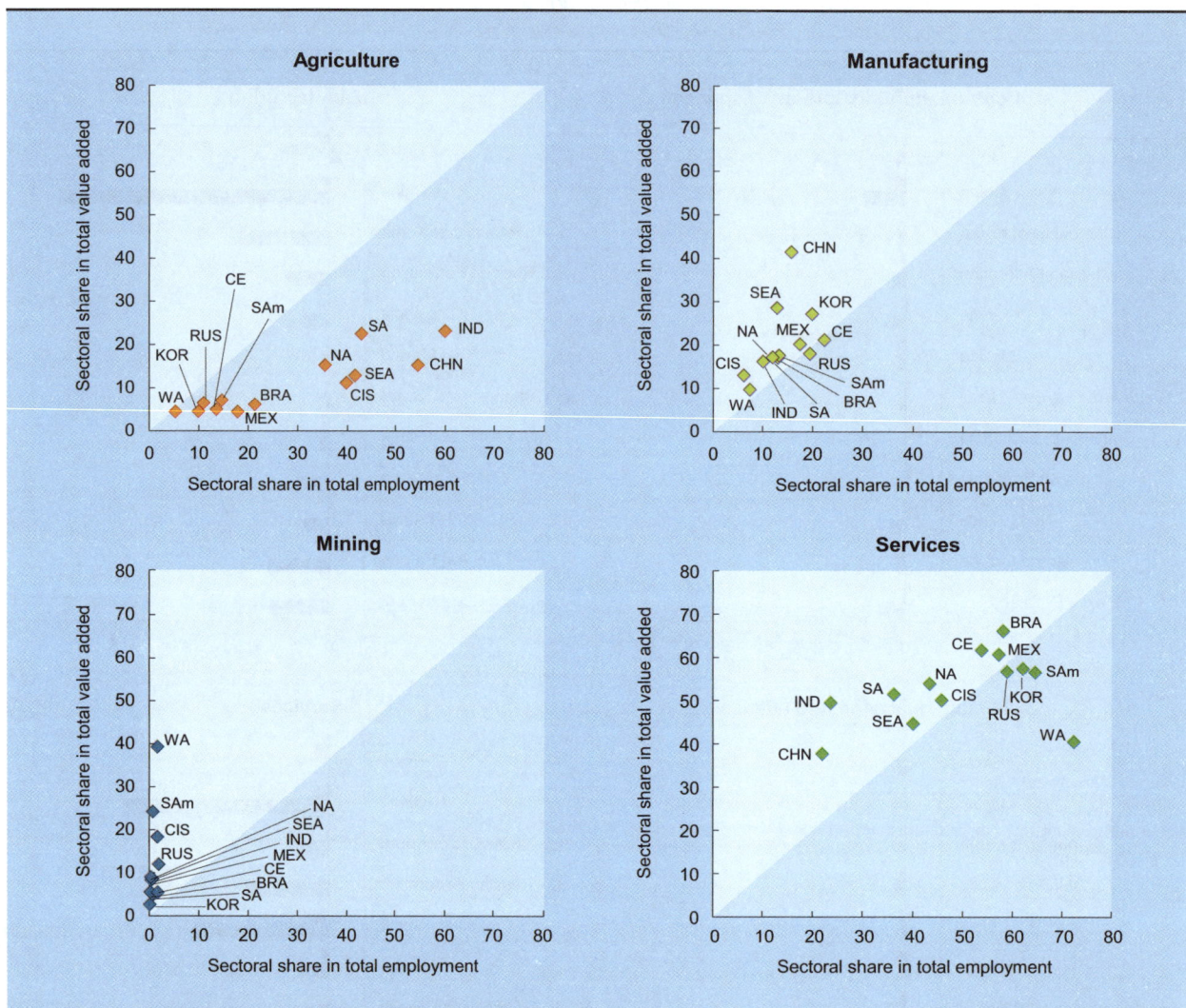

Source: See chart 4.2.

Note: For mining in China see note to chart 4.1. See chart 4.2 for the countries included in the regional groups listed below. BRA: Brazil; CHN: China; IND: India; MEX: Mexico; KOR: Republic of Korea; RUS: Russian Federation; SEA: South-East Asia; SA: South Asia; WA (West Asia): Qatar and Saudi Arabia; SAm: South America; NA: North Africa; CE: Central Europe; CIS: Commonwealth of Independent States.

services are both supplied and demanded predominantly in urban areas. This might also explain why the share of agricultural employment remains very high, though its productivity is very low compared to other sectors, in particular services in India and manufacturing in China.

Structural heterogeneity of employment thus remains a central feature of developing countries,

with wide differences between and within countries and regions. In addition, the evidence on structural change shows that even if the most dynamic sectors are manufacturing and services, as expected by development theory, the generation of good quality employment in these sectors has generally been insufficient to absorb the available labour force. Moreover, the productivity gains through labour reallocation to relatively high-productivity sectors have been minor.

Therefore, the strategy of improving labour conditions and raising the aggregate productivity of labour should not only concentrate on the modern sectors. In addition to increasing formal employment in these sectors, improving the productivity of informal work should also be a central concern of public policy (Pollin, Heintz and Mwangi, 2008). And those activities that presently employ much of the low-productivity labour force deserve special attention.

Thus investment in agriculture is essential. On the one hand, growth in agricultural productivity is indispensable for improving the living standards of a large segment of the population and for increasing domestic food production. On the other hand, efforts should be made to improve productivity in agriculture in such a way that it does not lead to accelerated migration to urban areas, where it is already difficult to absorb the existing flow of migrants. Therefore it is necessary to consider strategies for increasing productivity per hectare and not only per worker, such as through irrigation projects, better transport infrastructure, more rational use of fertilizers, better seeds and crop rotation, and access to credit at reasonable rates (Kalecki, 1976; Nkurunziza, 2007). Even if in the long run agricultural employment is projected to shrink, development policies aimed at improving production capacity and employment cannot afford to overlook agriculture and rural areas. Similarly, there needs to be a greater focus on improving technology and ensuring access to credit for small producers in manufacturing and services, many of whom are denied such access at present because of their informal status.

5. The extractive industries: employment impact and economic linkages

Many developing economies are highly dependent on the extractive industries, from which they derive a substantial share of their foreign exchange earnings and government revenues. Thus the sharp increases in prices of oil and mineral and metal products between 2003 and 2008 enabled these countries to achieve higher rates of economic growth. But since the extractive industries have very low employment elasticities (UNECA, 2010), the boom in commodity prices has not fully translated into generally higher standards of living for the population.

With technological advances and productivity increases there has been a steady decline in the number of people employed in mining in the 1990s, a decline exacerbated by the processes of privatization and restructuring of the sector through mergers and acquisitions (ILO, 2002). In most producing countries, direct employment in the extractive industries accounts for no more than 1 or 2 per cent of total employment.[11] The International Labour Organization (ILO) estimates that the mining sector accounts for about 0.5 per cent of the world's workforce.[12] The small labour generation by these industries is in stark contrast to their important contribution to export earnings, government revenues and GDP in many developing countries. Most of the formal employment data available refer to employment by large-scale mining companies, which dominate production. However, in a number of the poorest producing countries, small-scale artisanal mining can still be an important source of employment, although difficult to quantify because it mainly takes the form of informal employment.[13]

It is likely that the activities in the extractive industries lead to important increases in employment at the initial stages of projects, mainly at the time of construction and in relation to the supporting infrastructure, for instance to transport the oil and mineral products or to provide power supply. While this infrastructure is useful, it is mostly oriented to the export sector and not to the physical integration of different regions within the countries. Furthermore, once the mines or the oil projects become operational, the number of employees is considerably reduced. For instance, in the United Republic of Tanzania it is estimated that employment in construction related to the extractive industries peaked at 6,600 workers in 2009, but fell to about 3,100 in 2010, and total direct employment peaked at 12,000 workers, stabilizing later to 7,000–8,000 workers (ICMM, 2009). In the Chad-Cameroon oil pipeline project, employment in Chad amounted to over 7,600 workers in 2002, but by the end of 2009 it had fallen to 5,747 Chadian workers (Leibold, 2010; Esso, 2010). In addition, most of the local workers tend to be hired to perform the less sophisticated activities, which require a lower skill base, while it is normally expatriate employees who perform the more specialized managerial tasks and those requiring higher skills.[14]

The extractive industries can also generate indirect employment stemming from increased consumer demand by the directly employed workers who may be earning wages that are higher than average, and also from the provision of goods and services to these companies by local businesses. According to some estimates, employment multipliers in African economies may be three or more indirect jobs for every directly created job in the mining sector (ICMM, 2009). In Peru, it is estimated that each direct employment generates four indirect jobs (Instituto de Ingenieros de Minas de Perú, 2010).[15] However, again, as many of the services needed are highly specialized and have a strong technological content, they are usually provided by foreign firms.

In analysing the employment effects of the mining sector it is also important to look at what happened during the privatization phase in the 1990s. While the positive direct employment effects of large-scale mining are negligible, in some countries such as Zambia, privatization led to a steep decline in employment, and to the casualization of labour in this sector. Employment in the mining sector increased in the 2000s, but many workers shifted to service providers and were subcontracted under worse labour conditions (Lungu, 2008; Fraser and Lungu, 2007; Simutanyi, 2008). Furthermore, in the United Republic of Tanzania, for example, the introduction of large-scale mining had a strong social impact by forcing many small-scale miners out of business and into unemployment. It is estimated that the sector employed between 500,000 and 1.5 million people in the late 1990s, mainly small-scale miners, and by 2006 there were only around 170,000 small-scale miners in that country (Curtis and Lissu, 2008).

Regarding the economic linkages of the extractive industries with the rest of the economy,

> The extractive industries offer limited opportunities for employment and for direct linkages with the rest of the economy.

transnational corporations (TNCs) often source their inputs and equipment from foreign suppliers, particularly for products and services with a high technological content. This is because many producing countries often lack the industrial capabilities to supply these goods. The opportunities for backward linkages are therefore limited, and are mainly concentrated in non-specialized goods and services, such as housing, catering, cleaning and retailing. Although this may enable some learning spillovers, their effect remains marginal. In most producing developing countries, there are also few, if any, forward linkages related to adding value to the metals and oil products, such as refining. For instance, many African countries export crude oil, but have to import the refined petroleum.[16]

Therefore, since the extractive industries offer limited opportunities for employment and for backward and forward linkages, they often tend to create enclave situations, with hardly any connections with the rest of the economy. Consequently the only means of establishing linkages between these industries and other economic activities, and deriving benefits from these industries for the society at large, is through economic policies, particularly through the generation and efficient use of government revenues. While proactive policies may encourage some transformation of raw materials, and regulations may require the use of more domestic inputs with higher local content requirements, as well as the hiring of a specified proportion of local nationals, this is generally insufficient. The main domestic impact of production in the extractive industries will depend on the capacity of the State to appropriate a significant share of the natural rent and use it for development financing (an issue examined further in chapter V).[17]

C. Impact of globalization and reforms on employment in developing countries

This section examines the impact of globalization and policy reforms on employment in developing countries in the 1980s and 1990s. Reforms involved a reorientation of macroeconomic policies, with priority given to combating inflation and attracting foreign capital inflows, as well as structural adjustment programmes that aimed at greater openness to trade and capital flows, market liberalization (including of financial and labour markets) and a smaller economic role for governments.

According to the new policy orientation, the hierarchy of sectors that were supposed to lead development was altered: industry, to which the lead role was formerly assigned, was replaced by whichever sector was seen as reflecting a country's comparative advantage. Previous industrial policies were sometimes blamed for fostering an inefficient manufacturing sector and encouraging the use of capital-intensive technologies that were considered partially responsible for employment problems. In this view, opening up and liberalization would therefore permit a reallocation of productive resources from protected, inefficient sectors to export-oriented competitive sectors that were supposedly more labour-intensive.

The proponents of liberalizing reforms acknowledged that the reallocation of resources would necessarily involve costs, in particular in the form of temporary unemployment, since capital and labour "released" from the firms and sectors affected by the new policies could not be re-employed immediately in the firms and activities that were supposed to lead development. However, they believed such costs would be moderate and short-lived (World Bank,

1987: 107). Therefore one critical aspect of the case for reform was the relative importance of employment created in sectors that were the "winners" when compared with the jobs lost in sectors that were "losers", not only in quantitative terms, but also when assessed in terms of the kinds of jobs won and lost and the timing of employment destruction and creation. If this process actually destroyed formal employment (typically in manufacturing and the public sectors) and the expected employment creation in the internationally competitive sectors did not rapidly create at least an equivalent amount of jobs, the "transition period" involving higher unemployment may be longer than expected and exert downward pressure on domestic wages and domestic demand. Unless foreign demand was dynamic enough to offset this negative impact, global growth would be affected in the medium term, together with job creation.

In addition, financial liberalization gave rise to recurrent economic crises, which in turn altered growth trajectories in ways that were inimical to employment generation. Typically, recessionary episodes with high unemployment weakened the bargaining power of organized workers, lowered their share in income distribution and favoured reforms that provided for greater labour flexibility. Subsequent recoveries did not in general restore the pre-crisis distribution of income and employment conditions (ILO, 2008b: 15). Rather, the availability of a large unemployed or underemployed workforce willing to work without social security or labour protection increased de facto labour flexibility, which made it easier to establish *de jure* labour flexibility in the formal sector.

It has been pointed out that globalization also contributed to this shift in economic power (Jomo, and Baudot, 2007; Ocampo and Jomo, 2007). One of the reasons was that the increased international mobility of goods and factors – the core of the whole process – was very uneven: capital appears to have been much more mobile than labour, which increased the former's bargaining power. This asymmetry was no doubt partly due to technical factors (no person can move easier, faster and farther than a wire transfer), but it also partly resulted from differences in regulations: capital controls have been greatly relaxed over the past few decades, while the movement of workers has remained tightly controlled, especially in developed countries. In these countries the threat of delocalization became a powerful argument for wage moderation (Scarpetta, 2009). The mobility of capital and immobility of labour also tended to generate competition among developing countries for foreign direct investment (FDI), causing them to engage in a race to the bottom through concessions made to TNCs in terms of tax rebates, subsidies and relaxation of labour regulations (Cornia, 2005). To what extent all these factors actually affected employment and income distribution in the long run is discussed in more detail below.

1. Latin America: stagnation and deterioration of labour markets in the 1980s and 1990s

Although the policy shift towards liberalization and global integration was widespread, its timing and intensity were quite diverse. The first developing region to embrace the new policy orientation was Latin America and the Caribbean, its three Southern Cone countries (Argentina, Chile and Uruguay) having adopted radical liberal reforms in the mid-1970s. After the debt crisis of the 1980s and the subsequent policy adjustments required to access international liquidity, other Latin American countries followed their example in the early 1990s (Sáinz and Calcagno, 1992).

However, between 1980 and 2002, these policies failed to deliver a combined growth of GDP, employment and productivity, as the policy regimes between 1950 and 1980 had been able to do. The average annual rate of GDP growth slowed down to 2.4 per cent between 1980 and 2002 from 5.4 per cent between 1950 and 1980, unemployment increased and average annual labour productivity declined by 0.5 per cent in the later period, which contrasts with the robust annual increase of 2.5 per cent recorded in the earlier period (Palma, 2010). Thus the main objectives of structural reforms were not met. It was only after 2003 that a virtuous cycle of increasing GDP, employment and productivity was achieved, although progress in the latter has remained modest (chart 4.4). By that time several countries had departed from a neoliberal policy orientation.

In the past three decades, labour markets in Latin America have gone through four distinct phases, associated with changing macroeconomic frameworks and policy stances: a long recession in the 1980s, followed by a recovery during the period 1990–1997; then a new recession between mid-1998 and 2002, and rapid economic growth since 2003. So far, the 2008-2009 crisis seems to be more of a pause than a breaking point in this last period.

Of course, not all the countries underwent this sequence of change with the same intensity and at the same time, but overall the region experienced a highly synchronized succession of economic ups and downs, owing to common external shocks and similar domestic policies. For example, most countries devalued and adjusted their domestic spending during the 1980s, in response to the debt crisis and the conditionality attached to assistance by international financial institutions. During the 1990s, almost all the countries embarked on (or deepened) liberal structural reforms and cut inflation through currency appreciations. This was facilitated by a renewed access to capital inflows, which eased import restrictions and spurred growth. However, they also experienced an increase in domestic and foreign indebtedness, deterioration in their competitiveness and large trade deficits, making the continuation of growth dependent on a permanent flow of foreign capital (ILPES, 1998: 13–15). The 1997-1998 financial crises dried up capital inflows and affected almost the whole region. In several countries, restrictive monetary and fiscal policies accentuated the recession. In addition, many primary exporters were affected by deteriorating terms of trade. It was only after 2003 that the region was able to return to rapid GDP growth as a result of better international conditions and a significant reorientation of economic policies, which restored competitiveness and

Chart 4.4

EMPLOYMENT, UNEMPLOYMENT, GDP AND LABOUR PRODUCTIVITY, SELECTED REGIONS, 1980–2009

(Index numbers, 2000 = 100, and per cent)

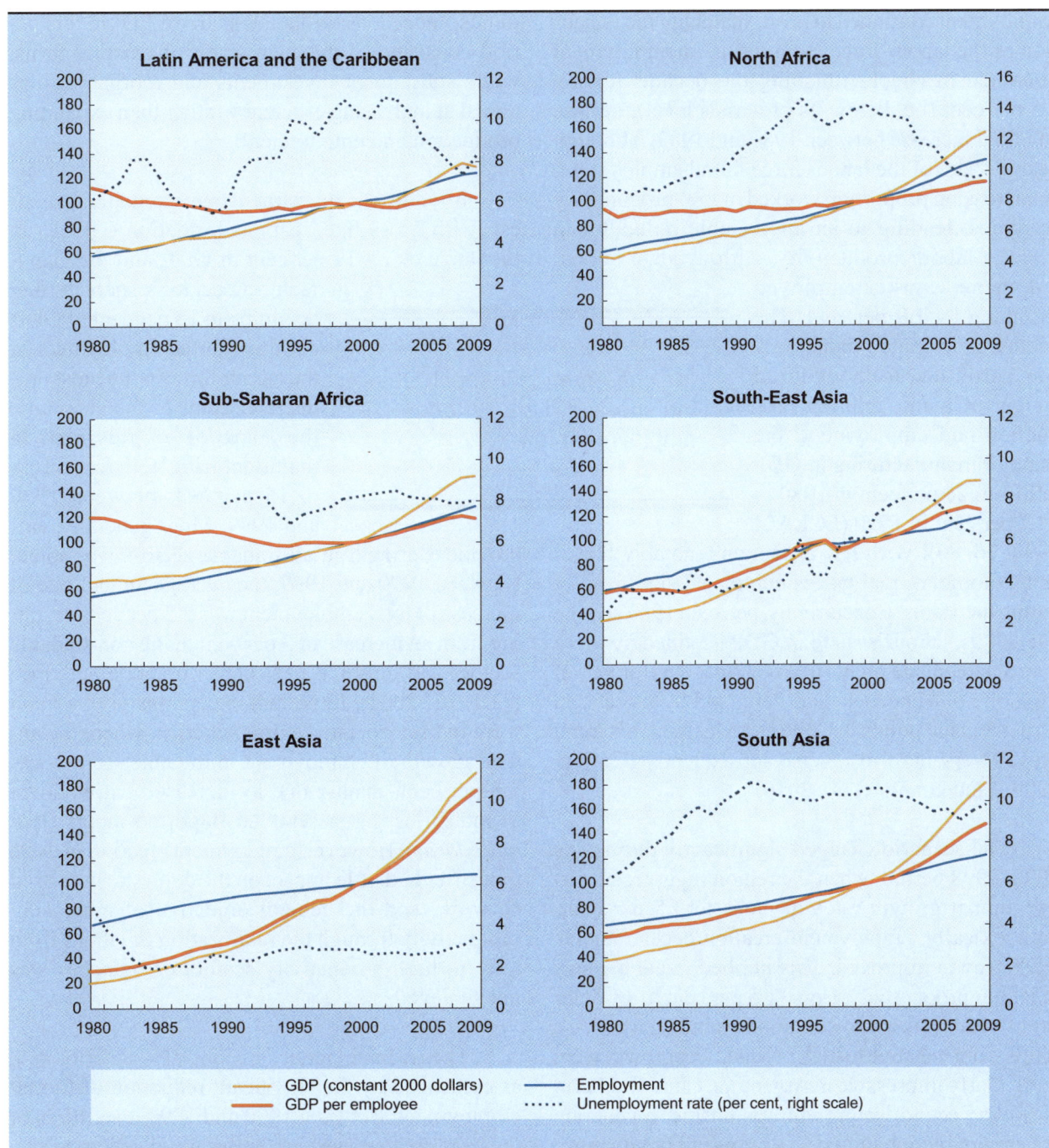

Latin America and the Caribbean

North Africa

Sub-Saharan Africa

South-East Asia

East Asia

South Asia

— GDP (constant 2000 dollars) — Employment
— GDP per employee ······· Unemployment rate (per cent, right scale)

Source: UNCTAD secretariat calculations, based on table 1.1; ILO, *LABORSTAT* and *Key Indicators of the Labour Market* (*KILM*) databases; OECD, *Stat Extracts* database; ECLAC, *CEPALSTAT* database; Economist Intelligence Unit, *EIU CountryData* database; UN/DESA, *World Population Prospects. The 2008 Revision*; and national sources.

Note: Latin America and the Caribbean comprises: Argentina, the Bolivarian Republic of Venezuela, Bolivia, Brazil, Chile, Colombia, Costa Rica, Ecuador, El Salvador, Guatemala, Honduras, Jamaica, Mexico, Nicaragua, Panama, Paraguay, Peru, Trinidad and Tobago, and Uruguay. North Africa comprises: Algeria, Egypt, the Libyan Arab Jamahiriya, Morocco, Sudan and Tunisia. South-East Asia comprises: Indonesia, Malaysia, the Philippines, Singapore and Thailand. East Asia comprises: China, Hong Kong (China), the Republic of Korea and Taiwan Province of China. South Asia comprises Bangladesh, India, Islamic Republic of Iran, Pakistan and Sri Lanka.

enlarged the space for expansionary public policies. All these shocks and changing policies had a strong impact on the region's labour markets.

During the 1980s, GDP grew at a meagre 1.5 per cent a year (implying a fall in per capita GDP), but employment continued to grow, matching the expansion of the labour force. As a result, unemployment remained in check, finishing the decade at only 5.5 per cent (i.e. below its pre-crisis level), despite an initial increase between 1980 and 1983. Although a large share of the labour force found employment, an increasing proportion worked in low-productivity activities, leading to an appreciable reduction in average labour productivity, with average annual output per worker employed shrinking by 1.9 per cent. The decline in average productivity was partly due to the reduced weight of manufacturing production and employment: the share of manufacturing in GDP fell from 26 per cent in 1980 to 23.7 per cent in 1990 (ECLAC, 1996: 76–80). With few exceptions (notably Brazil and Colombia), real wages contracted significantly during the 1980s. Concurrently, between 1980 and the late 1980s, labour's share in GDP declined by more than 5 percentage points in Argentina, the Bolivarian Republic of Venezuela and Peru, and by more than 10 percentage points in Chile and Mexico. This trend proved very hard to reverse subsequently (Cornia, 2009; Lindenboim et al., 2010).

The scenario changed significantly during the 1990–1998 period, when the region registered average annual growth rates of close to 3.5 per cent. Paradoxically, employment creation decelerated as GDP growth improved. This implied sizeable gains in labour productivity, from -1.5 per cent to +1.5 per cent a year for the whole region (excluding Mexico). Shifts from negative to high productivity growth were particularly impressive in Argentina, Chile and Peru. However, economic growth was unable to generate the employment required – in terms of both quantity and quality – to sustain durable and comprehensive productivity gains and expanding domestic demand. Productivity gains only partially responded to new investment and technology upgrading. To a large extent, those gains were a one-off result of the use of idle productive capacity and rationalization, which in many cases led to labour retrenchments. In order

to gain efficiency and adapt to international competition, many firms in tradable sectors replaced labour by capital and domestic inputs by imported inputs, taking advantage of lower tariffs and appreciating domestic currencies. The increasing penetration of TNCs in services and manufacturing reinforced these trends. Indeed, a substantial share of FDI in this period consisted of the acquisition of existing firms, while subsequent investments and reorganizations aimed at increasing efficiency rather than expanding production and employment.

In addition, investment rates remained modest, with gross fixed capital formation (GFCF) in the range of 17–19 per cent of GDP, and the manufacturing sector's share further declining to 18 per cent of GDP. All this limited employment of the labour force in the most productive sector of the economy: the share of employment in manufacturing fell from 16.8 to 15 per cent between 1990 and 1999. More generally, employment growth in all tradable sectors was weak. Between 1990 and 1999, the average annual rate of increase of total employment was 2.2 per cent, resulting from an increase of 3 per cent in the non-tradable sectors and only 0.8 per cent in tradable activities (ECLAC, 2004). Important exceptions to this trend were in Mexico and Central America, where the annual growth of employment in tradable sectors was 1.8 per cent, mainly due to increased employment in industries that assembled imported inputs (*maquiladoras*). However, employment creation in these industries had little impact on the domestic industrial network, and the general objective of increasing productivity through the reallocation of labour from low- to high-productivity sectors or branches was not achieved.[18]

The average quality of jobs also deteriorated, as evidenced by the significant reduction of formal employment. Between 1990 and 1999, two thirds of the jobs created were in the informal sector, which increased its share in total urban employment from 41 per cent to 46.3 per cent (table 4.8). At the same time, the share of the public sector in total urban employment declined from 16 per cent to 12.9 per cent, and that of wage earners in the formal private sector fell from 40.6 per cent to 36.9 per cent. In the informal sector, the share of unqualified self-employed

> In Latin America in the 1990s the share of manufacturing employment fell.

Table 4.8

EMPLOYMENT AND INCOME INDICATORS, SELECTED COUNTRIES IN LATIN AMERICA, 1980–2008

(Per cent, unless otherwise indicated)

	Population employed in low-productivity activities (Percentage share in urban employment)				Unemployment rate					Employment-density of households (Number of occupied in number of household members)				Average income of occupied wage earners in the private sector, in urban areas (In number of poverty lines)				Income distribution (Ratio D10 / D1 to D4)				
	1990	1998	2002	2008	1980	1990	1998	2002	2008	1990	1999	2002	2008	1990	1998	2002	2008	1980	1990	1998	2002	2008
Argentina	44.4	41.3	42.4	41.0	3.7	10.6	14.8	21.8	7.7	40.0	42.0	37.0	45.0	4.7	5.2	3.1	4.4	9.9	13.5	16.4	20.0	13.8
Bolivia	58.5	65.6	66.7	62.5	5.9	7.3	6.1	8.7	6.7	..	..	51.0	..	3.5	3.7	3.6	3.4	..	17.1	26.7	30.3	22.2
Brazil	40.7	47.4	46.2	42.0	6.3	4.3	7.6	11.7	7.9	45.0	46.0	48.0	52.0	3.7	3.4	3.2	3.8	25.3	31.2	31.9	32.2	23.8
Chile	38.9	34.3	31.7	30.7	11.7	9.2	6.4	9.8	7.8	36.0	39.0	41.0	43.0	3.7	5.4	5.2	5.1	..	18.2	19.1	18.8	15.9
Colombia	32.9	40.9	45.1	42.6	10.0	10.5	15.3	18.1	11.5	41.0	41.0	..	45.0	2.7	3.3	3.2	3.4	..	26.8	22.3	24.2	25.2
Costa Rica	36.9	39.5	40.3	37.1	6.0	5.4	5.4	6.8	4.8	38.0	41.0	..	..	4.5	5.0	6.2	5.3	..	10.1	12.6	13.7	12.4
Ecuador	54.5	54.0	56.4	57.4	5.7	7.0	11.5	9.2	6.9	41.0	43.0	46.0	48.0	2.8	2.7	3.1	3.2	..	11.4	17.2	15.1	14.0
Mexico	40.7	44.3	47.1	43.7	4.5	2.7	4.7	3.9	4.9	37.0	44.0	45.0	46.0	3.3	2.9	3.1	3.0	10.6	17.2	18.4	15.1	16.1
Peru	..	61.0	63.8	59.3	7.1	8.3	8.5	9.4	8.4	..	..	50.0	55.0	..	3.6	3.0	3.6	..	..	17.9	15.6	12.8
Uruguay	36.8	42.4	45.7	42.8	7.4	8.5	10.1	17.0	7.9	40.0	41.0	39.0	48.0	3.6	4.7	3.9	3.8	10.7	9.4	8.8	..	9.0
Venezuela, Bolivarian Republic of	39.1	48.1	56.5	49.8	6.0	10.4	11.3	15.8	7.4	36.0	41.0	43.0	47.0	3.6	2.8	2.4	3.5	7.8	12.1	15.0	14.5	8.4
Latin America	41.0	46.3	48.4	45.4	6.2	5.8	10.3	11.1	7.4	39.0	42.0	44.0	48.0	3.6	3.9	3.6	3.9	..	16.7	18.8	20.0	15.8

Source: UNCTAD secretariat calculations based on ECLAC, *Social Panorama* statistical database; and national households surveys.
Note: When data were missing for a specific year, they were replaced by the closest year for which data were available (no more than two years). Income distribution refers to the average of per capita household income of the richest decile (D10), divided by the average of per capita household income of the four poorest deciles (D1 to D4).

workers (mainly in trade and services) in total urban employment increased from 22.3 per cent to 25.8 per cent (ECLAC, 2004; Sáinz, 2007). As a result, productivity gains were concentrated in too few firms or sectors, which meant that not enough employment could be generated for their dynamism to have an impact on the entire economy. Some economic agents, including a number of well-qualified employees, gained higher incomes and benefits, but an increasing share of the labour force had to work in low-productivity, informal activities or remained unemployed. Indeed, during these years of economic growth, open unemployment in the region practically doubled, to almost 10 per cent of the labour force.[19]

Employment problems worsened between mid-1998 and 2002, when most countries in the region entered a new recessionary phase. During these years investment rates dropped to 16 per cent of GDP – a historic low. Employment creation slowed down even further, productivity growth turned negative once more and unemployment averaged more than 11 per cent. Real remuneration for employed wage workers stagnated or declined in most countries, and the quality of employment further deteriorated, with informal employment close to 50 per cent (table 4.8). Thus, after more than two decades of liberalization there were greater disparities in productive and social structures in a region that was already viewed as having the largest inequalities in the world, and little if any progress in achieving sustained capital accumulation and growth or an improved employment situation.

> The employment situation improved substantially after 2003.

A major problem in the 1980s and 1990s were the weak linkages between the export sector and the rest of the economy, due to the lack of industrial policies, inappropriate macroeconomic policies and income concentration. As a result, domestic markets and domestic productive capacities were undermined. Two factors mitigated the social cost of these outcomes. One was the progressive increase in the number of employed relative to the size of households ("employment density") which had become smaller as a result of demographic trends. Higher employment density was also a response to declining real revenues. In most countries, instead of being discouraged by the labour market conditions, more members of poorer households, including women,

began to participate in low-productivity activities (ECLAC, 2004: 47–48). Where the new entrants to the labour market were young and had been obliged to abandon their education, this was a less positive development. Another factor that contributed to alleviating the social costs was the progressive increase in social spending by governments since the early 1990s, both as a percentage of GDP and in constant value per capita. This may have helped prevent further increases in the poverty level, though by 2002 this level was still higher than that in 1980, at 44 per cent of the total population compared with 40.5 per cent respectively.

The employment situation improved substantially after 2003 as a result of renewed economic growth and a new policy orientation. Several governments abandoned the "trickle-down" approach and directly addressed the problems of unemployment, informalization of employment, falling wages of unskilled workers and other social problems such as reduced social security coverage and the weakening of institutions for wage negotiation and dispute settlement (Cornia, 2009). They adopted specific measures for the labour market, including sizeable increases in minimum wages, reactivation of collective bargaining bodies and the launching of public works and programmes for the unemployed. Following a rise in fiscal revenues, governments were able to increase their social spending significantly, and many countries improved public salaries. Fiscal revenues rose rapidly not only because higher incomes and imports augmented the tax base, but also because of new sources of revenue. In particular, several countries were able to appropriate part of the very high rents from the export of oil and natural gas, mining products and/or agricultural commodities, either through export duties or new taxes, or by increasing public sector participation in the extractive industries. A number of countries also began to tax financial transactions, clamped down on tax evasion and improved the collection of direct taxes, and made the tax system less regressive. As a result, the share of fiscal revenues in GDP increased in almost all the countries, particularly in Argentina, Bolivia, Brazil and Colombia (by between 8 and 10 percentage points of GDP) and the Bolivarian Republic of Venezuela (by 6 points). This enabled the reduction of budget deficits (or even a switch to fiscal surplus) and of the public debt as a percentage of GDP, while increasing public spending.

Most governments also adopted a more accommodative monetary policy and a flexible approach to exchange rates: instead of the "corner solutions" of the previous years (i.e. free floating or totally fixed exchange rate regimes), they opted for a managed floating regime. In a context of trade surpluses and renewed capital inflows, central banks had to intervene to prevent (or set limits to) currency appreciation, which also led to the accumulation of international reserves. However, in some cases, their interventions were not strong or systematic enough to prevent some revaluation of real exchange rates. In the countries where more competitive exchange rates could be sustained, production in a number of labour-intensive tradable sectors increased (mainly in manufacturing). In addition, a number of production linkages were re-established within those countries (i.e. by substituting imported inputs with domestically produced ones), which increased employment in some of the non-exporting sectors. Even if competitive exchange rates may have only a moderate effect in boosting exports, especially in countries that are specialized in primary commodities, they amplify the positive effects of those exports on the rest of the economy. One outstanding example is that of Argentina, which undertook a massive devaluation in 2002: even though exports did not immediately respond to new relative prices, production and employment surged in all the economic sectors, most notably in manufacturing, which increased its share in total employment for the first time in 25 years. In just five years, open unemployment dropped from 22 per cent to 8 per cent. Similarly in Chile in the late 1980s and early 1990s, after a huge devaluation, jobs were not created by export-oriented activities per se – indeed, new employment in activities such as mining, fishing, and fruit production was negligible – but as a result of the domestic spending related to them. Export-related investment (mainly in construction) and fiscal expenditure (funded by the revenues obtained through the State-owned copper company) strongly increased domestic demand primarily for domestically produced goods and services, owing to the competitive exchange rate. This in turn had a strong multiplier effect on employment: in five years, one

million new jobs were created, causing employment to jump from 3.9 to 4.9 million people, essentially in domestic-oriented activities such as commerce, manufacturing and construction (ECLAC, 1994).

The employment intensity of economic growth also rose. Between 2002 and 2008, unemployment in Latin America and the Caribbean fell by almost 4 percentage points, to reach its lowest levels since the early 1990s. With a few exceptions, the share of formal employment increased vis-à-vis informal and low-productivity jobs. The participation of wage-earners rose while that of non-qualified self-employed workers fell. Household incomes also grew along with employment density, real remuneration and better quality of employment. In addition, several governments improved social security coverage, partly by expanding the formal sector and partly by providing basic benefits to previously excluded segments of the population (i.e. unemployed, workers in the informal sector and their families). These included non-contributory minimum pensions and conditional transfer programmes in which monetary subsidies were given to low-income households provided their children attended school and used the public health services. All these factors helped to reverse the trend of income inequality which had been widening continuously since the 1980s. Income inequality, measured as the ratio between the per capita average income of the top 10 per cent of rich households and the bottom 40 per cent of poor households, has narrowed the most in Argentina, the Bolivarian Republic of Venezuela, Bolivia and Brazil since 2003 (table 4.8). The combination of a higher average income and its better distribution brought about a significant reduction in poverty ratios, which fell from 44 per cent of the population in 2002 to 33 per cent in 2008. The concomitant rebound of domestic markets provided the impetus for continued growth and employment creation. Together with a strong recovery of fixed investment (from 16.5 per cent of GDP in 2002-2003 to 21.9 per cent in 2008), this may help to restore a virtuous circle of employment expansion, growth and productivity increase.

The recent global economic and financial crisis may test the durability of these advances. Rather than resorting to procyclical adjustments, most

> The share of wage earners in total employment rose while that of non-qualified self-employed workers fell.

countries have been supporting domestic demand, including through monetary transfers to vulnerable populations. In some cases, they have introduced specific programmes for safeguarding employment. For instance some governments have committed to assuming part of the labour costs for a period of time, if firms in difficulty refrain from laying off workers. The combination of countercyclical macroeconomic policies and specific pro-employment measures may not have been able to prevent a rise in unemployment, but they have certainly mitigated it, as the rate only increased from 7.4 per cent in 2008 to 8.3 in 2009. The future evolution of employment conditions and income distribution – which continues to be highly inequitable – will be critical for the success of the policy reorientation towards a development strategy that places a greater emphasis on domestic markets, and, within these markets, on workers' demand.

2. Africa: persistence of a large informal sector despite structural adjustment policies

Output growth in Africa in the past few decades has been low and unstable, partly as a result of wars and civil strife, but also because of fluctuations in international prices of primary commodities, which remain the region's most important exports. In addition, the overall policy orientation has played a major role. During the 1960s and 1970s, when African economies pursued mainly import-substituting policies, economic activity improved in North Africa, but it was weak in sub-Saharan Africa. Even so, the average regional performance was considerably better than in subsequent years when structural adjustment programmes associated with the Washington Consensus (described earlier in this chapter) were undertaken in the 1980s which continued in the early 2000s. The 1980s to the end of the 1990s was a period of stagnation and decline for most of the countries of the region. In North Africa, GDP growth slowed down and labour productivity failed to grow for 20 years, while the growth rate of employment was not rapid enough to absorb the fast expanding labour force. As a result, unemployment surged to two-digit levels in the 1990s. In sub-Saharan

Africa, per capita GDP actually fell during the 1980s and 1990s, which, for the majority of the countries, implied falling productivity, except in mining. In the subregion as a whole, labour productivity dropped by 20 per cent (chart 4.4), but there was little change in open unemployment, which indicates that recession in these countries affected the quality and productivity of employment but not its volume. For the subregion as a whole, excluding South Africa, these years of decline resulted in a slump in manufacturing, from 10 per cent of total value added in the early 1980s to 8 per cent 20 years later. By the end of the 1990s the production structure of the subregion had become reminiscent of the colonial period, consisting overwhelmingly of agriculture and mining.

While there are several reasons for this disappointing performance, the combination of external instability and relatively inflexible production systems, aggravated in many countries by civil conflict, greatly increased the problems of economic management in the sub-Saharan region. Nearly all the countries pursued orthodox macroeconomic policies advocated by the International Monetary Fund (IMF) and the World Bank, both of which played a major if not decisive role in their policy-making. During nearly half of the 1990–2009 period, the governments of 46 sub-Saharan countries were managing their economies with IMF assistance. Two countries, Burkina Faso and Mali, submitted to IMF conditionality throughout that period, except for one year, and two others – Mozambique and Senegal – for eight years. The impacts of the macroeconomic policy conditions of the World Bank were no less important in all but a handful of sub-Saharan countries: Botswana, Equatorial Guinea, Eritrea, Namibia, South Africa and Sudan.

In Africa, tight monetary policies dampened growth and employment creation.

At the end of the 1990s growth began to recover, rising faster and remaining higher than population growth during the period 2002–2008. However, there is little evidence to suggest that liberalized trade and investment rules, combined with "sound macro fundamentals" in the form of reduced deficits and tight monetary policies, as required by the IMF, World Bank and other creditors and donors, were responsible for the recovery. Rather, on examining the evolution of fiscal deficits across the sub-Saharan region during the 1990s and 2000s, it is possible to make the general observation that, except in some extreme cases, deficits were reduced through output growth, not through fiscal austerity (Weeks, 2010). Fiscal balances in oil-exporting countries tended to be in surplus whenever oil prices rose. In other countries, deficits were substantially reduced in the mid-2000s when growth rates rose, largely due to the positive elasticity of revenue with respect to national income, rather than to conscious deficit reduction measures. Similarly, tight monetary policies are likely to have dampened economic activity instead of creating a favourable macroeconomic climate for investment. High real interest rates, driven by a single-minded focus on "inflation targeting" rather than one aimed at balancing the different needs of inflation control relative to output expansion and employment creation, served to raise the cost of borrowing and inhibited private investment.

Therefore, more than 20 years of so-called policy reforms seem to have had a relatively limited impact on strengthening the potential for rapid and sustainable growth in Africa, particularly in the sub-Saharan region; indeed, they may even have reduced that potential by hindering crucial investments in physical and social infrastructure. The main drivers of the recovery during the second half of the 2000s appear to have been a commodity price boom, debt relief and fewer domestic conflicts. The growth of demand for imports, a major factor that had previously hampered economic growth, may have become an even more binding constraint, given the lower level of industrialization in the 2000s compared with the previous 20 or 30 years.

The emphasis of the Washington Consensus-related policies on static comparative advantage virtually amounted to a prescription for non-development in the sub-Saharan region. Since exports in most sub-Saharan economies were based on natural resource endowments, volatile global commodity prices caused volatile exchange rates in response. Further, the lack of diversification of national production (in other words, the lack of industrialization) reduced the tax base, especially in economies dominated by agriculture. In mineral-exporting countries, the reliance on taxation of companies involved in natural resource extraction resulted in unstable public revenues due to fluctuations in commodity prices.

These trends in turn were reflected in employment patterns, or, more precisely, in the lack of

Table 4.9

EMPLOYMENT INDICATORS IN AFRICA, 1996 AND 2008

(Per cent)

	North Africa		Sub-Saharan Africa	
	1996	*2008*	*1996*	*2008*
Employment by sector				
Agriculture	33.4	30.3	68.1	63.0
Industry	19.1	20.0	9.0	8.8
Services	47.5	49.6	22.9	28.2
Vulnerable employment	42.9	37.9	80.9	75.5
Working poor	19.9	13.6	66.5	58.6
Unemployment rate				
Men	11.3	8.2	7.6	7.6
Women	18.2	14.8	8.9	8.5
Youth	27.3	23.5	12.6	12.3

Source: ILO, *Global Employment Trends*, various issues; and ILO, 2007.
Note: Employment by sector in 2008 refers to 2006 data.

change in these patterns, since slow economic growth and deteriorating productivity prevented significant improvements in labour markets. Participation and employment rates (i.e. labour force and employment as a share of the working age population) have remained stable and comparatively high in sub-Saharan Africa over the past 20 years: with participation rates of 71–72 per cent and employment rates of 65–66 per cent, which is consistent with an almost constant unemployment rate of 7–8 per cent. The unsolved problem in this subregion is not a shortage of employment in absolute terms, but rather inadequate employment, or insufficient decent and productive jobs (ILO, 2007).[20] A proxy for assessing the quality of employment is the ILO's concept of "vulnerable employment", which consists of the self-employed and contributing (but usually unpaid) family members. It is used as a basis for estimating informal jobs, although not all the wage earners and employers are necessarily employed in the formal sector. In sub-Saharan Africa very little has changed in this respect in the last 15 years: three out of four jobs correspond to "vulnerable" positions and, unsurprisingly, most of the employed are classified as "working poor" (table 4.9).

This lack of improvement is reflected in the sectoral composition of employment: jobs in manufacturing remain at very low levels (less than 10 per cent of the employed population). In addition, part of the employment in manufacturing recently created in export promotion zones, mainly in garment industries, consists of precarious jobs with little possibility for promotion or the acquisition of marketable skills (ILO, 2007). Employment in agriculture, which is characterized mainly by informal occupations, has diminished somewhat, in line with progressive urbanization, but it is still clearly predominant. In 1996, it accounted for 68 per cent of total employment, while the rural population was 69 per cent of the total sub-Saharan population, and in 2006 these shares were 63 and 64 per cent respectively. The counterpart to this moderate drop in the share of agricultural employment was increasing employment in services, mainly in the informal sector (including small-scale retail trade). It is estimated that the informal economy accounted for 78 per cent of non-agricultural employment, 61 per cent of urban employment and 93 per cent of new jobs created in the African continent (Xaba, Horn and Motala, 2002).[21] The low rate of employment generation in the formal sector can largely be attributed to insufficiency of aggregate output growth, combined with low labour intensity of production in the formal sector (Pollin et al., 2006). The low labour intensity of production is the converse of the productivity increases discussed in Chapter III, and reinforces the argument made there, that sectoral productivity gains may not necessarily translate into aggregate economy-wide gains if the benefits are not distributed in a manner that leads to more rapid increases in aggregate demand.

Labour market characteristics in North Africa have also remained largely unchanged since the 1990s with respect to participation rates and the sectoral composition of employment. Participation rates increased marginally, and in the late 2000s were about 44 per cent of the working age population (and 33 per cent of the total population). This was largely owing to low female participation in the labour market, although it increased more rapidly than in other developing regions. Agriculture still accounts for almost one third of total employment, with half of the population living in rural areas. Industrial employment represents some 20 per cent of the total, and has been showing a slightly upward trend. Correspondingly, the share of manufacturing in total value added has increased from 9 per cent to 12–13 per cent over the past 30 years. As a result, although this region is not highly industrialized, it

does not show any sign of deindustrialization either. Services account for approximately 50 per cent of both value added and total employment.

Acceleration of GDP growth in the 2000s has led to an improvement in several labour indicators, including aggregate labour productivity. The incidence of vulnerable employment has declined, as also that of the working poor. Unemployment has shrunk, although, at close to 10 per cent, it remains high relative to many other developing regions. Much of the improvement is attributable to the sharp fall in the unemployment rate in Algeria, from 30 per cent in 2000 to 11 per cent in 2009. Despite these improvements, unemployment continues to be a serious problem, especially for young people and women (table 4.9).

3. South, South-East and East Asia: growth and employment before and after the 1997-1998 financial crisis

The experiences of East, South and South-East Asian countries with liberalization were quite different from those of Latin America and Africa. In most of the Asian countries, liberalization in the 1980s and 1990s did not lead to deindustrialization. This was because the approach they adopted was more successful in increasing exports of manufactures and improving the trade balance, and because they typically began to open up only after they had developed their domestic capacities following many years of infant industry protection.[22] All three Asian subregions have experienced rapid economic growth over the past 30 years, interrupted, as is well known, only by the financial crisis in the late 1990s. Even so, this has not prevented an increase in open unemployment in South Asia and South-East Asia (mainly in the 1990s), partly because the opportunities for employment in urban areas have been insufficient to absorb all the migrants from the rural areas.

Fixed investment grew significantly in the three subregions, boosting productivity and output growth, as well as employment creation in manufacturing. In the 10 years before the Asian financial crisis average annual productivity increased at more than 5 per cent and total employment at more than 2 per cent. Real wages rose in line with productivity gains in Indonesia, Malaysia, the Philippines and the Republic of Korea, but at a significantly slower rate than productivity in China, Thailand and Viet Nam (table 4.10).

While the Asian countries generally liberalized trade in a gradual and strategic way, many governments failed to manage integration into global financial markets with the same prudence and skill. With capital account deregulation, several countries in South-East Asia (and the Republic of Korea) ended up exposed to the vagaries of capital flows and short-term speculation. Capital inflows caused an appreciation of their real exchange rates, shifted incentives within their economies from tradables to non-tradables, generated bubbles in asset markets and led to current-account deficits. This sowed the seeds for the financial crisis of 1997-1998, resulting in a wave of bankruptcies. The adoption of procyclical policies as part of IMF-led stabilization strategies worsened the situation by causing asset deflation and thereby exacerbating the downturn in output and employment.

In Asia, fixed investment boosted manufacturing employment.

Following the crisis, most countries, many of them under IMF pressure, continued with financial liberalization, although now they adopted proactive exchange-rate policies aimed at keeping their exchange rates low after the sharp depreciation of their currencies during the crisis. The currency depreciation enabled a rapid recovery of exports, which had suffered during the crisis. In Indonesia, for example, exports grew by more than 30 per cent in 2000 alone.

GDP growth also recovered, but in general less rapidly and with greater volatility than in the pre-crisis period. Underlying this loss of dynamism was an abrupt adjustment in investment rates in all the crisis-hit countries. They were cut by almost half in Malaysia and Thailand, for example. Subsequently, there was a partial recovery in those rates, but in general they have not returned to their pre-crisis levels. Fiscal policies contributed to a large extent to the reduction of aggregate investment. Even though the crisis in these countries was essentially caused by the profligacy of private investors

Since 2002, employment recovered but has not reached pre-crisis growth rates.

in an environment of financial liberalization, in its aftermath, governments in these subregions came under pressure to cut back on spending and reduce their deficits or increase their fiscal surpluses (Ghosh and Chandrasekhar, 2009).

How did these macroeconomic trends affect the labour market? In the post-crisis period from 1998 to 2002 there was a sharp deceleration of growth in both employment and labour productivity in the crisis-affected economies, compared with the pre-crisis period of the early 1990s.[23] By comparison, no such deceleration was evident in countries not affected by the Asian financial crisis, such as Cambodia, China, India or Viet Nam. The unemployment rate in the crisis-affected South-East Asian countries almost doubled between 1997 and 2003, to 8 per cent, but fell thereafter. Since 2002, employment creation, productivity and economic growth have recovered significantly, although they have not reached their pre-crisis growth levels (chart 4.4). Moreover, real wages have clearly lagged behind productivity gains in the crisis-hit countries, including Indonesia, Malaysia, the Philippines, the Republic of Korea and Thailand (table 4.10). It seems that this group of countries made deliberate efforts to avoid running large current-account deficits again, and opted for an export-led economic recovery supported by competitive exchange rates, while also containing labour costs.

These broad macroeconomic trends, in particular the decline of investment rates, also set back the structural changes that had accompanied the phase of rapid industrialization during the pre-crisis boom. In most South-East Asian countries, growth rates of manufacturing output fell, typically to less than half the previous rates. The lower output growth rates were accompanied by increases in labour productivity, such that employment elasticities of manufacturing growth declined dramatically, and in some cases even turned negative (table 4.10). It is worth noting that, even though the share of manufacturing in total value added and employment stopped growing in several countries, it remained relatively high. Moreover, in other lower income

Table 4.10

EMPLOYMENT INDICATORS, SELECTED ASIAN COUNTRIES, 1985–2008

(Per cent)

| | Share in total employment in | | | | | | | | | Overall productivity growth | | | Productivity growth in manufacturing | | | Real wage growth | | | Value added growth in manufacturing | | | Employment elasticity in manufacturing | | |
| | Agriculture | | | Industry | | | Services | | | | | | | | | | | | | | | | | |
	1995	2002	2008	1995	2002	2008	1995	2002	2008	1985–1997	1998–2002	2003–2008	1985–1997	1998–2002	2003–2008	1985–1997	1998–2002	2003–2008	1985–1997	1998–2002	2003–2008	1985–1997	1998–2002	2003–2008
Bangladesh	63.2	51.7	48.1	9.6	13.7	14.5	25.0	34.6	37.4	1.9	3.0	4.2	5.9	0.3	3.3	..	..	..	5.5	5.5	8.6	0.1	1.0	0.6
China^a	48.5	44.1	..	21.0	17.7	..	12.2	16.1	..	8.2	7.0	10.0	11.9	11.9	..	4.2	14.1	12.0	12.5	9.3	11.7	0.1	-0.3	..
India^a	63.3	57.4	55.7	11.2	11.8	12.8	21.3	25.1	25.0	3.5	3.1	6.4	..	..	..	-1.8	1.1	0.7	7.0	4.4	9.3	..	..	..
Indonesia	44.0	44.3	40.3	18.4	18.8	18.8	37.6	36.9	40.8	4.9	-0.2	3.7	4.6	-0.7	3.7	4.4	6.1	-0.6	11.0	2.1	5.3	0.6	1.3	0.2
Malaysia	20.0	14.9	14.0	32.3	32.0	28.7	47.7	53.1	57.4	4.7	0.9	4.0	4.7	2.6	7.8	4.5	2.6	1.3	12.5	4.5	5.9	0.6	0.4	-0.1
Pakistan	46.8	42.1	43.6	18.5	20.8	21.0	34.6	37.1	35.4	3.0	1.5	2.1	6.2	-1.7	6.7	..	-2.2	3.0	5.0	5.3	9.4	-0.1	1.3	0.4
Philippines	44.1	37.0	35.3	15.6	15.6	14.8	40.3	47.4	49.9	0.4	1.5	3.5	-0.1	1.5	4.1	0.1	1.4	0.2	3.1	2.8	5.0	1.0	0.4	0.1
Republic of Korea	12.4	9.3	7.4	33.3	27.3	25.9	54.3	63.3	66.7	5.1	3.6	3.0	6.9	9.3	8.3	7.9	7.0	-0.8	9.1	9.4	7.0	0.2	0.0	-0.2
Sri Lanka	37.3	34.5	32.7	23.4	16.5	18.9	33.6	33.7	33.6	2.3	0.8	5.5	..	..	..	0.4	0.8	-2.3	..	..	..	..	..	..
Thailand	52.0	46.1	42.5	19.8	19.8	19.6	28.3	34.0	37.9	6.5	0.9	3.7	5.4	0.1	5.4	2.8	-0.9	0.5	12.6	3.8	6.9	0.5	1.0	0.2
Viet Nam	64.8	62.0	57.9	11.6	14.7	17.4	23.7	23.3	24.8	3.8	3.9	6.0	..	6.6	..	2.0	2.0	2.0	6.1	10.5	12.0	..	0.4	..

Source: UNCTAD secretariat calculations, based on ILO, *Global Wage* and *LABORSTAT* databases; National Bureau of Statistics of China, *China Statistical Yearbook 2005*; UN/DESA, *National Accounts Main Aggregates* database; and EIU, *EIU CountryData* database.

a   Employment in agriculture, industry and services does not add up to 100 per cent due to non-classified employment.

countries in the region (e.g. Cambodia and Viet Nam) the manufacturing sector expanded rapidly.

The two Asian economic and demographic giants – China and India – recorded exceptionally high GDP and productivity growth rates, but less impressive employment outcomes. In both countries, their most dynamic economic activities (manufacturing and modern services respectively) contributed significantly to GDP growth, but still account for a relatively small proportion of employment.

China's economy, backed by investment rates often exceeding 40 per cent of GDP, has expanded at an average annual rate of almost 10 per cent since 1980, and its manufacturing sector by 11.5 per cent. However, such a large increase has not resulted in an equivalent rise of employment in manufacturing; indeed employment in that sector has been declining since the mid-1990s, in relative and absolute terms. As a result, manufacturing currently generates 43 per cent of total value added but only about 15 per cent of total employment.[24]

China's labour market has undergone profound changes, owing not only to accelerated economic growth, but also to structural reforms. Beginning in 1978, the framework for rural employment changed radically with the authorization of family farming for agricultural production, and the creation of township and village enterprises (TVEs). In urban areas, there was increasing diversification of enterprises and forms of employment, including private and cooperative enterprises, small-scale firms and individual businesses. On the other hand, employment in State and collective enterprises declined significantly from the mid-1990s. Job losses of more than 60 million in State and collective enterprises between 1994 and 2002 outnumbered job creation in new formal enterprises. Rural migrants – many of whom did not have official permission for permanent urban residence – added to the newly unemployed in the urban areas, which significantly increased the number of informal workers in those areas. Total employment has increased in line with the labour force, but has changed in nature: all the new jobs tend to be in urban areas and are in largely informal activities, while employment in rural areas, although still predominant, is stagnating.

The contrast between the very rapid increase of GDP and the much slower increase of employment

has resulted in a significant growth of labour productivity (chart 4.4). Productivity gains led to higher real wages for skilled workers after 1996, especially in urban formal enterprises (Ghose, 2005: 14–15). However, the continued presence of surplus labour constrained the growth of real income in low-skilled, non-farm occupations, and contributed to rising income inequality (Jomo, 2006).

In India, the growth of modern services such as information technology (IT) and IT-enabled services, communication services and financial services has not been accompanied by a proportionate growth in employment. This reflects an increase in labour productivity, which makes India's growth trajectory in services more positive in terms of productivity, though less positive in terms of unemployment and underemployment in a labour-surplus economy. Moreover, technological changes and developments have enabled the export of a number of services through various modes of supply such as digital transmission. Thus, in IT and IT-enabled services in India, the expansion of output is being driven by the expansion of exports, with positive effects on the country's balance of payments.[25] As a result, the services sector as a whole has come to dominate the Indian economy, accounting for more than half of its GDP and contributing overwhelmingly to its relatively high rate of growth in recent years.[26] However, only half of the services sector's GDP consists of modern activities. By 2005, knowledge-intensive market and non-market services, including education and health services accounted for 17.7 per cent of GDP. If the 8 per cent contributed by the railways, defence and public administrations is added, the total comes to 25.7 per cent. To this could be added an equal percentage of substantially unorganized services that offer extremely low wages (Chandrasekhar and Ghosh, 2010).

Furthermore, despite the expansion of the services sector, employment growth in this sector has been limited: while the sector accounted for 50 per cent of GDP in 2004/05, it employed only 25 per cent of the work force. Between 1999/00 and 2004/05, employment in the sector increased by only 22 per cent, whereas the sector's contribution to GDP at constant prices increased by 44 per cent. A typical example is the contribution of the IT sector to employment, which is far below its contribution to income and foreign exchange. Employment in computer-related activities which increased from around 314,000 in

1999/00 to about 963,000 in 2004/05, accounted for only 0.2 per cent of the workforce (Government of India, 2010); in business services, including financial intermediation, real estate renting and business activities, the share of employment was just 1.7 per cent. This explains to a great extent the large disparity between the services sector's respective contributions to GDP and employment.

Similarly, the rapid rate of output growth in the organized manufacturing sector[27] has not been accompanied by any noticeable expansion of decent work opportunities for India's labour force. Formal employment in this sector (involving explicit contracts, including a minimum level of work security and social protection) actually stagnated between 1999/00 and 2004/05, signifying a decline from 9.3 per cent to 7.5 per cent of total employment. Since the share of employment in manufacturing in total employment remained at around 12 per cent during this period, the manufacturing sector's contribution to organized employment was not only small relative to the total, but it even declined slightly. This happened despite the rapid growth of production in manufacturing in the period after 2001/02, in large measure due to increases in private consumption and investment in housing, which were driven by rapid income growth in the top deciles of the population and in urban areas. Real aggregate consumption in urban areas increased by 22 per cent, much faster than the 5.5 per cent rate of increase in rural areas between 1999/00 and 2004/05 (Chandrasekhar and Ghosh, 2010). Another factor driving demand was the sharp increase in credit-financed investment in housing and consumption of durable goods, facilitated by financial liberalization. Exports also provided a stimulus, especially as India became drawn into the export-oriented manufacturing hub dominated by East Asia. In recent years, the share of India's traditional manufactured exports (such as textiles, gems and jewellery, and leather) in its total manufactured exports has declined, while that of chemicals and engineering goods has risen significantly. As a result, recent industrial growth in India has been driven by the metal and chemical industries. The metal industries have gained from new export opportunities, and from credit-financed construction and the surge in demand for consumer goods such as automobiles, television receivers and computing equipment, while the chemical industries, such as refined petroleum

products, provide inputs into luxury products for which there is growing demand. All these industries, which tend to be capital-intensive and are characterized by relatively high productivity and high rates of productivity growth, create much less direct employment than those more oriented to the production of goods consumed by the lower income groups. Moreover, real wages in India have not followed productivity gains (table 4.10).

Summing up, most Asian countries have experienced strong economic growth over the past few decades, based on rapid productivity growth in manufacturing and, increasingly, also in modern services. Despite these achievements, employment problems persist: a large proportion of the labour force is still employed in informal and low-productivity employment, either in agriculture or in traditional services. The dynamic modern sectors boosted GDP and overall productivity growth without absorbing a substantial part of the surplus labour force. Moreover, informal employment and even open unemployment have increased in recent years, owing to lack of sufficient job creation in the urban areas to absorb rural migrants. The Asian financial crisis in 1997-1998 and the global crisis in 2008-2009 have exacerbated this situation. Several of the crisis-hit countries managed to restore productivity gains, particularly in manufacturing, but these have not translated into higher wages. In addition, employment creation in manufacturing has remained weak. This situation may not only widen the gap in income distribution in the region; it could also render economic recovery fragile and overdependent on uncertain export performance.

In the long-term, a sustainable development strategy, high investment and productivity gains are of the utmost importance, as discussed in chapter III, but they need to be complemented with rising wages, better incomes for non-wage earners, and the creation of more and better employment. This is critical for rebalancing the structure of demand. As stated by the ILO, in reference to the crisis-affected countries of the Association of Southeast Asian Nations (ASEAN), the crisis has highlighted the importance of reducing excessive dependence on exports to drive growth in some countries in the region, and of strengthening domestic and regional demand through deeper regional integration for sustainable recovery and development (ILO, 2010b: 15).

Notes

1   Vulnerable employment is defined as the sum of own-account workers and contributing family workers.

2   For instance, official statistics for Senegal estimate that in 2001–2002, 25 per cent of the rural population was underemployed because they mainly worked in agricultural activities, which only take place for 5 to 7 months a year, depending on the geographical zone (Agence Nationale de la Statistique et de la Démographie, *Situation Economique et Sociale du Sénégal Edition 2005*, at: www.ansd.sn).

3   Around 2005, urban unemployment rates were 31 per cent in Mozambique, 26.1 per cent in Ethiopia, 22.5 per cent in Senegal, 17.9 per cent in Cameroon (Yaoundé), 13.8 per cent in Morocco, 8.4 per cent in Rwanda (Kigali) and 6.9 per cent in Uganda. In contrast, rural unemployment rates were 12.9 per cent in Mozambique, 4.5 per cent in Senegal, 3.7 per cent in Morocco, 0.6 per cent in Rwanda and 1.1 per cent in Uganda, while rural unemployment figures were not available for Ethiopia and Cameroon.

4   It may become more important to generate employment opportunities in small cities and rural areas, as the positive agglomeration effects that are found in urban areas are becoming increasingly limited by congestion and inadequate urban infrastructure.

5   The greater role of services in output and employment observed in recent data may partly be an accounting problem. Outsourcing of services to specialized service providers has become important, leading to the statistical effect that services which used to be performed within a manufacturing firm were counted under manufacturing, while the same services now performed by a specialized provider are counted under services.

6   Construction is not included in this analysis because developments in the real estate sector are often affected by financial factors unrelated to productivity and employment, which would blur the analysis.

7   For these decomposition exercises, see also UN/DESA, 2006 and Rada and Taylor, 2006.

8   Due to data limitations, resource shifts within these four sectors cannot be accounted for. This may be an important shortcoming in the analysis of the services sector, which presents substantial variations across sub-categories with respect to both their level of labour productivity and their productivity growth potential.

9   Due to data limitations, sub-Saharan Africa is not included in charts 4.2 and 4.3.

10   One estimate indicates a shortfall of 21 percentage points for China, and 19 percentage points for India, relative to what would be expected from a cross-country comparison (IMF, 2006: table 3.1). However, this estimate may be unreliable because the underlying predictions are based partly on population size. Given that the populations of China and India are so much larger than those of the next largest country, reliable extrapolations based mainly on data for other countries become impossible. Another study, using different controls and comparator countries, estimates a lower but still substantial shortfall of 9 percentage points for China (Guo and N'Diaye, 2009: 12).

11   In some cases, the share of employment in mining in total employment is even below 1 per cent. In Ghana, the mining sector provides only 0.7 per cent of total employment (Akabzaa, 2009). In Angola, employment in the petroleum sector is about 0.3 per cent of total employment (Government of Angola: Programa de Governo 2009, available at: http://mirror.undp.org/angola/Offical-Documents.htm).

12   The ILO estimates that this accounts for 11 million people in large mining enterprises. In addition, 11.5 million to 13 million people work in small-scale mines (see ILO, at: http://www.ilo.org/public/english/dialogue/sector/sectors/mining/emp.htm).

13   For instance, in Zambia in 2005, while formal employment in the mining sector was about 8 per cent of total formal employment, the share of employment in mining in total employment was only 1.4 per cent, because informal employment in the mining sector accounted for over 30 per cent of total employment in that sector (van Klaveren et al., 2009).

14   For the example of Ghana, see Akabzaa, 2009.

15   Employment multipliers differ by project and country. Some other examples are provided in UNCTAD's *World Investment Report 2007*: 135.

16   For a more detailed discussion on the limited linkages between foreign affiliates of TNCs in the extractive

industries and domestic companies, see UNCTAD, *World Investment Report 2007*, chapter V.

17 Sturmer and Buchholz (2009) provide some estimates of potential revenues in the mining sector up to 2015 for Ghana, Namibia, Mozambique and Zambia. They conclude that government revenues from the extractive sector can greatly contribute to financing efforts towards meeting the Millennium Development Goals (MDGs). See also Sturmer, 2008; and ODI, 2005.

18 ECLAC studies on the Latin American industry have shown that productivity gains were realized within each industrial sector rather than through reallocations between sectors, and that such increases in productivity without structural change were associated with a low generation of jobs in manufacturing in the 1990s. Instead of generating a virtuous cycle of growth in which productivity gains go along with structural changes, production expansion, diversification and strong employment creation, employment and productivity actually evolved in opposite directions, and the productivity gap with developed countries' industries widened (Cimoli et al., 2005; Holland and Porcile, 2005).

19 Unemployment figures are estimates by ECLAC's CEPALSTAT, *Social Statistics and Indicators*, which adjusted historical data to the new series in Argentina, Brazil, Chile and Mexico.

20 Participation rates are of course lower when the labour force is compared with total population, as in table 4.2, instead of with the working age population.

21 South Africa is somewhat of an exception in this regard, with around 64 per cent of workers in the formal sector, but it also has high rates of open unemployment (NALEDI, 2004).

22 The share of manufacturing in total value added eventually declined slightly in Singapore and in Taiwan Province of China, but this was more a process of "normal" reduction, owing to relatively high income levels, rather than "premature" deindustrialization caused by badly handled trade liberalization.

23 The only exception seems to be Thailand, which recorded low employment growth and high labour productivity growth even in the pre-crisis period. However, employment statistics may be muddied by the impact of unrecorded migration. In Thailand there appear to be a large number of migrant workers from Myanmar, who are not included in employment statistics, which means that labour productivity indicators may be exaggerated.

24 Figures calculated by the UNCTAD secretariat, based on ILO, *LABORSTAT* database.

25 The Central Statistical Organisation has estimated that the share of ICT services in total GDP increased from 3 per cent in 2000/01 to 6 per cent in 2007/08. Regarding their contribution to the balance of payments, gross exports of software, business, financial and communication services amounted to 5.3 per cent of GDP at market prices in 2007/08, with exports of software services amounting to 3.4 per cent of GDP. By comparison, the ratio of merchandise exports to GDP was 14.2 per cent (see Reserve Bank of India, at: http://rbidocs.rbi.org.in/rdocs/Bulletin/PDFs/T%2042%20[Trade%20and%20Bal].pdf; and Central Statistical Organisation, at: http://mospi.gov.in/qr_estimate_gdp_curr_prices_12march09.pdf).

26 Services (excluding construction) accounted for 56 per cent of the increase in GDP at factor cost between 1996/97 and 2006/07 (computed from figures reported by the Reserve Bank of India, 2008).

27 "Organized sectors" are defined as including all enterprises with electricity employing 10 or more workers, and those without electricity employing 20 or more workers and which are subject to the Factories Act.

References

Akabzaa T (2009). Mining in Ghana: Implications for national economic development and poverty reduction. In: Campbell B, ed. *Mining in Africa: Regulation and Development.* The International Development Research Centre.

Baumol WJ, Blackman S and Wolff EN (1989). Productivity and American leadership: the long view. Cambridge, MIT Press.

Bosworth B and SM Collins (2008). Accounting for growth: comparing China and India. *Journal of Economic Perspectives,* 22(1): 45–66.

Çağatay N and Özler S (1995). Feminization of the Labor Force: The Effects of Long-Term Development and Structural Adjustment. *World Development,* 1883–1894.

Chandrasekhar CP and Ghosh J (2010). Aspects of growth and employment in India. UNCTAD Discussion paper. Forthcoming.

Chenery H, Robinson S and Syrquin M (1986). *Industrialization and Growth: A Comparative Study.* Washington, DC, World Bank.

Cimoli M et al. (2005). Cambio Estructural, Heterogeneidad Productiva y Tecnología en América Latina. In: Cimoli M, ed., *Heterogeneidad Estructural, Asimetrías Tecnológicas y Crecimiento en América Latina.* Santiago, Chile, ECLAC-BID, November: 9–39.

Cornia GA (2005). Policy reform and income distribution. DESA Working Paper no. 3, ST/ESA/2005/DWP/3, New York, United Nations, October.

Cornia GA (2009). Income Distribution under Latin America's New Left Regimes. Dipartimento di Scienze Economiche Università degli Studi di Firenze. Working Paper no. 16/2009, November.

Curtis M and Lissu T (2008). *A golden opportunity? How Tanzania is failing to benefit from gold mining.* Christian Council of Tanzania, National Council of Muslims in Tanzania and Tanzania Episcopal Conference. Dar es Salaam, October.

Dasgupta S and Singh A (2007). Manufacturing, Services and Premature Deindustrialization in Developing Countries. A Kaldorian Analysis. In: Mavrotas G and Shorrocks A, eds. *Advancing Development: Core Themes in Global Economics.* Houndsmill and New York, Palgrave Macmillan.

ECLAC (1994). El crecimiento económico y su difusión social: el caso de Chile de 1987 a 1992. LC/R.1483, Santiago, Chile, 27 December.

ECLAC (1996). Quince años de desempeño económico, América Latina y el Caribe 1980–1995.

ECLAC (2004). Una década de desarrollo social en América Latina, 1990–1999. Santiago, Chile, March.

Eichengreen B and Gupta B (2009). The two waves of service sector growth. Working Paper No. 14968, National Bureau of Economic Research, May.

Esso (2010). Chad-Cameroon Development Project. Project Update no. 27, Annual Report 2009.

Fraser A and Lungu J (2007). For whom the windfalls? Winners & losers in the privatization of Zambia's copper mines. Civil Society Trade Network of Zambia and Catholic Centre for Justice, Development and Peace. Lusaka, March.

Ghose AK (2005). Employment in China: Recent trends and future challenges. Employment Strategy Papers, 2005/14, International Labour Office, Geneva.

Ghosh J (2004). Globalization, export-oriented employment for women and social policy: A case study of India. In: Razavi S and Pearson R, eds. *Globalization, export-oriented employment and social policy: Gendered connections.* London, Palgrave: 91–125.

Ghosh J and Chandrasekhar CP (eds.) (2009). *A Decade After: Financial Crisis and Recovery in East Asia.* New Delhi, Tulika Books.

Government of India (2010). Ministry of Statistics and Programme Implementation, National Statistical Organisation, Central Statistics Office, Value Addition and Employment Generation in the ICT Sector in India, Delhi.

Guo K and N'Diaye P (2009). Employment effects of growth rebalancing in China. Working Paper No. 09/169, International Monetary Fund, Washington, DC, August.

Holland M and Porcile G (2005). Brecha Tecnológica y Crecimiento en América Latina. In: Cimoli M, ed., *Heterogeneidad Estructural, Asimetrías Tecnológicas y Crecimiento en América Latina.* Santiago, Chile, ECLAC-BID, November: 40–71.

Horton S (1999). Marginalization Revisited: Women's Market Work and Pay, and Economic Development. World Development, 27(3): 571–582.

ICMM (2009). Mining in Tanzania – What future can we expect? The challenge of mineral wealth: using resource endowments to foster sustainable development. International Council of Mining and Metals. October.

ILO (2002). The evolution of employment, working time and training in the mining industry. Document TMMI/2002. International Labour Office, Geneva, October.

ILO (2007). African employment trends. Geneva, April.

ILO (2008a). Global employment trends for women. Geneva, March.

ILO (2008b). *Global Wage Report 2008/09*. Geneva, International Labour Office.

ILO (2010a). Unemployment reached highest level on record in 2009: Somavia calls for the same policy decisiveness that saved banks to save and create jobs. *Press Release* ILO/10/01, 26 January.

ILO (2010b). Labour and Social Trends in ASEAN 2010. Sustaining recovery and development through decent work.

ILPES (1998). Reflexiones sobre el Desarrollo y la Responsabilidad del Estado. Instituto Latinoamericano y del Caribe de Planificación Económica y Social. Naciones Unidas, Santiago, Chile.

IMF (2006). Asia rising: patterns of economic development and growth. World Economic Outlook, chapter 3, September.

Instituto de Ingenieros de Minas de Perú (2010). Minería peruana: Contribución al desarrollo económico y social. Lima.

Jomo KS (2006). Growth with equity in East Asia? DESA Working Paper no. 33, ST/ESA/2006/DWP/33, United Nations, New York, September.

Jomo KS (2009). Export-oriented industrialisation, female employment and gender wage equity in East Asia. *Economic and Political Weekly,* 45(29), January.

Jomo KS and Baudot J (eds.) (2007). *Flat world, big gaps. Economic liberalization, globalization, poverty and inequality*. Orient Longman, Zed Books and Third World Network in association with the United Nations.

Kalecki M (1976). *Essays on Developing Economies*. Hassocks, Sussex, The Harvest Press Limited.

Kuznets S (1966). Modern Economic Growth. Structure and Spread. New Haven, Yale University Press.

Leibold AM (2010). Aligning incentives for development: Lessons learned from the Chad-Cameroon oil pipeline, Yale Law School Student Scholarship Papers.

Lindenboim J, Kennedy D and Graña JM (2010). La relevancia del debate sobre la distribución funcional del ingreso. UNCTAD Discussion Paper. Forthcoming.

Lluch C, Powell A and Williams R (1977). *Patterns in Household Demand and Saving*. Oxford, Oxford University Press.

Lungu J (2008). Socio-economic change and natural resource exploitation: a case study of the Zambian copper mining industry. *Development Southern Africa*, 25(5): 543–560.

Maroto-Sánchez A and Cuadrado-Roura JR (2009). Is growth of services an obstacle to productivity growth? A comparative analysis. Structural Change and Economic Dynamics, 20(4): 254–265.

NALEDI (National Labour and Economic Development Institute) (2004). Highlights of current labour market conditions in South Africa. Global Policy Network, January. Available at: http://www.gpn.org/data/south-africa/south-africa-analysis.doc.

Nayyar G (2009). The nature of employment in India's services sector. Exploring the heterogeneity. Discussion Paper 452, Department of Economics, University of Oxford, September.

Nkurunziza J (2007). Generating rural employment in Africa to fight poverty. In: Ocampo JA and Jomo KS, eds. *Towards Full and Decent Employment*. New York, London, Penang and Hyderabad, Orient Longman Pvt. Ltd., Zed Books, Third World Network, in association with the United Nations.

Ocampo JA and Jomo KS (eds.) (2007). *Towards full and decent employment*. Orient Longman, Zed Books and Third World Network in association with the United Nations.

ODI (2005). Does the sustained global demand for oil, gas, and minerals mean that Africa can now fund its own MDG financing gap? ODI briefing note no. 6, September.

Palma JG (2010). Why productivity growth stagnated in most Latin American countries since the neo-liberal reforms? Cambridge Working Papers in Economics (CWPE) 1030, May. Available at: http://www.econ.cam.ac.uk/dae/repec/cam/pdf/cwpe1030.pdf.

Pollin R, Heintz J and Mwangi WG (2008). *An Employment-Targeted Economic Program for Kenya*. Cheltenham, United Kingdom and Northampton, MA, Edward Elgar Publishing.

Pollin R et al. (2006). *An Employment-Targeted Economic Program for South Africa*. Northampton, MA, Edward Elgar Publishing.

Prebisch R (1963). *Hacia una dinámica del desarrollo latinoamericano*. Fondo de Cultura Económica. Mexico D.F.

Rada C and Taylor L (2006). Developing and transition economies in the late 20th century: diverging growth rates, economic structures, and sources of demand. DESA Working Paper No. 34, Document ST/ESA/2006/DWP/34, New York.

Reserve Bank of India (2008). Handbook of Statistics on the Indian Economy, Mumbai, RBI.

Sáinz P (2007). Equity in Latin America since the 1990s. In: Jomo KS and Baudot J, eds. *Flat Word, Big Gaps*. New York, London, Penang and Hyderabad, Orient Longman Pvt. Ltd., Zed Books and Third World Network in association with the United Nations: 242–271.

Sáinz P and Calcagno A (1992). In search of another form of development. *ECLAC Review* 48: December.

Scarpetta S (2009). La globalisation a fait baisser la part du salaire dans la valeur ajoutée. Interview in *Le Monde de l'Economie*, 21 December.

Simutanyi N (2008). Copper mining in Zambia. The developmental legacy of privatization. Institute for Security Studies Paper No. 165, July.

Sturmer M (2008). Financing for development series: Increasing government revenues from the extractive sector in Sub-Saharan Africa. German Development Institute Briefing Paper 9/2008.

Sturmer M and Buchholz P (2009). Government revenues from the extractive sector in Sub-Saharan Africa – A potential for funding the United Nations Development Goals? Federal Institute for Geosciences and Natural Resources. Hannover, June.

Syrquin M (1986). Productivity growth and factor reallocation. In: Chenery HB, Robinson S and Syrquin M eds. *Industrialization and Growth*. New York, Oxford University Press.

UNCTAD (2007). *World Investment Report 2007* – Transnational Corporations, Extractive Industries and Development. United Nations Publications, Sales No. E.07.II.D.9, New York and Geneva.

UN/DESA (2006). World Economic and Social Survey 2006. United Nations Department of Economic and Social Affairs, New York.

UNECA (2010). *Economic Report on Africa 2010*: Promoting high-level sustainable growth to reduce unemployment in Africa. Jointly published by the United Nations Economic Commission for Africa and the African Union. Addis Ababa.

Van Klaveren M et al. (2009). An overview of women's work and employment in Zambia. Decisions for Life MDG3 Project Country Report No. 4. University of Amsterdam, Amsterdam Institute for Advanced Labour Studies. Amsterdam, September.

Weeks J (2010). Employment, productivity and growth in Africa south of Sahara. UNCTAD Discussion Paper. Forthcoming.

World Bank (1987). *World Development Report 1987*. New York, Oxford University Press.

Xaba J, Horn P and Motala S (2002). The informal sector in sub-Saharan Africa. Available at: http://www.wiego.org/papers/2005/unifem/29_ILO_WP_10_IS_Sub-Saharan_Africa_Horn.pdf.

REVISING THE POLICY FRAMEWORK FOR SUSTAINED GROWTH, EMPLOYMENT CREATION AND POVERTY REDUCTION

A. Introduction

Widespread unemployment in the global economy over the past 30 years has become the most pressing social and economic problem of our time, because it is closely related to poverty, on the one hand, and social peace and political stability on the other. Observers generally agree that the fallout from the global financial and economic crisis has further aggravated the labour market situation in most countries, as millions of workers have lost their jobs or suffered wage cuts. There is a particularly close link between unemployment and poverty in developing countries, where public social security systems are rare and workers are forced into more vulnerable jobs and into informal sector activities for fear of descending into poverty.

The employment performances of different groups of developing countries discussed in chapter IV of this *Report*, the theoretical considerations presented in chapter III, as well as the risk of a deflationary trend in the global rebalancing process discussed in chapters I and II, all suggest that for employment-creating development strategies to succeed, it will be necessary to go beyond the policy prescriptions of the past, which relied primarily on market liberalization and on exports for development and employment creation. This chapter argues for an alternative public policy approach to solve the pressing employment problems, based on the premise that output and demand expansion is a precondition for employment generation, in developed and developing countries alike. It suggests that labour markets do not function in the same way as goods markets: in principle, price flexibility causes demand to match supply on individual markets for goods and services, but wage flexibility does not prevent a rise in unemployment. This is because wages are not only a cost factor but also a key determinant of the level of domestic demand in any economy.

Therefore faster employment creation, particularly in developing countries which have a large amount of surplus labour, requires appropriate macroeconomic policies and development strategies for accelerating growth of productive capacities and domestic demand. This, in turn, calls for a reassessment of priorities in macroeconomic policies. Monetary policies geared to keeping the inflation rate low and attracting foreign capital inflows, and fiscal policies aimed at balancing budgets, combined with liberalization of goods, financial and labour markets, have not yielded the results hoped for in terms of growth and employment. Achieving more satisfactory outcomes for employment creation – and thus also for poverty reduction – therefore requires widening the scope of policy instruments beyond what was deemed appropriate under the development paradigm of the past 30 years.

A promising strategy for rapid employment generation would be one that focuses more on the investment dynamics that drive growth of productive capacity, while at the same time ensuring that productivity gains are distributed in a way that leads to a commensurate increase in domestic demand. Such a strategy would use fiscal policy as an instrument of demand management and support for private fixed capital formation. In the design of monetary policy, the exclusive focus on inflation control would be replaced by a greater emphasis on growth and employment creation. Such an employment-friendly monetary policy would aim at maintaining low costs of credit for investment in fixed capital and avoiding currency overvaluation.

In addition, an incomes policy that links increases in labour income to productivity growth in such a way that the wage share does not fall and domestic demand expands at more or less the same rate as domestic supply capacities will ensure that a sufficient number of new jobs are created to compensate for the labour-saving effects of productivity growth. The policy will also provide incentives for further investment in fixed capital, thereby helping to establish a virtuous cycle of productivity growth, domestic demand expansion and enlargement of productive capacity.

By shifting the emphasis of monetary policy to growth and employment creation, the scope for central banks to control inflation will be reduced. However, an incomes policy can serve not only to generate greater domestic demand, but also to prevent labour costs from rising faster than productivity, thereby helping to control inflation. Together, monetary, fiscal and incomes policies would then provide

considerable scope for demand management to fight unemployment – both structural and cyclical – while controlling inflation.

Section B of this chapter first reviews how policy approaches to employment creation have changed since the immediate post-war era. It examines the shifting priorities in the economic policy goals of developed countries based on the policy experiences and the changing theoretical propositions of the 1970s and early 1980s. During this period, the economic policy regime moved from interventionism, involving an active role of the State, to broad deregulation and liberalization with a diminished role of the State. The priority of macroeconomic policy shifted from employment creation to achieving and maintaining a low level of inflation. Section C offers recommendations, including reviving proactive fiscal and monetary policy instruments in support of development, and introducing a new kind of incomes policy. It emphasizes that such a policy should aim at reducing the dependence of developing countries on export markets for employment growth, as these markets are likely to be more sluggish in the foreseeable future. Instead, employment growth should be based on a steady increase of domestic demand in line with productivity growth. Section D highlights the need for creating and strengthening institutions to support an incomes policy aimed at faster employment creation, bearing in mind that such institutions have to be adapted to the specific conditions of each country. It also discusses the need for measures to link the expansion of the modern sector and successful export industries with the rest of the economy, including the informal and rural sectors. Examples of such measures include appropriate forms of taxation and public spending, as well as agricultural support institutions. These measures are of particular importance in countries where formal wage employment constitutes a relatively small share of total employment. Finally, section E briefly discusses how a new assignment of national macroeconomic policies in favour of faster employment creation can be supported by appropriate exchange-rate policies and capital-account management.

B. Employment creation as a goal of economic policy in retrospect

1. Full employment in the "golden age of capitalism"

In response to the experience of high unemployment during the Great Depression in the 1930s and the subsequent long period of instability and war, many major industrialized countries established full employment as a goal in law, and committed themselves to implementing proactive macroeconomic policies. In the post-war era up to the mid-1970s, a period often referred to as the "golden age of capitalism" (Marglin and Schor, 1990; Singh, 2009), unemployment in developed countries was at historically low levels. In Japan as well as several Western European countries that even absorbed a large number of migrant workers from Southern Europe, it was a period of what is considered full employment (table 5.1).

During that period, governments actively guided the growth process through fiscal and monetary policies which aimed at preventing a repetition of the catastrophic economic downturn of the Great Depression. Equally important was cooperation between workers, employers and governments according to certain rules which ensured high rates of investment and parallel growth of productivity and earnings (Glyn et al., 1990; Singh, 2009). This cooperation was based on strong labour-market and social-security institutions, which had been part

of the structural change that accompanied the process of industrialization. In this process, collective bargaining on wages and labour conditions helped to ensure that productivity gains from investment in the fast-growing economies were distributed in such a way that the share of wages in total income remained fairly stable. Trade unions, employers' associations and government guidance played an important role in this process.

Proactive fiscal policies to maintain high employment were justified on the grounds that employment was a crucial determinant of prosperity, and was therefore too important to be left entirely to an inherently unstable market of decentralized private agents. With the experience of the Great Depression in mind, and influenced by Keynesian theory, which attributed rising unemployment to insufficient aggregate demand, policymakers focused on maintaining robust aggregate demand through income stabilization policies and public expenditures. The willingness of governments to pursue counter-cyclical fiscal policies, and to incur budget deficits if necessary in order to stabilize demand and employment, created a macroeconomic environment of relatively low uncertainty. It also fostered incentives for private investment and consumption. This in turn contributed to an employment-generating growth process (Glyn et al.,1990: 62; and Epstein and Schor, 1988: 22).

> During the "golden age of capitalism" unemployment was historically low, even though labour markets were more regulated than they are today.

Table 5.1

UNEMPLOYMENT RATES, SELECTED ECONOMIES, 1956–2008

(Average, per cent)

	1956–1973	*1974–1985*	*1986–2000*	*2000–2008*
Developed economies	2.9	5.9	7.2	6.6
United States	5.0	7.5	5.7	5.1
Japan	1.4	2.2	3.1	4.6
EU-15	2.5	6.8	9.7	7.7
of which:				
Germany	1.3	4.9	7.5	9.1
France	1.7	6.0	9.8	8.3
United Kingdom	1.8	7.2	8.3	5.1
Developing economies	..	5.2	6.0	6.7

Source: UNCTAD secretariat calculations, based on *Annual Labour Force Statistics*, ALFS Summary tables in *OECD.Stat Extracts* database; ILO, *LABORSTAT* and *KILM* databases; ECLAC, *CEPALSTAT* database; and Taiwan Province of China, *Labor Force in MacroEconomics* database.

Equally important, monetary policy was used as a tool of macroeconomic management to foster growth and to achieve the goal of full employment. In the aftermath of the Second World War, central banks in nearly all developed countries were given the responsibility not only for ensuring price stability, but also for contributing to stable and satisfactory output growth and maintaining a high level of employment. This created the monetary conditions necessary for rapidly rebuilding their economies and expanding productive capacities through an enlargement of the fixed capital stock and productivity increases. Besides low interest rates, direct measures (e.g. credit controls and credit allocation techniques) were temporarily employed to influence the allocation of resources and to channel finance to key economic sectors. This model of central banking gave governments a high degree of leverage over the financial system and facilitated the pursuit of their priorities (Epstein, 2005: 13–14).

For the major industrialized countries, the quarter century following the Second World War was a period of strong and sustained growth accompanied

> Central banks were responsible not only for price stability but also for ensuring a high level of employment.

by high employment rates. Especially for Western European economies, the period of the Bretton Woods system until 1973 was associated with virtually full employment. Growth was centred on the domestic market. Capital accumulation boosted productivity growth that was paralleled by an equally fast growth in real wages, which in turn strengthened aggregate demand (Singh, 2009: 59–61).

The objective of keeping unemployment low became a more serious challenge for economic policy during the 1970s. With the breakdown of the Bretton Woods system and the first oil price shock in 1973, the macroeconomic environment changed dramatically, at both national and international levels. Higher oil import costs accelerated the increase in the general price level. At the same time global economic growth slowed down sharply for various reasons. First, the oil-price-related shift in the terms of trade and redistribution of incomes led to a net decline in aggregate demand, as the imports of oil-exporting countries did not immediately compensate for the fall in effective demand by the oil-importing countries.

Other factors contributing to the economic slowdown were the response of trade unions in some major industrialized countries to the initial price shock and macroeconomic policy reactions to the newly emerging "stagflation". The price shock intensified the conflict over income distribution as rising import prices led to higher consumer prices that squeezed real wages. Trade unions were unwilling to accept this fall in real wages and successfully fought for nominal wage increases rising in line with past inflation rates, based on the assumption that this would restore real wages to the level they had been before the price shock. But as these nominal wage increases by far exceeded productivity growth, unit labour costs were pushed up, a process that ushered in an inflationary wage-price spiral without ever restoring workers' real wages.

Stagflation in turn, provoked overly restrictive monetary policies. Of course, central banks could do nothing about rising import prices, but growing unemployment weakened the power of trade unions in wage negotiations and helped to bring the rise in unit labour costs under control. With interest rates and unemployment rising, public finances deteriorated sharply and governments were increasingly reluctant to apply expansionary fiscal policies. Nonetheless, in the late 1970s, G-7 countries agreed on a coordinated effort to revive global growth, but the resulting recovery was only brief. It was derailed once more by a second oil-price shock, which pushed inflation rates even higher. This time the policy response was led by the United States in the form of ultra-tight monetary policy.

The 1970s produced a decisive break in the post-war process of capital formation in the leading industrialized countries. Investment rates plummeted, and have never recovered to the levels of the "golden age". It should be borne in mind that by reducing fixed capital formation and output growth, tight monetary policy itself contributes to stagflationary forces by squeezing productivity growth. Furthermore, if high unemployment is allowed to persist, the resulting budgetary pressures can have similarly adverse effects on growth to the extent that rising tax rates and falling public investment worsen supply conditions.

> In the mid-1970s macro-economic policies started to focus on price stability and balanced budgets.

2. Paradigm shift in the 1980s

The radical shift in the orientation of macroeconomic policies in the late 1970s and early 1980s had a massive impact on the future course of the world economy. In the United States it provoked a double-dip recession in the early 1980s, in Western Europe it led to a severe recession and record high unemployment rates together with budget crises, and in developing countries it triggered the debt crises of the 1980s.

The policy responses to the global slump as well as the longer term economic consequences differed widely across countries. Developing countries, especially those in Latin America, found their policy space highly constrained, as discussed in chapter IV. The United States economy experienced long periods of expansion in both the 1980s and 1990s, with low unemployment rates, and monetary policy took precedence over fiscal policy in managing domestic demand. By contrast, most governments in Western Europe began to move away from macroeconomic demand management beyond what automatic stabilizers would do.

In the policy debate the "Phillips curve" featured prominently. The curve was originally a record of empirically observed combinations of rates of inflation with rates of unemployment in the United Kingdom (Phillips, 1958). Subsequently, it became associated with Keynesian thought through its influential application by Samuelson and Solow (1960) to show an inverse relationship between unemployment and inflation in the United States. To many observers, this result suggested the existence of a stable trade-off that could guide Keynesian policymakers in choosing their policy priorities. Critics led by Friedman (1968) and Phelps (1967) argued that expectations of inflation would adapt to changes in actual inflation, and the supposed trade-off would therefore disappear "in the long run".

With unemployment and inflation rising simultaneously in the 1970s, Keynesianism seemed at a loss to explain the phenomenon of stagflation. Reflecting the gradual rise of "monetarism", Friedman (1968) had reasserted the pre-Keynesian vision of an economy that, if left to its own devices, would tend towards full employment. He employed the theoretical notion of the "natural rate of unemployment", which he defined as the level of unemployment that would exist in equilibrium given agents' preferences and labour market imperfections. In order for the alleged tendency towards full employment to run its course, it would be necessary, in particular, to reduce the discretionary element in monetary policy. This was to be done by subjecting central banks to the famous "k-per cent rule" of steady expansion of the monetary base, irrespective of business cycles, while letting financial markets freely determine all interest rates. The "rational expectations revolution" took these monetarist ideas to their "new classical" level in asserting that any systematic stabilization policies would be ineffective, since agents that formed the "rational expectations", guided by the "true model" of the world, would fully anticipate the impact of such policies and could only be fooled by policy surprises. These results were shown to be true in models based on a set of highly unrealistic assumptions, including perfect price flexibility.

The idea of an inherent tendency towards full employment was supposed to be captured by research on the concept of the "non-accelerating inflation rate of unemployment" (NAIRU). In this context, full employment was considered to be solely dependent on labour-market institutions and beyond the reach of macroeconomic policies (Palley, 2007). However, NAIRU estimates would vary over time together with actual unemployment levels, which are undeniably related to macroeconomic policies.

Stark contrasts in practical policy-making have been observed between the United States and European experiences. When actual unemployment levels fell well below the prevailing NAIRU estimates in the United States in the second half of the 1990s, policymakers ignored the supposed inflation threat and allowed the boom to continue. The NAIRU estimates were reduced accordingly, and prominent critics rejected the concept altogether (Galbraith, 1997; Stiglitz, 1997). In the European

> There was a widespread belief that full employment was beyond the reach of macroeconomic policy ...

> ... and that jobs could be created only by reducing the price of labour.

context, researchers coined the term "hysteresis" to describe the finding that NAIRU estimates had been adjusted upwards as actual unemployment rose in the absence of policies to counter the trend towards high unemployment.

The influence of the paradigm shift in economic theory on practical policy-making differed among countries. In the United States, it primarily meant replacing regulation by trust in free or self-regulating markets, but it also meant the continued flexible application of macroeconomic policies to stabilize domestic demand growth. In Western Europe, neoliberalism signified enthusiasm for deregulation to varying degrees, but it was combined with a more far-reaching retreat from demand management, with macroeconomic policies becoming focused on price stability and balanced budgets.[1] Perhaps the greatest impact of the rise of neoliberalism was in the developing world, where policy prescriptions for structural adjustment, in line with what came to be called the "Washington Consensus", meant a sharply reduced role of the State together with an excessive focus on competitiveness and export orientation.

The new approach, which considered the experience of stagflation in the 1970s as proof of the distorting effect of State discretion, promoted a post-golden age economic model. This model advocated the abandonment of State intervention in order to prevent the consequences of government failures. By the end of the 1970s, almost all developed countries adopted that model of economic thinking, including reducing government intervention aimed at maintaining high levels of employment. The change in the priorities of macroeconomic policy in the late 1970s and the declining role of government for stabilizing the business cycle are also reflected in the shift to money supply and inflation targeting in all major developed economies, thus subordinating fiscal policy to monetary policy (Epstein and Schor, 1988: 44).

Since then, most governments have relied on the hope of a self-stabilizing market, based on the belief that unemployment is an inevitable outcome of structural transformation, involving changes in production techniques, consumer demand and the location of production, and that the only way to create jobs is through changes in relative factor prices (i.e. by reducing the price of labour). Thus, increasing labour market flexibility and reducing labour regulations was combined with informal or formal inflation targeting by central banks, which abandoned their previously active role in supporting growth and employment creation in the hope that economic growth and employment creation would result as a by-product of the fight against inflation (IMF, 2006; Epstein, 2009: 1–3).

Nevertheless, except for a short period in the early 1980s, monetary policy in the United States followed a clearly accommodative approach involving fine-tuning the interest rate. Whereas the Federal Reserve System of the United States is responsible for both inflation and employment, monetary policy in the EU followed a monetarist approach for much longer, focused on inflation control. As a result, output growth and employment creation were slower than in the United States (see also chapter III, charts 3.1 and 3.2).

In developing countries, before the 1980s, engaging in a developmental role was widely seen as an important aspect of the mission of the central banks. Consequently, these banks employed a wide range of instruments in support of growth and investment, including keeping real interest rates low, financing government deficits and using capital controls to prevent currency overvaluations. They also used direct tools such as credit allocation and interest ceilings (Epstein, 2005 and 2007). Control over the financial sector and regulation of credit allocation were also deemed essential in the absence of an efficient system of financial intermediation and sufficiently deep financial markets, as well as to ensure that the financial sector served the needs of the real economy and conformed to national objectives. Governments assumed a central role in driving the development process towards outcomes perceived as responding to prevailing social and human needs and the requirements of long-term development. They pursued these objectives using a variety of price controls and intervention in resource allocation.

Many governments also considered public ownership of enterprises necessary in the absence of a critical mass of private capitalist entrepreneurs.

3. Structural adjustment and globalization

Since the early 1980s, development policies and macroeconomic policies in developing countries have been shaped largely by the policy prescriptions of the international financial institutions. As the current-account deficits of developing countries widened as a result of sharply rising interest rates on their external debt and weakening exports – both largely due to the marked shift in United States monetary policy aimed at combating inflation – the number of IMF-supported stabilization programmes rose from an annual average of 10 during the 1970s to 19 in 1980 and to 33 in 1985 (Jespersen, 1992).

Subsequently, a Structural Adjustment Facility (SAF) and later the Enhanced Structural Adjustment Facility (ESAF) for low-income countries that faced protracted balance-of-payments problems were created, which provided a longer time horizon for IMF support. Through them the role of the IMF was extended beyond that of financing external deficits of its members to one of becoming increasingly involved in development policy issues. Loans provided under the SAF/ESAF were accompanied by stringent conditions, generally including cuts in public spending, restrictive monetary policies and exchange-rate adjustments; in many cases, they also included structural conditions, such as import liberalization, privatization and deregulation of the domestic economy. Their main objectives were to reduce government interference in the allocation of resources and to contain inflation (Schadler et al., 1993: 9). However, the conditionality did not adequately address the questions of how to increase productive capacity and generate employment, which would have required a more balanced mix of monetary and fiscal measures.

Similarly, World Bank lending for structural adjustment placed emphasis on price stability, limited

> IMF conditionality did not adequately address the question of how to increase productive capacity and employment.

Chart 5.1

SHARE OF COMPENSATION OF EMPLOYEES IN NATIONAL INCOME, SELECTED COUNTRY GROUPS, 1980–2008

(Per cent)

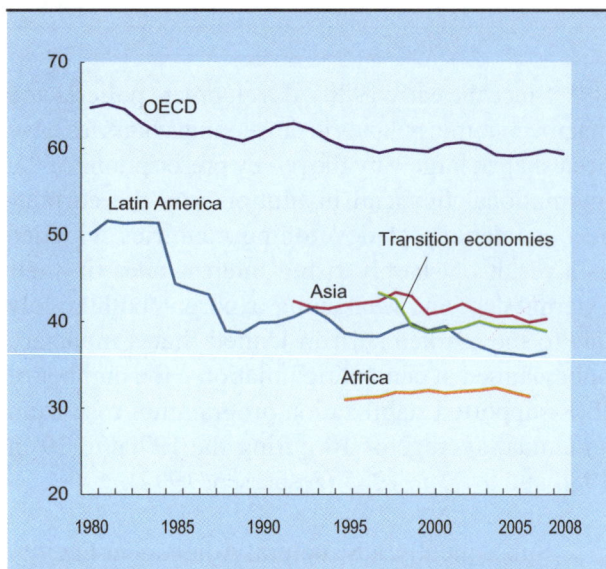

Source: UNCTAD secretariat calculations, based on UN/DESA, *National Accounts Official Country Data* database, table 4.1; *OECD.Stat Extracts* database; and Lindenboim et al., 2010.

Note: Unweighted averages. Data refer to net national income for OECD countries and to gross national income for other country groups.
Latin America comprises: Argentina, Brazil, Chile, Colombia, Mexico and Peru; Asia comprises: Bahrein, China, Hong Kong (China), the Philippines and the Republic of Korea; Africa comprises: Egypt, Kenya, Mozambique, Namibia, Niger, Senegal, South Africa and Tunisia; Transition economies comprises: Armenia, Azerbaijan, Belarus, Kazakhstan, Kyrgyzstan, the former Yugoslav Republic of Macedonia, the Republic of Moldova, the Russian Federation, Serbia and Ukraine; OECD comprises: Australia, Austria, Belgium, Canada, Denmark, Finland, France, Germany, Iceland, Ireland, Italy, Japan, Luxembourg, the Netherlands, New Zealand, Norway, Portugal, Spain, Sweden, Switzerland, the United Kingdom and the United States.

intervention – including through fiscal instruments –, reduced State involvement, greater reliance on market forces and a rapid opening up to international competition as key to unlocking an economy's growth potential. This orientation of structural policies, and the policy programme that came to be known as the Washington Consensus approach to development, represented a shift away from the previous focus on capital accumulation to an almost exclusive reliance on the efficiency-enhancing potential of

improved factor allocation generated by market forces. Moreover, with the general shift to export-led growth strategies and the accelerated pace of trade liberalization, output growth and employment creation became increasingly dependent on external markets. At the same time, productivity growth had to rely more on foreign direct investment (FDI) rather than efforts aimed at strengthening domestic demand and domestic investment.

While in several countries these policies were successful in bringing down inflation, they did not live up to expectations with regard to their impact on growth and diversification (see, for example, Muqtada 2010). While inflation was brought down considerably, growth and investment remained weak, with attendant effects on employment. The failure of the reform programmes was due in large part to the fact that they were typically initiated during a crisis situation, when, in a context of slow global expansion, fiscal and monetary policies were tightened to bring down inflation, rather than adopting an expansionary stance to stabilize domestic demand and employment. There were sizeable cuts in spending on productive infrastructure and the provision of social services. Contrary to expectations that the cuts in public sector deficits would "crowd in" private investment and that a reduced State presence in economic activity would unleash a fresh wave of private entrepreneurial initiatives, private investment remained depressed. In most cases the process of capital accumulation came to a halt, and in some net investment even became negative.

Data on the long-term evolution of the share of wages in national income in developing countries is scarce. Nevertheless the data that is available suggests that this share has been on a declining trend over the past three decades in both developed and developing countries, except in Africa, where it has traditionally been the lowest in the world (chart 5.1). According to van der Hoeven (2010), based on research by Harrison (2002), the wage share has been falling in many countries since the 1960s; this trend accelerated and occurred in more countries since the 1990s: the share of labour fell, on average, by more than 0.3 percentage points annually between 1993 and the early 2000s in a group of poorer countries and by 0.4 percentage points in a group of richer countries. This is explained partly by a trend towards greater export orientation, which tended to limit increases in wages to boost international competitiveness, and partly by the fact that the share of labour in gross national income recovers more slowly in an upturn when overall GDP increases than it falls in a crisis situation (van der Hoeven and Saget, 2004; ILO, 2008). A study of the manufacturing sector in a large sample of developing countries revealed that the decline in real wages and in the wage share of value added in most non-Asian developing countries in the 1980s and the 1990s was due to wage compression, with workers having to bear the burden of manufacturers losing competitiveness in international markets (Amsden and van der Hoeven, 1996). This loss of competitiveness was the result of an inappropriate monetary policy of high interest rates to attract foreign capital, which led to currency overvaluation while at the same time discouraging domestic investment.[2]

> Workers had to bear the burden when manufacturers lost international competitiveness.

By 1994, the World Bank officially recognized that the removal of distortions in product and factor markets alone would be insufficient to "put countries on a sustained, poverty-reducing growth path", and that this would require "better economic policies and more investment in human capital, infrastructures, and institution building, along with better governance" (World Bank, 1994: 2). The Bank did not, however, revise its definition of "good economic policies" by giving more weight to macroeconomic and sectoral policy measures aimed at strengthening productive private investment for faster growth and accelerating employment creation for poverty reduction. Thus, monetary conditions for private investment remained unfavourable in many developing countries, resulting in the lack of both infrastructure investments and the provision of public goods and services, both of which create important positive externalities for a wide range of productive activities (*TDR 1993*, chaps. II and III).

In the late 1990s, given the disappointing results of almost 20 years of policy reforms in developing countries, an enlarged policy agenda, sometimes called the "post-Washington Consensus" or "second-generation reforms" (Kuczynski and Williamson, 2003), emphasized poverty reduction and the mitigation of its effects as immediate objectives of development policies, which required direct government involvement. It was accompanied by a new emphasis on supply-side measures in health,

education and infrastructure improvements to reduce poverty. However, macroeconomic policies that would promote fixed investment, productivity growth and employment creation continued to be neglected. Similar to structural adjustment programmes, reforms undertaken in the poorer developing countries in connection with Poverty Reduction Strategy Papers (PRSP) starting in 1999 continued to focus on price stabilization (Khan, 2006; Muqtada, 2003; UNCTAD, 2002), while emphasizing the need for reallocation of public expenditure to areas such as primary health care and education. Such measures were destined to fail in their attempt to achieve sustained poverty reduction in the absence of accelerated structural change and sufficient capital accumulation, which could have boosted growth and created productive employment (World Bank, 2005).

Since the end of the hyperinflation phase in the second half of the 1980s and the early 1990s, most countries in Latin America and Africa adopted a "sound" monetary policy that sought to prevent inflation by keeping real interest rates consistently higher than growth rates, with the result that output growth remained subdued (chart 5.2). Consequently, the development gap widened and the catching up of these two regions lagged behind East and South-East Asian countries that had started industrializing from similar or even lower levels of development. It was only by drawing lessons from the experience of the Asian financial crisis in the late 1990s and the Argentinean debt crisis in 2001–2002 that the majority of Latin American countries adopted more accommodative and even expansionary monetary policies which led to stronger overall growth. A notable exception was Brazil, where monetary policy continued to resemble the orthodox approach, but the negative impact of high interest rates on development and structural change in that country was at least partly compensated by interest subsidies for loans from the national development bank for financing fixed capital formation.

Thus, over the past 30 years, adherence to the dogma of a flexible labour market, combined with a focus on keeping inflation rates low, prevented many developing countries from pursuing development strategies aimed at promoting investment in productive capacities and employment creation. And

Chart 5.2

REAL INTEREST RATES AND REAL GDP GROWTH RATES, SELECTED COUNTRIES IN AFRICA, ASIA AND LATIN AMERICA, 1990–2009

(Per cent)

A. Africa

Egypt

Mauritius

South Africa

B. Asia

China

Malaysia

Republic of Korea

C. Latin America

Argentina

Brazil

Chile

.... Real interest rate ——— Real GDP growth rate

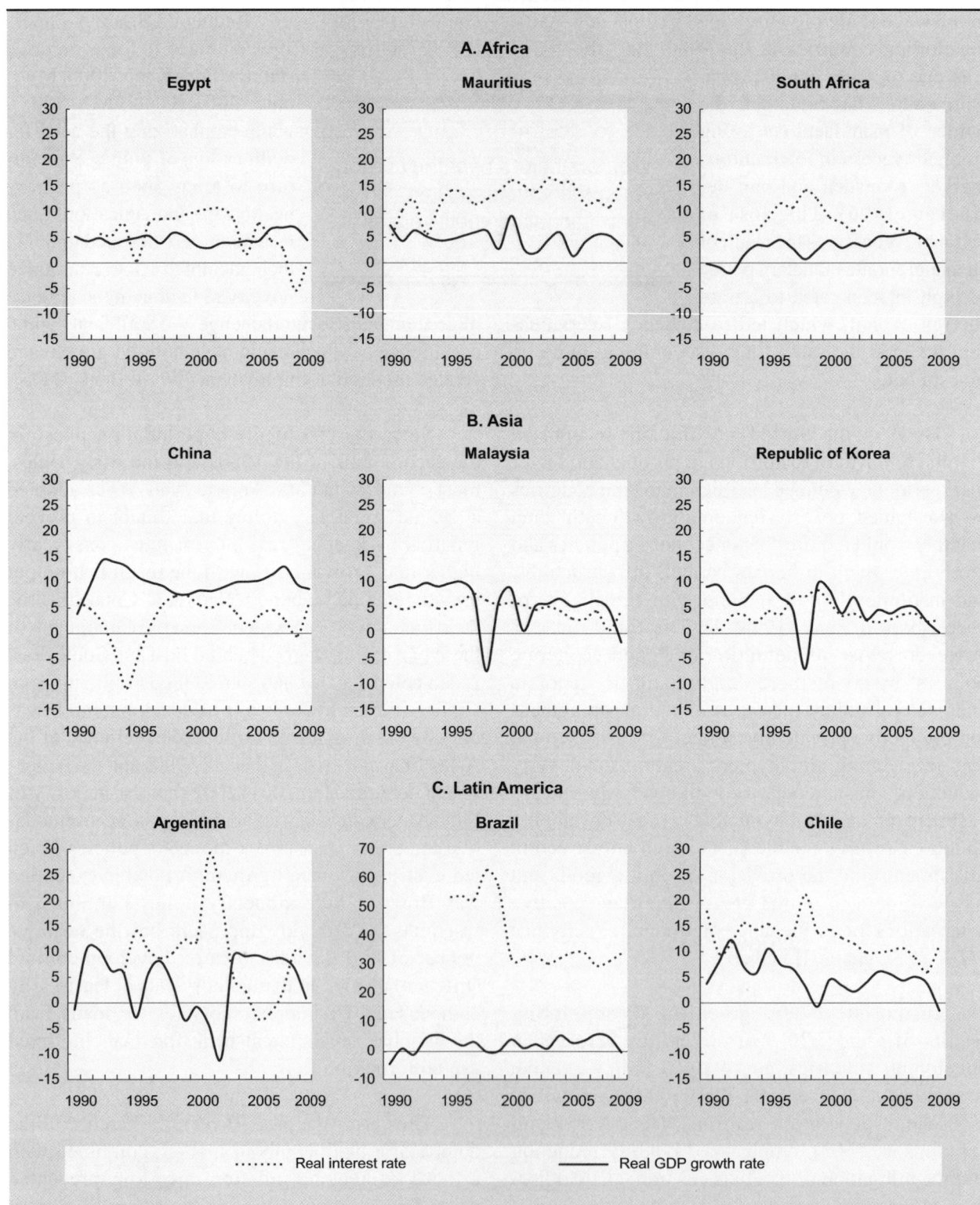

Source: UNCTAD secretariat calculations, based on table 1.1; IMF, *International Financial Statistics* database; and ECLAC, *CEPALSTAT* database.

for the same reason, they did not establish effective labour-market organizations and institutions.

4. Experience with heterodox policies

The most successful cases of economic catching up, all of which were in Asia, never strictly adhered to the principles of "sound macroeconomic policy" as advocated by the Washington Consensus. In practically all these countries private sector development and dynamic growth processes were bolstered by investment-friendly macroeconomic policies, a broad array of fiscal and regulatory instruments in support of capital accumulation and technological upgrading, effective institutions to coordinate private and public-sector activities, as well as redistributive policies and considerable investment in education (Chang, 2002; Amsden, 2001; Onaran and Stockhammer, 2005). Fiscal policy was used pragmatically to stimulate demand whenever that was required by cyclical developments. No doubt, their economic policies also gave importance to price stabilization, but it was pursued through various instruments other than high interest rates, the preferred ones being a government incomes policy and/or direct government intervention in the goods and labour markets.

Low interest rates are a key policy factor contributing to the dynamics of investment in fixed capital, growth and catching up (*TDR 2003*). Distinct from Africa and Latin America, in both real and nominal terms the lending interest rates in East and South-East Asia over the past 20 years, except during the Asian financial crisis, have been consistently lower than the GDP growth rate. As a result, they have acted as a driver of the strong investment dynamics in those two subregions (chart 5.2).

In addition to fiscal and monetary policies more favourable to domestic capital formation and productivity growth, the principles governing the functioning of labour markets in most countries in East and South-East Asia, beginning with Japan and the Republic of Korea, were also quite different, and often just the opposite of the "hire-and-fire" principle. The principle that employers assume responsibility for their employees and that employees enter into a lifelong relationship with "their" company served as the cornerstone of a sustained investment-led growth path, but was contradictory to the Washington Consensus. Furthermore, the East Asian form of labour-market organization has involved a process of participatory wage determination that could also serve development elsewhere.

C. Reassignment of macroeconomic policies for employment creation

1. The need for a new policy approach

As discussed in the context of the theoretical considerations in chapter III, a successful strategy for growth and employment depends on investment in fixed capital. In a market economy with a dominant private sector, such investment is strongly influenced by growth of demand for the goods and services that are produced with that capital, on the one hand,

and on the conditions to finance such investment on the other. Public policies can support investment on both sides.

The experience with the reform agendas of the 1980s and 1990s has shown that capital accumulation, productivity enhancement and more jobs do not automatically result from a purely market-determined allocation of resources; successful strategies for economic growth, catching up and sustained improvements in welfare for all groups of the population require much more than integration into the international division of labour.

Widening the scope of policy instruments beyond those that were deemed acceptable under the development paradigm of the past 30 years would not only allow the pursuit of additional goals, potentially it would also increase the number of combinations of instruments. In many cases this will be decisive in determining the success or failure of a strategy. For example, productivity-enhancing measures in agriculture will not translate into significant acceleration of growth and alleviation of poverty if rural workers that eventually become redundant cannot be absorbed into industrial production due to unfavourable conditions for investment in real productive capacity. Most frequently, it is excessively high interest rates for investment loans or an overvalued exchange rate that put domestic firms in the tradables sector at a disadvantage. Similarly, higher government outlays for education will not be sufficient for reducing unemployment if the better educated cannot be employed productively due to a lack of demand for higher skilled labour in a stagnating economy. And public expenditure for research and development related to activities in the manufacturing and services sector is unlikely to fuel growth if the results of these activities are not translated into innovation at the production level because financing conditions for investment are unfavourable. However, good financing conditions alone may not lead to the desired take-off led by private fixed capital formation if the demand expectations of potential investors are unfavourable or if essential public infrastructure is lacking. These examples illustrate that a key aspect of successful catch-up experiences seems to have been "the connection between macropolicy and structural policy, in which the links between sectoral policies, trade and macroeconomic growth contributed significantly to economic dynamism" (Bradford, 2005: 14).

> It is necessary to reassess the priorities of macroeconomic policies and to enlarge the range of policy instruments.

> During the latest crisis, countercyclical fiscal policy has been rediscovered.

Mainstream economic thinking and policy-making over the past few decades has focused almost exclusively on the conditions that determine behaviour on the supply side of markets. However, stabilizing employment at a high level and creating new jobs in the growth process require a macroeconomic approach that gives greater attention to conditions on the demand side. In such an approach, monetary and fiscal policy instruments again aim to serve the employment objective. The need for such a reorientation has been emphasized by many authors (see, for example, Epstein, 2005, 2007 and 2009; Muqtada, 2010; Pollin, Heintz and Githinji, 2007; Weeks, 2010), but the discussion has largely remained confined to the existing choice of policy instruments, and has argued mainly for a reassessment of the priorities in using those instruments.

In this section, it is argued that while such a reassessment of priorities is essential if faster growth and employment generation are to be achieved in developing countries, it is also important to enlarge the range of policy instruments. There is a need not only for appropriate fiscal and monetary policies, but also for an incomes (or wage) policy that will influence wages and the demand for wage goods in support of employment creation. Together, monetary, fiscal and incomes policies would then provide considerable scope for demand management to fight unemployment – both structural and cyclical – while keeping a lid on inflation. What matters from the employment perspective is that sufficient demand should be generated for goods and services to be produced in new activities that employ the same amount of labour as becomes redundant in the process of technological upgrading. This reassignment of macroeconomic policy should be part of a more fundamental reorientation in economic thinking based on an overall philosophy of capitalism, where capital serves the well-being of the society at large (the majority of which lives on incomes from labour) rather than the other way around.

2. Fiscal policy and the role of the public sector

Public finances, through variations in the levels of spending or taxation, can help stabilize aggregate demand, and, in times of recession, compensate for a shortfall of private demand relative to production potential. While reducing public spending is a direct way to curb excess demand in times of fast overall demand growth, debt-financed increases in public spending are essential to revive a stalling economy and protect employment in times of economic slowdown.

In the midst of the financial crisis, most governments have rediscovered the role of countercyclical fiscal policy in stabilizing aggregate demand, as reflected in the unprecedented stabilization packages that were launched to prevent another Great Depression. It would be highly beneficial for growth and employment if the principles underlying these policy decisions continued to serve as a basis for a revised approach to fiscal policy. By contrast, if public finances are governed by the same principles as the financial behaviour of private agents, it amplifies economic fluctuations and crises of confidence.

In an effort to attract foreign capital flows, governments of emerging-market economies often curtailed government spending to demonstrate their "fiscal discipline" to participants in financial markets and rating agencies. But the curtailment of government spending under the Washington Consensus concept of fiscal discipline has been partly responsible for output growth and employment falling short of their potential owing to insufficient investments in infrastructure. Such investments are often a precondition for private investment to become viable. Similarly, public expenditure on education and training can influence the quality and skills structure of the labour force and the potential of labour to contribute to productivity growth. This in turn allows the payment of higher wages that feed back into output growth and employment creation.

It should also be pointed out that fiscal balance per se is not a useful indicator of the effects of fiscal policy on employment creation: the same fiscal balance can have different effects, depending on how public revenue is raised and spent. For example, on the revenue side, tax income from high-income groups, and changes in the tax rates for these groups, typically have a small impact on domestic demand, as these income groups save a larger part of their income and spend a greater share of their household incomes on luxury goods, most of which are imported. On the expenditure side, public investment in transport infrastructure or credit subsidies for private investment in real productive capacity will have a much greater impact on employment creation than the bailing out of banks or spending on imports of military equipment and sophisticated vehicles used to transport officials.

The public sector, typically the largest purchaser of goods and services and the largest employer in an economy, has a significant influence on the expansion and functioning of goods and labour markets. Public sector employment can therefore play a major role in employment policy, especially in developing countries with a large amount of surplus labour. Taxation and public spending are potentially key instruments for establishing linkages between companies in the modern sectors, export industries and the rest of the economy. These aspects of the role of the State for employment creation are discussed further in section D.

3. Monetary and financial policies

Insufficient investment in fixed capital is often attributed to low savings, given the macroeconomic identity between savings and investment. According to this view, the scope for increasing savings, particularly household savings, is very small in most developing countries, so that there is also very little scope for increasing investment unless a country has access to "foreign savings". In this line of reasoning, foreign capital has to be attracted by high interest rates. However, this view is not supported by a comparison of the actual experiences of countries where monetary policy was tight but the economy stagnated, as in Africa and Latin America, and countries where monetary policy was expansionary and growth and employment creation were fast, as in East and South-East Asia. The combination of expansionary monetary policy and fast growth in developed countries in the "golden age of capitalism" also leads to the same conclusion.

An increase in household savings at a given level of income implies a decline in the demand for consumer goods and services, which discourages investment in additional productive capacity. On the other hand, fixed investment will result from positive demand expectations combined with favourable financing conditions. For sustained income and employment growth, proactive and permanent short-term management of monetary, financial and overall demand conditions is needed to ensure that planned investment exceeds planned savings. In such an environment, savings will rise even if the propensity of households to save remains unchanged (see also Gordon, 1995; Pollin, 2002). The higher savings, which correspond to the higher investment in the macroeconomic equilibrium equation, are eventually generated by higher profits. The initial real investment can be financed by bank credit if the central bank allows credit expansion through an appropriate monetary policy. Higher profits resulting from the temporary pioneer rents of innovative investors provide the funding for the investments and for repayment of the initial bank credit (see also *TDR 2006*, chap. I, annex 2).

The central bank, through its provision of liquidity and determination of the short-term interest rate, can provide an important expansionary stimulus, and at least indirectly influence long-term interest rates according to its assessment of the economic situation. Thus the positive effect of its expansionary monetary policy on investment in fixed capital supports employment creation. Monetary policy that is permanently and exclusively used for fighting protracted or inertial inflation, a priori, hampers employment creation and sustainable income growth. Therefore the macroeconomic policy instruments recommended to developing countries over the past three decades as the only rational choice, in line with the Washington Consensus, need to be revised in the light of the greater priority now being given to employment creation.

Central banks can do more for stable growth than keeping inflation low; they can function as agents of development by shifting their focus to employment. Moreover, monetary and financial policies have a bearing on

> Central banks can do more for stabilizing growth than keeping inflation low – they can establish favourable conditions for investment and employment creation.

the exchange rate, and thus on the competitiveness of domestic vis-à-vis foreign producers and employers. There are numerous examples of successful experiences in this respect in countries such as France, Germany, India, Japan, the Republic of Korea, the United Kingdom and the United States, where central banks played an essential role in public policies in support of growth and structural change by maintaining low interest rates, exerting capital controls to help stabilize exchange rates at competitive levels and sometimes engaging in direct lending for selected projects (Epstein, 2007). More recently, several proposals have been made for "employment targeting" in various countries, including Kenya, the Philippines and South Africa (Lim, 2006; Pollin et al., 2006; Pollin, Heintz and Githinji, 2007).

A monetary policy that focuses on creating favourable conditions for the financing of private investment can be complemented by the promotion of investment lending by private financial institutions and by the provision of credit through public financial institutions. State investment banks have played an important role in providing cheap credit to investors and channelling capacity creation in a socially desirable direction, for example in Argentina, Brazil, Malaysia, the Republic of Korea and Taiwan Province of China (Amsden, 2001 and 2007).

4. An incomes policy for wage-led growth

Supportive monetary, financial and fiscal policies are required to achieve a strong growth dynamic based on fixed capital formation that provides the additional employment opportunities required to absorb surplus labour. But the task of monetary, financial and fiscal policies to support employment growth can be greatly facilitated by the additional use of an incomes policy that builds on certain rules for determining mass incomes in a growing economy. A well-designed incomes policy

> An incomes policy can pave the way for a steady expansion of domestic demand.

can make a major contribution to employment growth by paving the way for a steady expansion of domestic demand.

When unemployment rises, and many workers that lose their jobs in the formal labour market shift to the shadow or informal labour market, the power of employers tends to strengthen, forcing the laid-off workers to accept much lower wages than they would have if unemployment had not risen. This would be acceptable if the fall in wages was the right remedy for redressing the labour market disequilibrium. But the downward flexibility of wages causes a fall in demand, leading to even further wage cuts without stimulating employment creation through investment. Thus, unlike price flexibility in goods markets that causes demand to match supply for individual products, wage flexibility does not stop the rise in unemployment (see also chapter III, section B). Indeed, the outcome is just the opposite: the fall in wages increases the number of unemployed and underemployed, reduces the incentives to invest in productive capacity and results in a downward spiral in the overall standard of living of the society, as experienced by many developing countries during the era of the Washington Consensus, as discussed in chapter IV.

In this context, it is important to realize that if labour income does not rise in line with productivity growth, it does not mean that profits will automatically rise more. Profits are residual incomes, and will rise only when demand expands sufficiently, which is unlikely to happen when mass incomes do not rise in line with production. Moreover, increases in profit incomes tend to contribute less to employment growth than increases in labour incomes, because profit earners, on average, have a higher propensity to save than wage earners, and they tend to consume more imported luxury goods. Therefore, development strategies based on wage-led growth have a potential to maximize increases in output, productivity and employment.

Thus, in order to attain a sustainable trajectory, productivity gains need to be distributed in a way that allows labour income to grow at the same pace as productivity. As these income increases are largely spent on consumption, any job losses resulting from productivity gains at the level of the individual firm through the use of technologically more advanced production processes will be compensated by an additional demand for labour in the economy as a whole. As demand would grow at a similar rate as the supply potential, it would also serve as an inducement to additional fixed investment, and as a stimulus for industrial growth and the creation of jobs to absorb the surplus labour in the economy.

The incentive for dynamic entrepreneurs to invest in fixed capital and product or process innovation is even stronger when wages follow the average productivity growth of the entire economy, rather than the wages in every firm following the productivity growth in that same firm. The former would result in a greater differentiation of profits between capitalist firms. More dynamic entrepreneurs would be rewarded for their investments or innovations by greater pioneer rents than in a situation where they pass on the gains from their firms' enhanced productivity either to their own workers or to their customers through price cuts.

In a market economy, the implementation of such an incomes policy requires an institutional framework adapted to the stage of development, economic structure and cultural and historical specificities of each country, as discussed further in section D below. Such an institutional framework is all the more important as an incomes policy can serve not only as an instrument for employment generation, but also as a means to control inflation.

5. Incomes policy and inflation control

A frequently made argument against a monetary policy that aims at the provision of investment financing at low cost is its alleged inflationary impact. Undoubtedly, low inflation is critical for macroeconomic stability. Countries that are prone to high and accelerating inflation will find it more difficult to start and sustain a process of development and catching up because of the frequent need to tighten monetary and

> Productivity gains need to be distributed in a way that allows labour income to grow at the same rate as productivity.

Chart 5.3

ANNUAL GROWTH RATES OF UNIT LABOUR COSTS AND INFLATION RATES, 1970–2008

(Per cent)

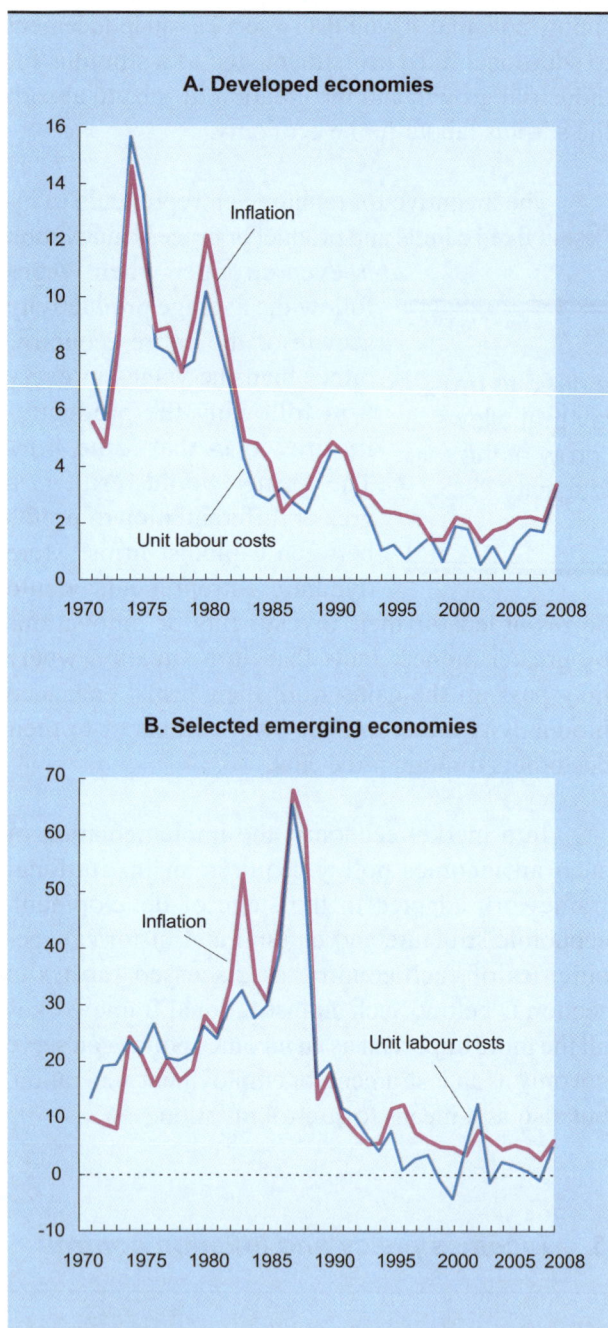

A. Developed economies

B. Selected emerging economies

Source: UNCTAD secretariat calculations, based on United States Bureau of Labor Statistics, *International Labor Comparisons* database; *OECD.Stat Extracts* database; IMF, *International Financial Statistics* database; OECD database; and ILO, *LABORSTAT* database.

Note: Selected emerging economies comprises Argentina (2000–2006), Brazil (1996–2006), Mexico (1975–2006), the Philippines (2001–2007), the Republic of Korea (1971–2008), Singapore (1991–2008) and Taiwan Province of China (1991–2007).

credit conditions. It is also true that monetary policy will be overburdened if it has to simultaneously keep inflation low and provide low-cost finance for investment in real productive capacity that would create new employment opportunities. This would amount to pursuing too many objectives with too few policy instruments. Here too, the application of incomes policy instruments can provide a solution.

Wage growth based on the productivity rule would contribute to keeping inflation low by preventing a rise of unit labour costs and an increase in demand in excess of the supply potential. For example, in the aftermath of the oil price hikes of the 1970s, nominal wages in many countries were adjusted by applying some form of backward-looking indexation: they were increased in line with past consumer price inflation, based on the erroneous assumption that this would give workers quick compensation for the negative real income effect of the falling terms of trade. But, as mentioned in section B above, this practice led to long disputes about income distribution as employers tended to react to the higher labour costs by raising prices, which caused an acceleration of inflation and higher unemployment. Inflationary risks were managed better in those oil-importing countries where nominal wages were not adjusted to past inflation but grew more in line with productivity growth. Although the immediate fall in real wages was larger, the medium- to long-term impact on growth and employment was positive since an acceleration of inflation could be avoided.

As wages are the most important determinant of the overall cost of production in a vertically integrated market economy, the importance of avoiding excessive nominal wage increases for stabilizing the inflation rate cannot be overestimated. In developed economies, where the share of labour in total income typically exceeds 60 per cent, the growth rates of unit labour costs (i.e. wage increases exceeding productivity growth) are very closely correlated with price level movements (chart 5.3A). The data coverage is much less comprehensive for developing countries, but to the extent that comparable data is available, it suggests that the correlation is very similar in a number of emerging-market economies (chart 5.3B). Unless there is broad acceptance throughout the economy that an increase in the wage share is desirable, inflation can be kept in check only if wages rise at a rate that corresponds approximately to the rate of productivity growth augmented by a target rate of inflation that is deemed acceptable, thereby anchoring inflationary expectations.

In developing countries, a rule for growth of labour income to be consistent with such an inflation target may be of particular importance for stabilizing the economy, on both the real and nominal side. Many developing countries have a history of very high inflation, or even hyperinflation, due to bouts of accelerating inflation spilling over into nominal wage increases through indexation mechanisms. This has proved to be extremely costly, because for central banks to bring inflation down to their target level against permanent upward price pressures from the cost side, they are obliged to apply shocks to the economy time and again through interest rate hikes. This implies

> Inflation can be kept in check if labour compensation rises approximately in line with productivity.

sacrificing real investment and employment for the sake of nominal stabilization. In this case, anchoring nominal wages to the productivity growth trend is extremely important.[3]

Applying the rule of increasing labour compensation in line with average productivity growth plus a targeted rate of inflation implies that the share of labour in total income remains unchanged. However, there may be situations when it is desirable to change a given distribution of income between capital and labour in an effort to redress inequities and national inequalities. In this case, more far-reaching adjustments of labour compensation should be subject to explicit negotiations as part of a social compact (van der Hoeven and Saget, 2004).

D. Institution building and the role of the State in developing countries

1. Collective bargaining and the role of labour and employer organizations

The recognition that labour compensation is not only a cost factor but also the most important single determinant of domestic demand, and that, consequently, real wages rising in line with productivity are a precondition rather than a hindrance to successful development, points to the importance of building appropriate institutions that support an incomes policy (as outlined in subsections C.4 and 5 above). In this regard, some lessons can be learned from the policy experiences of developed countries during the golden age of capitalism between 1950 and 1973, when very low rates of unemployment were achieved while labour markets were much

more regulated than today (Epstein and Schor, 1988; Singh, 2009).

An important institutional development in this context is the creation and empowerment of trade unions. While their primary mission is to represent the interests of workers, their role in collective bargaining and wage formation is also in the interests of the economy as a whole, including the owners of capital. As one side in collective bargaining negotiations – with employer associations on the other – trade unions can be instrumental in nurturing a process of domestic-demand-led growth.[4]

Trade unions have often been criticized for their exaggerated attempts to stabilize or increase the purchasing power of workers even in periods of supply shocks, as discussed in the previous section. Such attempts are indeed counterproductive, as they fuel inflation and unemployment instead of protecting workers. But at the other extreme, the current dogma of labour market flexibility, which aims at minimizing the role of trade unions and at getting "prices right", overlooks the important role that workers' and employers' associations can play in stimulating a dynamic process of investment, productivity growth and employment creation. This is provided that collective wage negotiations are conducted within a framework of rules designed to ensure that wage growth neither substantially exceeds nor substantially falls short of a rate that ensures stability of both prices and employment. Tripartite arrangements involving government representation in collective wage negotiations, or government recommendations or guidelines for an incomes policy, have helped many countries in the past to focus economic policy on investment in fixed capital and to preserve their overall international competitiveness.

> Workers' and employers' associations can be instrumental in promoting domestic-demand-led growth.

It is undoubtedly difficult to expect the establishment of sophisticated labour-market institutions in poor developing countries where governments are often not even able to protect the poor against hunger and sickness. But the laissez-faire approach of the past has failed the test, and in many developing countries the share of wages in national income has been extremely "flexible" downwards without solving investment, employment and poverty problems. Thus some appropriate form of labour-market institutions may be the only way to solve the unemployment problem, and therefore deserves to be given much greater priority in institution building and governance reforms in developing countries than in the past.

2. Minimum wages

The realization of an institutional framework for a dynamic investment-productivity-employment nexus is especially difficult in developing-country environments where the degree of labour protection and organization of the labour force and employers is very low, and where structured negotiations for determining wages and employment conditions are rare or absent. Since the creation of responsible institutions representing workers and employers may require considerable time, the establishment of minimum wages is a tool that governments can activate more rapidly. It may also serve as a complement to collective bargaining (ILO, 2008).

The problem here is to determine the right level of the minimum wage from the perspective of the macroeconomic relevance of wages as a determinant of private consumption. In many countries, it has been observed that, as a consequence of structural adjustment and liberalization policies and the declining power of trade unions and labour-market institutions, minimum wages have been set at very low levels. Making formal labour cheaper in this way has been part of efforts to create additional formal employment and reduce informal employment. However, apart from the fact that extremely low minimum wages do not contribute to poverty reduction, they are also unlikely to help job creation because they do little to raise mass purchasing power.

In other countries, minimum wages are relatively high – sometimes referred to as "maxi minimum wage" (Saget, 2008) – which is often attributed to poorly developed collective bargaining. This may result from the fact that minimum wage consultations are the only forum where trade unions can make their demands known. In these cases, the legal minimum wage is closer to the actual wage earned by most formal workers. In such a process, several goals are pursued with a single policy instrument: the minimum wage is used as a reference to fix wages, to get a grip on inflation and to promote social dialogue.

It has been argued that minimum wages that are excessively low or high are an indication of malfunctioning labour markets (van der Hoeven, 2010), in the sense that they do not fulfil the function of ensuring the participation of labour in overall income growth that would contribute to poverty reduction without jeopardizing employment and economic growth. Indeed, whether minimum wages help employment creation and macroeconomic stabilization by supporting wage-led growth is best judged by their relationship with productivity growth and inflation.

If they are adjusted regularly in line with the actual average productivity growth of an economy and the targeted rate of inflation, rather than arbitrarily in response to the varying influences of interest groups on political decisions, they can have a positive effect on the investment-productivity growth dynamic. Poverty will then be reduced not so much by lifting the income of those that actually earn the minimum wage, but much more by the additional employment that is created in response to higher demand and higher profits in those firms where productivity growth exceeds the average.

> Minimum wages and public employment schemes can be effective tools of an incomes policy.

3. Public employment schemes

It is well known that in most low-income developing countries, informal jobs and self-employment constitute the bulk of employment in a context where a large reserve of surplus labour exists. Competition between the employed and the unemployed and underemployed tends to drive down earnings and worsen other conditions of work. Thus, while the long-term effort in such contexts must be one of expanding the share of formal employment in total employment, the emphasis for the foreseeable future must also be on mechanisms to improve both earnings and conditions of work in the informal sector and in the "self-exploitative" segment where workers are self-employed.

One way of doing this is to implement public employment schemes, such as those introduced in Argentina and India (see box 5.1), which establish an effective floor to the level of earnings and working conditions by ensuring the availability of "on demand" jobs that offer the minimum employment terms. These terms should be improved over time at a rate that appropriately reflects the average growth of productivity in the entire economy and the increase in tax revenues in a growing economy. There are a number of benefits to such a scheme. First, to the extent that

> Public employment schemes can be successfully implemented even in very low income countries.

it is successfully implemented, it would ensure that employment outside the scheme would be on terms that are better than the minimum standards set by the scheme. Second, the demand for goods and services generated directly and indirectly – through a multiplier effect – by the scheme would help expand markets and drive output growth, so that the restraining effect of productivity increases on employment are neutralized by an enhanced pace of demand growth. Third, the scheme itself would tend to be self-selecting, since only those unable to obtain this minimum level of wages and working conditions would demand and be provided with such employment. Fourth, since the operation of the scheme would expand domestic demand and increase employment elsewhere through multiplier effects, it would, ideally, reduce workers' demand for such employment over time, so that there would be endogenous limits on the budgetary outlays needed to implement this policy. Fifth, the scheme would act as an automatic stabilizer of consumption demand in periods of recession or downswing, and therefore serve to moderate the economic cycle, which is extremely important given that such stabilizers are relatively few in most developing economies. Finally, over time, by eroding the ability of firms to compete based on low wages and poor working conditions, it would help increase the share of formal sector employment in total employment, reduce the differential between the formal and informal sectors with respect to terms of employment, and improve the average terms of employment in the system as a whole.

Public sector employment schemes can be successfully implemented even in very low income countries. In Sierra Leone, one of the poorest countries in the world, a World Bank supported public works programme after the disastrous civil war prevented thousands from suffering starvation. In 2008–2009 the government extended this programme as a measure to counter the international recession that reduced demand for export crops. The success of this programme demonstrates that emergency and countercyclical public employment schemes can play an important role even when administrative capacity is limited (Weeks, 2009).

Box 5.1

EMPLOYER OF LAST RESORT PROGRAMMES IN ARGENTINA AND INDIA

The National Rural Employment Guarantee Scheme in India

Under this scheme, launched in February 2006, every rural household is guaranteed up to 100 days of unskilled manual wage employment per year, at the statutory minimum wage for agricultural workers. This is a demand-driven scheme that recognizes the legal right to employment. If employment is not provided within 15 days, the applicant is entitled to an unemployment allowance. The scheme, with a budgetary provision of around 0.6 per cent of GDP, has been extended to all rural districts in India. It aims to provide work on labour-intensive projects focusing on rural infrastructure at the local level. Nearly 4.3 million public works have been undertaken so far, about half of which were for water conservation, 15 per cent for rural connectivity and 12 per cent for land development. Thus far, it has provided some employment to more than 50 million households, and nearly 2.6 billion person days of employment have been generated.

The enhanced wage earnings have contributed to strengthening the livelihood resource base of the rural poor in India, reduced distress migration, and become an extremely important buffer against both the employment shocks generated by the economic crisis (as migrant workers returned home to their villages) and the drought that swept across large parts of the country in the summer of 2009. In 2008 and 2009, nearly 70 per cent of the expenditure under the scheme was in the form of wages paid to the labourers. The programme is affecting the labour market in some parts of the country quite significantly. It has raised the de facto minimum wage by 10–15 per cent in some areas and changed seasonal migration patterns to some extent. It has reduced the migration of unskilled workers in the agricultural sector within India, and there is evidence that the remuneration of construction work has risen, as rural workers are able to find some gainful employment during the lean season (Chandrasekhar and Ghosh, 2010).

Another effect of the scheme is that it raises agricultural incomes as the demand for food rises. At the same time it contributes to productivity gains in agricultural and other rural activities, albeit with some time lag, as the public works projects help to improve irrigation, water harvesting, soil quality and transport infrastructure.

A support programme for household heads in Argentina

In 2002, in the midst of a deep economic crisis, when 21.5 per cent of the labour force was out of work and the income of more than 50 per cent of the population was below the poverty line, the Government of Argentina launched a programme for providing a subsistence income to unemployed heads of households (Programa Jefas y Jefes de Hogar) with at least one child. In exchange, these persons work for a minimum of 20 hours a week in small projects that help improve local and community infrastructure. Another condition is that children attend school and enrol in a vaccination programme. As in India, the programme is implemented by local and regional administrations.

In May 2003, when resort to the programmes was at its peak, its fiscal cost amounted to about 1 per cent of GDP. About 2 million households, more than 70 per cent of which are headed by women, have benefited from the scheme. The impact on poverty and economic recovery has been very significant. As the beneficiaries consume most of the income derived from the programme, and their consumption has a relatively low import content, the programme has had a huge multiplier effect. According to an estimate by the Ministry of Labour based on 2003 data, the programme's contribution to GDP was 2.5 times the amount of the initial expenditure on the programme (Tcherneva and Wray, 2005). With faster growth of the national economy in the subsequent years and the reduction in unemployment to 8 per cent in 2008, the number of beneficiaries fell to 500,000 at the end of 2008. Some of the former beneficiaries found more stable jobs, while others are now covered by new programmes designed to facilitate their insertion into the labour market through education and vocational training.

Another approach to stabilizing employment and income is the Argentinean Programme for Production Recovery. Under this programme, the Government assumes, for a period of one year, part of the wage bill paid by private employers in difficulty, who present a plan for redressing the economic problems of their firms and make a commitment not to lay off their workers. This has helped to preserve tens of thousand of jobs, mainly in small and medium-sized enterprises, and to avoid not only the social costs of higher unemployment, but also the economic costs of losing human capital and depressing domestic demand, which would have made the labour market situation even more precarious.

In most developing countries there is a pressing need to increase public sector provision of essential social services, especially those concerned with nutrition, sanitation, health and education. This is important not only for the obvious direct effects in terms of improved material and social conditions, but also for macroeconomic reasons. The public provision of such services tends to be labour-intensive, and therefore also has considerable direct effects on employment.

4. Improving incomes of small producers

In many developing countries, informal employment and self-employment account for large shares of total employment. It is therefore important for these countries to complement employment-enhancing policies and institution building as discussed in the preceding sections with measures to raise incomes and purchasing power of the informally and self-employed.

Measures to strengthen the capacity of small-scale farmers to purchase productivity enhancing intermediate goods and equipment are needed in any case to raise food security and to gradually improve the living conditions of the rural population (Mittal, 2009). But mechanisms that link agricultural producer prices to the overall productivity growth in the economy would also contribute to an increase in demand by those segments of the population who tend to purchase consumer goods that can be produced locally. Such mechanisms have been applied successfully in all developed countries for decades. Productivity in the agricultural sector could be enhanced through public investments in agricultural research and rural infrastructure and with the help of publicly assisted agricultural support organizations. Such organizations were frequently dismantled in connection with structural adjustment programmes in the 1990s. If they are revitalized with appropriate governance structures, they can play an important role in raising agricultural productivity and incomes, for example by providing extension services, disseminating information about productivity-enhancing investments and efficient marketing, and facilitating access of small farmers to affordable credit. Ensuring the participation of the agricultural sector in overall productivity growth may also require protecting farmers against the impact of competition from highly subsidized agricultural products imported from developed countries.

But the development of rural areas cannot rely on the agricultural sector alone (Nkurunziza, 2007; Davis and Bezemer, 2003), and informal and self-employment is also widespread in urban areas. Small producers in non-agricultural activities often cannot raise their productivity due to difficulties in obtaining credit to finance even small investments that would improve their supply capacity and access to markets. Private micro-finance schemes can meet these financing needs only partially, since they charge very high interest rates. Small-scale farmers and the self-employed pursuing non-farm activities in both rural and urban areas are therefore particularly dependent on financial support schemes such as credit subsidies and guarantees, and the provision of public credit for selected projects through national development banks (see also McKinley, 2009).

5. Taxation: finding the right balance

As mentioned above, taxation and government spending are key instruments for establishing important linkages between export industries – be they traditional extractive or modern manufacturing industries – and the rest of the economy, where such linkages are not created by market forces. For example, effective taxation of extractive industries' profits may often be the only way to ensure that huge gains from an increase in international commodity prices are channelled into domestic demand and into greater investment in diversification of production and job creation.

(a) Distribution of rents from the extractive industries

Natural resources on their own are neither a curse that perpetuates underdevelopment of a country, nor a blessing that helps its rapid economic development. But their exploitation generates rents (i.e. the difference between the sales value and the cost of exploitation of these resources) which, if effectively used, can serve as a basis for structural change and fixed capital formation, and hence the creation of employment opportunities. Thus, managing the distribution and use of the rents generated by the extractive industries needs to be integrated into the national development strategies of the producing countries, so that they contribute to the process of diversification out of the natural resources sector, as these finite resources will eventually be depleted (Sachs, 2007; Auty, 2007; Pineda and Rodríguez, 2010).

From the point of view of employment generation it is important that the use of this income either increases imports of capital goods for the creation of productive capacity in other sectors of the economy or generates demand for locally produced goods. To this end, where the extraction companies are not State-owned, appropriate fiscal treatment of their income is an important instrument.

The boom in prices of oil and mineral and metal products between 2003 and 2008 led governments in the developing countries producing these commodities to increasingly re-examine the fiscal treatment of companies in the extractive industries (UNECA-AfDB, 2007; UNECA, 2009). There were growing concerns that while the returns on investment of these companies were soaring as a result of higher prices, the share of the rents that stayed in the country remained unchanged, or even fell.

The analysis of the distribution of these rents is complicated due to the scarcity and fragmentation of data on government revenues and the costs of production in this sector. But the data available for a number of countries may give an approximate idea of the magnitudes involved, and enables drawing some conclusions (table 5.2).[5]

There are large variations in the distribution of the rents from extractive activities across countries and sectors, reflecting differences in the role of State-owned enterprises and fiscal regimes. In countries where State-owned enterprises play a major role in the extractive industries, such as Angola, the Bolivarian Republic of Venezuela, Chile and Mexico, the share of the rents captured by the government is much higher than in countries where these companies have been privatized and where the fiscal treatment is relatively liberal, such as Peru, the United Republic of Tanzania and Zambia. In particular, government revenues in the form of income taxes have been low as a percentage of the total rent from oil and mining.

The distribution of the rents, especially in mining, tends to be biased in favour of transnational corporations (TNCs). This is because many governments offered very favourable fiscal regimes in order to attract FDI in mining, particularly during the period of privatization of the sector in the 1980s and 1990s. It was also due to the imbalances of bargaining power in the negotiations of the contracts between the governments of poor countries and powerful TNCs. The latter often enjoyed low royalty rates,[6] and benefited from lower tax rates and shorter depreciation periods than domestic firms. In addition to these advantages, TNCs can also reduce their taxable income by using certain accounting practices, such as transfer pricing. Since all these factors bear on investment decisions taken with a relatively long time horizon, the contractual arrangements between governments and TNCs are often difficult to adjust to changing market conditions (see, for example, OSISA et al., 2009). In general, therefore, a significant proportion of the sharply rising proceeds of the extractive industries, as a result of the commodity boom since 2002, was mostly repatriated to the TNCs' home countries or reinvested in the same mines; only a small share would revert to the country in the form of government revenues to be used for the development of other industrial activities and domestic employment creation.

Only since 2006 have the governments of a number of countries partly been able to revise their fiscal regimes and renegotiate contracts with TNCs in the extractive industries.[7] Such renegotiations have been an issue especially in Africa (Custers and Matthysen, 2009), but also in Latin America and Australia.[8]

> **Taxation may be the only way to ensure that the huge gains from commodity price increases are channelled in ways that boost domestic demand.**

> **Countries should avoid a race to the bottom in offering fiscal incentives to FDI.**

Table 5.2

SHARE OF GOVERNMENT REVENUES IN RENTS FROM THE EXTRACTIVE INDUSTRIES, SELECTED COMMODITIES AND COUNTRIES, 2002–2009

(Per cent)

	2002	2003	2004	2005	2006	2007	2008	2009
Oil								
Angola	72.7	76.1	72.8	61.7	69.3	66.3	62.4	48.7
Azerbaijan	..	41.5	30.0	27.6	29.6	31.6	58.2	..
Bolivarian Republic of Venezuela	59.0	62.0	62.0	58.0	69.0	67.0	75.0	..
Chad	..	28.8	19.6	16.2	36.5	43.1	55.9	31.3
Copper								
Chile	43.2	72.8	49.0	53.3	50.2	44.3	62.6	..
Indonesia	46.0	44.0	42.0	45.0	42.0	..	..	..
Zambia	..	..	..	1.0	3.0	7.9	12.0	..
Gold								
Mali	..	..	20.9	18.3	11.1	34.4	33.3	..
Peru	21.8	27.9	26.3	30.0	28.5	29.7	27.4	..
United Republic of Tanzania	19.2	13.1	18.7	32.0	10.1	13.2	16.3	10.3

Source: UNCTAD secretariat calculations, based on annual reports of producing companies; UNCTAD, *Commodity Price Statistics Online* database; IMF, *Country Reports*, various issues; IMF, *International Financial Statistics* database; World Bank, *Global Commodity Markets*, various issues; *United States Energy Information Administration* database; BGS, 2010; Mpande, 2009; Curtis and Lissu, 2008; Thomas, 2010; and national sources.

Note: Rent is defined as the difference between the sales value and the cost of production, including capital depreciation. 2008 data for Chad include anticipated 2009 payments to the Government.

But the recent global economic crisis and downturn in commodity prices at the end of 2008 again reduced the bargaining power of governments in producing countries. In some cases they were forced to go back on their decisions to introduce fairer regimes for sharing the rents from the extractive industries, as mines were closing down and laying off workers.[9] Indeed, the global financial crisis took a heavy toll on employment in the mining sector in many developing countries, particularly countries such as Bolivia, the Democratic Republic of the Congo, the United Republic of Tanzania, and Zambia (SARW, 2009; and ODI, 2010).

Prices of oil and minerals and metals recovered in 2009 and 2010, and may remain relatively high on account of continuously growing demand from emerging developing countries, particularly China. In this context, and quite independently of short-term price developments, there is a fundamental need to achieve the right balance between the objective of generating income from the exploitation of natural resource endowments with the help of FDI, on the one hand, and government appropriation of a fair share of the rents accruing from the higher prices in the extractive industries on the other. In particular, governments should avoid engaging in a "race to the bottom" in fiscal as well as environmental rules in order to attract FDI (see *TDR 2005*; and UNCTAD, 2007).

An equitable distribution of the rents from the extractive industries between governments and TNCs is a necessary, but not sufficient, condition for the benefits from the exploitation of the natural resources to be translated into higher incomes and improved employment conditions for the population, especially in highly commodity-dependent economies. It is equally important that the revenues accruing to governments from these activities, in the form of either profits of State-owned enterprises or royalties and taxes paid by private companies, are used efficiently.

Strategic spending of these revenues could create a link between the extractive industries, which often operate in enclaves, and the rest of the economy.

Government revenues from the extractive industries could be used not only for public investments in infrastructure, health and education, but also for the provision of fiscal incentives and improved public services under industrial policies aimed at diversification of economic activities. This would reduce countries' dependence on natural resources – which are finite and the prices of which are volatile – while enabling an expansion of activities in manufacturing, services and agro-industry, where employment elasticities are much higher (UNECA, 2010).

(b) Rents from FDI in manufacturing industries

A large part of FDI by TNCs is attracted to developing countries because of low local labour costs. Such FDI typically implies the transfer of more advanced technology and the introduction of more capital-intensive production techniques than are available in the host country. Such investment may thus contribute substantially to raising the average level of productivity in the low-wage country.

From the perspective of the TNC, the relocation of production to a developing country will normally result in a dramatic drop in its unit labour costs, since differences in the wage level between the host country and the TNC's home country are large. The TNC combines advanced foreign technology with cheap local labour. Unit profits can therefore be many times higher than those realized in the home country. Alternatively, the TNC can substantially reduce the sales price and thereby gain market shares. In both cases, most of the host country's "comparative advantage" of abundant cheap labour will be captured by the foreign investor in the form of higher profits, or by foreign consumers in the form of lower purchasing prices.

The policy challenge for countries that have manufacturing industries with a strong presence of

> High profits of TNCs based on low labour costs should be taxed sufficiently to create linkages between a successful export sector and the rest of the economy.

TNCs producing for the world market is comparable to some extent to that of countries that host TNCs in extractive industries. They need to ensure that an appropriate share of the "rent" remains in the country, and that some form of linkage is established between the advanced export industry and the rest of the economy. In some countries that pursue a coherent industrial policy, the market mechanism may lead foreign companies to purchase intermediate inputs for their production from the local market, and thereby generate some output growth and employment in the economy of the host county. In many cases, however, the market mechanism may not generate such linkages, in which case local content requirements in investment agreements might help, provided that the necessary supply capacities exist. If this is not the case, or in addition to those requirements, adequate taxation of high profits resulting from the low labour costs – which attracted the TNCs in the first place – can be instrumental in ensuring that linkages are created with the rest of the economy. Those linkages can lead to the creation of domestic demand, which in turn can generate additional employment.

As unit labour costs are the most important determinant of competitiveness between regions with relatively immobile labour, the rents or the gains in market shares that the investor is able to realize by cutting prices up to the full extent of the cost reduction can be extremely high in most cases of FDI in low-wage countries. Even in China, with its robust economy, where FDI is an important contributor to the huge jumps in productivity and induces sharply rising nominal and real wages in manufacturing, the quasi-monopoly positions of foreign investors will taper off only slowly. This is because the process of catching up takes many years, or even decades, given the low original level of wages and capital stock in China, as in many other developing countries, compared with the developed countries.

The absolute competitive advantage gained by the foreign investor that is able to combine high technology with low wages in a low-wage environment is an advantage vis-à-vis those competitors with the same level of capital equipment in developed economies and vis-à-vis those competitors that benefit from low prices of labour in developing economies but have less, if any, access to advanced technologies.

Consequently, the catch-up strategy of some successful industrializers in Asia (i.e. Japan and the Republic of Korea) was to combine the advantage of a well-educated domestic labour force with imported advanced technology, thereby allowing domestic producers to gain most of the quasi-monopoly rents. This strategy, which had strong government support, proved to be very effective. A similar effect could be achieved if governments in developing countries were to adequately tax quasi-monopoly rents appropriated by TNCs and use the proceeds to increase domestic demand for domestically produced goods, either directly through purchases by the public sector or indirectly through wage subsidies, public employment programmes and/or financial support for local private investors. However, appropriation of a large share of the rent can only be successful if such a strategy is applied by most countries with similar levels of wages and well-educated workforces. If developing countries compete with each other by offering lower taxes to attract FDI, footloose foreign investors may move to the lower tax locations. This would be at the expense of all the countries that entered into such tax competition, an effect similar to that resulting from international wage competition.

E. The external dimension

Strengthening domestic demand to drive employment creation and relying less on exports for growth than many countries have done in the past must not be equated with a retreat from integration into the global economy. Developing countries need to earn the foreign exchange necessary to finance required imports, especially of capital goods and their embedded advanced technologies. Moreover, international competition among firms can also spur innovation and investment in tradable goods industries. However, in many countries, export-oriented strategies have made growth performance and employment creation overly dependent on global growth and on the ability to gain global market shares while reducing policy options to boost domestic demand based on increases in productivity-related growth of labour compensation.

In some developing countries the strategy of strong dependence on external markets has succeeded because they have been able to maintain lower costs of production than their competitors by keeping wages and domestic consumption low. But not all countries can simultaneously generate demand for their growing output by improving the international competitiveness of their producers in this manner. When productivity gains are used to reduce prices, it may temporarily help a country's firms to successfully compete in external markets, but this will be at the expense of other countries' products, and thus adversely affect the level of employment in these latter countries. The latter may therefore respond by reducing unit labour costs through wage cuts in order to remain or regain their competitive position internationally, thereby leading to an unsustainable race to the bottom in terms of wages. This is a systemic problem that could be mitigated through a multilateral framework for exchange-rate management that aims at keeping the real exchange rate relatively stable. Under such a system, nominal exchange rates would be adjusted according to differentials in the changes in unit labour costs (or inflation rates), so that there would be less incentives for firms to engage in international wage competition. The incentive for speculative capital flows would also be reduced, thereby alleviating pressures from capital markets on the exchange rate. Monetary policy can then focus primarily on domestic objectives, in particular that of achieving a high and stable level of investment in fixed capital (*TDR 2009*: chap. IV, sect. E; see also Frenkel and Taylor, 2006; and Epstein, 2007).

In the absence of effective multilateral arrangements for exchange-rate management, post-crisis policies in many developing countries whose growth and employment performance suffered in the past from currency overvaluation have shifted to an exchange-rate policy that aims at avoiding a repetition of that experience. They are intervening in foreign exchange markets and seeking to accumulate foreign exchange reserves, not only as a means of maintaining or improving their international competitiveness, but also to keep domestic interest rates low in order to foster investment and employment creation.

> Not all countries can simultaneously improve their international competitiveness.

In principle, policies in support of employment creation are possible under a regime of open capital markets as long as interest rates can be kept low so that there is no incentive for speculative capital inflows aimed at arbitrage profits. This is possible if inflation control is facilitated by appropriate incomes policies. But it is also true that a number of emerging-market economies have been able to regain greater autonomy in macroeconomic policy-making through the use of capital controls. Chile, for example, resorted to capital controls to reduce the share of short-term capital inflows in total inflows (Gallego, Hernández and Schmidt-Hebbel, 1999; and De Gregorio, Edwards and Valdés, 2000). In some countries, controls on outflows were imposed, which in the case of Malaysia appear to have enabled the stabilization of exchange rates and interest rates during the East Asian crisis and a faster recovery from that crisis, while limiting the decline in real wages and employment (Edison and Reinhart, 2001; Kaplan and Rodrik, 2001). Moreover, since global finance favours a deflationary rather than an expansionary fiscal stance, retaining the policy space needed to adopt the latter stance requires reducing dependence on global finance. To this end, capital controls not only help better management of exchange rates and monetary policy, they also prevent excessive inflows of capital that erode policy space of the kind needed to improve labour market conditions. ∎

Notes

1 The practical application of the neoclassical theory in macroeconomic policy can be illustrated by a statement of then British Prime Minister James Callaghan to the Labour Party Conference in September 1976: "We used to think that you could spend your way out of a recession and increase employment by cutting taxes and boosting government spending. … [T]hat option no longer exists, and in so far as it ever did exist, it only worked … by injecting a bigger dose of inflation into the economy, followed by a higher level of unemployment" (Labour Party Annual Conference Report 1976: 188, at: http://en.wikiquote.org/wiki/James_Callaghan).

2 Currency appreciation was even seen as a positive outcome because it contributed to disinflation and forced governments to advance with their "pro-market" reforms, which were expected to restore the international competitiveness of their domestic tradables sector.

3 It has also been suggested that in developing countries a higher rate of inflation may be acceptable when central banks provide more favourable

financing conditions for investment and growth than are often advocated in standard policy prescriptions. This is based on empirical research over the period 2000–2006 which has shown that, particularly in developing countries with underutilized capacities, growth can be compatible with – or even supported by – a moderate rate of inflation (Muqtada, 2010). It is estimated that the threshold rate of inflation for developing countries (i.e. the rate above which real GDP growth could be compromised) is 11–13 per cent (Khan and Senhadji, 2001), but it is bound to differ across countries depending on their specific circumstances.

4   For an account of recent developments in collective wage bargaining, see ILO, 2008.

5   The data has been compiled in connection with an ongoing project by the UNCTAD secretariat on the distribution of rents from the extractive industries. Initial results of this research and the methodology used were discussed in *TDR 2005*.

6   An IMF study on mineral taxation in developing countries found that royalty rates varied between 2 per cent and 30 per cent; the most common range was 5–10 per cent (Baunsgaard, 2001). A number of countries in Africa applied rates that were well below that common range.

7   For instance, the Democratic Republic of the Congo revised its mining licences and renegotiated contracts which did not meet required standards. In Zambia, in 2008 the Government raised the effective royalty rate paid by TNCs from 0.6 per cent to 3 per cent of the value of production, and the income tax from 25 per cent to 30 per cent (Ley, 2010; and Lungu, 2009). It also introduced a windfall tax and a variable profit tax, and reduced the capitalization allowance from 100 per cent to 25 per cent. In the United Republic of Tanzania, in April 2010 royalties payable on minerals were raised from 3 per cent to 4 per cent, and in new projects the Government will become a shareholder. In Ghana, the Government passed new mining laws that double royalties on mining to 6 per cent. In Madagascar, the new Government moved to suspend all mining contracts and in 2009 announced a review of all tax and royalty arrangements. Sierra Leone also passed new laws in December 2009 which increased royalties and community benefits. In Namibia, the Government established a State-owned company to take advantage of the mineral wealth. In South Africa, profit-based royalties were introduced only in 2009, and there is even an ongoing political debate on the nationalization of the mining sector (see *Mining Weekly*, 2010; *Mining Journal,* 2010; OSISA et al., 2009; UNCTAD, 2007; Custers, 2008; Johnston, 2008).

8   The Chilean Government established a royalty-like fee in 2006, of 0.5–5 per cent of the production value (depending on the volume of production); and there has been a recent proposal to increase this tax for funding reconstruction from the earthquake in early 2010. In Ecuador, the Government plans to renegotiate oil contracts to convert them into service arrangements (see La Hora, El Gobierno de Ecuador prevé comenzar renegociación contratos petroleros en julio, 10 May 2010; for a more detailed account of mineral tax reforms in Latin America, see Christian Aid, 2009). In early May 2010, the Government of Australia announced the introduction of a new Resource Super Profits Tax of 40 per cent to be applied from 2012 (Commonwealth of Australia, 2010), while in South Australia, royalties have been doubled to 7 per cent (Roubini, "Australian Mining Enters the Crosshairs of Tax Authorities", 11 May, available at: http://www.roubini.com).

9   For instance, in 2009 the Government of Zambia removed the windfall tax that had been introduced the year before, and reintroduced the 100 per cent capitalization allowance (Christian Aid, 2009). However, it also announced intentions to increase its shareholdings in foreign-owned mining companies to 35 per cent, and drafted a revised mineral empowerment policy to encourage greater participation by Zambians in the mining industry (Ernst & Young, 2009). The United Republic of Tanzania might also be rethinking its plans to increase taxes on mining operations. In Ghana, most companies reported that they were protected by stability agreements and did not expect to pay the new 6 per cent royalty rate (*Financial Times*, Mining fails to produce golden era for Ghana, 22 March 2010).

References

Amsden A (2001). The Rise of "the Rest": Challenges to the West from the Late-Industrializing Economies. Oxford, Oxford University Press.

Amsden A (2007*)*. Escape from Empire: The developing World's Journey Through Heaven and Hell. Cambridge, MA, Massachussets Institute of Technology.

Amsden A and van der Hoeven R (1996). Manufacturing output, employment and real wages in the 1980's: Labour's loss until century's end. *Journal of Development Studies,* 32(4): 506–530.

Auty RM (2007). Natural resources, capital accumulation and the resource curse. *Ecological Economics*, 61(4): 627–634, March.

Baunsgaard T (2001). A primer on mineral taxation. International Monetary Fund Working Paper WP/01/139, Washington, DC.

BGS (2010). World Mineral Production 2004–2008. British Geological Survey. Keyworth, Nottingham.

Bradford C (2005). Prioritizing economic growth: Enhancing macroeconomic policy choice. G-24 Discussion Paper No. 56. New York and Geneva, UNCTAD, June.

Chandrasekhar CP and Ghosh J (2010). Aspects of growth and employment in India. UNCTAD Discussion paper. Forthcoming.

Chang HJ (2002). Kicking Away the Ladder - Development Strategy in Historical Perspective. London, Anthem Press.

Christian Aid (2009). Undermining the poor: Mineral taxation reforms in Latin America, September.

Commonwealth of Australia (2010). The resources super profits tax: a fair return to the nation. Available at: http://www.deewr.gov.au/Department/Documents/ Files/Announcement%20document.pdf.

Curtis M and Lissu T (2008). *A golden opportunity? How Tanzania is failing to benefit from gold mining.* Christian Council of Tanzania, National Council of Muslims in Tanzania and Tanzania Episcopal Conference. Dar es Salaam, October.

Custers R (2008). L'Afrique révise les contrats miniers, in *Le Monde diplomatique*, July.

Custers R and Matthysen T (2009). Africa's natural resources in a global context. International Peace Information Service. Antwerp, August.

Davis JR and Bezemer D (2003). Key emerging and conceptual issues in the development of the RNFE in developing countries and transition economies. Natural Resource Institute Report 2755. University of Greenwich, Chatham Maritime, United Kingdom, July.

De Gregorio J, Edwards S and Valdés R (2000). Controls on capital inflows: Do they work? *Journal of Development Economics,* 63 (1): 59–83.

Easterly W (2002). The lost decades: Developing countries stagnation in spite of policy reforms 1980–1998. Washington, DC, World Bank.

Edison H and Reinhart C (2001). Stopping hot money. *Journal of Development Economics,* 66(2): 533–553, December.

Epstein G (2005). Central banks as agents of economic development. Working Paper No. 104. Political Economy Research Institute, University of Massachusetts, Amherst, MA.

Epstein G (2007). Central banks as agents of employment creation. In: Ocampo JA and Jomo KS, *Towards Full and Decent Employment.* New York, London, Penang and Hyderabad, Orient Longman Private Ltd, Zed Books, Third World Network and United Nations: 92–122.

Epstein G (2009). Rethinking monetary and financial policy: Practical suggestions for monitoring financial stability while generating employment and poverty reduction. Employment Working Paper 37, International Labour Office, Geneva.

Epstein G and Schor J (1988). Macropolicy in the rise and fall of the Golden Age. Working Papers, World Institute for Development Economics Research of the United Nations University (UNU-WIDER), Helsinki.

Ernst & Young (2009). 2009: The year of survival and revival – Mergers and acquisitions in the mining and metals sector.

Frenkel R and Taylor L (2006). Real exchange rate, monetary policy, and employment. DESA Working Paper 19. New York, United Nations Department of Economic and Social Affairs, February.

Friedman M (1968). The role of monetary policy. *American Economic Review,* 58(1): 1–17.

Galbraith JK (1997). Time to ditch the NAIRU. *Journal of Economic Perspectives*, 11(1): 93–108.

Gallego F, Hernández L and Schmidt-Hebbel K (1999). Capital controls in Chile: Effective, efficient? Central Bank of Chile Working Paper 59.

Glyn A et al. (1990). The rise and fall of the Golden Age. In: Marglin S and Schor J, eds., *The Golden Age of Capitalism*. Oxford, Clarendon Press: 39–125.

Gordon D (1995). Putting the horse (back) before the cart: disentangling the macro relationship between investment and saving. In: Epstein G and Gintis H, eds., *Macroeconomic policy after the conservative era*. Cambridge, United Kingdom, Cambridge University Press.

Harrison A (2002). Has globalisation eroded labor's shares? Some cross country evidence. National Bureau of Economic Research, Cambridge, MA. Mimeo.

ILO (2008). *Global Wage Report 2008/09*. Geneva, International Labour Organisation.

ILO (2009). Protecting people, promoting jobs. A survey of country employment and social protection policy responses to the global economic crisis. Geneva, International Labour Office.

IMF (2006). Inflation targeting and the IMF. IMF Working Papers 01/31. Washington, DC.

Jespersen E (1992). External shocks, adjustment policies and economic and social performance. In: Cornia GA, van der Hoeven R and Mkandawire T, eds., *Africa's Recovery in the 1990s: From Stagnation and Adjustment to Human Development*. Basingstoke, United Kingdom, Macmillan: 9–90.

Johnston D (2008). Changing fiscal landscape. *Journal of world energy law & business*, 1(1): 31–58.

Kaplan E and Rodrik D (2001). Did the Malaysian capital controls work? NBER Working Paper 8142, National Bureau of Economic Research, Cambridge, MA.

Khan AR (2006). Integrating employment growth into the PRSP process: An analysis of issues and a suggested methodology (unpublished). Geneva, International Labour Office.

Khan MS and Senhadji AS (2001). Threshold effects in the relation between inflation and growth. IMF Staff Papers, 48(1): 1–21.

Kuczynski PP and Williamson J, eds. (2003). *After the Washington Consensus: Restarting Growth and Reform in Latin America*. Washington, DC, Institute for International Economics.

Ley E (2010). Exhaustible resources and fiscal policy: Copper mining in Zambia. Background paper for the Public Expenditure Review, World Bank, Washington, DC.

Lim J (2006). Philippine monetary policy: A critical assessment and search for alternatives. PERI Working Paper, Political Economy Research Institute, University of Massachussetts, Amherst, MA.

Lindenboim J, Kennedy D and Graña JM (2010). La relevancia del debate sobre la distribución fun-cional del ingreso. UNCTAD Discussion Paper. Forthcoming.

Lipumba N (1995). Structural adjustment policies and economic performance of African countries. In: *International Monetary and Financial Issues for the 1990s*, V. United Nations publication, sales no. E.95. II.D.3, New York and Geneva: 35–64.

Lungu J (2009). The politics of reforming Zambia's mining tax regime. Southern Africa Resource Watch. Resource Insight. Issue no. 8, August.

Marglin S and Schor J (1990). *The Golden Age of Capitalism*. Oxford, Clarendon Press.

McKinley T (ed.) (2009). *Economic Alternatives for Growth, Employment and Poverty Reduction*. London and Basingstoke, United Kingdom, Palgrave Macmillan.

Mining journal (2010). A supplement to Mining Journal, Mining Indaba 2010, February.

Mining weekly (2010). Investors reject Tanzania's distorted mining law, 28 April.

Mittal A (2009). The 2008 Food Price Crisis: Rethinking Food Security Policies. G-24 Discussion Paper No. 56. New York and Geneva, UNCTAD, June.

Mpande MM (2009). Management of mineral economies. Background paper on problems of the Zambian mining industry. EAZ Public Discussion Forum on "Mining Taxation", December.

Muqtada M (2003). Macroeconomic stability, growth and employment: Issues and considerations beyond the Washington Consensus. Employment Paper 2004/48. International Labour Office, Geneva.

Muqtada M (2010). The crisis of orthodox macroeconomic policy: the case for a renewed commitment to full employment. *Employment Working Paper* 53, International Labour Office, Geneva.

Nkurunziza J (2007). Generating rural employment in Africa to fight poverty. In: Ocampo JA and Jomo KS, eds. *Towards Full and Decent Employment*. New York, London, Penang and Hyderabad, Orient Longman Private Ltd., Zed Books, Third World Network and United Nations: 158–190.

ODI (2010). The global financial crisis and developing countries. Phase 2 Synthesis. Overseas Development Institute Working paper 316.

Onaran Ö and Stockhammer E (2005). Two Different Export-Oriented Growth Strategies. Accumulation and Distribution in Turkey and South Korea. *Emerging Markets Finance and Trade*, 41(1): 65–89.

OSISA et al. (2009). Breaking the curse. How transparent taxation and fair taxes can turn Africa's mineral wealth into development. Open Society Institute of Southern Africa, Johannesburg; Third World Network Africa, Accra; Tax Justice Network Africa, Nairobi; Action Aid International, Johannesburg; and Christian Aid. London, March.

Palley T (2007). Reviving full employment policy. Challenging the Wall Street paradigm. Briefing Paper 191, Economic Policy Institute, Washington, DC.

Phelps ES (1967). Phillips curves, expectations of inflation and optimal employment over time. *Economica,* 34(3): 254–281.

Phillips AW (1958). The relationship between unemployment and the rate of change of money wages in the United Kingdom, 1861–1957. *Economica,* 25(2): 283–299.

Pineda J and Rodríguez F (2010). Curse or blessing? Natural resources and human development. United Nations Development Programme. Human Development Research Paper 2010/04, New York.

Pollin R (2002). Saving. In: King JE ed. *The Elgar Companion to post Keynesian Economics.* Cheltenham, United Kingdom, Edward Elgar Publishing.

Pollin R et al. (2006). An employment-targeted economic programme for South Africa. Amherst, MA, UNDP and Political Economy Research Institute.

Pollin R, Heintz J and Githinji M (2007). An employment-targeted economic programme for Kenya. Amherst, MA, UNDP and Political Economy Research Institute.

Sachs J (2007). How to handle the macroeconomics of oil wealth. In: Humphreys M, Sachs J and Stiglitz J, eds. *Escaping the resource curse.* Columbia University Press, New York.

Saget C (2008). Fixing minimum wage levels in developing countries: Common failures and remedies. International Labour Review, 147(1): 25–42.

Samuelson PA and Solow RM (1960). Analytical aspects of anti-inflation policy. *American Economic Review,* 50(2). Papers and Proceedings of the Seventy-second Annual Meeting of the American Economic Association, May: 177–194.

SARW (2009). Impact of the global financial crisis on mining in Southern Africa. Southern Africa Resource Watch, Johannesburg.

Schadler S et al. (1993). Economic adjustment in low-income countries: experience under the Enhanced Structure Adjustment Facility. IMF Occasional Paper, no. 106. Washington, DC, June.

Singh A (2009). Historical examination of the golden age of full employment in Western Europe. In: Arestis P and McCombie J, eds., *Missing Links in the Unemployment Relationships.* Basingstoke, Palgrave Macmillan.

Stiglitz J (1997). Reflections on the natural rate hypothesis. *Journal of Economic Perspectives,* 11(1): 3–10.

Tcherneva P and Wray LR (2005). Employer of last resort program: a case study of Argentina's Jefes de Hogar Program. CFEPS Working Paper No. 41. Center for Full Employment and Price Stability. Kansas City, April.

Thomas S (2010). Mining taxation: An application to Mali. IMF Working Paper WP/10/126, International Monetary Fund.

UNCTAD (2002). *Economic Development in Africa:* From Adjustment to Poverty Reduction: What's New? United Nations Publications, Sales no. E.02.II.D.18, New York and Geneva.

UNCTAD (2007). *World Investment Report 2007*: Transnational Corporations. Extractive Industries and Development. United Nations Publications, Sales no. E.07.II.D.9, New York and Geneva.

UNCTAD (various issues). *Trade and Development Report.* United Nations publications, New York and Geneva.

UNECA (2009). Africa Review Report on Mining. United Nations Economic Commission for Africa, E/ECA/CFSSD/6/7. Addis Ababa.

UNECA (2010). *Economic Report on Africa 2010*: Promoting high-level sustainable growth to reduce unemployment in Africa. Jointly published by the United Nations Economic Commission for Africa and the African Union. Addis Ababa.

UNECA-AfDB (2007). The 2007 Big Table. Managing Africa's Natural Resources for Growth and Poverty Reduction. Summary Report. United Nations Economic Commission for Africa and African Development Bank, 1 February. Available at: http://www.uneca.org/thebigtable/.

van der Hoeven R (2010). Income inequality and unemployment revisited: Can one make sense of economic policy? *Journal of Human Development and Capabilities,* 11(1): 67–84.

van der Hoeven R and Saget C (2004). Labour market institutions and income inequality: What are the new insights after the Washington Consensus? In: Cornia A, ed. *Inequality, Growth and Poverty in an Era of Liberalization and Globalization.* Oxford, Oxford University Press: 197–220.

Weeks J (2009). The Impact of the Global Financial Crisis on the Economy of Sierra Leone. Country Study 18. UNDP and International Policy Centre for Inclusive Growth. Brasilia, September.

Weeks J (2010). Active Macro Policy for Accelerating Achievment of the MDG Targets. New York, UNDP. Forthcoming.

World Bank (1994). Adjustment in Africa: Reforms, Results and the Road Ahead. New York, Oxford University Press.

World Bank (2005). Economic Growth in the 1990s: Learning from a Decade of Reform. Washington, DC.

UNITED NATIONS CONFERENCE ON TRADE AND DEVELOPMENT

Palais des Nations
CH-1211 GENEVA 10
Switzerland
(www.unctad.org)

Selected UNCTAD Publications

Trade and Development Report, 2009
Responding to the global crisis
Climate change mitigation and development

United Nations publication, sales no. E.09.II.D.16
ISBN 978-92-1-112776-8

Trade and Development Report, 2008
Commodity prices, capital flows and the financing of investment

United Nations publication, sales no. E.08.II.D.21
ISBN 978-92-1-112752-2

Trade and Development Report, 2007   United Nations publication, sales no. E.07.II.D.11
Regional cooperation for development   ISBN 978-92-1-112721-8

    Chapter   I   Current Issues in the World Economy

                    Statistical annex to chapter I

    Chapter   II   Globalization, Regionalization and the Development Challenge

    Chapter III   The "New Regionalism" and North-South Trade Agreements

    Chapter IV   Regional Cooperation and Trade Integration Among Developing Countries

    Chapter   V   Regional Financial and Monetary Cooperation

                    Annex 1   The Southern African Development Community

                    Annex 2   The Gulf Cooperation Council

    Chapter VI   Regional Cooperation in Trade Logistics, Energy and Industrial Policy

Trade and Development Report, 2006   United Nations publication, sales no. E.06.II.D.6
Global partnership and national policies for development   ISBN 92-1-112698-3

    Chapter   I   Global Imbalances as a Systemic Problem

                    Annex 1: Commodity Prices and Terms of Trade

                    Annex 2: The Theoretical Background to the Saving/Investment Debate

    Chapter   II   Evolving Development Strategies – Beyond the Monterrey Consensus

    Chapter III   Changes and Trends in the External Environment for Development

                    Annex tables to chapter III

    Chapter IV   Macroeconomic Policy under Globalization

    Chapter   V   National Policies in Support of Productive Dynamism

    Chapter VI   Institutional and Governance Arrangements Supportive of Economic Development

Trade and Development Report, 2005   United Nations publication, sales no. E.05.II.D.13
New features of global interdependence   ISBN 92-1-112673-8

    Chapter   I   Current Issues in the World Economy

    Chapter   II   Income Growth and Shifting Trade Patterns in Asia

    Chapter III   Evolution in the Terms of Trade and its Impact on Developing Countries

                    Annex: Distribution of Oil and Mining Rent: Some Evidence from Latin America, 1999–2004

    Chapter IV   Towards a New Form of Global Interdependence

Trade and Development Report, 2004   United Nations publication, sales no. E.04.II.D.29
Policy coherence, development strategies   ISBN 92-1-112635-5
and integration into the world economy

    Part One   Global Trends and Prospects

         I   The World Economy: Performance and Prospects

        II   International Trade and Finance

    Part Two   Policy Coherence, Development Strategies and Integration into the World Economy

        III   Openness, Integration and National Policy Space

        IV   Fostering Coherence Between the International Trading, Monetary and Financial Systems

                    Annex 1: The Concept of Competitiveness

                    Annex 2: The Set-up of Econometric Estimates of the Impact of Exchange Rate Changes on
                                      Trade Performance

                    Conclusions and Policy Challenges

Trade and Development Report, 2003
Capital accumulation, growth and structural change

United Nations publication, sales no. E.03.II.D.7
ISBN 92-1-112579-0

<table>
<tr><td>*Part One*</td><td></td><td>Global Trends and Prospects</td></tr>
<tr><td></td><td>I</td><td>The World Economy: Performance and Prospects</td></tr>
<tr><td></td><td>II</td><td>Financial Flows to Developing Countries and Transition Economies</td></tr>
<tr><td></td><td>III</td><td>Trade Flows and Balances</td></tr>
<tr><td></td><td></td><td>Annex: Commodity prices</td></tr>
<tr><td>*Part Two*</td><td></td><td>Capital Accumulation, Economic Growth and Structural Change</td></tr>
<tr><td></td><td>IV</td><td>Economic Growth and Capital Accumulation</td></tr>
<tr><td></td><td>V</td><td>Industrialization, Trade and Structural Change</td></tr>
<tr><td></td><td>VI</td><td>Policy Reforms and Economic Performance: The Latin American Experience</td></tr>
</table>

Trade and Development Report, 2002
Developing countries in world trade

United Nations publication, sales no. E.02.II.D.2
ISBN 92-1-112549-9

<table>
<tr><td>*Part One*</td><td></td><td>Global Trends and Prospects</td></tr>
<tr><td></td><td>I</td><td>The World Economy: Performance and Prospects</td></tr>
<tr><td></td><td>II</td><td>The Multilateral Trading System After Doha</td></tr>
<tr><td>*Part Two*</td><td></td><td>Developing Countries in World Trade</td></tr>
<tr><td></td><td>III</td><td>Export Dynamism and Industrialization in Developing Countries
Annex 1: Growth and classification of world merchandise exports
Annex 2: United States trade prices and dynamic products
Annex 3: International production networks and industrialization in developing countries</td></tr>
<tr><td></td><td>IV</td><td>Competition and the Fallacy of Composition</td></tr>
<tr><td></td><td>V</td><td>China's Accession to WTO: Managing Integration and Industrialization</td></tr>
</table>

* * * * * *

The Global Economic Crisis:
Systemic Failures and Multilateral Remedies
Report by the UNCTAD Secretariat Task Force
on Systemic Issues and Economic Cooperation

United Nations publication, sales no. E.09.II.D.4
ISBN 978-92-1-112765-2

<table>
<tr><td>Chapter</td><td>I</td><td>A crisis foretold</td></tr>
<tr><td>Chapter</td><td>II</td><td>Financial regulation: fighting today's crisis today</td></tr>
<tr><td>Chapter</td><td>III</td><td>Managing the financialization of commodity futures trading</td></tr>
<tr><td>Chapter</td><td>IV</td><td>Exchange rate regimes and monetary cooperation</td></tr>
<tr><td>Chapter</td><td>V</td><td>Towards a coherent effort to overcome the systemic crisis</td></tr>
</table>

* * * * * *

These publications may be obtained from bookstores and distributors throughout the world. Consult your bookstore or write to United Nations Publications/Sales Section, Palais des Nations, CH-1211 Geneva 10, Switzerland, fax: +41-22-917.0027, e-mail: unpubli@un.org; or United Nations Publications, Two UN Plaza, DC2-853, New York, NY 10017, USA, telephone +1-212-963.8302 or +1-800-253.9646, fax: +1-212-963.3489, e-mail: publications@un.org. Internet: http://www.un.org/publications.

G-24 Discussion Paper Series

Research papers for the Intergovernmental Group of Twenty-Four
on International Monetary Affairs and Development

No. 59	June 2010	Andrew CORNFORD	Revising Basel 2: The Impact of the Financial Crisis and Implications for Developing Countries
No. 58	May 2010	Kevin P. GALLAGHER	Policy Space to Prevent and Mitigate Financial Crises in Trade and Investment Agreements
No. 57	December 2009	Frank ACKERMAN	Financing the Climate Mitigation and Adaptation Measures in Developing Countries
No. 56	June 2009	Anuradha MITTAL	The 2008 Food Price Crisis: Rethinking Food Security Policies
No. 55	April 2009	Eric HELLEINER	The Contemporary Reform of Global Financial Governance: Implications of and Lessons from the Past
No. 54	February 2009	Gerald EPSTEIN	Post-war Experiences with Developmental Central Banks: The Good, the Bad and the Hopeful
No. 53	December 2008	Frank ACKERMAN	Carbon Markets and Beyond: The Limited Role of Prices and Taxes in Climate and Development Policy
No. 52	November 2008	C.P. CHANDRASEKHAR	Global Liquidity and Financial Flows to Developing Countries: New Trends in Emerging Markets and their Implications
No. 51	September 2008	Ugo PANIZZA	The External Debt Contentious Six Years after the Monterrey Consensus
No. 50	July 2008	Stephany GRIFFITH-JONES with David GRIFFITH-JONES and Dagmar HERTOVA	Enhancing the Role of Regional Development Banks
No. 49	December 2007	David WOODWARD	IMF Voting Reform: Need, Opportunity and Options
No. 48	November 2007	Sam LAIRD	Aid for Trade: Cool Aid or Kool-Aid
No. 47	October 2007	Jan KREGEL	IMF Contingency Financing for Middle-Income Countries with Access to Private Capital Markets: An Assessment of the Proposal to Create a Reserve Augmentation Line
No. 46	September 2007	José María FANELLI	Regional Arrangements to Support Growth and Macro-Policy Coordination in MERCOSUR
No. 45	April 2007	Sheila PAGE	The Potential Impact of the Aid for Trade Initiative
No. 44	March 2007	Injoo SOHN	East Asia's Counterweight Strategy: Asian Financial Cooperation and Evolving International Monetary Order
No. 43	February 2007	Devesh KAPUR and Richard WEBB	Beyond the IMF
No. 42	November 2006	Mushtaq H. KHAN	Governance and Anti-Corruption Reforms in Developing Countries: Policies, Evidence and Ways Forward
No. 41	October 2006	Fernando LORENZO and Nelson NOYA	IMF Policies for Financial Crises Prevention in Emerging Markets
No. 40	May 2006	Lucio SIMPSON	The Role of the IMF in Debt Restructurings: Lending Into Arrears, Moral Hazard and Sustainability Concerns
No. 39	February 2006	Ricardo GOTTSCHALK and Daniela PRATES	East Asia's Growing Demand for Primary Commodities – Macroeconomic Challenges for Latin America
No. 38	November 2005	Yilmaz AKYÜZ	Reforming the IMF: Back to the Drawing Board
No. 37	April 2005	Colin I. BRADFORD, Jr.	Prioritizing Economic Growth: Enhancing Macroeconomic Policy Choice

G-24 Discussion Paper Series
Research papers for the Intergovernmental Group of Twenty-Four
on International Monetary Affairs and Development

No. 36	March 2005	JOMO K.S.	Malaysia's September 1998 Controls: Background, Context, Impacts, Comparisons, Implications, Lessons
No. 35	January 2005	Omotunde E.G. JOHNSON	Country Ownership of Reform Programmes and the Implications for Conditionality
No. 34	January 2005	Randall DODD and Shari SPIEGEL	Up From Sin: A Portfolio Approach to Financial Salvation
No. 33	November 2004	Ilene GRABEL	Trip Wires and Speed Bumps: Managing Financial Risks and Reducing the Potential for Financial Crises in Developing Economies
No. 32	October 2004	Jan KREGEL	External Financing for Development and International Financial Instability
No. 31	October 2004	Tim KESSLER and Nancy ALEXANDER	Assessing the Risks in the Private Provision of Essential Services
No. 30	June 2004	Andrew CORNFORD	Enron and Internationally Agreed Principles for Corporate Governance and the Financial Sector
No. 29	April 2004	Devesh KAPUR	Remittances: The New Development Mantra?
No. 28	April 2004	Sanjaya LALL	Reinventing Industrial Strategy: The Role of Government Policy in Building Industrial Competitiveness
No. 27	March 2004	Gerald EPSTEIN, Ilene GRABEL and JOMO, K.S.	Capital Management Techniques in Developing Countries: An Assessment of Experiences from the 1990s and Lessons for the Future
No. 26	March 2004	Claudio M. LOSER	External Debt Sustainability: Guidelines for Low- and Middle-income Countries
No. 25	January 2004	Irfan ul HAQUE	Commodities under Neoliberalism: The Case of Cocoa
No. 24	December 2003	Aziz Ali MOHAMMED	Burden Sharing at the IMF
No. 23	November 2003	Mari PANGESTU	The Indonesian Bank Crisis and Restructuring: Lessons and Implications for other Developing Countries
No. 22	August 2003	Ariel BUIRA	An Analysis of IMF Conditionality
No. 21	April 2003	Jim LEVINSOHN	The World Bank's Poverty Reduction Strategy Paper Approach: Good Marketing or Good Policy?
No. 20	February 2003	Devesh KAPUR	Do As I Say Not As I Do: A Critique of G-7 Proposals on Reforming the Multilateral Development Banks

* * * * * *

G-24 Discussion Paper Series are available on the website at: www.unctad.org. Copies of *G-24 Discussion Paper Series* may be obtained from the Publications Assistant, Macroeconomic and Development Policies Branch, Division on Globalization and Development Strategies, United Nations Conference on Trade and Development (UNCTAD), Palais des Nations, CH-1211 Geneva 10, Switzerland; fax +41-22-917-0274.

UNCTAD Discussion Papers

No. 199	June 2010	Ugo PANIZZA, Federico STURZENEGGER and Jeromin ZETTELMEYER	International government debt
No. 198	April 2010	Lee C. BUCHHEIT G. MITU GULATI	Responsible sovereign lending and borrowing
No. 197	March 2010	Christopher L. GILBERT	Speculative influences on commodity futures prices 2006–2008
No. 196	Nov. 2009	Michael HERRMANN	Food security and agricultural development in times of high commodity prices
No. 195	Oct. 2009	Jörg MAYER	The growing interdependence between financial and commodity markets
No. 194	June 2009	Andrew CORNFORD	Statistics for international trade in banking services: requirements, availability and prospects
No. 193	Jan. 2009	Sebastian DULLIEN	Central banking, financial institutions and credit creation in developing countries
No. 192	Nov. 2008	Enrique COSIO-PASCAL	The emerging of a multilateral forum for debt restructuring: The Paris Club
No. 191	Oct. 2008	Jörg MAYER	Policy space: What, for what, and where?
No. 190	Oct. 2008	Martin KNOLL	Budget support: A reformed approach or old wine in new skins?
No. 189	Sep. 2008	Martina METZGER	Regional cooperation and integration in sub-Saharan Africa
No. 188	March 2008	Ugo PANIZZA	Domestic and external public debt in developing countries
No. 187	Feb. 2008	Michael GEIGER	Instruments of monetary policy in China and their effectiveness: 1994–2006
No. 186	Jan. 2008	Marwan ELKHOURY	Credit rating agencies and their potential impact on developing countries
No. 185	July 2007	Robert HOWSE	The concept of odious debt in public international law
No. 184	May 2007	André NASSIF	National innovation system and macroeconomic policies: Brazil and India in comparative perspective
No. 183	April 2007	Irfan ul HAQUE	Rethinking industrial policy
No. 182	Oct. 2006	Robert ROWTHORN	The renaissance of China and India: implications for the advanced economies
No. 181	Oct. 2005	Michael SAKBANI	A re-examination of the architecture of the international economic system in a global setting: issues and proposals
No. 180	Oct. 2005	Jörg MAYER and Pilar FAJARNES	Tripling Africa's primary exports: What? How? Where?
No. 179	April 2005	S.M. SHAFAEDDIN	Trade liberalization and economic reform in developing countries: structural change or de-industrialization
No. 178	April 2005	Andrew CORNFORD	Basel II: the revised framework of June 2004
No. 177	April 2005	Benu SCHNEIDER	Do global standards and codes prevent financial crises? Some proposals on modifying the standards-based approach

UNCTAD Discussion Papers

No. 176	Dec. 2004	Jörg MAYER	Not totally naked: textiles and clothing trade in a quota free environment
No. 175	Aug. 2004	S.M. SHAFAEDDIN	Who is the master? Who is the servant? Market or Government?
No. 174	Aug. 2004	Jörg MAYER	Industrialization in developing countries: some evidence from a new economic geography perspective
No. 173	June 2004	Irfan ul HAQUE	Globalization, neoliberalism and labour
No. 172	June 2004	Andrew CORNFORD	The WTO negotiations on financial services: current issues and future directions
No. 171	May 2004	Andrew CORNFORD	Variable geometry for the WTO: concepts and precedents
No. 170	May 2004	Robert ROWTHORN and Ken COUTTS	De-industrialization and the balance of payments in advanced economies
No. 169	April 2004	Shigehisa KASAHARA	The flying geese paradigm: a critical study of its application to East Asian regional development
No. 168	Feb. 2004	Alberto GABRIELE	Policy alternatives in reforming power utilities in developing countries: a critical survey
No. 167	Jan. 2004	R. KOZUL-WRIGHT and P. RAYMENT	Globalization reloaded: an UNCTAD perspective
No. 166	Feb. 2003	Jörg MAYER	The fallacy of composition: a review of the literature
No. 165	Nov. 2002	Yuefen LI	China's accession to WTO: exaggerated fears?
No. 164	Nov. 2002	Lucas ASSUNCAO and ZhongXiang ZHANG	Domestic climate change policies and the WTO
No. 163	Nov. 2002	A.S. BHALLA and S. QIU	China's WTO accession. Its impact on Chinese employment
No. 162	July 2002	P. NOLAN and J. ZHANG	The challenge of globalization for large Chinese firms
No. 161	June 2002	Zheng ZHIHAI and Zhao YUMIN	China's terms of trade in manufactures, 1993–2000
No. 160	June 2002	S.M. SHAFAEDDIN	The impact of China's accession to WTO on exports of developing countries
No. 159	May 2002	J. MAYER, A. BUTKEVICIUS and A. KADRI	Dynamic products in world exports
No. 158	April 2002	Yilmaz AKYÜZ and Korkut BORATAV	The making of the Turkish financial crisis

* * * * * *

UNCTAD Discussion Papers are available on the website at: www.unctad.org. Copies of *UNCTAD Discussion Papers* may be obtained from the Publications Assistant, Macroeconomic and Development Policies Branch, Division on Globalization and Development Strategies, United Nations Conference on Trade and Development (UNCTAD), Palais des Nations, CH-1211 Geneva 10, Switzerland; fax +41-22-917-0274.

QUESTIONNAIRE

Trade and Development Report, 2010

In order to improve the quality and relevance of the Trade and Development Report, the UNCTAD secretariat would greatly appreciate your views on this publication. Please complete the following questionnaire and return it to:

Readership Survey
Division on Globalization and Development Strategies
UNCTAD
Palais des Nations, Room E.10009
CH-1211 Geneva 10, Switzerland
Fax: (+41) (0)22 917 0274
E-mail: tdr@unctad.org

Thank you very much for your kind cooperation.

1. What is your assessment of this publication?

	Excellent	*Good*	*Adequate*	*Poor*
Overall	☐	☐	☐	☐
Relevance of issues	☐	☐	☐	☐
Analytical quality	☐	☐	☐	☐
Policy conclusions	☐	☐	☐	☐
Presentation	☐	☐	☐	☐

2. What do you consider the strong points of this publication?

_____
_____
_____

3. What do you consider the weak points of this publication?

_____
_____
_____

4. For what main purposes do you use this publication?

Analysis and research	☐	Education and training	☐
Policy formulation and management	☐	Other (*specify*) _____	

5. Which of the following best describes your area of work?

Government	☐	Public enterprise	☐
Non-governmental organization	☐	Academic or research	☐
International organization	☐	Media	☐
Private enterprise institution	☐	Other (*specify*) _____	

6. Name and address of respondent (*optional*):

_____
_____
_____

7. Do you have any further comments?

_____
_____
_____